D1072543

CHARLES FENTON MERCER

and the Trial of National Conservatism

Charles Fenton Mercer

and the Trial of National Conservatism

Douglas R. Egerton

UNIVERSITY PRESS OF MISSISSIPPI
JACKSON AND LONDON

The paper in this book meets the guidelines for permanence
and durability of the Committee on Production Guidelines
for Book Longevity of the Council on Library Resources.

Library of Congress Cataloging-in-Publication Data

Egerton, Douglas R.
    Charles Fenton Mercer and the trial of national conservatism / by
Douglas R. Egerton.
        p.   cm.
    Includes index.
    Bibliography: p.
    ISBN 0-87805-392-1
    1. Mercer, Charles Fenton, 1778–1858.   2. Legislators—United
States—Biography.   3. United States—Politics and
government—1815–1861.   4. Virginia—Politics and
government—1775–1861.   5. Conservatism—United States—
History—19th century.   6. Whig Party (U.S.)—Biography.
7. Federal Party (U.S.)—Biography.   I. Title.
E340.M5E36   1989
973.5'092'4—dc19
[B]   88-36545
                                                                    CIP

British Library Cataloguing in Publication data is available.

For my Mother
and the memory of my Father

Contents

Preface

In far less sophisticated times, it was an unassailable tenet of Jacksonian historiography that the Whigs were the party of conservatism. This thesis found its most compelling and colorful presentation in Arthur M. Schlesinger, Jr.'s, *Age of Jackson*, published in 1945. The book met with overwhelming popular and critical acclaim and inspired new interest in the period, which ironically produced a wave of scholarship in opposition to Schlesinger's thesis. Anxious to shout down the idea that the early stages of industrialism wrought havoc on the young nation, a generation of consensus historians went over the book line by line, gleefully isolating Schlesinger's more egregious errors, exaggerations, and omissions. Within several decades the Whigs were lauded as the party of optimism, reform, and big government; the consensus historians crowed that they had laid the foundations of "modern liberalism."

The pro-Whig historians especially faulted the earlier view that there was a direct link between the Federalist and National Republican/Whig parties; both groups, the earlier historians insisted, were made up of wealthy, reactionary men. Indeed, it was suspected that former Federalists marched en masse into the Whig coalition. Consensus historians rejected this crude assumption. They insisted that no direct link existed between Federalist and Whig theories of political economy. Federalists, they observed, were elitist, antidemocratic, and mercantile-oriented, whereas the Whigs merely borrowed the Federalist idea of a strong central government to produce a new synthesis, the positive liberal state in which all groups would profit from the new industrial wealth.

The corrective was welcome. But the consensus school failed to recognize that the Whig party could be both progressive and con-

servative. That the Whigs were "modern" in their economic thinking and political method is now beyond doubt. But it is equally true
that there was a dark side to their modernity. Ready to take their
chances in the new capitalist age, the Whigs, except for their
glowing rhetoric, did not care about those who might not emerge
from the maelstrom as successfully as they had. There was also a
dark side to the American System, the vaunted Whig economic
program, for lurking beneath the glittering and nationalistic label
lay elements of control that betrayed the social limitations of Whig
thought. Indeed, many of their reforms were either pursued for
profoundly conservative reasons, like education, or appear to be
anything but "optimistic" (the term adopted by many consensus
historians to replace the ahistorical "liberal"), like colonization.

Stranger still is the consensus penchant for insisting that the
political economy of Whiggery was so different from that of
Federalism. The distinctions these historians make are valid, but
only if one concentrates on the older generation of Federalists who
were driven from power in 1800. The young men who took control
of the party during the era of Thomas Jefferson displayed ideas
quite unknown to their fathers. It was this generation, not that of
Alexander Hamilton, that would be active in the early years of the
Whig party. And it was this generation that pioneered political and
economic theories that resembled nothing so much as the American System. That all of these Federalists did not become Whigs is
hardly the point; the point is that they created and promoted the
idea of the national conservative industrial state.

The life of Charles Fenton Mercer of Virginia provides an ideal
opportunity for exploring these foundations of modern American
conservatism. A Federalist from the time of his college days during
the Quasi War, Mercer laid the groundwork in his native state for
what later became Whiggery. When Henry Clay, who is often
depicted as the personification of Whiggery, was opposing the rechartering of the Bank of the United States, Mercer was busy
creating an American System in miniature in Virginia. Virtually all
the pieces were in place, for Mercer sponsored an interlocking
program of state banking—while also supporting the national
bank—internal improvements, public education, and black colonization. Mercer worked hard to garner public support for his
program and to democratize his party, or at least to make it appear
to be democratic, by producing in 1812 the most modern state
convention in the South before the Jacksonian period. It was small

wonder that this former Federalist was the driving force behind the Virginia constitutional convention of 1829.

In significant ways Mercer is a far better example of pure Whiggery than those men traditionally identified with the party. Consistent to the end of his life, Mercer was first and last a nationalist. He did not, like Daniel Webster, begin his political career in the states' rights camp. Nor did he, as did Clay when devising the tariff of 1833, ever compromise his principles for political expediency. In a state hostile to his ideas Mercer was safe in his staunchly nationalistic district. But despite his great ambition, he could go no further than the House of Representatives, and so he was allowed the luxury of ideological purity. Mercer's long service in the political wars allows one to examine Whiggery over time; when he left Congress, he had served more consecutive terms than all but one other man up to that date.

Unlike Webster, whose golden voice served as a substitute for the actual creation of legislation, Mercer drafted bills at an astonishing rate. As brilliant as Webster and Clay, with political skills superior to those of his friend John Quincy Adams, and despite his usual position in the political minority, Mercer passed an astounding number of bills. Strangely, many of those bills—even those that failed—continue to attract attention even though Mercer himself is forgotten. The mention of his bill for public education is virtually a requirement for any survey of education in America, and his slave trade bill of 1819 is discussed as often as it is misunderstood. His act declaring the slave trade piracy has also received great attention, and Washingtonians today who have never heard his name enjoy biking along his most beautiful, if unfortunate, creation, the Chesapeake and Ohio Canal.

That Mercer has been forgotten is strange, for during his long life he counted most of the leading men of the day as his intimates. Among his close friends and political associates were James Monroe, Henry Clay, James Barbour, Richard Rush, Francis Scott Key, John Randolph, and, after several false starts, John Quincy Adams. His enemies, and this unhappy man appears almost to have gathered more enemies than friends, included Benjamin Watkins Leigh, Andrew Jackson, Virginia jurist John Scott, Louis McLane, Abel Upshur, and (he could be found in both categories) John Randolph. Mercer also counted his father's friend George Washington as his patron and adviser.

Recently, Mercer has begun to reappear in history, mentioned in monographs on colonization or internal improvements. Yet he has no biographer. Unlike the more romantic and eccentric men of the Tidewater, Mercer's long and important life has never been treated in full. Only in the *Dictionary of American Biography* can one find a biography of Mercer (written by Charles Francis Adams, Jr.), and it is but a seventh the length of John Randolph's. That men like Randolph were important is not at issue. Yet it is strange that unlike those who could only "tear down," to borrow Monroe's words, this Tidewater-raised man of northern principles has been so overlooked.

Perhaps those historians who have dealt with some aspect of Mercer's career have shied away from a longer treatment because of two apparently irreconcilable strains in his thought. Although Mercer was often a pioneer in social or political reform movements, his letters are filled with pessimistic and conservative assessments. Clement Eaton, for example, has termed Mercer a "Southern liberal," although as an advocate of big government Mercer fits neither the nineteenth- nor the twentieth-century meaning of the term. Eaton is also hard-pressed to explain away the Virginian's unrelentingly gloomy memoir, filled as it is with bitter attacks on the lower classes. Perhaps, too, Mercer has been ignored because his personal papers were unavailable. When Union troops occupied the Alexandria school in which he died, Mercer's trunks were torn open and the contents carried north by soldiers eager to sell the autographs. It is only within recent years that the majority of his papers have become accessible.

Because Mercer was a highly educated man, and because I wish to convey a sense of the time in which he lived, I have made no attempt to modernize his spelling or grammar. I have also avoided the admonitory [sic] except when quoting recent historians.

I have incurred many debts in the writing of this book. In its beginnings the advice of Richard R. Duncan and Ronald M. Johnson was just right, giving me room to explore my ideas but always keeping me firmly on course. I appreciate their encouragement, patience, and wise counsel. Marcus Rediker shared with me his rich knowledge of social history and helped clarify many of my opinions. James H. Broussard, Robert J. Brugger, Daniel Walker Howe, and Robert M. McColley read all or parts of the manuscript and saved me from more than one error of fact and judgment. Alan Gallay supplied telling criticism of the early chapters, but it is for his long friendship and untiring support that I am truly grateful.

My thanks also go to the Department of History of Georgetown University for granting me a teaching fellowship that allowed me to revise my manuscript and helped me to gain my footing as a historian.

I am especially grateful to Seetha Srinivasan, Associate Director of the University Press of Mississippi, for her efficient assistance and support, and to Trudie Calvert, whose editorial skills helped to turn a manuscript into a book. Parts of Chapters 7 and 8 appeared in the *Journal of the Early Republic* and the *Virginia Magazine of History and Biography* and are reprinted here with the kind permission of their editors, Ralph D. Gray and Nelson D. Lankford.

Most of all I wish to thank my wife, Linda. She patiently listened to endless stories about Mercer, pored over yellowed letters and papers at various archives, read numerous drafts of my manuscript, and even tramped through high grass at the old Leesburg cemetery in a fruitless search for Mercer's grave. She alone knows how much of this book is really hers.

PART ONE

The Golden Age 1778–1802

1

Fredericksburg

"Old age is not without its enjoyments," he mused, "and among them is reflection on the past." It was dawn, and below the old man's apartment the Paris streets were beginning to come to life. Charles Fenton Mercer sat at the writing table in his parlor, scratching into his journal by the yellow candlelight. The date was June 16, 1855, his birthday, and he was seventy-seven years old. His health was good, he thought happily, although he needed glasses to read and his sore lip worried him. He paused in his writing and thought about his long and extraordinary life.[1]

Mercer thought about the amazing time in which he was born. In the early summer of 1778 the newly independent states of the American South faced an unprecedented crisis. It had been just three years since fighting had broken out between British soldiers and American colonists at Lexington and Concord and almost two since the Declaration of Independence had been adopted in Philadelphia. Now the British were evacuating the North and planning a major southern assault, and the author of that declaration was anxiously trying to obtain information. On June 14 Thomas Jefferson wrote James Mercer of Marlborough and nervously inquired whether he had "any news of the British army's departure, a French war declared, or any other important event." But if Mercer was not concentrating on the war he could be forgiven, for his wife, Eleanor, was about to give birth to their fourth child.[2]

Two days later the child was born and named Charles Fenton. The birth took place in the sleepy Tidewater village of Fredericksburg, Virginia, very near Marlborough plantation, which was also the birthplace of James Mercer and the longtime home of the boy's recently deceased grandfather, John Mercer.[3]

Although Charles Fenton was the younger son of a younger son, he did belong to an important and aristocratic family. John Mercer was born in 1704, in Dublin, Ireland. His parents, John Mercer and Grace Fenton, were of some means, and the boy was given a good education at Trinity College. But in 1720,at the age of sixteen, he emigrated to the colony of Virginia. At first in the New World he was a merchant, at which he prospered, but in 1728 he began to practice law. In this he also did well, but, though brilliant, John Mercer was also more than a little mad, and either his temper or his tactics at the Prince William County court earned him disbarment. Reinstated six months later by the council, he soon made enough money to begin investing heavily in land. He bought up vacant lots in and around around the hamlet of Marlborough in Stafford County, where he built his plantation house. He prided himself on achieving success without aid, for he later told one of his sons that "except [for] my education I never got a shilling of my father's or any other relations estate; every penny I ever got has been on my own industry."⁴

John Mercer arrived in Virginia much later than the powerful first families—the Byrds, Carters, Masons, and Randolphs—who had come to America in the mid-seventeenth century. But like them, he was from a substantial and cultured British background. And also like them, although he practiced law, he began to buy large numbers of slaves. Planters, not lawyers or merchants, dominated the colony's political life. To obtain entrance into the charmed circle of first families he would have to emulate their pretensions. Mercer purchased at least sixty-nine Africans between 1731 and 1746. One of these demonstrated his opinion of his new life and the erratic and often violent behavior of his master by hanging himself, an act of defiance that impeded Mercer's acquisitions not at all.⁵

Mercer's land and slaves were only two signs of his prosperity; the third was the name of his wife: Catherine Mason. This marriage, made in his twenty-first year, brought him acceptance into the tight circle of eminent families; socially one could rise no higher in colonial Virginia. They were married in 1725, and in the next quarter-century ten children were born to them. In 1750, at age forty-three, Catherine died a very old woman. The robust John was properly disconsolate, but after five months he roused himself enough to marry Ann Roy of Essex County. "Tho . . . not so young" as his new bride, John fathered nine more children, the last one born in the last year of his life.⁶

John's third son by his first wife was James Mercer, born on

February 26, 1736, and named for an uncle. After receiving several years of education at home, James entered the College of William and Mary in Williamsburg. His education there was interrupted by the French and Indian War, for his father volunteered his services as an officer. When the fighting ended, James was free to seek his fortune. Like his father, he studied the law, but also like his father, James was not one to follow a single path to wealth and prestige. He therefore joined his father and older brother George in land speculation through the Ohio Company. This partnership, founded in 1747 by Thomas Lee, was the largest and most influential of the firms investing in the West, and its membership consisted entirely of the best Virginia gentry. Besides the three Mercers its members included George Washington, George Mason, and Robert Carter. John Francis Mercer, one of John's sons by Ann Roy, joined later.[7]

Following military service and business success, James continued his rise in Virginia society by entering politics. In 1762 he was elected to represent the county of Hampshire in the House of Burgesses (although he continued to call the family plantation of Marlborough his home). He held that post for almost fifteen years and also served Virginia in several other capacities. But they would not be quiet years.[8]

The French and Indian War had driven the hated French out of North America, but it had also brought a new set of problems, especially the question of how Britain was going to pay for its newly won empire. Parliament decided to impose a stamp tax on its American subjects not unlike one already levied on those at home. But the American colonists responded to the tax with a storm of abuse. On May 29, 1765, Patrick Henry made his celebrated resolutions against the Stamp Act in the House of Burgesses. No record was kept of the individual voting on those resolutions, but it is almost certain that James Mercer voted for them, for his father had already acted against the tax. Indeed, John Mercer not only wrote one of the first tracts against the act, he was a member of the Stafford County Court that resigned in protest over the bill.[9]

But the Stamp Act met a mixed reaction in the colonies and in the Mercer family. George Mercer defended the abused tax and became a central character in the controversy. In 1763 George, James's senior by three years, was sent to England on behalf of the Ohio Company to protest the Proclamation Line, which threatened the company's future by outlawing immigration across the Appalachian crest. He had little success on the land issue, but he did apply for and receive a Stamp Act commission, under which he would distribute the stamps for Maryland and Virginia and realize a tidy profit in the bargain. Clearly, George Mercer was out of touch with the political climate in America. Even as he sailed home, Virginia Governor Francis Fauquier decided that the unpopular act was unenforceable. When Mercer and the stamps arrived in Williamsburg he was met by a hostile crowd screaming for his blood and that of the governor. After just twenty-four hours of this abuse, including being burned in effigy, Mercer wrote Lord Rockingham in England that he was resigning his commission "as the only step."[10]

The uproar over the "cussed" act divided the powerful Mercer clan politically, but it did not damage their fierce personal loyalty to one another. Both James and John were loud in their defense of George, and when James discovered that Richard Henry Lee, who had organized the burning in effigy of George, had applied unsuccessfully for the post of stamp distributor, he published the fact in a newspaper. A vitriolic newspaper debate with Lee turned into a challenge, but when nothing came of that James, perceiving that any Lee would do, fell into a "skirmish" with Arthur Lee. James obviously got the best of it, for as John Mercer gleefully reported to George, "Your bro. without receiving any damage broke [Lee's] head, & closed his eyes in such a manner as obliging him to keep [in] his house sometime."[11]

George did not consider such plebeian behavior the path to vindication, and he felt it was necessary to return to England and defend his conduct. Parliament clearly did not consider him at fault, for just before he sailed word arrived that he had been offered the post of lieutenant governor of North Carolina. But Mercer declined the bid. He went to Britain, never to return to America but destined to wreck the finances of his yet unborn nephew Charles Fenton. By 1766 he was in London, where he appeared twice before the committee investigating the disturbances and generally made life miserable for fellow witness Benjamin Franklin.[12]

But James Mercer, who displayed no such Tory inclinations, had more on his mind than imperial affairs and the misfortunes of his royalist brother. During this period he became engaged to Eleanor Dick, the vivacious daughter of Charles Dick of Fredericksburg. Eleanor was not as good a social catch as John Mercer had made, but her father had served as the Virginia commissary in the last colonial war and made a great deal of money manufacturing arms and ammunition. The thirty-six-year-old James and the much younger Eleanor wed on June 4, 1772.[13]

His new family connections and the established Mercer name helped James rise in prominence. At the same time, as tensions continued to worsen between Britain and its colonies, James's position in the House of Burgesses became more important. In 1775 the royal government of Virginia dissolved, and the General Convention at Richmond created the Committee of Public Safety to conduct the defense of the colony during its recesses. Eleven men were named to this body. One of them was James Mercer.[14]

During the following year James Mercer participated in the writing of a new constitution for Virginia, and when the first General Assembly met following its adoption Benjamin Harrison and Mercer were chosen as delegates to represent the state in the national Congress. James declined. His long service in the Burgesses and the convention had forced him to neglect his part of the family fortune. And what was worse, his brother George was creating new problems.[15]

When George sailed for England following the Stamp Act fiasco, he evidently had no intention of returning to America. Nontheless, he continued to own a great deal of property in Virginia and in the disputed Ohio region. (The Ohio Company had collapsed in 1763, but the holdings were in legal limbo.) James was expected to watch over George's interests, but he was neglecting his own holdings and could not adequately oversee his brother's estate. George accused James of cheating him, and he fired off letter after letter to their Virginia friends, who began to take sides. One who found against the family Tory was George Washington, who was "well persuaded, that Mr. James Mercer hath not intentionally wronged" his brother. Still, the lord of Mount Vernon was forced to admit that "appearances may be against him."[16]

Unfortunately, the family estate was nearly impossible for James Mercer to untangle, at least partly because his father had borrowed so lavishly. James owed money to Washington, who advised his friend to mortgage some of his land, especially if he was unwilling to sell any of his slaves. But Washington was "content notwithstanding" to hold a "fresh Mortgage on the same Negroes if they are still living." James stubbornly refused to sell any of his land or the 122 slaves he had inherited and instead hoped to pay his debts with the profit from his crops. In the meantime, heavy interest continued to accumulate not only on his debts but also those of "the old Gentleman's," which were "still unpaid."[17]

Circumstances finally became so desperate that James was forced to sell about half of his human property. In 1777 he advertised for sale at public auction in Fredericksburg "thirty-six choice slaves." He later upped the number of sixty-three, with "a dozen more to hire out." A more tragic situation could not be imagined by a southern aristocrat.[18] And if this were not enough, the British were now planning a major southern invasion. Such was the situation when Eleanor Dick Mercer gave birth to Charles Fenton on June 16, 1778. Charles had been preceded by a brother, John Fenton, born in October 1773, and two sisters, Mary Eleanor Dick, born in the fall of 1774, and Lucinda.[19]

Charles Fenton Mercer was born into a unique social environment in eighteenth-century Tidewater Virginia. The Tidewater was the low and often marshy land that bordered the Chesapeake, and its planters controlled the commonwealth. It set the social tone, provided the political leaders, and dominated the precapitalist, agrarian economy. It was here that the large plantations and ancestral manors existed and that the first families of the state resided.[20]

The first families reigned atop a society that attached considerable importance to rank. They were members of the gentry, a group of perhaps 10 percent of Virginia's population. Class distinctions needed no explanation in this world. There were, as Patrick Henry stated, four classes: the "well-born" planters, the middle-class yeomen (who worked their own farms), the "lower orders," the landless poor whites (about 30 percent of the population), and finally the slaves (about 40 percent of Virginia's population but not included in the potential political equation). Yet the class consciousness that pervaded the state was not based on hereditary aristocracy alone but also on property and land, which naturally induced great power in an agrarian society. Birth and property combined to determine class structure.[21]

Virginia's social structure was supported by a number of elements, one of which was the Episcopal church, the established religion before the Revolution. Even after the break with Britain, membership in this essentially English institution continued to designate gentry, especially in the Tidewater, and the Mercers were good Episcopalians. A gentleman was recognizable not only by the church he attended but also by the wig he wore, the carriage he rode in, the cut of his clothes, and the manners he affected.[22]

The social world that served the Mercer family was also supported by the state's political framework. The state constitution of

1776 was a profoundly conservative document that made no break from the act of 1736 that established conditions for voting. One must own either fifty acres or twenty-five acres and a house, a qualification that could be met by approximately half of the adult white males. It also allowed men who, like James Mercer, owned land across the state to vote in more than one county. It was a document designed to favor the interests of the large planters over the small farmers, the Tidewater over the west, and the rich over the poor.[23]

The conservative constitution mirrored the political and philosophical outlook of James Mercer. Like most southern planters, following the Revolution Mercer expected to retain his prewar rank in society, and he was apprehensive about the social changes that accompanied the break with Britain. The lord of Marlborough was especially unnerved by the violent expression of grievances filed by the impoverished revolutionary soldiers weary of waiting for the settlement of their military claims. "Unless some Examples are made of those Rebels lately in arms," this generous patriot warned, "we shall have but anarchy for all the Treasure & Blood expended these eight years."[24]

Not surprisingly, considering the social outlook of James Mercer's peers, he was soon elected for a second time to a position of power: the Continental Congress. His election came on June 18, 1779, almost a year to the day from the birth of his youngest child. Despite his diminishing financial resources, Mercer accepted. In late August he rode north to Philadelphia, where he took his seat on September 9. Among those elected with him from Virginia were Edmund Randolph and Patrick Henry.[25]

But Mercer was not pleased with the situation in Philadelphia. He considered his fellow delegates grasping and argumentative, and he quickly came to believe that he could accomplish very little. Part of the problem lay in the weak structure of the Continental Congress, and he perceived "that a still greater change must hapen in Men and Measures, to make it either Hon'ble or Safe to continue in Congress." He requested the Virginia House of Delegates to allow him to resign his post and return home. He added, in a nasty aside, that the General Assembly might "reduce the number of Delegates to three, [and to] let these be Men of Integrity and Diligence, and abilities too if to be had."[26]

Despite his resignation and less than subtle public attack on his fellow delegates, the pessimistic Mercer was still considered a man of ability. Jefferson soon requested that he work to achieve a financial settlement with the Philadelphia government for funds owed the state. Mercer declined, but he felt "not a little uneasiness" in refusing to help Virginia so soon after resigning his seat in Congress, and he told the governor the real reason for his refusal: his "peculiar Domestic situation." Eleanor, his wife, was deathly ill. "Nothing but the frequent and critical situation of my wife should have induced me to quit congress," Mercer wrote. He could not "say how soon after I cou'd be from home for any length of time.[27]

Tragically, there was nothing James could do, and on March 28, 1780, the frail Eleanor quietly slipped away. Her youngest son was not yet two years old. Unlike his father, James never remarried. He accepted the sole responsibility of raising his four children. "I lost my mother in infancy," Charles Fenton later wrote, "but my surviving and venerated parent was the mother, as well as the father, of his children." James Mercer never again left home that he did not take his cherished youngest son with him.[28]

James Mercer's self-imposed retirement from national politics did not mean that he ceased to follow important questions. In 1787 Charles Fenton heard his father, who had denounced the Articles of Confederation as too weak to protect property, attack the new Constitution on the grounds that the president could be reelected without restriction. Nor did Mercer lose interest in state politics, and when in 1789 he was elected to the state's highest court, the reorganized court of appeals, he accepted the honor. He promptly departed for Richmond, taking Charles Fenton with him, but not, apparently, any of his other children. The eleven-year-old boy must have found the Richmond spectacle fantastic after life at Marlborough, for the court was one of Virginia's most visible signs of civil authority. The judges were the elite of the commonwealth, and their short session was accompanied by great pomp and ceremony. The court presided over a wide range of affairs, and at its meeting people gathered from across Virginia for pleasure as well as business.[29]

When the court was not in session the Mercers, father and son, returned to Marlborough. Despite his financial problems, James continued to spend money in the ostentatious manner typical of the Virginia gentry. Charles Fenton later remembered that his father's "hospitable table [was] spread every day, and abundantly provided, [and] rarely, if ever, without guests, who, tho often invited, needed no invitation to welcome them." Every evening at dusk, almost without exception, cards and chess boards were brought out, and the guests were encouraged to play. These games

were as much a part of patrician life as riding and politics, and
James taught his son the game of piquet while other members of
the family taught the bright boy to play chess at a very young age.
But gambling for money, an important aspect of Virginia life, was
never allowed on the Mercer plantation, and a supper served
promptly at ten put an end to the evening of games.[30]

Life on the plantation must have seemed idyllic for the young
Virginian. The property provided a peaceful pastoral setting that
looked down on the Rappahannock River, and the manor house
was as magnificent as any in the state. Wide halls ran through the
structure both from side to side and front to rear, cutting the house
into quarters. All the work on the plantation was performed by
slaves, although the servant population was much smaller than
that enjoyed by John Mercer. The system could have only reinforced Charles Fenton's growing perception that he held a charmed
and special position in society, and though in later life he came to
loathe the idea of slavery, he never completely turned against it or
manumitted the few slaves he inherited.[31]

The relationship between Charles Fenton and his father grew
extremely close in the years following Eleanor's death. The busy
jurist and planter always found time to join his youngest son in
some "boyish amusement," whether it was sailing a toy boat or
floating a balloon they built. "My father was the mother of all his
children," Charles Fenton later remarked, "but mine especially."[32]

Charles Fenton was with his father in Richmond in the early fall
of 1793 when the Mercer family traveled south to attend the
annual court. There, on October 30, James suddenly fell ill and died
at the age of fifty-six. His youngest child was fifteen. The next day
"his remains were deposited in the silent grave" in St. John's
churchyard, attended by the officers of the grand lodge, as well as
friends, family, and most of the General Assembly.[33]

Charles Fenton did not return to Marlborough. It had been almost impossible for James to retain and run the family manor, for
he had not paid off his considerable debts. The sudden death of
Charles Fenton's father ended the boy's childhood, his tranquil and
contented "waste of time." It not only removed him from the seat
of his "happy boyhood" but rudely informed him that he likely
faced a grim "life of poverty" that could destroy his status as a
gentleman.[34]

The family decided that the boy would go to live with his oldest
sister, Mary Eleanor, who had done very well for herself by marrying James Mercer Garnett, her first cousin. James Mercer had

stipulated in his will that Garnett was to be Charles Fenton's guardian even though there were more immediate family members. One of them, John Francis Mercer, James's younger half-brother, who was then serving in the House of Representatives from Maryland, was passed by because he had broken with James over the messy question of family finances. Two years before, the two brothers had quarreled violently on the Richmond streets when John Francis accused James of being "greatly indebted both to [himself] & George."35

James Garnett had married Mary Eleanor in September 1793, only one month before his father-in-law's death. Though he was only twenty-three years old, he was well placed, having inherited Elmwood, his father's English-style estate in Essex County, Virginia. He already had made several important social and political connections, including James Madison and James Monroe.36

When Charles Fenton arrived at Elmwood, heading up the long road that gave way to fertile fields tilled by slaves and stables crowded with thoroughbreds, the boy realized that the plantation was even more elegant than Marlborough. The manor house was a handsome two-story brick with a front broken by twenty windows. He stepped through the main door into a white-paneled hall that ran the width of the house and was decorated by a carved frieze and a frescoed ceiling. Before him stood a tremendous, heavily carved mantle of deep pink marble.37

Mercer lived happily at Elmwood. There in January 1795 his sister Lucinda wed Solomon Betton of Loudoun County, Virginia. Lucinda unknowingly carried on the unfortunate family tradition of marrying into financial disaster, but on her wedding day she received the three hundred pounds sterling willed her by her father, as well as one hundred guineas that should have been hers immediately upon James Mercer's death.38

Also at Elmwood Charles Fenton received the remainder of his private education. Virginia patricians held that a southern gentleman should be accomplished in riding, dancing, and conversation. A knowledge of the law, of agriculture, and of military strategy was also important, although an understanding of the ancient classics was more so. Latin and Greek were prized subjects in the plantation home, and Mercer learned these languages in "laborious, but delightful" sessions with an older cousin. These studies, Mercer later claimed, "formed [his] character."39

The Mercer family finances continued to be an unfathomable

tangle, but by early 1795 James Garnett, the administrator, and Benjamin Harrison, the executor, began to probate James Mercer's will. Final settlement with George Mercer was left to a future date, but in the meantime Charles Fenton received nearly three hundred acres of good farmland in the Piedmont county of Loudoun. Best of all, a small amount of money was put aside for the education of all four children. Charles Fenton, now seventeen, would be able to afford college, which would enable him to make his own way in the world.⁴⁰

Charles Fenton chose to attend the College of New Jersey in the small town of Princeton. He probably decided on this institution over the closer College of William and Mary because the quality of instruction at the Williamsburg school was undistinguished. His father and his uncles George and John Francis had attended William and Mary, but now that the state capital had been moved to Richmond there was little reason to patronize the Virginia college. Perhaps even more important, Princeton, a bastion of tradition and religious conservatism, was viewed by the Virginia gentry as a safe school. Almost half of its enrollment came from the South.⁴¹

In the fall of 1795 Mercer left Essex and traveled north. Probably he took the winding lowland road across the Rappahannock, Potomac, Susquehanna, and Delaware rivers to Philadelphia. For a young man who had never been beyond the boundaries of undeveloped Virginia, the city, with its paved streets and stone sidewalks, must have been an astonishing sight. If he made good time, Mercer's trip to Princeton took ten days.⁴²

The seventeen-year-old youth who arrived in Princeton was slight of build and shorter than most of his classmates. He was not handsome but delicate, almost pretty. Enormously self-assured, he was well aware of his intellectual prowess. And despite his meager resources, Mercer habitually affected the dress of a southern gentleman: a tightly fitted coat with a high collar and a ruffled shirt with a long silk tie.⁴³

The regimented life of a Princeton student began immediately. The morning after arrival all freshmen presented their applications at the president's home and faced the ordeal of entrance examinations. But young Mercer was well prepared. The entrance board of professors and tutors informed him that he could enter the junior class. Mercer hurried back to the school to secure a room and await his new roommate, a person of considerable importance in the college. He was placed with John Henry Hobart, who was several years Mercer's senior and already serving as a tutor. Hobart found the young Virginian both "amiable" and possessing "the tenderness and affection of the warmest heart." The two became lifelong friends.[44]

At Princeton Mercer was one of about ninety students. Each of these young men paid a yearly tuition of eight pounds and an additional five pounds for room and board. There were few comforts, and most of the students, coming from privileged backgrounds, found the living conditions difficult and the food spartan. Breakfast consisted of bread, butter, milk, and coffee. The afternoon meal was rich in both quality and quantity, but the evening meal was again bread, butter, and milk.[45]

The strict regimen was the result of the connection between the college and the Presbyterian church, and indeed religion played a very important part in the life of Princeton students. Mercer was already a deeply religious young man, but southern Episcopalians did not frown on a little high living, and doubtless he had to adjust to the dour Presbyterian style. Every morning at five the students were awakened by the sharp sound of a horn blown in the halls. Flying out of bed, they scampered to wash their faces and hands, dress, and join the group pouring into the prayer hall.[46]

Academic life at the college was no less strict. The emphasis at Princeton, as at all other eighteenth-century colleges, was on Latin and Greek, although courses in arithmetic had recently been added. The books they were assigned to read were fascinating, but the method of study, which emphasized recitation over understanding, bored even the best students. But in addition to the works of Horace and Cicero, the school library contained the works of Shakespeare, Defoe, Bacon, Newton, and Locke. Best of all, there were recent histories of the American colonies and of the Revolution, as well as works by contemporary scholars such as David Hume and Adam Smith.[47]

Both the books and the professors at Princeton had a considerable impact on young Charles Fenton Mercer. He wrote later that he entered college with his political opinions unsettled. But the works of William Godwin, "whose Political Justice and Inquiries were among [his] favourite volumes," gave him a different outlook than he had learned in regional-minded Virginia. Intrigued by Godwin's image of nature and man in the 895-page *Political Justice,* Mercer learned that government could be a powerful instrument for promoting social and individual change. The seed of service and duty was planted in the impressionable boy's mind. Such ideas led him away from a sectional view toward more nationalistic, worldly notions; they taught him that he "was to live not for my country, but in a sense more enlarged, for mankind." Godwin's political theories, combined with his teachers' economic opinions, began to change Mercer's provincial ideas toward distinctly northern conceptions of business and mercantile capitalism. Clearly, Princeton was not as safe as Garnett believed.[48]

Mercer's growing estrangement from planter ideology is evident in a drawing he did while at Princeton. Entitled "Progress of Reason," it depicted a youth being directed upward to the difficult path of study and away from the path of ease. It was at once a claim to deference from the illiterate Virginia yeomen—his due as a son of the gentry—and a dismissal of the Tidewater ideal of leisure. Mercer well understood that a few hundred acres of Piedmont farmland would support no pretensions to position; his path to greatness would be different and far more arduous. The words of Godwin ordered him to serve his nation as well as his state. The drawing served notice that he intended to do just that and that his claims of class were as legitimate if not more so than those of the localist, idle planters.[49]

But life at college was not all work for Mercer, nor was it a headlong rush away from his southern notions. Social life at Princeton centered around the two rival debating societies, the Whigs and the Cliosophians. No real ideological differences separated these two groups, although the former tended to be dominated by southerners and the latter by northerners. The Whigs prided themselves on their upper-class origins and adopted a condescending air toward the inferior Clios.[50]

Both societies quietly judged the unsuspecting freshmen during the first few weeks of the term, not only on their scholarship but also on their habits, manners, and conduct. A handful of students, however, were more sought after than observed, as both societies labored to recruit the best; each hoped to capture the freshman who would become the class valedictorian. After several weeks the societies made their choices known. In this year, the Whigs were lucky, for they successfully recruited Mercer, whom one Whig believed would be "a good and highly valuable member of the society."[51]

There were other diversions for the students, a highlight being the visit of some famous person or the Fourth of July celebration. On that special day all classes were canceled, and the students assembled early in the prayer hall for the reading of the Declaration of Independence. Later, all sat down for a special dinner, certainly a welcome change from the usual meager fare. The students, many of whom, like Mercer, were born during the Revolution, were deadly serious about this occasion. "How patriotic were we not in those days every 4th of July," laughed one of Mercer's friends much later in life, "in firing off cannon, in sight of that old revolutionary battle ground near the town?"[52]

The students also found time to engage in sports, some of which were new to the Virginia boys. By midwinter the Millstone River usually was frozen solid enough for skating. Mercer, despite his small size, discovered that he excelled at this sport as in most others. "Hard a student as you were then," remembered classmate Richard Rush, "you could also beat most of us at [ice] skating and other pastimes; going ahead in those things as you did of us in the recitation room."[53]

When the weather turned warm, many of the students enjoyed taking long walks around the college. At these times they could shut out the world and engage in rambling, tranquil discussions. On such occasions, Mercer preferred to walk with his good friend Hobart, and both "enjoyed the highest pleasures" of these almost daily strolls. Mercer saw the other students as hurdles to be overcome, rivals to be defeated in an ever-present battle for deference. But Hobart was older and a tutor (and a northern man); there was no competition in their relationship. Clearly Hobart, the senior partner in this friendship, acted as both teacher and companion. The two youths grew intimate. Charles Fenton was Hobart's "much-loved Mercer," and the younger man more than returned "the endearments of a friendship so pure, so tender."[54]

But John Hobart was an unusually melancholy young man, and his gloomy outlook on humankind and his own fate fed a similar trait in the orphaned and impoverished Mercer. Although Mercer did not have to struggle with Hobart, the older boy nonetheless confirmed the Virginian's penchant for struggle. Like his roommate, Hobart was a pious and devout Episcopalian, but his religion was far from life-affirming and led him to adopt an appallingly grim view of human nature. He regarded "this world as the scene of so much vice and misery and containing no bliss" that he looked forward "with triumph [on] the prospect of leaving it." Both youths were relatively happy as long as they were preoccupied with their studies, and Mercer tried his best to "counsel" and sympathize with his friend. But Hobart never tired of reminding Mercer that "disappointment and affliction" would ever stalk his path, and he found only slight comfort in their friendship amid life's "many, many sorrows."[55]

By the fall of 1797 Mercer was ready to receive his Bachelor of Arts degree, and the college rewarded his two years of academic toil by naming him class valedictorian in a unanimous vote. His literary reputation was so great, Samuel Southard recalled, that younger students remembered him "in after years." At the end of September the class graduated, and Mercer gave his fellow Whigs something to lord over the Clios by receiving the "first honours" and delivering the Latin address. Yet Mercer was not prepared to leave Princeton; all but bred to the law, he had decided to stay and work toward a graduate degree in jurisprudence.[56]

Two short, hectic years at Princeton made a tremendous impression on Mercer. He lost many of his provincial attitudes and precapitalist agrarian economic notions. He also proved himself both mentally and physically by heading a class of intelligent and talented young men. There was no question that he could now make his own way in the world. But the cost had been high; he had befriended a man who reinforced his own growing suspicion that the world was a loathsome and unfriendly place. This idea would lead him away from Princeton into a web of politics and world conflict. For by the time of his graduation Mercer was no longer concentrating on his studies; he had "heard the sound of the trumpet & the alarm of war."[57]

Notes

ABBREVIATIONS

ACS	American Colonization Society
CFM	Charles Fenton Mercer
COCC	Chesapeake and Ohio Canal Company
DAB	*Dictionary of American Biography,* ed. Allen Johnson and Dumas Malone, 21 vols, 1928–1936.
JQA	John Quincy Adams
JSH	*Journal of Southern History*
LC	Library of Congress
NJHS	New Jersey Historical Society

NYHS   New-York Historical Society
PRO, FO Great Britain, Public Record Office, Foreign Office
UVA   University of Virginia
VHS   Virginia Historical Society
VMHB   *Virginia Magazine of History and Biography*
VSL   Virginia State Library
WMQ   *William and Mary Quarterly*

1. CFM Journal, June 6, 1855, Mercer-Hunter Papers, VSL.
2. Thomas Jefferson to James Mercer, June 14, 1778, in Julian P. Boyd, ed., *The Papers of Thomas Jefferson,* 20 vols. to date (Princeton, 1950–82), 2:199.
3. CFM, Autobiographical Sketch dated March 14, 1849, Mercer-Hunter Papers.
4. Biographical-Geographical Glossary, in Robert A. Rutland, ed., *The Papers of George Mason, 1725–1792,* 3 vols. (Chapel Hill, 1970), 1:1xxix; "Journals of the Council," *VMHB* 14 (January 1970): 232 n.; Malcolm C. Watkins, *The Cultural History of Marlborough, Virginia* (Washington, D.C., 1968), 24; John Mercer to George Mercer, December 22, 1767, in Lois Mulkearn, ed., *George Mercer Papers Relating to the Ohio Company of Virginia* (Pittsburgh, 1954), 204.
5. Virginius Dabney, *Virginia: The New Dominion* (New York, 1971), 46–47; Allan Kulikoff, "The Origins of Afro-American Society in Tidewater Maryland and Virginia. 1700–1790," *WMQ,* ser. 3, 35 (April 1978) : 242; Charles S. Sydnor, *Gentlemen Freeholders: Political Practices in Washington's Virginia* (Chapel Hill, 1952), 6; Watkins, *Cultural History of Marlborough,* 41.
6. DAB, 12:543; James M. Garnett, "James Mercer," *WMQ,* ser. 1, 17 (1908): 85–89; John Mercer to George Mercer, December 22, 1767, in Mulkearn, ed., *George Mercer Papers,* 188.
7. Garnett, "James Mercer;" "Education in Colonial Virginia," *WMQ,* ser. 1, 7 (1898 : 2–7; Eugene M. Papa, "The Royal Proclamation of 1763: Its Effect upon Virginia Land Companies," *VMHB* 83 (October 1975): 407–8; John Mercer, Articles of Agreement for the Ohio Company, May 22–24, 1757, in Rutland, ed., *Papers of Mason,* 1:13.
8. DAB, 12:542.
9. Garnett, "James Mercer," 91–92; J. A. L. Lemay, "John Mercer and the Stamp Act in Virginia, 1764–1765," *VMHB* 91 (January 1983): 37.
10. George Mason to James Mercer, January 13, 1772, in Rutland, ed., *Papers of Mason,* 1:140–42; Papa, "Royal Proclamation," 409; Dumas Malone, *Jefferson and His Time,* 6 vols. (Boston, 1948–81), 1:94–95; George Mercer to the Marquis of Rockingham, January 7, 1766, in CFM Papers, NJHS.
11. Lemay, "John Mercer," 7; John Mercer to George Mercer, December 22, 1767, in Mulkearn, ed., *George Mercer Papers,* 186, 203.
12. William Garnett Chisolm, "The Garnetts of Essex County and Their Homes," *VMHB* 42 (January 1934): 81; J. E. Tyler, "Colonel George Mercer's Papers," *VMHB* 60 (July 1952): 405.
13. *DAB,* 12:542.
14. Virginia Committee of Safety to James Madison, October 2, 1775, in Charles F. Hobson et al., eds., *The Papers of James Madison,* 14 vols. to date (Chicago, 1962–83), 1:163–64; CFM, Autobiographical Sketch, Mercer-Hunter Papers.
15. Garnett, "James Mercer," 208.
16. Papa, "Royal Proclamation," 408–10; George Washington to Edward Montague, April 5, 1775, in John C. Fitzpatrick, ed., *The Writings of George Washington,* 39 vols. (Washington, D.C., 1931–44), 3:283–86.
17. George Washington to James Mercer, July 19, 1773, in Fitzpatrick, ed., *Writings of Washington,* 3: 146–47; John Mercer to George Mercer, December 22, 1767,

in Mulkearn, ed., *George Mercer Papers*, pp. 186–219; George Mason to George Washington, December 21, 1773, in Rutland, ed., *Papers of Mason*, 1:185–86.

18. Garnett, "James Mercer," 212.

19. Ibid., 209–10.

20. Rhys Isaac, "Preachers and Patriots: Popular Culture and the Revolution in Virginia," in Alfred F. Young, ed., *The American Revolution: Explorations in the History of American Radicalism* (De Kalb, Ill.: 1976), 129; Daniel P. Jordan, *Political Leadership in Jefferson's Virginia* (Charlottesville, 1983), 7. See also Eugene Genovese, *The Political Economy of Slavery: Studies in the Economy and Society of the Slave South* (New York, 1966), and his *The World the Slaveholders Made: Two Essays in Interpretation* (New York, 1969), for a view of the South as an anti-bourgeois, noncapitalist social system.

21. Isaac, "Preachers and Patriots," 131: Jackson Turner Main, *The Anti-federalists: Critics of the Constitution, 1781–1788* (Chapel Hill, 1961), 2–3; J. R. Pole, "Representation and Authority in Virginia from the Revolution to Reform," *JSH* 24 (February 1958): 29.

22. Clement Eaton, *The Growth of Southern Civilization, 1790–1860* (New York, 1961), 3; Jordan, *Political Leadership*, 7; Sydnor, *Gentlemen Freeholders*, 61.

23. Pole, "Representation in Virginia," 17; Main, *Antifederalists*, 31.

24. James Mercer to John Francis Mercer, July 15, 1783, in John M. Jennings, ed., "Letters of James Mercer," *VMHB* 59 (January 1951): 189.

25. *DAB*, 12:542; Thomas Jefferson to Cyrus Griffin, June 19, 1779, in Boyd, ed., *Papers of Jefferson*, 3:4. Jefferson presumably wrote an identical letter to James Mercer.

26. James Mercer to Benjamin Harrison, October 1, 1779, in Edmund C. Burnett, ed., *Letters of Members of the Continental Congress*, 8 vols. (Washington, D.C., 1921–26), 4:464–65.

27. James Mercer to Thomas Jefferson, January 8, 1780, in Boyd, ed., *Papers of Jefferson*, 3:261–62.

28. CFM to Maria H. Garnett, December 8, 1854, Mercer-Hunter Papers.

29. James Madison to Thomas Jefferson, October 24, 1787, in Hobson, ed., *Papers of Madison*, 10:217; Edmund Randolph to James Madison, September 30, 1787, ibid., 181–82; James Mercer to John Francis Mercer, July 15, 1783, in Jennings, ed., "Letters," 189; Hardin Burnley to James Madison, November 28, 1789, in Hobson, ed., *Papers of Madison*, 12:456; Isaac, "Preachers and Patriots," 135–36.

30. Dabney, *Virginia*, 107; CFM to Maria H. Garnett, December 8, 1854, Mercer-Hunter Papers.

31. Alfred P. James, *George Mercer of the Ohio Company: A Study in Frustration* (Pittsburgh, 1963), 9.

32. CFM to Maria H. Garnett, June 6, 1856, Mercer-Hunter Papers.

33. *Virginia Gazette and General Advertiser* (Richmond), November 6, 1793; John J. Maund to Robert Carter, November 9, 1793, in Kate Mason Rowland, ed., "Letters of John James Maund," *WMQ*, ser. 1, 20 (1916): 276.

34. Watkins, *Cultural History of Marlborough*, 63–64; CFM to Maria H. Garnett, June 6, 1856, Mercer-Hunter Papers. Since 1956 the Smithsonian Institution has conducted considerable excavation on Marlborough.

35. Guardian Bonds, Will Book E, in William A. Crozier, ed., *Spotsylvania County Records, 1721–1800* (1905; rpt. Baltimore, 1965), 81; James Mercer to John Francis Mercer, January 19, 1791, Mercer Family Papers, VHS.

36. James M. Garnett, *Biographical Sketch of Hon. James Mercer Garnett, with Mercer-Garnett and Mercer Genealogies* (Richmond, 1910), 4–5, 16; James Monroe to James Madison, June 7, 1790, in Hobson ed., *Papers of Madison*, 8:241.

37. Chisholm, "The Garnetts of Essex County," 179.

38. Deed Book O, 1794–97, in Crozier, ed., *Spotsylvania County Records*, 473.

39. Eaton, *Growth of Southern Civilization*, 114; CFM to Maria H. Garnett, June 6, 1856, Mercer-Hunter Papers.

40. Will Book E, 1772–98, in Crozier, ed., *Spotsylvania County Records*, 51; CFM, Autobiographical Sketch, Mercer-Hunter Papers.

41. Harry Ammon, *James Monroe: The Quest for National Identity* (New York, 1971), 4; *Historic Princeton* (Princeton, 1940), 59; Sydnor, *Gentlemen Freeholders*, 3.

42. Ralph Ketcham, *James Madison, A Biography* (New York, 1971), 25.

43. This description is based on a small painting of Mercer as a young man now in the possession of the VHS and on the reminiscences of his great-nephew James Mercer Garnett, ed., *Biographical Sketch of Hon. Charles Fenton Mercer, 1778–1858* (Richmond, 1911), 56. Garnett, who knew Mercer only very late in life, described him as "stout in proportion to his height." The painting, however, depicts a slim youth.

44. Thomas J. Wertenbaker, *Princeton, 1746–1896* (Princeton, 1946), 184; CFM, Autobiographical Sketch, Mercer-Hunter Papers; John H. Hobart to Hannah Hobart, August 28, 1797, in Garnett, ed., *Biographical Sketch*, 26.

45. John MacLean, History of the College of New Jersey, 1746–1854 (1877; rpt. New York, 1969), 7–25.

46. Wertenbaker, *Princeton*, 189.

47. Linda K. Kerber, *Fedralists in Dissent: Imagery and Ideology in Jeffersonian America* (Ithaca, 1970), 111; Lawrence A. Cremin, *American Education; The National Experience, 1783–1876* (New York, 1980), 404.

48. Peter H. Marshall, *William Godwin* (New Haven, 1984), 94–105; CFM to Maria H. Garnett, June 6, 1856, Mercer-Hunter Papers.

49. Rhys Isaac, *The Transformation of Virginia, 1740–1790* (Chapel Hill, 1982), 289–90, 421.

50. Ketcham, *Madison*, 35.

51. Whig Society Circular to CFM, March 23, 1802, DeCoppet Collection, Princeton University Library; Ebenezer Grant to John H. Hobart, June 1, 1797, in John McVicar, ed., *The Early Life and Professional Years of Bishop Hobart* (Oxford, 1838), 115.

52. Wertenbaker, *Princeton*, 208, 210; Richard Rush to CFM, April 26, 1853, Richard Rush Papers, LC.

53. Wertenbaker, *Princeton*, 194; Richard Rush to CFM, April 26, 1853, Rush Papers.

54. John H. Hobart to CFM, May 15, 1798, November 5, 1797, in Garnett, ed., *Biographical Sketch*, 30–32, 28; CFM to Hobart, June 23, 1804, in Arthur Lowndes, ed., *The Correspondence of John Henry Hobart*, 6 vols. (New York, 1912), 3:433; Hobart to CFM, July 11, 1799, in McVicar, ed., *Early Life of Hobart*, 172.

55. John H. Hobart to CFM, March 18, 1801, July 24, 1798, in Lowndes, ed., *Correspondence of Hobart*, 1:cxix–cxx, 2:89–91; Hobart to CFM, November 5, 1797, in Garnett, ed., *Biographical Sketch*, 28.

56. CFM, Autographical Sketch, Mercer-Hunter Papers; John H. Hobart to Hannah Hobart, August 28, 1797, in Garnett, ed., *Biographical Sketch*, 26; Samuel Southard, undated speech in Charles Fenton Mercer, ed., *The Farewell Address of the Hon. C. F. Mercer to His Constituents* (N.p., 1839), 15. Southard's comments about Mercer's reputation are part of a speech given at a testimonial dinner on the latter's retirement from Congress, but since Mercer finished first in his class the statement is probably accurate.

57. John H. Hobart to CFM, July 24, 1798, in Lowndes, ed., *Correspondence of Hobart*, 2:89–91.

2

The Good Soldier

The trumpet Charles Fenton Mercer heard in the fall of 1797 was the conservative call to arms against world radicalism. President John Adams, who had taken office the previous March, inherited the European war, French attacks on American shipping, and the question of how the new minister, Charles Cotesworth Pinckney, would be received in Paris. The French Directory confounded Adams by refusing to accept the reactionary Pinckney and announced that all American sailors captured on British vessels, even if they had been the victims of impressment, would be hanged as pirates. Adams decided to follow the example of his predecessor and send a special mission to France. Elbridge Gerry and moderate Virginia Federalist John Marshall joined Pinckney in Paris on October 4, around the time Mercer received his diploma.[1]

The crisis with revolutionary France came at a time when Mercer's philosophical and political outlook was undergoing considerable metamorphosis. Cut adrift from his southern political and economic moorings, and influenced by new and challenging ideas and imperious professors, Mercer began to perceive the world in a new way. He had seen unsettling scenes in Philadelphia that he had never witnessed in rural Virginia, which, combined with the influence of his gloomy roommate and his own tendency toward melancholy, gave the young man a new social philosophy. At the same time the war between Britain and France was helping Americans to see their own social world in sharper focus. In this ideological debate the Federalist Adams administration sought to portray its hostility toward France as the response of the stable, the propertied, and the socially established toward a world gone mad.[2]

As a young patrician in the safe world of Virginia, Mercer had accepted his exalted social position as wholly natural. His plantation upbringing had led him to adopt the philosophy of decentralized government supported by the agrarian-minded Republicans, of whom James Mercer Garnett was an increasingly important member. But the urban disorder Mercer witnessed in Philadelphia and the power of the French mobs he read about led him to a new conclusion. A "weak government," he decided, could not "stay the hand of the violent and reckless" and would be forced to "shrink from the ruthless action of mobs and rioters."[3] The Federalist party with its orientation toward a strong central government was the logical home for Mercer, a decision that horrified his brother-in-law. Mercer tried to calm his guardian's fears, writing that the "uneasiness you express at a change which you suppose my political opinions to have undergone since I left Virginia" was unnecessary. He especially denied falling under the influence of his professors "on either moral or political questions," although he did admit that he was "under the instruction of a teacher fully qualified by the possession of the highest talents . . . to support any opinions he might care to entertain."[4]

There were other reasons behind Mercer's political conversion that he neglected to tell his Virginia relations. One was that he had come to admire John Adams, which would have appalled Garnett, who was an ardent supporter of Vice-President Thomas Jefferson. Mercer had concluded that Adams was "a patriot as pure as any," and he especially admired the way the president boldly interpreted the Constitution "so as to render the Federal government respectable at home and abroad."[5]

What most led to Mercer's change of heart was his fear of social upheaval. To the young aristocrat, France symbolized mob control, Britain social stability. This feeling was influenced by an example near at hand. Philadelphia, which Mercer passed through on every trip home, was filling up with unruly Irish immigrants. The working-class Irish were openly hostile to Britain, and with the adoption of Jay's Treaty they had become overwhelmingly Republican. Because of this, and because they represented a threat to established order, the Federalists as a party were antagonistic to the Irish. This made great sense to Mercer. He believed that unless they were controlled, the Irish with their "unclean hands" would "pollute and deface every thing sacred to the cause of freedom." Like most Americans, Mercer surveyed both the social scene and the international arena and picked his party accordingly. Unlike most Americans, however, the nineteen-year-old Mercer was ready to fight to support his new beliefs.[6]

By November 1797, the American envoys had been in Paris for a month, and Congress was preparing to convene in Philadelphia. With the news that the danger of plague had finally passed, President Adams and most members of Congress traveled through the raw weather to the capital. Also making the trip was Charles Fenton Mercer. He knew that Adams was likely to ask Congress for an expanded army and navy in case the American envoys failed in their mission, and he desperately wanted to be in that army. He had made arrangements to stay with John Hobart's mother, who lived in poverty in Philadelphia. Hannah Hobart was already burdened with a seriously ill daughter, but she doted on her gloomy son and wanted very much to accommodate the young man she had heard so much about. "I have concluded to put your room in as decent order as I can," she told John, with the hope that Mercer would "excuse what may not be so agreeable as might be wished."[7]

The winter of 1797 was uncommonly severe, and the icy wind tore through Mercer as he followed the southern road into Philadelphia. But he could not be discouraged. He sincerely desired a commission—as an officer, of course—to fight the French should war come, and he understood the importance of being in the capital. Should Adams grant him a commission, his presence in Philadelphia would allow him to accept on the spot, and because it would be returned immediately he would be ahead in rank of those officers who had to mail their letters of acceptance back to the president.[8]

Mercer evidently decided at the last moment not to stay with Hannah Hobart, as by the end of November she had still not seen him, and in early December she wrote her son, "Mr Mercer is not yet come." Mercer chose instead to room with another of Hobart's sisters when one of her boarders moved out, for in early January Hannah informed John that she had not known Mercer "was in town till yesterday afternoon [when] your Sister sent to let me know." She also mentioned that Mercer planned to return to Princeton soon. But events were to change the young gentleman's plans.[9]

The long-anticipated dispatches from the three American envoys arrived in Philadelphia on March 4, 1798. Far from solving the outstanding problems, the negotiations had broken down. The Americans had been met by three agents of Charles M. de Talleyrand, the French foreign minister, who informed them that they would not be received until they repudiated President Adams's statements on France, paid a bribe of fifty thousand pounds sterling, and agreed to a loan of 12 million livres. The indignant

Americans refused, and when their correspondence was laid before
Congress the nation was electrified. Federalist extremists called for
an immediate declaration of war. The Republicans, who were correctly perceived as being soft on France, were in a state of disarray
and panic.[10]

The Republicans had reason to be nervous. Addresses shouting
support for firmness against France flooded in from all over the
nation. Mayors, aldermen, lawyers, and even students sent their
encouragement to the suddenly popular Adams. To all this Mercer
bore witness, and although the excitement made it likely that the
army would indeed be increased, he made no headway in obtaining
a commission. On April 18 he abruptly decided to return to Princeton and rally the school and its environs behind the Federalists.
Mercer honestly wished to draw his college behind what he believed to be the banner of stability and sanity, but it must also have
occurred to him that his school could provide an avenue to the
military position he craved.[11]

There may have been a deeper reason for Mercer's new and
emotional attachment to the government. He was an orphan far
from home, and it is possible that his revised conception of government authority—Godwin's conception—had become a kind of sur-
rogate parent. His poor financial situation made it unlikely he
would ever become a power in planter society, but under the protective wing of centralized government he would win the deference due him. The state had taken over the role of father. Now that
new father was under attack from within and without, and Mercer
was ready to fight back.

By the time Mercer reached Princeton he found the community
already seething at the French insult. A mass meeting had been
planned for April 21, the very day of his return. He "hastily" sat
down that morning and composed an oration. With little time to
polish his handiwork, the speech was "Begun, finish'd and committed to memory between the hours of ten in the morning and
four in the afternoon."[12]

By the hour of the meeting Mercer was ready. As the crowd
quieted he rose to address his "fellow citizens." But quickly it
became apparent that he was speaking not to all Americans, and
certainly not to the treasonous faction that supported Jefferson,
anarchy, and France, but to "every true American." He warmed to
his subject quickly, pausing briefly to provide an inventive history
of the Anglo-French conflict, Jay's Treaty, and the undeniably poor
"conduct of Genet, Fauchet and their successor." He attacked

France for impressing American seamen, carefully avoiding any mention of the even larger number of his countrymen carried off by English ships, and denounced the French war effort as "a policy whose object it is to reduce you to beggary, to deprive you of the means of defence, and then to rule you with a rod of iron." Her ultimate plan, Mercer told his audience, was to "cross the Atlantic" and invade the United States.

Mercer next turned to the conduct of the Adams administration. He touched upon the president's numerous attempts to negotiate, his patience in the face of Pinckney's rejection, and his willingness to listen to "groundless" French complaints. Here Mercer demonstrated a surprising flair for stump speaking. Talleyrand had rejected not just Pinckney, had spurned not just Adams, but had "refused to listen to you." The French had turned their backs not just on the Federalist administration's policies; they had rebuked each and every American. "The French government has confided in the intelligence it has received that you are a divided people," he cried. "Step forward and tell them you are not so." They had once offered to lay down their lives for independence, Mercer reminded them, and now that true Americans were being threatened both from within and without he called upon them to do so "a second time." The "first effort towards it," he concluded, "should be made by publickly approving the conduct of your executive in foreign affairs."[13]

It was a brilliant speech, and its logical construction and tight organization revealed the young man's talents at oratory. It also revealed that Mercer had traveled much farther from Fredericksburg than simple geography would indicate. He had become a passionate Federalist, prepared to fight for country and class, prepared to see all who opposed him as dangerously unpatriotic. It was also another triumph for Mercer at Princeton. But this time was not one of complete happiness, for his good friend John Hobart was preparing to be ordained and leave for New York. Despite Hobart's pervasive gloominess, he was a young man of wisdom, and without his good advice—which was for Mercer to stay in school—Charles Fenton came close to ending his political career long before it began.[14]

On May 27, just about the time Hobart left Princeton, the Federalist majority in Congress forced through several measures that stopped just short of declaring war on France. They empowered American naval vessels to capture all French cruisers in

American waters and created a ten-thousand-man army to augment the regular army of three thousand. A provisional paper army
of another fifty thousand men was created in case of actual invasion. The bills passed along party lines and came, interestingly, not
from a recommendation of President Adams but from private citizen Alexander Hamilton, the leader of the reactionary High
Federalist faction.[15]

In the meantime, Mercer busily prepared his fellow students for
invasion. Even as they continued in their studies, they hired a
retired revolutionary war officer to teach them the basics of military strategy and exercises. Should war come, Mercer and his corps
could volunteer as a unit. But a better possibility suddenly appeared. He could use his family connections to receive a commission. He had made little headway in Philadelphia, but now George
Washington was called out of retirement to head the greatly expanded military force. Accordingly, on July 4, amid the pomp and
celebration, Mercer addressed a letter to his father's old friend and
creditor, making known his desire to serve in the enlarged army.[16]

But no sooner had Mercer mailed his letter to Washington than
he began to think better of it. This change of heart was motivated
by the superior political judgment of John Hobart. Hobart had long
known of his friend's desire to join the military, but he had heard of
the Virginian's letter to Washington only after the fact. Hobart was
horrified at his friend's naiveté. He quickly wrote a long and blunt
letter to Mercer in an attempt to dissuade him, stating frankly that
failure to receive a commission from the president might "not be
any cause for regret." Hobart flattered his friend, saying that he
well understood his desire to be "a good soldier, a zealous patriot, &
an upright and noble youth." But he reminded Mercer of what a
commission could do to the political career the Virginian was
planning. Had he thought about "how far your plan may interfere
with your advancement in [public] life," Hobart questioned,
"should you settle in Virginia, & should party spirit continue to be
violent [?]"[17]

Unfortunately for the noble youth, at the same moment that
Hobart was warning him of the folly of his course, George Washington wrote to tell him that he would indeed get a commission.
Washington informed Mercer of his "very sincere regard" for both
his father and grandfather, and he warmly applauded his desire to
do battle with "a Power which disregards all Law." Washington
announced that he had already written to the secretary of war on
Mercer's behalf. As a soldierly afterthought, the old general advised

Mercer always to be a gentleman and to avoid "the dissipations which are but too common in a Camp."[18]

Washington was as good as his word. If anything, his letter to James McHenry was even more effective than the one he had written to Mercer. "I have heard him exceedingly well spoken of by others," recalled the former president. Mercer was a fine "young man of Education; a Gentleman's son who was able to give him little besides it." Best of all, in Washington's opinion, Mercer was a Federalist "and sound in his Politic's, notwithstanding the example of his nearest relative[s]; who are, I believe," on "the opposite scale." Washington ended by suggesting that the youth would make "an Excellent Artillery Officer."[19]

The friendship between Washington and the Mercer family was certainly important, but it was Charles Fenton's political conversion that won him a commission. By the summer of 1798 the heated debate over war with France was more than ever a party question, and Washington was determined to purify his army. Adams had been willing to provide a few commissions to moderate Republicans (such as Aaron Burr) as a conciliatory gesture, but when James McHenry returned to the capital from Mount Vernon with Washington's list of general officers, the new president discovered that all were staunch Federalists.[20]

In October Mercer took advantage of Princeton's postgraduation break to ride south into Virginia. He had decided that he no longer wanted a commission and was determined to speak with Washington. On October 28 he dined with Washington at Mount Vernon and discovered that he was too late. The former president was preparing to set out for Philadelphia, where he would spend the next five weeks selecting officers for the twelve new regiments. But his long list had already gone out to the secretary of war. Washington grilled Mercer on his politics lest any Republicans accidentally "poison the army."[21]

Exactly two months later, on December 29, John Adams wrote out the list of officers from the names submitted to him since the previous July. "I nominate the following persons," he informed the Senate, six of whom were to be made lieutenants. The first name on the list was "Charles F. Mercer, Virginia." On Tuesday, January 8, 1799, the Senate confirmed the appointments. It was now up to Mercer to accept or decline.[22]

The decision could not have been easy. Mercer knew that Hobart's advice was sound, but he also knew that a military background could provide a basis for a political future, although only if he remained in the North. He had spent the last year of his life using every device and connection available to him trying to obtain a commission, and finally it was within his grasp. But more than anything else he longed to return to Virginia and live on the land left to him by his father. The answer would have to be no. Yet having come to that difficult conclusion, Mercer discovered that the president had unintentionally further complicated his life. Washington's nephew Lawrence Lewis had declined his captain's commission, and Adams routinely passed it to the next man in line. On March 3, the Senate again approved a commission for Charles Fenton Mercer.[23]

Again, Mercer turned down the commission. He declined, he wrote later, "as all probability of actual war had ceased, and it had never been his intention to make arms his profession for life."[24] But in fact Adams had not announced his second attempt to negotite with France until February 18, long after Mercer declined his first commission. Indeed, Adams kept his plans secret because he knew that Timothy Pickering, his disloyal secretary of state, and other members of his cabinet who took their marching orders from Hamilton, wished to keep him firmly on an anti-French course. The truth was that the public fury that followed the publication of the diplomatic papers had passed, and Mercer had no desire to tie his political career to a cause that was becoming unpopular even in the Federalist-dominated North.[25]

One reason for the sudden downturn in Federalist fortunes was the four acts conservatives pushed through Congress during the previous summer. These measures dealt with naturalization, friendly and enemy aliens, and, most of all, "the Punishment of Certain Crimes," a sedition law that made all criticism of the president or Congress, even private criticism, illegal. The acts were nothing less than a blatantly partisan attempt to outlaw the Republican party. But the Sedition Act was increasingly unpopular, even in the North, and it concerned many moderate Federalists like Mercer. "When I read Porcupines [antiadministration] paper I lament that the freedom of the press will not permit him to be silenced," Mercer told Garnett, "without establishing a precedent that would be dangerous to liberty."[26]

On his trips between Princeton and Virginia, Mercer could not have failed to note the changing mood of the republic. Pamphlets sold on the streets of Philadelphia told of southern opposition to the acts, and the papers detailed the jailing of a Vermont congressman for writing in a private letter that Adams had "an unbounded thirst for ridiculous pomp." The "courts that executed the sedition law were very odious," Mercer later admitted, "and the popular clamor born down the popularity of Mr. Adams, and with all his pure patriotism branded him with the epithets of aristocrat, [and] tyrant."[27]

Moreover, Mercer surely knew that the great partisan counterattack, the Virginia and Kentucky Resolutions, originated in his home state. It is even possible, though unlikely, that he knew that James Madison and Thomas Jefferson had secretly written the reports. Madison had consulted often with John Taylor of Caroline while writing his resolution, and the two men frequently met in the Richmond hotel room of James Mercer Garnett, who was himself deeply embroiled in politics. In any case, Mercer was doubtless informed by his brother-in-law that the House of Delegates voted along strict party lines to condemn the four acts and that he himself voted with the majority.[28]

But if Mercer had saved his political hide he had antagonized those who helped him obtain his commissions. Washington was furious not only with Mercer for turning down the first appointment but with Adams for giving the young man a second opportunity. "I find by the Gazettes (I have *no other* information of these matters)," Washington fumed, "that Lieutt Mercer, of the Light Dragoons, is promoted to the Rank of Captn." He was aghast that "a boy" of "20 or 21 years of age" would be chosen "over a Lieutent. of 30, in *every other respect his equal.*" He did not, Washington hastened to add, "mean to derogate from the merits or deserts of this young Gentleman," even though "his whole family are *bitter* in their enmity to the General Government." He simply thought it unwise to offer a captaincy to "a youth fresh from College."[29]

When a month passed and Washington still received no word of explanation from either Adams or Mercer, the frustrated former president fired off another salvo to the secretary of war. With "respect to young Mercer's promotion," he stormed, "I cannot but express my regrets; notwithstanding the high opinion I have of his merit and the sincere regard I entertained for his deceased father." The squire of Mount Vernon noted that "a Lieutenancy was conceived to be a handsome appointment" for a student with almost no military training. A higher post was "radically wrong."[30]

Washington's second letter sent James McHenry scrambling to explain himself. Significantly, he wrote not to Washington or Adams but to Alexander Hamilton, who had been made second in command to the aged former president in the new army. The facts were, the secretary bleated, "that Mr. Mercer had declined the Lieutenancy and was afterwards appointed as a new man to a vacant Captaincy." It was not a promotion from an officer who had accepted a lower rank. Even though Mercer was tactfully trying to distance himself from the post he had craved, McHenry had considered his "a stronger case" and thus had offered the commission.[31]

At about the same time that McHenry was defending his actions Washington discovered that Mercer had turned down the second offer. He was livid, not only because of his efforts in the young man's behalf, but because it appeared to him that the aristocratic student was holding out for yet a third offer more befitting his social station. "I am glad he has refused it," Washington roared. "But, in the nature of common modesty, what did this young Gentleman expect? the command of the Regimt.?" The general was wrong about the reasons for Mercer's refusals, although had he known the truth he certainly would have been no happier.[32]

Whether Mercer knew for sure or simply guessed of Washington's wrath, he decided that the time had come to pay another call at Mount Vernon. In early July he left Princeton and galloped south into Virginia, where he also spent some time mending ties with his estranged family. On August 7 Mercer dined with the former president and assuaged his patron's anger. Also eating with the two men that day was Dr. James Craik, who would bleed his lifelong friend to death the following December.[33]

By September Mercer was back in Princeton. It had been two years since his graduation and he needed to complete the last work of his legal internship for a master's degree in the law. With his first involvement in national politics and world affairs behind him, Mercer devoted himself to his studies. In the fall of 1800, for a second time, he received the honor of finishing at the top of his class and being chosen to give the commencement speech. Yet all that he had seen and heard in Philadelphia was not forgotten, and the address he gave, which was delivered before an audience that included recently fired Secretary of State Timothy Pickering, was one he had written in the winter of 1798. His topic, the need for establishing a large and permanent navy, was so powerful that with Mercer's permission it was published in 1802 and again in 1813 under the title "The Voice of Prophecy."[34]

Mercer's address demonstrated the extent to which he had become a northern, mercantile-minded Federalist. He began by tweaking his fellow Virginians for believing their interests were "to be found in a system unfavourable to foreign commerce." This, he believed, was the basis of "Antifederalism." But, he declared, "it is in vain to contemplate a destruction of our foreign trade." The nation demanded international commerce and would fight to protect it. Here Mercer foreshadowed the argument for a mixed and interlocking economy that would be the heart of the American System he would champion in later years. The nation relied on industry and trade, he argued, and foreign efforts to control it would wield a "paralytic power" felt "through every department of the community." And a nation that required trade required a strong navy. "When we relinquish our navigation," he shouted, "we shall virtually relinquish our independence." Prophetically, Mercer warned his audience that the seemingly endless rivalry of England and France would once more draw the United States into war. "Again," Mercer warned, "our commerce is plundered by the greatest naval powers of Europe." Should the power of France be defeated, "what may we not apprehend from the unrivalled Navy of Britain?" In such a war, the expanse of ocean would be no defense. "A single month will transport an army across the Atlantic; the [same] period it would consume on land in marching from Charlestown to Washington." To delay building a navy, Mercer concluded, was to invite attacks on American shipping and American sailors and thus invite another war.[35]

With his second degree in hand, Mercer had to leave Princeton. Late in life, he spoke of the five years spent at Nassau Hall as his "Golden Age," the only time in his long life he would be "willing to pass over again." It had been a time of success. Twice he had surpassed a class of able and talented young men to win the greatest honor Princeton could bestow, and he had ventured into the turbulent world of national politics and emerged with two generous offers of military position from the president. He had blossomed at Princeton. Now he would return home to accept his reward and prosper in Virginia in the fashion of his father and grandfather.[36]

But Virginia and the nation were changing. The hatred of the Alien and Sedition Acts, the opposition toward the direct property tax (to pay for the enlarged army), and the split in the Federalist party swept the Republicans into power in the election of 1800. Jefferson's triumph was complete. The Federalists lost forty seats in the House, and only one of nineteen members elected from Virginia was a Federalist. But the defeat of the old conservatives did not mean the death of Federalism; it only drove the generation of

Adams and Washington from public life. Younger and more flexible men such as Mercer could bring new life and new methods to the conservative cause.[37]

Just days after the election Mercer bade farewell to his friends at Princeton and rode south toward Virginia. It had been five years since he had lived in the South. Now he "left Nassau Hall" a Federalist and a "Christian"—the terms were synonymous to him—ready to do battle with the "infidel" Jefferson and his infernal crew in their very stronghold.[38]

Upon his return to Virginia, however, Mercer chose to live not on the land in Loudoun County left to him by his father but in the city where his father had sat on the court. The town that seemed so exciting and wonderful a decade past must have appeared much different to the young man who had witnessed both the splendor and squalor of Philadelphia. Turn-of-the-century Richmond was a town of but five thousand people. The massive capitol building gave the dusty hamlet whatever elegance it had, for most of the streets were dung-ridden and unpaved, and when it rained the gullies and ruts in the roads turned into small streams. No gaslights burned in the streets, although most of the houses were new and built of brick.[39]

Despite its foul condition and small population, Richmond was the logical choice for Mercer. Its population was growing rapidly, and it had become an important port. More crucial was that the city remained a Federalist island in a Republican sea. Even following the disastrous election of 1800, the Federalists retained power in the ports of Richmond and Norfolk, which came as close to commercial and mercantile centers as existed in the Old Dominion. Virginia society may have been uncontaminated by businessmen, but its largest urban center was becoming a significant manufacturing hub. The city increasingly reflected the economic mix that Mercer had come to endorse. If he were to enter public life, Richmond would be as good a place as any to start.[40]

Indeed, Mercer knew exactly what he was about. The Richmond superior court system provided the most lucrative legal practice in the state. The cost of living was very high, and he would have to compete with the established lawyers of the city's brilliant bar, but Mercer was not cowed. He had a high opinion of his intellectual and legal abilities, and rightly so. He probably also hoped that the memory of James Mercer would bring business to his door.[41]

Mercer's three-years training in Princeton had perhaps overqualified him for the Virginia bar. The standards of the state were none too high, and a majority of the lawyers had not received any college instruction in the law. Most read with an established lawyer or studied for the bar on their own. Yet Mercer was determined to be well prepared, and he spent almost another full year in diligent study. During this time he had no income and relied on loans from Garnett's friend James Monroe, then serving as governor. By mid-1802 Mercer thought himself ready and appeared before Judges Edmund Pendleton, Edward Carrington, and Spencer Roane; the latter had replaced his father on the bench. Not surprisingly, he breezed through the questions and was granted a license to practice.[42]

But before Mercer could enter his profession—or embark on a political career, his ultimate objective—he had to deal with his family's tangled finances. The chronic overspending of Mercer's grandfather had been compounded by the legal ambiguity created by the Proclamation Line of 1763 and George Mercer's expatriation. When George died in London in 1784 he still owned several parcels of land in Virginia and the Ohio Valley. An unrecorded, unprobated will dated 1770 had been sent from Britain. But George had married in England, and both another will and another claim contested the American Mercers' right to the property. The claims were so complicated that it became clear to the family that a lawyer would have to sent to London to obtain clear title, at least to the potentially lucrative Ohio lands. Charles Fenton was the obvious choice. Because of his excellent legal training and his lack of an established career, it made sense that the young man represent the extensive Mercer clan. Moreover, he could combine his business with a grand tour of England and France, an absolute necessity for any young gentleman.[43]

In October 1802, Mercer left Richmond and anxiously rode north for New York. He intended to spend a few days in the city with John Hobart before he left, and so he wrote to his friend, asking him to obtain passage on an English packet. It was a long trip, but he evidently rode hard, for he made it in less than fifteen days. At the end of the month, the twenty-four-year-old Mercer boarded the ship for Falmouth.[44]

Charles Fenton Mercer's youth truly was his golden age. Except for family fortune, he had received everything he could have possibly received as a child. He had lost his mother at so young an age that he could not remember her, but a devoted father and two doting sisters had eased that loss. Indeed, his awareness that he was his father's favorite child (combined with an understanding of his genuinely superior abilities) possibly led to the massive ego he so often demonstrated in later life. The influence of his father was enormous, and in crucial ways he more resembled a man of his father's generation than one of his own. It was, in fact, the clue to his character.

Like his father, Mercer emerged from his plantation upbringing conservative and antidemocratic. In his settled world class consciousness was understood. The years at Princeton and his travels through the North modified his earlier social and political views. He relinquished his precapitalist, agrarian views, although he did not forsake his other aristocratic attitudes. At the same time, the turbulent world of international politics and the bitter party warfare of the late 1790s introduced into his mind the first stirrings of class conflict. But it was an idea that was not yet strong; the deferential social world of his youth was still too powerful.

Charles Fenton Mercer had become the quintessential Federalist. He had developed a clear understanding of American social and economic structure, his place in it, and its place in the larger world economy. He had logically decided for the party and the method of government that would best serve and protect that understanding. All that was missing was an appreciation of how the economy and the political structure of his country might change and how he and those like him would have to adapt to retain their position. But those were lessons to come. As the packet sailed out of New York harbor, Mercer turned his back on the city and looked to the east. He was turning from his past to his future.

Notes

ABBREVIATIONS

ACS	American Colonization Society
CFM	Charles Fenton Mercer
COCC	Chesapeake and Ohio Canal Company
DAB	*Dictionary of American Biography*, ed. Allen Johnson and Dumas Malone, 21 vols., 1928–1936.
JQA	John Quincy Adams
JSH	*Journal of Southern History*
LC	Library of Congress
NJHS	New Jersey Historical Society
NYHS	New-York Historical Society
PRO, FO	Great Britain, Public Record Office, Foreign Office
UVA	University of Virginia
VHS	Virginia Historical Society

VMHB   *Virginia Magazine of History and Biography*
VSL   Virginia State Library
WMQ   *William and Mary Quarterly*

1. James T. Flexner, *George Washington, Anguish and Farewell* (Boston, 1969), 379; Keith I. Polakoff, *Political Parties in American History* (New York, 1981), 50.
2. William N. Chambers, *Political Parties in a New Nation: The American Experience, 1776–1809* (New York, 1963), 43–44.
3. Charles Fenton Mercer, *An Exposition of the Weakness and Inefficiency of the Government of the United States of North America* (N.p., 1845), 207. Although written much later, this work is autobiographical, and Mercer indicated that it was at this point in his life that he reached such a conclusion.
4. CFM to James M. Garnett, June 18, 1798, CFM Papers, NYHS.
5. Mercer, *Exposition*, 236–37.
6. David H. Fischer, *The Revolution of American Conservatism: The Federalist Party in the Era of Jeffersonian Democracy* (New York, 1965), 163; Edward C. Carter, "A 'Wild Irishman' under Every Federalist's Bed: Nationalization in Philadelphia, 1789–1806." *Pennsylvania Magazine of History and Biography* 94 (July 1970): 333, 342; Mercer, *Exposition*, 325.
7. Page Smith, *John Adams*, 2 vols. (New York, 1962), 2:944–945; Hannah Hobart to John H. Hobart, November 10, 1797, in Arthur Lowndes, ed., *The Correspondence of John Henry Hobart*, 6 vols. (New York, 1912), 1:314–15.
8. Hannah Hobart to John H. Hobart, December 17, 1797, in Lowndes, ed., *Correspondence of Hobart*, 1:342; George Washington to James McHenry, May 5, 1799, in John C. Fitzpatrick, ed., *The Writings of George Washington*, 39 vols. (Washington, D.C. 1931–44), 37:201–2.
9. Hannah Hobart to John H. Hobart, November 30, December 17, 1797, January 7, 9, 1798, in Lowndes, ed., *Correspondence of Hobart*, 1:326, 342–44, 2:3–4, 6.
10. Smith, *Adams*, 2:952–53; John C. Miller, *The Federalist Era, 1789–1801* (New York, 1960), 210–12; Ralph A. Brown, *The Presidency of John Adams* (Lawrence, 1975), 48–51.
11. Smith, *Adams*, 2:962–63; Hannah Hobart to John H. Hobart, April 18, 1789, in Lowndes, ed., *Correspondence of Hobart*, 2:48–49.
12. Thomas J. Wertenbaker, *Princeton, 1746–1896* (Princeton, 1946), 208–9; CFM to James M. Garnett, June 18, 1789, CFM Papers, NYHS.
13. CFM, Speech of April 21, 1798, CFM Papers, NYHS.
14. John H. Hobart to CFM, May 15, 1798, in James Mercer Garnett, ed., *Biographical Sketch of Hon. Charles Fenton Mercer, 1778–1858* (Richmond, 1911), 30–32.
15. *Annals of Congress*, 5th Cong., 1772 (Philadelphia, 1799); *Gazette of the United States* (Philadelphia), June 21, 1798; *Aurora*, (Philadelphia) May 28, 1798.
16. CFM, Autobiographical Sketch, Mercer-Hunter Papers, VSL.
17. John H. Hobart to CFM, July 24, 1798, in Lowndes, ed., *Correspondence of Hobart*, 2:89–91.
18. George Washington to CFM, July 25, 1798, in Fitzpatrick, ed., *Writings of Washington*, 36:367.
19. George Washington to James McHenry, July 25, 1798, ibid., 366.
20. Brown, *Presidency of Adams*, 68: Dumas Malone, *Jefferson and His Time*, 6 vols. (Boston, 1948–81), 3:427.
21. George Washington Diary, October 28, 1798, in Donald Jackson and Dorothy Twohig, eds., *The Diaries of George Washington*, 6 vols. (Charlottesville, 1976–79), 6:359; George Washington to James McHenry, October 21, 1798, in Fitzpatrick, ed., *Writings of Washington*, 36:505.

22. John Adams to the Senate, December 29, 1798, in *Journal of the Executive Proceedings of the Senate*, 3 vols. (Washington, D.C., 1828), 1:298, 303–4; *Gazette of the United States* (Philadelphia), January 10, 1799.

23. *Journal of the Executive Proceedings* 1:322–23.

24. CFM, Autobiographical Sketch, Mercer-Hunter Papers. Mercer wrote this short autobiography in 1849 when attempting to convince President Zachary Taylor and Secretary of State John Clayton to name him minister to one of the German states. Mercer's superior memory for events and dates makes it a useful guide to his public career, although it is obvious that he attempted to put the best face on his actions. Other evidence in this case indicates that Mercer was not being completely honest in stating why he declined the commissions.

25. *Gazette of the United States*, February 28, 1799; Smith, *Adams*, 2:999; Flexner, *Washington*, 426.

26. CFM to James Mercer Garnett, June 18, 1798, CFM Papers, NYHS; Norman Risjord, "The Virginia Federalists," *JSH* 33 (November 1967): 503. In addition to thinking the act unconstitutional he thought it impolitic. See Mercer, *Exposition*, 74.

27. *Aurora*, (Philadelphia) March 15, 1799; James Morton Smith, *Freedom's Fetters: The Alien and Sedition Laws and American Civil Liberties* (Ithaca, 1956), 221–46; Mercer, *Exposition*, 237–38.

28. James M. Garnett, *Biographical Sketch of Hon. James Mercer Garnett, with Mercer-Garnett and Mercer Genealogies* (Richmond, 1910), 5–6; Chambers, *Political Parties*, 140.

29. George Washington to James McHenry, March 25, 1799, in Fitzpatrick, ed., *Writings of Washington*, 37:161–63.

30. Washington to McHenry, April 23, 1799, ibid., 191–92.

31. James McHenry to Alexander Hamilton, August 30, 1799, in Harold C. Syrett, ed., *The Papers of Alexander Hamilton*, 26 vols. (New York, 1961–79), 23:361–65.

32. George Washington to James McHenry, May 5, 1799, in Fitzpatrick, ed., *Writings of Washington*, 37:201–2.

33. John H. Hobart to CFM, July 14, 1799, in Garnett, ed., *Biographical Sketch*, 32; George Washington, Diary, August 7, 1799, in Jackson and Twohig, eds., *Diaries of Washington*, 6:359.

34. Hannah Hobart to John H. Hobart, September 10, 1799, in Lowndes, ed., *Correspondence of Hobart*, 2:162: CFM, Autobiographical Sketch, Mercer-Hunter Papers; CFM to Timothy Pickering, January 27, 1817, Pickering Papers, LC. The question of who wrote "An Address to the People of the United States" has long been disputed, although the *National Union Catalog* now lists Mercer as one of the possible authors. There is no reason to dispute his Autobiographical Sketch in this case. Moreover, former student Samuel Southard, in Charles Fenton Mercer, ed., *The Farewell Address of the Hon. C. F. Mercer to his Constituents* (N.p., 1839), 15–16, recalled the speech Mercer "delivered when he presented himself to receive his second honorary degree, which address, Mr. S[outhard]. remembered, embraced, among other topics an eloquent and patriotic argument for the Navy."

35. [Charles Fenton Mercer], "An Address to the People of the United States, on the Policy of Maintaining a Permanent Navy" (1802), *Magazine of History* 18, no. 3, extra no. 71 (1921): 140–70.

36. CFM to Maria H. Garnett, June 6, 1856, Mercer-Hunter Papers.

37. Miller, *Federalist Era*, 273–74; Fischer, *Revolution of American Conservatism*, 29.

38. CFM to Maria H. Garnett, June 6, 1856, Mercer-Hunter Papers; CFM to Eliza Garnett, April 5, 1843, Mercer Family Papers, VHS.

39. CFM, Autobiographical Sketch, Mercer-Hunter Papers; Virginius Dabney, *Richmond: The Story of a City* (New York, 1976), 78–82.

40. Harry Ammon, *James Monroe: The Quest for National Identity* (New York, 1971), 184; Daniel P. Jordan, *Political Leadership in Jefferson's Virginia* (Charlottesville, 1983), 17; Dabney, *Richmond*, 61–62.

41. Glyndon G. Van Deusen, *The Life of Henry Clay* (Boston, 1937), 14–15.

42. James Monroe to CFM, June 17, 1802, James Monroe Papers, UVA; CFM, Autobiographical Sketch, Mercer-Hunter Papers.

43. Alfred P. James, *George Mercer of the Ohio Company: A Study in Frustration* (Pittsburgh, 1963), *DAB*, 12:544; CFM, Autobiographical Sketch, Mercer-Hunter Papers.

44. CFM to John H. Hobart, October 14, 1802, in Lowndes, ed., Correspondence of Hobart, 3:98.

PART TWO

A New Era
1802–1817

3

Europe

The trip across the Atlantic in the dead of winter was miserable, yet December in London was even worse. After the country air of Princeton and the pervasive but sweet tobacco aroma of Richmond, Mercer must have found it difficult to adjust to the damp and smoky London climate. And the cost of living was almost more than he could afford. He had been forced to borrow to exist in Richmond, and prices in London were five times higher. Worse yet, Mercer's Federalist enthusiasm for Great Britain was quickly eroded by haughty English manners. "I have changed my opinion of the personages in the drama," he informed Hobart; his "reverence" for the British was gone. He was appalled by London, "this noisy, selfish and luxurious city," which greeted him with pride and suspicion. "I fear we have been deceived," he sighed.[1]

Mercer's patrician sensibilities were especially assaulted by the London working class. The Irish of Philadelphia and the mobs of Paris had helped turn him toward Federalism, but they were nothing compared to the horrors of Hanoverian London. The British people were known throughout Europe for their turbulence, and the common people of London shocked even American visitors with their lack of deference. The "unsocial city" filled with "rough inhabitants" put the melancholy Virginian into an unusually deep mood of "fretfulness and disgust."[2]

To ease his mind Mercer turned to the church. Surrounded by members of his own class, he found the sermons of the Anglican clergy soothing. He heartily endorsed one lecture that condemned the "indecency of dress among fashionable women, immoral conversation among men," and the loud and frequent "public violation of the sabbath" by "noisy festivity or midnight routes."[3]

Handling his uncle's tangled estate, however, turned out to be less wearing than he expected. Parker, the executor, was, if not especially agreeable, knowledgeable about the Mercer family finances. Despite a government pension, his uncle George had fallen upon bad times during his last years and had borrowed heaviy. He borrowed eight thousand pounds sterling from a man named Gravatt, to whom he gave his share of the Ohio land bonds as collateral. Evidently he died before he could repay the loan, and the bonds stayed with Gravatt. But then Gravatt, too, died, and settling the affair fell to Parker and his lawyer, a Mr. Fearon. It was not clear whether James Mercer owed his brother money or who owned the land to which Parker held the bonds.[4]

As the coadministrator of his father's estate, Mercer intended to obtain clear title to the Ohio lands and settle any outstanding debts. He quickly perceived that Parker had the better legal argument, and he therefore accepted a tentative agreement based on a compromise suggested by the executor. The Mercers would pay Parker six thousand pounds sterling (roughly twenty thousand dollars) for his entire claim, payable in six annual installments at 4 percent interest. Mercer sent this proposal to John Francis Mercer for his approval. Charles Fenton wrongly assumed that his family would accept his judgment in the matter.[5]

With the business that brought him to England settled, at least until he heard from his uncle, Mercer began his grand tour. Several months in France seemed an excellent idea to get away from the British and their damp climate. Early in 1803 Mercer departed for Paris in the company of a Mr. Shaw, an Englishman much older than himself. Mercer felt compelled to compete against those of his own age, but he harbored no such compulsion toward older men. (Perhaps that is why he felt no need to compete with Hobart.) To his great surprise, Mercer found that he truly enjoyed France, the demon with which he was so recently prepared to do battle. Immediately upon their arrival in Paris, Shaw called on St. Cyr Cocquard, an old friend from before the Revolution. Cocquard had left his chateau in Gascogny for the season, and he was delighted to join Mercer and Shaw in their "rambles" about Paris. The young patrician deeply admired the manners and habits of the old aristocrat. They "breakfasted on his prunes and wine, produced on his own estate, and brought by him to Paris." Best of all, Cocquard was willing to teach Mercer French, his fourth language. "Never was an instructor more patient," Mercer told Hobart, or "more anxious for the progress of his pupil."[6]

Cocquard had numerous friends and connections in the city, and through him Mercer became acquainted with bishops, noblemen, republican generals, legislators, and men of science. Day by day the old man became fonder of Mercer and tried to talk him into remaining in France. Cocquard's plan was for Mercer to live with him for a time, then the two men would roam the length of Europe, and finally they would cross the Atlantic and travel throughout the United States. Mercer was tempted, just as he was touched by the rich man's "peculiar" offer to "give five hundred guineas to the poor" as an incentive for him to stay.[7]

Mercer's growing friendship with Shaw and Cocquard, two life-long bachelors, did not sit well with the narrow-minded and religious Hobart, who saw something more than friendship in the relationship and told Mercer so. Mercer was quick to defend his new life. "You are under an error," he wrote peevishly, "which I ought to have guarded against when I mention'd the warm friendship [Cocquard] expressed for me." Mercer was unwilling to accept criticism from his old friend, especially now that Hobart was married. Mercer had reacted to that news with more than a hint of jealousy and as little enthusiasm as possible and in his letters stubbornly refused to recognize Hobart's wife's existence aside from a perennially cool request to "remember" him to "Mrs. Hobart." The two men were never again close. His cryptic but revealing denial to the contrary, it is possible that far from the restrictive atmosphere of home and school Mercer found himself and was happy for the first time in his life. Mercer's financial situation would not allow him to stay, although he did tarry long enough to join Cocquard and Shaw in watching Napoleon Bonaparte review his troops in the yard of the Tuileries. Cocquard was a friend of Jean Antoine Chaptal, the minister of the interior, who allowed them to watch the spectacle from his window, "the best situation to see it from." Mercer was no longer so certain in his views on Britain and France.[8]

Unlike the proud and suspicious British, the French had "an enchanting urbanity." They flattered him, poured him fine wines, and led him on long walks "admist the forsaken grandeur" of the palace of Versailles. Best of all, Cocquard had a seemingly endless number of friends, many of them with connections to Napoleon's emerging educational system. It was they who most influenced the young American's mind. Among them were Bernard de la Ville, the Comte de Lacépède, professors Joseph Louis Lagrante and Pierre Simon de Laplace, Joseph Jerome LeFrancais de Lalande, Antoine François, Gaspard Monge, and Fourcroix, the creator of three hundred elementary schools. Like Cocquard, these aged aristocrats, many of whom had become Bonapartists, took a liking to Mercer; they were, he wrote, not only "my masters, but my friends."[9]

What Mercer learned of Napoleonic education from his friends was like an answer to his prayers. The realization that all was not well in his tidy, class-conscious world had begun when he saw the dirty side streets of London. To the class consciousness he had learned from his father was added the idea of class conflict. But education might solve this problem. Napoleon, Mercer was told, saw a close connection between education and political stability; in a society hierarchized by property and money, education could discipline as well as enlighten, control as well as liberate. Napoleon's new system largely excluded primary education, an area Mercer would soon devote much time and effort to, but clearly the seeds for later action had been planted.[10]

By late fall the time had come for Mercer to return to England. St. Cyr Cocquard continued to press his young friend to stay with him and spend the summers in Gascogny and the winters in Paris, where Mercer would be tutored in French literature, history, and the sciences. But the "embarrassments" he continued to suffer "for want of regular remittances from home" forced him to spend no more time in Europe than it would take to receive an answer from his family and settle George Mercer's estate.[11]

But when he returned to England, he found no messages from his uncle. And after having been accepted in the highest circles in France, Mercer found London even more dreary and unkind than before. "The neglect of all strangers who are foreigners in London," he complained to Hobart, "I have had my full proportion." He considered returning to France. But on May 15 word reached London of "the termination of the [peace] negociation at Paris." Great Britain promptly issued "letters of marque." Europe was again at war.[12]

If the renewed conflict trapped Mercer in England, it also brought him an old friend in the person of James Monroe. Following his election, Jefferson had retained Federalist Rufus King as minister to Great Britain, and there Mercer met the New York conservative. But King had tired of the post after eight years, and with the outbreak of war Jefferson desired to have a more trusted friend in that crucial position. He appointed Monroe, who arrived on July 18, 1803. The best news for Mercer was that Monroe counted James Mercer Garnett as a warm friend and was willing to lend a hand in settling the family finances.[13]

Mercer was surely pleased to see a friendly face in the cold, unruly London crowd, but after several months had passed with still no word from his uncle he decided to leave the city and travel throughout the country. "In London you certainly see the English character at the worst," Mercer grumbled. But "among the genteel country families," he presumed, "it wears a very different and far more amiable aspect." Specifically, he wished to visit the Reverend Jonathan Boucher, a religious connection of Hobart's, who lived in the tiny country village of Epsom.[14]

In late July Mercer left London armed with a letter of introduction from Hobart. Boucher, a much older man, gladly took the young American in. With Boucher, a Tory who had once lived in Virginia, Mercer felt content in familiar society. "I believed, for a moment," Mercer gushed, "that I saw the old patriarchal simplicity revived." Indeed, in Epsom Marlborough and perhaps his father seemed to come alive again. Boucher's "gardens, his grounds, his house" all brought back childhood memories. Mercer was "especially pleased" with the library, the largest he had ever seen in a private home. For his part, Boucher was delighted to show his new friend his estate, and they ambled beneath the long row of evergreens and along the lake. The wealthy Boucher had broad interests in politics and economics—he had recently written a pamphlet on banking—and doubtless added new topics to Mercer's growing list of issues to ponder.[15]

After a week Mercer tore himself away from this charmed world, as he had from Cocquard, and returned to London in hopes of finding a letter from his uncle. He found nothing but his ever-increasing dislike of the city. "The English are certainly not quick in their feelings," Mercer fumed. It "is not easy to obtain a place in their hearts." But thinking of Boucher he admitted "that when a person once obtained a familiar footing with them, they would go great lengths to please him." Certainly as a nation they have "the means of doing so," he observed with more than a touch of jealousy.[16]

By September Mercer had still not heard from America. The war hindered the mails, but he evidently presumed that no news meant his family acquiesced in his legal handiwork. Again he decided to leave the city, this time on a longer journey. He would traverse

England "on foot," he wrote much later, "for the acquisition of knowledge I might render useful at home." Clearly, Mercer was again thinking of a career in politics. He began his journey by heading up the Thames toward Richmond and from there to Twickenham and Hampton Court. He had intended to continue by boat to Windsor, but low water forced him to abandon his plans and take a carriage to Brentford, from which he could easily reach Windsor. For two days he remained there with the family of the "worthy" James Ogilvie, the brother of the poet.[17]

Mercer next traveled northwest toward Oxford, where he presented a letter of introduction to John Gutch at Oxford University. Gutch was writing the history of the school, but he put aside his work to provide Mercer with a tour of "the Halls, libraries, and chapels." Like all Americans on a grand tour, Mercer took a coach to Stratford,where he visited "the House in which Shakespear was born." By September 27 he reached the port of Gloucester.[18]

Mercer briefly considered returning to London, but his curiosity pulled him northward. He was anxious to visit the manufacturing region of Birmingham of which he had heard so much. Two days later he was there. For some time he remained in Birmingham "employed in taking a cursory view of its celebrated manufactories." What he saw both fascinated and frightened him, for it was nothing less than "an elemental war with miners and forgers." Although it did not seem so to Mercer, Birmingham was hardly the most volatile industrial center in England.[19]

Mercer was fascinated by Birmingham. He wished to know more about the city's dynamics, and so he "mixed a great deal with the lower classes of the people." He decided, as did almost all observers of every political brand, that the factories were producing a new class relationship. A young man as perceptive as Mercer, raised in a society in which class consciousness was understood, well knew what he was seeing. It was not just the end of the old order, it was the future his own country faced.[20]

In early October Mercer returned to London, where again he found no communication from his uncle. Two weeks later, almost a year from the time he had sailed from New York harbor, Mercer stood on the dock, preparing to recross the Atlantic. The silence of his family and the emptiness of his purse led him to hope that he had settled the family business successfully. He was "quitting England without regret." He wished to escape not only the "noisy and sordid" London crowd but the "thousand anxieties" that pushed their way into his mind. The trip had changed him. His mind had been assaulted by revolutionary France, wild Irishmen, Philadelphia mobs, the Republican tide, and then the London crowd and the manufacturing district, where the process of industrialization was marked by exceptional violence. His sense of social harmony, a notion held by most Federalists of Washington's age, was gone forever. And to the class consciousness of his father's generation was added a new sense of class conflict, a concept southern Republicans associated only with manufactures.[21]

Europe ruined Mercer for the South, if Princeton had not already done so. Financial insolvency, he realized, was only one of his problems, one cause of his unhappiness. What he had witnessed in England made him uneasy, and his feelings were further complicated by Paris and his relationship with Cocquard. It seemed unlikely that he could find a satisfatory life in the Tidewater world that had nurtured him.

But if Mercer's year in Europe had cost him his peace of mind, it had also given him something of immense value: a glimpse into the future. He had seen industrial expansion in all its force and fury, and he well knew that it would reach his nation in time. The lessons of Europe, combined with his relative lack of position in Virginia and the seeds of duty planted in Princeton, compelled Mercer into a life in politics, a professional career almost unknown to his generation. He had not yet devised a plan of action, but in the next few years he would begin to prepare for that industrial revolution in a way that would benefit him personally, allow those like him to retain their position, and forge social relationships in a way that would, he hoped, minimize the sort of upheaval he had witnessed. The lessons would also aid him in doing this within the context of what he knew Jefferson had wrought: "A new era in the political history of the country."[22]

Notes

ABBREVIATIONS

ACS	American Colonization Society
CFM	Charles Fenton Mercer
COCC	Chesapeake and Ohio Canal Company
DAB	*Dictionary of American Biography,* ed. Allen Johnson and Dumas Malone, 21 vols., 1928–1936.

JQA   John Quincy Adams
JSH   Journal of Southern History
LC   Library of Congress
NJHS   New Jersey Historical Society
NYHS   New-York Historical Society
PRO, FO   Great Britain, Public Record Office, Foreign Office
UVA   University of Virginia
VHS   Virginia Historical Society
VMHB   Virginia Magazine of History and Biography
VSL   Virginia State Library
WMQ   William and Mary Quarterly

1. Harry J. Ammon, *James Monroe: The Quest for National Identity* (New York, 1971), 230; CFM to John H. Hobart, May 15, 1803, in Lowndes, ed., *The Correspondence of John Henry Hobart*, 6 vols. (New York, 1912), 3:200–205.

2. E. P. Thompson, *The Making of the English Working Class* (New York, 1963), 62; George Rude, *Hanoverian London, 1714–1808* (Berkeley, 1971), 184; CFM to John H. Hobart, June 13, 1803, in Lowndes, ed., *Correspondence of Hobart*, 3:224.

3. CFM to John H. Hobart, May 15, 1803, in Lowndes, ed., *Correspondence of Hobart*, 3:200–205.

4. CFM to John Francis Mercer, September 1804, Mercer Family Papers, VHS.

5. John T. Brooke to John Francis Mercer, October 2, 1803, ibid.

6. CFM to John H. Hobart, October 15, 1803, in Lowndes, ed., *Correspondence of Hobart*, 3:290–91.

7. Ibid., 291.

8. Ibid., 290–91.

9. CFM to John H. Hobart, June 13, 1803, ibid., 225–26.

10. Louis Bergeron, *France Under Napoleon*, trans. R. R. Palmer (Princeton, 1981), 32–33; Michel Foucault, *Discipline and Punish: The Birth of the Prison*, trans. Alan Sheridan (New York, 1979), 147, 149, 156–61, 166, 170–94.

11. CFM to John H. Hobart, June 13, 1803, in Lowndes, ed., *Correspondence of Hobart*, 3:225–26.

12. CFM to John H. Hobart, May 15, 1803, ibid., 204–5.

13. Ralph Ketcham, *James Madison, A Biography* (New York, 1971), 424; James Monroe to CFM, February 1, 1809, in Stanislaus M. Hamilton, ed., *The Writings of James Monroe*, 7 vols. (New York, 1898–1903), 5:92–93.

14. CFM to John H. Hobart, May 15, 1803, in Lowndes, ed., *Correspondence of Hobart*, 3:203; John H. Hobart to CFM, July 9, 1803, in John McVicar, ed., *The Early Life and Professional Years of Bishop Hobart* (Oxford, 1838), 234–35.

15. Leslie Stephen, ed., *Dictionary of National Biography*, 66 vols. (New York, 1885–1901), 6:3; John H. Hobart to Jonathan Boucher, November 22, 1802, in James Mercer Garnett, ed., *Biographical Sketch of Hon. Charles Fenton Mercer, 1778–1858* (Richmond, 1911), 33–34; CFM to John H. Hobart, July 29, 1803, ibid., 34–35.

16. John H. Hobart to CFM, July 9, 1803, in McVicar, ed., *Early Life of Hobart*, 234–35.

17. CFM to Lord Radstock, July 12, 1856, CFM Papers, NYHS; CFM to John H. Hobart, September 27, 1803, in Lowndes, ed., *Correspondence of Hobart*, 3:273.

18. CFM to Hobart, September 27, 1803, in Lowndes, ed., *Correspondence of Hobart*, 3:273–74.

19. Ibid., 274; Thompson, *Making of the English Working Class*, 239.

20. CFM to John H. Hobart, October 15, 1803, in Lowndes, ed., *Correspondence of Hobart*, 3:290.

21. Ibid., 288–91. David H. Fischer, *The Revolution of American Conservatism:*

The Federalist Party in the Era of Jeffersonian Democracy (New York, 1965), 34, argues that most younger Federalists "added a new sense of class conflict [to] the class consciousness of the old school." Mercer's experiences in Britain would have made his sense of turmoil stronger than most.

22. Charles Fenton Mercer, *An Exposition of the Weakness and Inefficiency of the Government in the United States of North America* (N.p., 1845), 239.

4

Aldie

The lessons of Europe did not lead to a full-blown plan of action in Mercer's mind. Rather they produced an evolution of thought that would slowly, over the next decade, reveal a sophisticated, interlocking economic program. This system was evolved through much serious thought, and over the next years Mercer was to have a great deal of time for contemplation. He first had to attempt to solve the seemingly endless problem of family finances, and he again had to establish a residence and stake his claim to social preeminence.

Instead of returning to Richmond, Mercer "finally resolved to settle" on the land left to him by his father in Loudoun County. The benefits of living on his own land in a rural district were obvious to a young man short of funds, but the decision also involved hard-headed political calculations. Like Richmond, the northern Piedmont county of Loudoun was a Federalist stronghold, and obtaining election from that district would be easy. Best of all, his property was only ten miles from the thriving country town of Leesburg and only thirty from the city of Washington. He would have little competition from other lawyers, for there were none there of his caliber and education. It would even be possible to practice law in Washington if he could get cases. By June 1804, Mercer was busy building a house, which he named Aldie, as tradition connected his family with the Mercers of Aldie castle, Scotland. Eventually the village that sprang up around his home adopted the name.[1]

Located on gently rolling land and watered by a deep creek, the plot James Mercer left his son consisted of 385 acres, 219 of them prime timberland. The acreage alone was impressive by northern Virginia standards; in a region of small, single-family farms, Mercer was one of the largest landholders. His fields would be worked by his handful of human property—they numbered less than ten in this period—which made him unusual although hardly unique in a county inhabited by antislavery Quakers. By the standards of his county, Mercer, despite his endless financial problems, was a very wealthy man. By the ostentatious standards of Marlborough and the rest of the plantation South, he was not. Yet because of his background and the promise of his future based on his education, Mercer placed himself—and was seen by others—firmly in the upper class.[2]

As Mercer watched his modest two-story clapboard house being constructed, he thought of all he had seen in Europe. As in England, class lines in the United States, and especially in Virginia, remained distinct. But the expanding American franchise forced the upper classes into a familiarity with the lower in a way unheard-of in Britain. Mercer understood that the retention of wealth was more crucial in America. Money could raise one up the social scale, just as the loss of it could drive a man like himself out of the upper class. Wealth was essential among the patrician element of Virginia, for gentlemen were expected to dress elegantly, spend lavishly, and conduct themselves in a fashion that marked them as men of noble birth. The Mercer name alone, although helpful, would not be enough.

All of this was disturbing to the young conservative. He had loathed London at least in part because it was so undeferential, and his charmed youth led him to expect deference as his just due. Mercer was increasingly aware that the American lower classes were beginning to act more and more like the unruly London crowd. Like most Federalists, he viewed the decaying of the old social habits with alarm, but because of his experiences in England he viewed the decline of deferential behavior with a different perspective. "This hatred of the higher classes goes further in the United States than in England," he grumbled, "because there they having no vote, do often consult their superiors and take advice from them, and become proud of their patronage."[3]

Mercer perceived that the franchise would change class relations in the United States. He saw the growing tendency toward the elimination of property restrictions on the vote as dangerous. To give the lower classes the vote, he thought, would only "bring down the government to their own standard." It was sheer madness. "Ignorant from birth and habit," he snorted, "they cannot judge of the wise and proper plans of improving the country." A man like himself would be lost in such a world because such voters "deride and hate all that is elegant, and civilized, and tasteful." The franchise brought a new element to Mercer's evolving equation. He would not only have to prepare his nation for the early stages of industrial growth—which was already under way in the North—to avoid the violence he had seen in England, but he would have to do it in a way that the lower classes would accept.4

This feat would have to be accomplished in the face of the primary agent of political madness in the United States: the Republican party. He knew that such a conservative program would not be easily accepted as long as "demagogues" like Jefferson provided the prople with an inflated sense of their own importance. The principal crime of the popular president, whose chief character traits, Mercer believed, were "fraud, hypocricy, [and] treachery," was that he told the lower classes "that they are not only as good as the independent and higher classes, but better, because they work and produce what others consume and profit by to grow rich upon." Most outrageous of all, the Republicans courted the common people and "invite[d] them to their political meetings and clubrooms."5

If Mercer well understood the problems he faced, he did not yet know how to implement the scheme that was growing in his mind. A vehicle would be needed to put his plans into action, but his beloved Federalist party was seriously damaged in 1804. The smoothly operating Republican organization, the relative calm of Jefferson's first term, and the defection of moderate Federalists had combined to produce a stunning victory that year. The Virginia Federalists did not even bother to nominate an electoral slate. If the Federalists were to compete with the Jeffersonians, they too would have to invite the common people into their clubrooms.6

It was evident that Charles Fenton Mercer and other Federalists would have to accept the concept of party, and tentatively the Virginia conservatives labored to establish a party machine. One of the first steps was the organization of Federalist clubs like the Washington Society of Alexandria, which resembled the Jacobin societies that Washington had so bitterly criticized in the previous decade. The club had been organized in early 1800; upon Mercer's return to Virginia he quickly joined. The group met four times a year and sponsored an annual parade through the streets of Alexandria on Washington's birthday. Yet the club's policies reflected the old Federalist ideas as well as the new, for membership dues were kept high enough to eliminate all but the "better sort." The society, however, did present one major speech a year, which served as the occasion for open convention and party planning. The speaker was chosen by ballot.[7]

In 1806 Mercer was chosen to speak. The choice of so young a man by a relatively aged group signaled not only the high esteem in which Mercer was held but probably also that he was deeply involved with both the society and the slowly emerging state party organization. It was an important day in Mercer's political career. The speech gave him the opportunity to outline some of his ideas to those in a position to do something to implement them. It also afforded him valuable exposure in both his region, and, considering the august nature of his audience, the state. It was his moment, and he did not intend to squander it.

The United States, he began ominously, was in danger. "The extension of commerce, and the progress of the [technical] arts," he warned, "create as much poverty, as opulence." The new class system created by industrialization, combined with the increase of population, which "expedites the division of property, multiplies the number of the indigent, even more rapidly, than that of the wealthy." The result, Mercer told his audience, was that a "corrupt mass" would arise, "easily set afloat by abandoned men, and as easily directed, by the impulse of passion, to the most destructive purpose." But the coming of the industrial order did not need to portend great violence. Remembering what he had learned in France, Mercer turned to the hope that public education held out, a hope that he would raise again and again in his public career. "Along side of the vast dungeons which you have built to incarcerate your fellow men," he implored, "erect humble schools." Prisons "can only punish." But schools developed along the lines of the French system could discipline and control. "It is Education, national education alone," Mercer suggested, "that can prevent crimes."[8]

Whatever the older Federalists may have thought of his speech, nothing came of it in Virginia, where public education remained among the lowest of priorities. The speech reflected Mercer's predilection to gloom, an unfortunate trait he would never lose. This outlook continued to feed his desire to enter politics so that he might enact some of his emerging plans. His pessimism was part of his political orientation; it wed him to the conservative cause. "I am sick," he whined to Hobart. "Indeed, I am weary of affairs, and almost so, of the world." He was, he admitted, of a "solitary and friendless" character. It was "not in [his] nature to be happy." These pronouncements were accepted by most of his family and friends with some humor, and his cousin Margaret Mercer laughingly tagged him with nickname of "Dick Doleful." A few of his friends, however, found his demeanor annoying. "I have just heard from Mercer. How much he indulges in gloom," one college friend reported to Hobart, adding: "He is very well."[9]

But Mercer could not yet devote himself fully to Federalist politics. Again he was sidetracked by his nagging financial problems. Although he had little money as yet, if the suit with his English creditors was settled he would inherit some of his father's land in the Ohio Valley, which he hoped to sell. In an attempt to discover just what his holdings might entail, he struck out in early 1804 on the treacherous two-hundred-mile journey across the mountains to the mouth of the Kanawha River. There, to his great dismay, Mercer discovered that the "quantity, as well as the quality" of the land was inferior to what he had been led to expect.[10]

Worse still, the lands were not yet his; the suit with his uncle's creditors was far from settled. Mercer had thought he had negotiated a fair compromise, but it was not final until agreed to by the rest of the American Mercers. Small details had to be concluded, although James Monroe, still in England, was kind enough to offer to act as agent in Mercer's absence. Even so, distance created a problem. Mercer not only had to ship long and detailed instructions to Monroe, he had to send them by way of New York, the port from which the English packets sailed. Hobart was willing to forward his letters and bills of exchange to London, but because the process was so lengthy, Mercer lived in fear that the delay would expose Monroe "to the most inconvenient embarrassment" and would "disgrace" Mercer.[11]

To make matters worse, Solomon Betton, his brother-in-law, was seriously in debt. The deficit was not originally his own but that of John Fenton, Charles Fenton's only brother, who was also anxiously awaiting the outcome of the English suit. But Betton was a true Mercer in that he could not recognize a bad bargain when he saw it, and he assumed the debt in exchange for some of John Fenton's unproductive land. Betton was unable to make a profit on the land, and he turned to his family for help. Betton's brother had "ready money at command" but would not aid his hapless sibling. Charles Fenton, despite his own problems, kindly loaned the talentless Betton what he needed. In exchange, Mercer obtained most of the worthless land.[12]

In early 1805, Mercer received news from London that Parker, the executor of Gravatt's estate, and Fearon, Parker's attorney, had made a new compromise offer of 4,750 pounds sterling. The compromise, however, did not extinguish the claims of a woman who had also made loans to George Mercer. Fearon promised Charles Fenton that Miss Wroughton, the claimant, had died without heirs, but Mercer thought Fearon of uncertain character and placed little faith in his word. Still, Mercer continued to think this the best deal that could be obtained under the law, and he tried to convince his doubting family. Monroe, meanwhile, waited apprehensively for a reply.[13]

Charles Fenton's uncle John Francis Mercer thought a better deal could be obtained, and he stubbornly refused to answer Mercer's letters or meet with him in Virginia. Mercer begged his uncle to discuss the case with him, telling him he would soon have to return to the Ohio River. He also informed his uncle that Monroe had obtained another concession from Fearon, the right to pay off the debt in five annual installments. Still no answer was forthcoming. To Mercer's mortification, Monroe then informed him that he was departing for Madrid and washing his hands of the affair. As he had not heard from Mercer, he sent on Fearon's last communication for Mercer to "accept or reject." Charles Fenton exploded, telling his silent uncle that he too was finished. "I am constrained to add that I cannot devote more of my time to this subject," wrote Mercer, "without absolute ruin to my profession."[14]

The threat was sufficient to convince his uncle that the time had come to settle, and with the suit behind him Mercer prepared to travel west. Although the land he had inherited was not rich, it was near a small but growing town, and Mercer hoped to obtain quick money by selling "a part of its suburbs." He abhorred these "solitary journey[s] over the waste of barren mountains," although, as he would discover, they were not all to be dull. For it was on his third trip to the Ohio in late 1806 that Mercer stumbled into the vortex of a storm that could have complicated his political ambitions: the Burr conspiracy.[15]

On November 1, 1806, as Mercer prepared to cross the Ohio River by boat, he spotted Joseph Alston, a classmate from Princeton. With Alston was Harman Blennerhassett, who was on his way to Kentucky. Blennerhassett was already famous for his "excentric and somewhat romantic mode of life," and Mercer was thrilled to find someone of "learning and taste" to travel with. (Doubtless Mercer was unaware that Blennerhassett had fled polite society after marrying his niece.) The two men talked for hours as they floated downriver, and when Blennerhassett left Mercer he invited him to come visit his famous island home, which was in the Ohio River but within the boundary of Wood County, Virginia. Mercer readily if unwisely accepted. He had heard the rumors that Blennerhassett and Aaron Burr were engaged in some "common enterprise" of a "highly criminal" nature, either to invade Spanish America or to separate the western states from the Union. But as these rumors "seemed to have arisen" from Republicans who were hostile to Jefferson's former vice-president, Mercer put little stock in them.

Mercer again stumbled across Blennerhassett in mid-November at the home of Andrew Lewis, and the former again invited him to visit his island. Blennerhassett was so open and friendly that Mercer felt at liberty to bring up the rumors. To Mercer's surprise, Blennerhassett confessed that he too had heard the stories but insisted that he would be the "last man in the world" to attempt the dissolution of the Union. He did admit that he was working with Burr to colonize a large tract of land on the Red River but insisted that they held a grant from the king of Spain. Impressed by Blennerhassett's bluff admission and elegant manners, Mercer was satisfied.[16]

On the evening of Saturday, December 6, as he was riding for home, Mercer was suddenly caught in a violent blizzard. He was, he realized, near Blennerhassett's island and, half frozen, he swam his horse across the Ohio. Blennerhassett took him in and gave him the run of his estate. As he toured the magnificent house Mercer noticed that everything was in disarray. Furniture was stacked high in each room, and Blennerhassett's books and clothes were boxed. His host explained that he was moving south for the winter and that only the "unfinished condition of the boats" delayed his departure. But Blennerhassett—or so Mercer said—did not show Mercer his boatyard, for his curious guest might have wondered why so many boats were needed.

Earlier the same day Comfort Tyler and Israel Smith, two of Burr's henchmen, arrived on the island with four boats and thirty-five men. Given the harsh weather, it appears improbable that the men did not stay in Blennerhassett's house. Yet Mercer later swore that he saw only his host's immediate family. Either Mercer lied to protect his growing legal practice and his future political career, which seems likely, or he spent one day and one night on the island without knowing that he was sharing his lodging with nearly forty conspirators.

Whatever the truth, Mercer admitted that Blennerhassett attempted to draw him into the scheme. He "pressed" Mercer "to become a participant," telling him that it would greatly enhance his meager fortune. As an inducement, Blennerhassett told his new friend that their society "would soon become the most select and agreeable in America" because it would have "Burr as the moral head of it." Mercer doubted that the man who had killed Alexander Hamilton was capable of being the moral head of anything, and he told his host so. But Blennerhassett stubbornly argued each point, and the increasingly sharp conversation ended only when Mercer insisted that his legal practice forced his return to the East.

Late the next day, Mercer and Blennerhassett rode north to Marietta, Ohio. On Monday morning the two men separated, Mercer heading east and Blennerhassett going a few miles farther north to check on more of his boats. Mercer briefly considered spending a few more days with his new friend because he dreaded the long and "dreary" journey east. It was well that he did not. Within hours Ohio Governor Edward Tiffin, acting in conjunction with Jefferson, seized ten of Blennerhassett's more than twenty boats and arrested several of Burr's agents. A few boats escaped from Blennerhassett's island, including one carrying the owner. The flight gave credence to Jefferson's charge that Burr intended to seize New Orleans and set up an independent union of western states. Of all this, however, Mercer was blissfully ignorant as he rode east. Had he remained with Blennerhassett, he would have surely been arrested. As it was, he only had to give evidence—probably perjured—at the Burr trial in Richmond a year later, at which James Mercer Garnett served as a juror. Mercer always insisted that Blennerhassett wore "the stamp of innocence." That Jefferson was of the opposite opinion was reason enough for him.

But if the naive Blennerhassett was wrong about Burr's character, he was absolutely correct in his assumption that Mercer was badly in need of money. Following his small role in the Burr trial, Mercer stretched his time and meager resources further by investing in milling. The milling of flour and cornmeal was the most common form of southern manufacture, although Loudoun County was badly in need of such a service. Typically, despite his financial problems, the ambitious Mercer was determined to create a model mill. As workers began construction on a three-building complex Mercer sent to France for four pairs of fine buhr millstones. The final product, which was built adjacent to Mercer's home, was a huge and lofty structure that featured unique twin overshot water wheels. Unfortunately, because of the high construction costs, it would be some time before Mercer would realize a profit.[17]

Mercer invested in yet another venture at the same time. Like most southern businessmen, who were less specialized than their northern counterparts, Mercer combined his less prestigious ventures with the traditional pursuits of farmer and lawyer, for businessmen were held in very low esteem in the turn-of-the-century South. He became heavily involved in internal improvements, especially toll roads. Roads were so wretched in much of the region that investors, if they could weather the initial investment, stood to make a good profit. Despite his lack of ready capital, Mercer helped to create the Little River Turnpike in 1806 and became a director of the Leesburg Turnpike Company in 1809. Like his mill, both of these were long-term investments that strained his current finances.[18]

But in the summer of 1807 Mercer was drawn back into politics. On June 22 Vice-Admiral George Berkeley of the Royal Navy, having learned that four deserters had signed aboard the American frigate *Chesapeake*, gave orders for his flagship to search her after she set sail from Norfolk. When the surprised American commander refused the request to be boarded, the British ship, the *Leopard*, opened fire. The *Chesapeake* was unprepared for battle and was forced to surrender, whereupon a British gang removed four of her sailors, three of whom were Americans previously impressed into English service. The battered *Chesapeake* then limped back into Norfolk, having suffered twenty-one casualties.[19]

As news of the "unexampled outrage" spread across Virginia and the rest of the country, a fever for war arose. At courthouses and taverns angry voices cried for retribution, and bellicose newspaper editors, such as Richmond's Thomas Ritchie, demanded that the president avenge the insult. But the Federalist party, as in the 1790s, regarded England as the last upright nation in Europe. Only the British navy, they believed, stood between the United States and Bonaparte. When notice of a public meeting in Richmond was posted, Mercer determined to be there.[20]

When Mercer arrived at the capitol on June 27, he found that nearly seven hundred men had already pushed their way into the House of Delegates chamber. Almost all were hostile to Britain. Spencer Roane and Thomas Ritchie were named chairman and secretary, a bad sign for the peace faction. A committee of seven was then chosen by Roane to prepare a set of resolutions, which took about an hour. It was then proposed to adopt the resolutions first. At that point, John Gamble, a Federalist ally of Mercer's, moved that a separate question be taken on the preamble, which, he claimed, implied that the English government was responsible for the outrage. How did they know, he wondered, that Berkeley was not acting on his own? Mercer rose to second the motion and support his friend's point. This act provoked catcalls and a sharp retort from Peyton Randolph, who caustically observed that Berkeley's conduct was perfectly in keeping with the policy of a government that refused to sign any treaty that outlawed impressment. Randolph's statement was met with loud applause.

Gamble again rose and insisted that all sides had a right to be heard. When the noise died away, Mercer again began to speak. He agreed that the attack was an outrage, he hurriedly assured the crowd, but thought that more information was necessary before demanding an explanation from England. Before he could continue, he was interrupted by Benjamin Watkins Leigh. "An explanation demanded by us!" Leigh shouted. "Are we to go across the Atlantic to request explanations[?]" The applause this outburst provoked pleased Leigh, so he expanded upon it: "It astonishes me to hear American youths, the descendants of American patriots saying, that we must now ask for explanations." Mercer tried to interject that he had been misunderstood, but Leigh insisted that he had understood all too well. Leigh added that he meant no "personal disrespect," leaving Mercer floundering. Above the din Gamble could be heard bawling that everyone had "a right to express his opinion."[21]

In the end Gamble's motion failed, with only Gamble and Mercer supporting it. The resolutions then passed unanimously; the two Federalists obviously felt they could do little more. Ironically, Mercer had taken the same position he had chided Garnett for taking during the Quasi War, when the latter had claimed there was no proof that Talleyrand's agents were acting in behalf of the French government. Mercer had thought that argument ludicrous because the agents' behavior was in keeping with French policy. Mercer was as right then as he was wrong now, and he allowed his desire to support Britain at all costs to lead him into foolish and legalistic subterfuges. He was badly burned, but he learned a valuable lesson—one the Republicans had learned a decade before and many Federalists never did grasp. Mercer now knew that in times of national crisis such arguments appeared disloyal.[22]

Little, however, came out of the Richmond resolutions. Neither president nor Congress was prepared for war, and Jefferson and

Secretary of State James Madison turned to the old concept of economic coercion. Congress agreed, and in December 1807, the Embargo Act became law. No goods could come in or out of the United States. The law demanded great sacrifice from all Americans, but Jefferson hoped that in time it would bring the British economy, already strained by war, to its knees.[23]

The embargo was incredibly destructive to the American economy, especially in the Northeast. Powerful merchants and workers of all classes who were involved in the shipping industry were badly hurt. In the South, urban merchants and planters were hardest hit; farmers and small industrialists like Mercer were not seriously wounded. But Mercer, with his northern principles, attacked the embargo as bitterly as any Boston merchant. "This fatal law," he fumed, "cast a general gloom over the land." Refusing to admit that it was the only alternative to a war he dreaded, he believed that the policy "cut off our own noses to spite our enemies." Mercer, of course, blamed Jefferson for the crisis and believed the embargo should "damn him to all time as a dangerous statesman." Had Jefferson "and his party done nothing else, they would have full title to the epithet of destroyers of their country."[24]

If Mercer could find anything to be pleased about in the embargo, it was that it aided the Federalist party by introducing chaos into Republican ranks. With Jefferson prepared to retire in 1809, the first significant intraparty struggle for leadership broke out between Madison and James Monroe. The latter had the support of Garnett's close friend John Randolph of Roanoke and the reactionary, strict agrarian Quids, who blamed Madison for the embargo. The dream of those like Mercer was that the majority Republicans would be so split between these two protégés of Jefferson that the Federalists could finally make political headway.[25]

To his dismay, Mercer discovered that his party was unable to capitalize on this schism, primarily because many Virginia Federalists, especially those in Richmond, approved of Monroe, who was believed to have a more favorable approach to Britain than Madison. Other Virginia conservatives wanted to support the national ticket of Charles C. Pinckney and Rufus King. Unable to reconcile the two factions, the Virginia party held two separate caucuses, the Richmond group endorsing Monroe, the other Pinckney. Mercer, who was coming to understand the need for a unified and strong party organization but was personally fond of Monroe, attended neither.[26]

The Virginia Federalists were also hampered by the Republican-created General Ticket Law, which submerged local Federalist majorities by requiring a statewide electoral vote. Pinckney might carry a few counties, but he obviously stood no chance against Madison. It therefore made sense to support Monroe in a desperate attempt to deprive Madison of the state's electoral tally. With no real state organization, local and state Federalist candidates, who ran on an antiembargo campaign, were on their own.[27]

Madison won in the closest election since 1800, handily defeating Monroe in Virginia, despite the latter's Federalist support; only 760 votes went to Pinckney. But the Federalists improved their numbers markedly. In Congress the minority party doubled its representation; the number of Virginia Federalists in the House jumped to five. In the state House of Delegates the Federalist ranks grew to thirty members. Best of all, the hated Jefferson, Old Scratch himself, was gone from the national scene. Madison, Mercer conceded grudgingly, was "a milder man," although still "of the Jeffersonian school of politics."[28]

This upturn in Federalist fortunes, combined with his growing desire to take the lead in building a formidable state organization, led to Mercer's decision finally to enter politics. Mercer was certain that the embargo, which continued on after the election in the guise of nonintercourse, was the answer to his prayers and the "prostration of the Jeffersonian influence." The Federalist party, he believed, "would be again called into power."[29]

Mercer knew that he could expect financial setbacks if he entered politics, for losses were inevitable. He was not completely out of debt. Solomon Betton and his brother continued in their ways of insolvency and constantly begged his aid. His mill had yet to show a profit, and his friend Monroe, hurt by the embargo, was "forc'd to add" to his problems by asking for a loan on the wheat he deposited in the mill.[30] But he had sold some of the Bull Run land he inherited from his father, as well as much of the land in the Ohio Valley. His uncle had finally agreed to Fearon's last offer, and the payments to Europe were almost complete. His law practice was flourishing, especially in Georgetown, and he had made a great deal of money buying and selling horses, a plebeian "traffick" that "heartily disgusted" the young aristocrat. In all, Mercer believed "his fortune sufficient to secure his independence," and he made it known that he was available for a seat in the Virginia House of Delegates.[31]

Campaigns in Virginia were short but hectic. Following notification of his availability, Mercer was thrown into a whirlwind of speeches at churches, taverns, and town halls. Like all candidates he traveled from house to house in search of votes, no easy task in his large rural district. He was also expected to provide food and drink for any group he addressed. His willingness to engage in canvassing demonstrated how far he had come in a decade, for Federalists of the old school loathed electioneering. In 1798 Mercer had urged Garnett not to seek office for precisely this reason. "The people of the South are accustomed to be courted for their votes," he had warned, and the winner would not be the best man "but he who will solicit their votes by adulation." Now Mercer was "much engaged in the election business." Like most of the younger, more pragmatic conservatives, he recognized the reality of the new era and was willing to cultivate the lower classes. This did not mean that he enjoyed it, and he characteristically continued to criticize the Jeffersonians for doing it better. "On the days of election [Republicans] offer them carriages to ride in, taverns to sleep and eat in, [and] all sorts of liquor to drink," he complained.[32]

All of this hectic activity culminated with election day. State elections were significant events in Virginia, partly because they provide an opportunity for the scattered populace to renew old ties, but mostly because of all the various offices, only the state House and Senate seats, along with those of the House of Representatives, were subject to popular election. The election was held on a convenient court day in early April at the county seat and was presided over by the sheriff. Mercer and the other candidates sat with the sheriff on a platform just outside the door of the Leesburg courthouse, and the voters came up one at a time and voted orally before the candidates and a large crowd of spectators. Mercer politely thanked his supporters for their votes. The voter was then free to dip into the punch bowl provided by the candidates and join the noisy throng.[33]

Because state races required only one polling place per district, the results were read to the crowd at soon as the voting had concluded. Late that evening the waiting Loudoun voters, illuminated by torch and lamp, knew what the *Enquirer* formally announced on April 17, 1810. Charles Fenton Mercer, along with veteran Federalist William Noland, had been elected by Loudoun County to serve in the next General Assembly.[34]

Notes

ABBREVIATIONS

ACS   American Colonization Society
CFM   Charles Fenton Mercer

COCC Chesapeake and Ohio Canal Company
DAB *Dictionary of American Biography*, ed. Allen Johnson and Dumas
   Malone, 21 vols., 1928–1936.
JQA John Quincy Adams
JSH *Journal of Southern History*
LC Library of Congress
NJHS New Jersey Historical Society
NYHS New-York Historical Society
PRO, FO Great Britain, Public Record Office, Foreign Office
UVA University of Virginia
VHS Virginia Historical Society
VMHB *Virginia Magazine of History and Biography*
VSL Virginia State Library
WMQ *William and Mary Quarterly*

1. James M. Garnett, "James Mercer," *WMQ*, ser. 1, 17 (1908): 86; CFM to John H. Hobart, June 23, September 22, 1804, in Arthur Lowndes, ed., *The Correspondence of John Henry Hobart*, 6 vols. (New York, 1912), 3:433–37, 504–5.

2. Asa Jackson surveys, VSL, pp. 9–11.

3. Linda K. Kerber, *Federalists in Dissent: Imagery and Ideology in Jeffersonian America* (Ithaca, 1970), 178; Charles Fenton Mercer, *An Exposition of the Weakness and Inefficiency of the Government of the United States of North America* (N.p., 1845), 52.

4. Mercer, *Exposition*, 362.

5. CFM to John Francis Mercer, October 12, 1810, Mercer Family Papers, VHS; Mercer, *Exposition*, 53.

6. James H. Broussard, *The Southern Federalists, 1800–1816* (Baton Rouge, 1978), 84.

7. David H. Fischer, *The Revolution of American Conservatism: The Federalist Party in the Era of Jeffersonian Democracy* (New York, 1965), 114; William B. McGroarty, "The Washington Society of Alexandria," *Tyler's Quarterly Historical and Genealogical Magazine* 9 (January 1928): 149–50.

8. Charles Fenton Mercer, *An Oration Delivered in the Episcopal Church on the Twenty-Second of February, 1806* (Alexandria, 1806), 26–27.

9. CFM to John H. Hobart, June 23, 1804, June 13, 1803, in Lowndes, ed., *Correspondence of Hobart*, 3:433, 225; CFM to John Francis Mercer, March 4, 1816, Mercer Family Papers; Frederick Beasley to John H. Hobart, December 2, 1805, in Lowndes, ed., *Correspondence of Hobart*, 5:69.

10. CFM to John H. Hobart, June 23, 1804, in Lowndes, ed., *Correspondence of Hobart*, 3:433–34.

11. CFM to John Francis Mercer, September 1804, Mercer Family Papers; CFM to John H. Hobart, September 22, November 1, 1804, in Lowndes, ed., *Correspondence of Hobart*, 3:504, 4:345–46.

12. Solomon Betton to John Francis Mercer, April 3, 1804, Mercer Family Papers.

13. CFM to John Francis Mercer, January 19, 1805, Mercer Family Papers; CFM to John H. Hobart, January 22, 1805, in Lowndes, ed., *Correspondence of Hobart*, 4:388–89.

14. CFM to John Francis Mercer, February 23, March 30, 1805; James Mercer Garnett to CFM, January 8, 1806, all in Mercer Family Papers.

15. CFM to unknown, October 25, 1805, Moore Autographs, Princeton University Library; CFM to Thomas Y. How, October 26, 1805, in Lowndes, ed., *Correspondence of Hobart*, 5:40–41.

16. The following paragraphs are based on Deposition of CFM, September 21, 1807, United States Circuit Court records, VHS; Dumas Malone, *Jefferson and His*

Time, 6 vols. (Boston, 1948–81), 5:252–66; Milton Lomask, *Aaron Burr: The Conspiracy and Years of Exile, 1805–1836* (New York: 1982), 189.

17. Ned Douglass, *The Aldie Mill* (N.p., n.d.). The mill is presently undergoing a $1 million restoration by the state of Virginia and will be open to the public. See "177-Year-Old Mill to Be Restored," *Washington Post,* October 24, 1983, sec. D, pp. 1, 7.

18. Clement Eaton, *The Growth of Southern Civilization, 1790–1860* (New York, 1961), 221, 242; CFM to (Governor) John Tyler, January 27, 1810, in H. W. Flourney, ed., *Calendar of Virginia State Papers and Other Manuscripts,* 11 vols. (1875–92; rpt. New York, 1968), 10:79.

19. *Richmond Enquirer,* June 24, 1807.

20. Edwin M. Gaines, "The Chesapeake Affair: Virginians Mobilize to Defend National Honor," *VMHB* 64 (April 1956): 138; Fischer, *Revolution of American Conservatism,* 173.

21. *Richmond Enquirer,* July 1, 1807.

22. *Virginia Argus* (Richmond), July 1, 1807; CFM to James Mercer Garnett, June 18, 1798, CFM Papers, NYHS.

23. *Richmond Enquirer,* December 31, 1807.

24. Mercer, *Exposition,* 247, 256, 243.

25. Ralph Ketcham, *James Madison, A Biography* (New York, 1971), 466–67; Samuel Eliot Morison, "The First National Nominating Convention," *AHR* 17 (July 1912): 761.

26. Harry Ammon, "James Monroe and the Election of 1808 in Virginia," *WMQ,* ser. 3, 20 (January 1963): 47, 37, 52–53.

27. Broussard, *Southern Federalists,* 98; Roger H. Brown, *The Republic in Peril: 1812* (New York, 1971), 21, 143.

28. Harry Ammon, *James Monroe: The Quest for National Identity* (New York, 1971), 277; Norman Risjord, "The Virginia Federalists," *JSH* 33 (November 1967): 509; Mercer, *Exposition,* 248.

29. Mercer, *Exposition,* 247.

30. Anthony F. Upton, "The Road to Power in Virginia in the Early Nineteenth Century," *VMHB* 62 (July 1954): 273; Payment receipt, September 28, 1809, John Francis Mercer Letterbook, and CFM to John Francis Mercer, June 22, 1810, Mercer Family Papers; John Minor to CFM, June 7, 1810, John Minor Papers, *VHS;* CFM to George Carter, May 12, 1809, Mercer-Hunter Papers, VSL; James Monroe to CFM, November 6, 1809, James Monroe papers, UVA.

31. David English to John H. Hobart, April 25, 1809, in Lowndes, ed., *Correspondence of Hobart,* 6:204; CFM to John Francis Mercer, October 12, 1810, Mercer Family Papers; CFM, Autobiographical Sketch, Mercer-Hunter Papers. Mercer wrote late in life that his "fortune" in 1810 was "80.000$." Considering other figures in contemporary letters, this seems high. See CFM to Nathan Appleton, February 20, 1852, Nathan Appleton Papers, Massachusetts Historical Society.

32. Broussard, *Southern Federalists,* 7; CFM to James Mercer Garnett, June 18, 1798, CFM Papers, NYHS; Frederic Beasley to John H. Hobart, April 19, 1810, in Lowndes, ed., *Correspondence of Hobart,* 6:398; John C. Vinson, "Electioneering in the South, 1800–1840," *Georgia Review* 10 (Fall 1956): 269; Daniel P. Jordan, "John Randolph of Roanoke and the Art of Winning Elections in Jeffersonian Virginia," *VMHB* 86 (January 1951): 392. Mercer, *Exposition,* 54.

33. Upton, "Road to Power in Virginia," 259; Rhys Isaac, *The Transformation of Virginia, 1740–1790* (Chapel Hill, 1982), 113.

34. *Richmond Enquirer,* April 17, 1810.

5

The Federalist

The General Assembly met annually on December 3. The roads were churned mud from the heavy autumn rains, yet a quorum was present in the House of Delegates. Among those present was Charles Fenton Mercer, finally beginning his long-delayed political career. At the age of thirty-three he was no longer a prodigy, and many delegates were far younger, but Mercer would at last get an opportunity to put some of his developing ideas into action. But if the legislation he planned to introduce in the next few sessions had its roots in the old Federalism, it also contained many new elements that hinted at a very different, politically astute form of conservatism.[1]

By 1810 the city of Richmond had become familiar to Mercer, although it had changed a great deal in the ten years since he had studied there for the bar. It had more than doubled in size, and it was more than ever the commercial center of the state. The city nonetheless had its frontier aspects. The political heart of Virginia, Capitol Square, was unkempt and unenclosed, with cattle grazing and pigs rooting in the tall grass. Dilapidated horse racks placed on either side of the building were used by the legislators to dry their wet laundry. Yet this glorified farmyard surely appeared wonderful to the young delegate from Loudoun.[2]

On the second day of the session, committee assignments were passed out, and Mercer was lucky enough to be placed on the committees of justice and finance. The second was one of the most powerful bodies in the legislature; perhaps he was chosen as a compliment to the Mercer name. But more important in Mercer's view was that it would allow him to play a role in shaping legislation regarding one of his greatest interests: banking. Centralized banking had been the hallmark of the Federalist party since the days of Alexander Hamilton, but it took on a new meaning for Mercer. He well understood the role the Bank of England had taken in aiding infant industrialism in Britain, and a similar institution could do the same in America. "Money is power," he observed, "and the loan of money, the transfer of power; power to command and set in motion all the sinews of labor, and to quicken all the efforts of industry."[3]

But the system of banking in Virginia was neither well developed nor statewide. The preferred system was the Scottish model, in which only a large "mother" bank with numerous branches was allowed to do business. It was in this form that the Bank of Virginia had been established in 1804. Although that bank had been an immediate success, the Republican majority in the legislature continued to view banks as politically dangerous institutions. It remained the only bank in the state, and it had very few branches in the western counties.[4]

An inherent complication in any plan Mercer might have for introducing new bank legislation was that the Bank of Virginia had fallen under Republican control, and partisan politics played a role in deciding where branches might be opened. The neglected western counties tended strongly toward Federalism, as both rising urban business elements and small farmers there believed that the developmental policies of that party would assist them. Unfortunately, by 1810 only seven of the thirty-five bank directors were Federalists. But Mercer was undaunted, and he soon saw a chance for action. On December 24 a petition arrived from the town fathers of Lynchburg, a hamlet about eighty miles west of Richmond, begging for a branch to be established in their town. The Piedmont town fit Mercer's plans completely. River falls there had recently led to the development of small-scale manufacturing, and a natural pass made the town a perfect commercial gateway to the valley beyond. The petition was ordered to the finance committee with instructions to bring in a bill.[5]

To Mercer's great surprise, the Republicans, normally hostile to the idea of more banks, for the most part supported Lynchburg's request. That the new branch would be only a part of the larger institution they firmly controlled certainly swayed them. Party moderates such as Wilson Cary Nicholas also recognized the growing commercial demands of Virginia's citizens and the potential threat of a Federalist resurgence should those demands not be met. Virginia Republicans thus closeted their principles. On January 2 the House and Senate formed a joint committee to examine the condition and future needs of the Bank of Virginia.[6]

The resulting joint report favored the Lynchburg request, and so with little fanfare and even less debate the House of Delegates agreed to the finance committee's bill on January 26 by a comfortable margin. It was then sent to the Senate, where it was expected to face little opposition.[7]

But the Senate was dominated by the Tidewater counties, even more so than the House, and the bill immediately ran into trouble. Enough votes were finally found in the upper chamber to pass, but only after the bill had been crippled by numerous amendments. The Senate demanded an extension of the present bank charter, additional capital of $1 million, and for yet another branch, this one to be located in Winchester. These amendments were so outrageous that they were doubtless designed to kill the bill by creating a hostile coalition of Federalists and Old Republicans. The former, Mercer feared, would oppose the bill as long as it extended the life of and gave greater power to a sharply partisan institution, and the agrarian-oriented latter would oppose the bill on ideological grounds.[8]

Mercer's prediction proved correct. When the bill was sent back to the House, the lower body refused to agree to the amendments. Senators retorted that they would not pass it otherwise. In an attempt to find a way out of this impasse the upper chamber requested "a free conference" with selected House members. A desperate House agreed and named Mercer and a handful of strong supporters of the bill. The Senate, however, revealed its true intention by naming six men hostile to banking, one of whom was Joseph Cabell. As Mercer would discover during his service in the legislature, the thirty-three-year-old Cabell was a formidable opponent. And as a protégé of Jefferson, the dogmatic young Republican viewed banks as hiding places for monocrats.[9]

The conference committee met on Saturday, February 9. For three hours the antagonists searched for ways to get the bill reported out but were unable to come to an agreement. Mercer and his colleagues were forced to trudge sadly back to the House with the recommendation that their body adhere to its original position. The Senate stubbornly continued to insist on its amendments, and the Lynchburg bill was dead for the year.[10]

It was the ill luck of the seemingly nonpartisan Lynchburg bill that it arrived in the Virginia Senate just as the issue of the National Bank was again heating up in Washington. Indeed, the question of Hamilton's creation, which was set to go out of existence in March 1811 unless rechartered, was perhaps the greatest domestic issue facing the nation that year. Federalists on the national level favored recharter, but most Republicans were opposed, in part because two-thirds of its stock was owned by British investors. As the crisis between England and the United States grew, so did animosity toward the bank.[11]

In Virginia the hostility toward the national insitution extended even to those Republicans who could stomach an expansion of state banking and was largely the result of partisan politics. The offices of the three southern branches, including the one in Norfolk, were dominated by Federalists. Thus the original distaste for the bank among Republicans never waned during its twenty-year charter. In addition, the Bank of Virginia viewed the Norfolk office, regardless of which party controlled it, as a rival and would gladly see it close so that a state branch could be opened in that busy commercial port.

Mercer saw no reason why the Virginia institution should view the National Bank as a rival, and he supported both. He continued to call for both recharter and more state banks throughout the session. Indeed, Mercer was the most vocal state supporter of the National Bank at a time when Henry Clay, who was most identified with it in later years, was leading the opposition to recharter in Washington. Mercer was in line with other Virginia Federalists on this issue. However they felt about giving the Republican Bank of Virginia more power, they favored recharter; one Federalist newspaper called the "annihilation of the National Bank" the "acme of Jacobinical Vandalism."[13]

Mercer supported recharter for the same reason he would twenty years later: it was crucial to American industrial growth. He favored the National Bank even though most industrial development was taking place outside of Virginia; if Mercer's stage was local, his perspective was national. Unlike most Virginia Federalists, who thought little of the virtues of manufacturing, Mercer both believed it inevitable and wished to make it benefit those like him. He well knew, as did others interested in manufacture, "that the supression of the B.U.S." would damage industrial progress in the commonwealth, for "the want of Capital" was the rural state's greatest problem.[14]

Mercer and the Virginia Federalists were badly outnumbered on the issue, however. On January 17 the House of Delegates voted on a resolution introduced by Andrew Stevenson that instructed Virginia's two senators, "as faithful representatives" of their state, to oppose renewal of the National Bank. The wisdom of killing the bank was argued, as was that of the legislature instructing its senators on how to vote. The bitter debate lasted almost four hours, but when the vote was taken Stevenson's resolution passed by a party-line vote of 125 to 35.[15]

If Mercer was unsuccessful in his advocacy of banking, his efforts went neither unnoticed nor unrewarded. It was crucial to his plans that the Federalist party become an active, modern organization that openly accepted the two-party system and rid itself of the old, frank, rhetoric. The older Federalists, placing themselves in the exalted role of the state itself, had refused to do so in the 1790s. Despite their spectacular lack of success in the elections of 1804 and 1808, they still continued to frown on the notion of party organization. Mercer, however, recognized that the Republicans had formed an excellent party organization, which was responsible for routinely beating the Federalists to a frazzle. The Republicans were little but "a set of clod-hoppers, whipped into the Jefferson policy by the rod of party," but they were wildly successful. Mercer was willing to take his party down the same path.[16]

Other young Federalists were willing to follow such a course—and such a leader. Mercer quickly began to gain adherents. "I love Mercer," gushed John Campbell, then in the state Senate. "He has given some of the finest manifestations of a virtuous heart and greatness of soul that I have almost ever witnessed." But if Mercer was gaining support in his own party, he had yet to find the way to appeal to the electorate at large or to moderate Republicans. His speaking style was still in keeping with the Princeton debating societies. Campbell, obviously a friendly critic, observed that Mercer's speeches contained great "information" but were not always "perspicuous."[17]

Mercer's chance to make his party—and hence its agenda—more appealing to moderate Virginians came even before the end of the session. The issue was James Monroe, then serving in the House of Delegates. As the year before, rumor had been rife that James Madison wished to remove his scheming and imcompetent secretary of state, Robert Smith. Should this happen, it was certain that Madison would offer the post to Monroe, which would serve to heal the principal split in the Republican ranks. This news horrified Mercer, who continued to admire Monroe. "How great will be my mortification," he told his uncle, "should Col. Monroe enter

into the administration only to head in the footsteps of his predecessors."[18]

As the rumors grew, Monroe continued his quest for political
rehabilitation by becoming a candidate for governor in early 1811.
Some Republicans believed that Monroe was not supportive
enough of the administration and planned to back his opponent.
Yet Monroe's alleged pro-British sympathies were precisely why
Mercer wished to elect him governor. He set to work with
Federalist Allen Taylor to unite the party behind Monroe, and with
much success. But Mercer's real opportunity to aid Monroe and to
increase the prestige of his beleagured party came during the debate over Monroe's election. After Samuel Blackburn had spoken
against Monroe, "Little Fenton Mercer" rose and, according to John
Campbell, "made one of the most eloquent speeches I ever listen'd
to in my life." Despite his party affiliation, Mercer shouted, he
"lov'd James Monroe from the bottom of his soul." He told his
audience: "You may call me a federalist or any thing else you please
yet Sir I love my country and a republican form of government as
much as any man within the walls of the House."[19]

With nearly unanimous Federalist backing Monroe became governor of the commonwealth. Madison observed this political maneuvering from Washington and offered Monroe the position of
secretary of state in less than a month. Mercer was disappointed
but not surprised. Monroe recognized the role Mercer had played in
his election and wrote him "a very friendly" letter explaining why
he was accepting Madison's offer. If nothing else, Mercer sighed,
Monroe's new position would lead to "a revival of the hopes of all
good citizens and all honest men." Mercer only prayed that Monroe
would not "bury himself, along with [Madison], under the ruins of
his country."[20]

By the time Monroe's carriage reached Washington the legislative session in Richmond had come to an end. Mercer's efforts on
behalf of banking virtually assured his reelection to the Federalist
stronghold of Loudoun County. Indeed, he so impressed his constituents that he even outpolled the languid William Noland, the
veteran delegate who also represented their district in the House.[21]

In the months before the next session Mercer attended to family
business. Unlike most Virginia statesmen, who combined casual
politics with other pursuits, often serving one or two terms before
voluntary retirement from public life, he intended to make politics
his lifelong vocation. He could not afford to let his financial burdens deprive him of his professional goals. He tied up the loose

ends of his father's estate and attended to Marlborough, the sale of which had never been finalized because of its shadowy title. Mercer even traveled again to the Ohio Valley. As always, this part of his life left him empty and depressed; his lot, he informed his uncle, was to be "wandering and uncomfortable."[22]

But December arrived quickly, and a happier Mercer arrived back in Richmond. Not surprisingly, the topic of banking was again in the air. The situation was more urgent than during the previous session. Chaos had followed the failure to recharter the National Bank. With no centralized banking system, credit began to tighten and specie reserves—hard money—began to flow into New England from the southern states as the latter bought manufactured goods. The Bank of Virginia found that its obligations nearly equaled the capital in its vaults. Mercer's "public duty" was never "so urgent," he told his uncle. "We have all our internal and external relations upon the anvil."[23]

Mercer did not have to make the first move. The crisis was so severe that the legislature had not even passed out committee assignments before it was flooded with petitions from the "merchants and traders" of Lynchburg crying for a branch bank. A similar petition came from the northern town of Winchester, also demanding either a branch or a completely new banking system. On December 7, Mercer rose and introduced a resolution calling for a joint committee from both houses to examine the "state of condition" of the Bank of Virginia. With little discussion the House appointed a committee of fifteen men. One of them was Mercer.[24]

As the committee pored over the bank's books, petitions clamoring for assistance continued to flow into Richmond. On December 20 the leaders of Portsmouth, in Norfolk County, demanded financial relief. Impressed by the growing number of memorials, the House turned the Portsmouth document over to the joint committee and instructed the House members of that group to "report thereupon by bill."[25]

The rising tide of petitions and the legislature's growing willingness to acquiesce in public opinion gave Mercer the opportunity he had long sought. Having watched a relatively insignificant bill fail the previous session, he abandoned caution and gambled on an ambitious plan. Late in the month he drafted and introduced a bill that did not just allow for branches in the distressed towns but audaciously created an entirely new "mother" bank called the Farmers' Bank. The measure also extended the charter of the Bank of Virginia and enlarged its capitalization. The bill, however, served to isolate Mercer from other members of his party. Federalist hostility to the partisan Bank of Virginia had not abated, and they objected not only to giving it more power but to creating a new bank that would eventually also fall under Republican planter domination.[26]

The Loudoun delegate was stubbornly optimistic. Virginia Republicans favored his bill. Those who had supported the Lynchburg act of the previous session were sure to support it, for essentially the same reasons the Federalists opposed it. Even many Republicans who were hostile to banking and had opposed recharter favored Mercer's bill, for they now recognized the chaos their previous handiwork had wrought. If Mercer could hold even a few of his Federalist followers in line, the bill would easily overcome any coalition of Federalist and Quid obstructionists. Willing House Republicans allowed the joint committee to dispense with the petitions already filed, as well as those that had recently arrived from Richmond and Manchester.[27]

While Mercer was waiting for his bill to come to the floor, his seemingly unending financial difficulties again intruded on his life in the person of Solomon Betton. Betton had finally given up on the Bull Run lands, and in late 1808 he moved to Georgia, leaving his family and most of his slaves in Virginia. But there were problems in Georgia as well. Betton was not able to return until December 1811. When he came for his wife, he brought several slaves with him, in the process breaking state law and incurring a heavy fine.[28]

Just as Mercer was approaching his moment of triumph he was forced meekly to introduce a petition begging that the fine be lifted in this one case. On January 6 the House found Mercer's request "reasonable" and allowed Betton to leave the state. The appeal was not unusual, and Betton had broken the law unintentionally. But Mercer was still embarrassed by the episode. He found the nagging problem of his finances distasteful, especially when they were paraded before the body he was trying so hard to impress.[29]

A month later more tragic family problems arose. In late February word reached Richmond "of the sudden & miserable death" of John Fenton Mercer, Charles Fenton's only brother. Just weeks before he had word that his brother's health was "much mended." The news hit Mercer hard and increased his tendency toward melancholy. But the bill he had labored over so long was coming up for consideration, and Mercer could spend only a few short moments at his brother's grave before galloping back to Richmond.[30]

The Farmers' Bank bill reached its first hurdle when the five resolutions of the joint committee preceded Mercer's measure to the floor of the House. These resolutions called for an unspecified increase of banking capital in the state, as well as for a new bank with branches in Lynchburg, Norfolk, Winchester, and Richmond. Mercer lobbied hard for the resolutions, arguing that increased banking would benefit all Virginians and not just the wealthy. Here there was some truth; loans would aid upward-looking western yeomen and small businessmen, both of whom identified with far richer eastern Federalists. Mercer discounted the "prevalent opinion, that the credit which a bank affords to its customers, is applicable only to the pursuits of commerce." It was false, he insisted innocently, that banks could not "subsist beyond the limits of large commercial towns, and are not calculated for the country." Even the name of the system, the Farmers' Bank, was chosen in a less than subtle attempt to identify it with the common people of rural Virginia. Mercer did not dwell upon the fact that its center would be in Richmond and its biggest branch in Norfolk, the two greatest commercial areas of the state.[31]

Mercer's efforts to clothe his comprehensive banking system in progressive rhetoric was immensely successful. At the very least it calmed the fears of those Republicans who tended to support state banking but were apprehensive about sustaining legislation written by so ardent a Federalist. On Saturday, January 18, when the resolutions came before the entire House, they passed by a safe margin. The vote meant that the House endorsed the system in theory and would be likely to do so when the formal act appeared.[32]

The final vote came on the morning of February 8. The complete bill, "Incorporating the Farmers' Bank in the City of Richmond," was read a third time and passed by a vote of 91 to 61, almost the same margin by which the resolutions had passed. But the vote demonstrated that however much Mercer might be admired, he was not yet the unquestioned leader of Virginia Federalists. Unable to hold the members of his party in line, Mercer watched with dismay as his party, which could be forgiven for not having shared his experiences in England, voted overwhelmingly against his bill.[33]

The bill then went to the Senate, where the Lynchburg act had faced so much opposition the year before. But confronted with a continuing drain on the state's hard-money reserves, the Senate was in a far different mood; Virginia Republicans were hardly deaf to the claims of property. With the hated National Bank gone,

Senate Republicans were more than willing to acquiesce in a state system that would fill that void, especially if it fell under their political control. The antibank attitude of the Republicans did surface, however, when they insisted that the Farmers' Bank, which had been capitalized at $2 million, could not become operative until the entire stock of twenty thousand shares was purchased. Several other minor amendments were made, and the bill was passed. Not wishing to engage in a battle like that of the previous term, especially over so small a point, the House of Delegates readily agreed. Mercer's bill had survived the gauntlet.[34]

But if the delegates to the state House thought they were through with banking they were wrong. During the previous session the House had instructed its United States senators to oppose renewal of the National Bank. But the two senators refused to obey their instructions. One of them, Richard Brent, voted in favor of renewal, and the other, William B. Giles, voted against recharter but publicly denied the right of the legislature to instruct him on how to vote. The failure of the bank to attain recharter aside, Virginia Republicans were outraged.[35]

Mercer, of course, supported Brent and Giles. The former had voted to preserve one of the last bastions of national Federalism, and both denied a state power Mercer believed was "at war with the spirit of the federal constitution." Lurking within the idea that legislatures could instruct their senators—who were elected not by the people but by the House—was the notion that the states dominated the federal government. Mercer was, first and last, a nationalist. That he had become so for conservative reasons was immaterial. What was important was that by attacking the antiquated idea of legislative instruction he was again siding with the progressive ideal. But when a Mercer resolution denouncing this power came to a vote on January 8, it was supported only by Federalists and lost, 148 to 28.[36]

The failure of Mercer's resolution, however, did not end the debate. Virginia Republicans wished to turn their view into legal doctrine. That task was entrusted to Benjamin Watkins Leigh, the sharp-tongued Republican who had attacked Mercer during the *Chesapeake* debate. After some research, Leigh informed the House that the right could be traced to the ancient House of Commons. That "branch of the English government, whatever it be now in practice," he proudly announced, "was in its origin, and in theory always has been, purely republican." The practice was neither new nor revolutionary. It was resolved, therefore, that no man should accept appointment to the Senate who did not "hold himself bound to obey such instructions."[37]

Mercer was annoyed by such bosh; he had little interest in romantic myths. "All of the learning here displayed," he groused, "will be found in *one* of Burgh's disquisitions."[38] But the savant had been poorly understood, Mercer thought, and he was as much annoyed by Leigh's lack of scholarship as he was by the Republicans' infernal doctrine. Grabbing his quill pen, he began a letter to Leigh, pointing out all his errors. The idea that the English House "was 'in its origin, purely republican,' is without a shadow of authority in any treatise on the English Government," Mercer snorted. All the British scholars meant, he continued, was that a man might consider it his duty to vote for a measure without admitting that he was bound to do so if the measure promoted "the welfare of his constituents."[39]

The letter was never mailed. It occurred to Mercer that he could use his knowledge not just to correct Leigh but to oppose the idea by writing a formal substitute to Leigh's resolution, a common practice in Virginia. The result was a thirty-one-page treatise that was a brilliant exposition of the new Federalism. Although unfailingly nationalistic in tone, it was a work that could not have been written by the Federalists of the 1790s, for it spoke the language of democracy. Senators, Mercer argued, represented not the states but "the people themselves." Based on the principle that "the people are sovereign," senators were bound by their responsibility to the public. Legislatures, by electing senators, had completed "a final act" and could not interfere with their relationship to the people. He thus resolved that the state had no right or power to instruct a senator.[40]

The ideological struggle was important to both sides. For the Republicans, it meant the enforcement of orthodoxy over "monarchical" ideas, and they were willing to go to oppressive extremes to obtain it. For the Federalists, it meant the right of minority ideas to survive, an idea they had not been noticeable advocates of before the election of 1800. Both sides published their resolutions as pamphlets in attempts to garner public support. And Mercer, who had once criticized politicians who "harangue [the people] on their sovereignty," did just that. But it was never even close. When Mercer's substitute reached the floor on February 19 it was overwhelmed by a vote of 103 to 13. Leigh then introduced his resolution, which was approved by the same margin. Many Federalists did not bother to vote.[41]

The next morning, Mercer was somewhat more successful with a much different bill, although one that was equally revealing. It had come to his attention that revolutionary war veteran George Rogers Clark was suffering through an old age of poverty and sickness. Years before, Clark had asked Virginia for a pension, and when it was denied him the old soldier broke his sword in anger and denounced the state. Mercer was not by nature a compassionate man; in the abstract he was unfeeling toward the plight of the poor. He was touched only when need was personified. Clark's situation also gave him further opportunity to ally his party with the lower classes. Just as the session was drawing to a close, Mercer asked for and received permission to bring in a bill concerning Clark.[42]

The bill was to grant Clark the half-pay of a colonel—four hundred dollars a year—for the rest of his life. It was also for a new sword to be made and presented (by Mercer!) to Clark. Despite the lateness of the session and the notorious disinclination of the House to approve money bills, the measure was hurried through. When it reached the floor, Mercer made an impassioned speech in its behalf. "Our house was dissolved in tears," Mercer reported to a friend of Clark's, "my voice was almost drowned in my own emotion." The largest pension then granted by the state easily passed both houses.[43]

The next day the session ended. Despite his failure to defeat Leigh's resolution, Mercer had seen some political triumph. The passage of his bank bill was an astounding victory, and he gained a small and completely undeserved reputation as a friend of the poor. Even his struggle with Leigh was not a complete loss, for his pamphlet that marveled in the sovereignty of the people was read across the state. By late April, when his reelection was announced in the Richmond papers, all of the shares of stock allotted to that city for the Farmers' Bank had already been subscribed for. Soon the bank would be in operation and would provide the state, he told Monroe, with capital enough to begin any "enterprise" of industry or internal improvement.[44]

Federalists had always been open in their admission that centralized banking was necessary to commercial pursuits, just as younger Federalists like Mercer acknowledged that banking was a necessary ingredient in the rise of the industrial order. But it was only now that the interconnection between an active government, banking, manufacturing, and internal improvement was put forward in America, although not yet in a completely cohesive fashion. The movement of raw materials and finished goods, which Mercer had observed to be so easy on England's numerous waterways, was crucial to industrial growth. When late in the session the House decided to send a small group of commissioners to examine the western rivers with an eye toward water transportation, it was not surprising that Mercer eagerly volunteered to go.

The expedition was led by Chief Justice John Marshall, then fifty-six years old. Marshall, Mercer, and four others planned to set out by boat on September 1, 1812, from Lynchburg to spend two months carefully surveying prospective routes from Lynchburg to the Ohio. Mercer, thrilled at the prospect of passing so much time in close quarters with the nation's leading Federalist, was willing to put aside his habitual dislike of wilderness activity.[45]

With the money gained from the Farmers' Bank stock and the reports from Marshall's expedition, Mercer was certain, he promised Monroe, that the next session would "give rise to a great plan of internal improvement." Indeed, Mercer would have great success with his plans for internal projects, although not in the next session. None of his bills would be brought to a vote for several years. He would not even be with Marshall when the expedition pushed upriver on September 1. By then the United States, for the second time in Mercer's short life, was again at war with Britain.[46]

Notes

ABBREVIATIONS

ACS	American Colonization Society
CFM	Charles Fenton Mercer
COCC	Chesapeake and Ohio Canal Company
DAB	*Dictionary of American Biography,* ed. Allen Johnson and Dumas Malone, 21 vols., 1928–1936.
JQA	John Quincy Adams
JSH	*Journal of Southern History*
LC	Library of Congress
NJHS	New Jersey Historical Society
NYHS	New-York Historical Society
PRO, FO	Great Britain, Public Record Office, Foreign Office
UVA	University of Virginia
VHS	Virginia Historical Society
VMHB	*Virginia Magazine of History and Biography*
VSL	Virginia State Library
WMQ	*William and Mary Quarterly*

1. *Richmond Enquirer*, December 4, 1810.

2. Charles D. Lowery, *James Barbour, A Jeffersonian Republican* (University, Ala., 1984), 63; Virginius Dabney, *Richmond: The Story of a City* (New York, 1976), 79.

3. *Journal of the House of Delegates of the Commonwealth of Virginia* (Richmond, 1811), 3–4; Charles Fenton Mercer, *Report on Banks* (Richmond, 1816), 5.

4. Joseph H. Harrison, Jr., "Oligarchs and Democrats—The Richmond Junto," *VMHB* 78 (April 1970): 194–95.

5. Robert J. Brugger, *Beverley Tucker: Heart over Head in the Old South* (Baltimore, 1978), 36; *Journal of the House*, 38.

6. Theodore Armistead to Wilson Cary Nicholas, March 10, 1811, Wilson Cary Nicholas Papers, LC; *Journal of the House*, 50.

7. *Journal of the House*, 81–82; *Richmond Enquirer*, February 5, 1811, puts the vote at 77 to 45.

8. *Journal of the Senate of the Commonwealth of Virginia* (Richmond, 1811), 69; *Richmond Enquirer*, February 19, 1811.

9. *Journal of the House*, 99; *Journal of the Senate*, 70; *The National Cyclopedia of American Biography*, 61 vols. (New York, 1906), 12: 139–40.

10. *Journal of the House*, 101; *Journal of the Senate*, 71; *Richmond Enquirer*, February 19, 1811.

11. Glyndon G. Van Deusen, *The Life of Henry Clay* (Boston, 1937), 65.

12. *Journal of the House*, 50.

13. Clement Eaton, *Henry Clay and the Art of American Politics* (Boston, 1957), 22; *Martinsburg Gazette*, March 22, 1811.

14. Theodore Armistead to Wilson Cary Nicholas, March 10, 1811, Nicholas Papers.

15. *Journal of the House*, 70; *Martinsburg Gazette*, February 1, 1811; *Richmond Enquirer*, January 26, 1811.

16. Charles Fenton Mercer, *An Exposition of the Weakness and Inefficiency of the Government of the United States of North America* (N.p., 1845), 247.

17. John Campbell to David Campbell, January 20, 1811, December 10, 1814, Campbell Family Papers, Duke University Library.

18. Virginia Moore, *The Madisons: A Biography* (New York, 1979), 236–37; Harry Ammon, *James Monroe: The Quest for National Identity* (New York, 1971), 281; CFM to John Francis Mercer, October 12, 1810, Mercer Family Papers, VHS.

19. James H. Broussard, *The Southern Federalists, 1800–1816* (Baton Rouge, 1978), 208; John Campbell to David Campbell, January 20, 1811, Campbell Family Papers.

20. CFM to John Francis Mercer, May 15, July 30, 1811, Mercer Family Papers.

21. *Richmond Enquirer*, April 23, 1811.

22. CFM to John Francis Mercer, June 12, July 30, May 15, 1811, Mercer Family Papers.

23. George T. Starnes, *Sixty Years of Branch Banking in Virginia* (New York, 1931), 38–40; CFM to John Francis Mercer, December 23, 1811, Mercer Family Papers.

24. *Journal of the House*, 10, 17.

25. *Richmond Enquirer*, December 31, 1811; *Journal of the House*, 43.

26. CFM, Autobiographical Sketch, Mercer-Hunter Papers, VSL.

27. *Journal of the House*, 48.

28. CFM to John Francis Mercer, December 23, 1811, Mercer Family Papers; *Journal of the House*, 53.

29. *Journal of the House*, 53, 66.

30. James M. Garnett to John Randolph, February 25, 1812, John Randolph Papers, LC; John Fenton Mercer to James Monroe, January 24, 1812, Mason Family Papers, Gunston Hall Archives; CFM to Joseph Hawkins, February 21, 1812, in

William H. English, *Conquest of the Country Northwest of the River Ohio. 1778–1783, and the Life of Gen. George Rogers Clark* (1896; rpt. New York, 1971), 878–90.

31. *Journal of the House*, 62–63; Mercer, *Report on Banks*, 9.

32. *Richmond Enquirer*, January 28, 1812; *Journal of the House*, 88.

33. *Richmond Enquirer*, February 8, 1812; *Journal of the House*, 112.

34. *Richmond Enquirer*, February 14, 1812.

35. Benjamin Watkins Leigh, *Substitute, proposed by Mr. Leigh, of Dinwiddie, to the Preamble and Resolution, on the Subject of the right of the State Legislatures to instruct their Senators in the Congress of the United States* (Richmond, 1811), 3; *Richmond Enquirer*, January 16, 1812.

36. *Journal of the House*, 69–70.

37. Leigh, *Substitute*, 3–16.

38. *Journal of the House*, 155. The comment is written in the margin in Mercer's hand. The journal, which has Mercer's name on the title page, was later was in the possession of the younger James Mercer Garnett and is now in the Rare Book Room, LC.

39. CFM to Benjamin Watkins Leigh, n.d., Rare Book Room, LC. The letter, which was never sent, was left in Mercer's copy of the 1811–12 journal. When the journal was rebound by the Library of Congress, the letter was accidentally bound with it.

40. Charles Fenton Mercer, *Substitute, proposed by Mr. Mercer, of Loudoun, by way of amendment to the Substitute proposed by Mr. Leigh, of Dinwiddie* (Richmond, 1812), 16–30.

41. CFM to James M. Garnett, June 18, 1798, CFM Papers, NYHS; *Journal of the House*, 144–160.

42. CFM, Autobiographical Sketch, Mercer-Hunter Papers; *Journal of the House*, 160–61.

43. CFM to Joseph H. Hawkins, February 21, 1812, in English, *Conquest of the Country*, 878–79; CFM to James Monroe, February 24, 1812, CFM Letters, UVA; CFM to George Croghan, February 21, 1812, in Temple Bodley, *George Rogers Clark: His Life and Public Services* (Boston, 1926), 370–71.

44. *Richmond Enquirer*, April 28, 1812; CFM to James Monroe, February 24, 1812, CFM Letters, UVA.

45. Virginus Dabney, *Virginia: The New Dominion* (New York, 1971), 213; Albert J. Beveridge, *The Life of John Marshall*, 4 vols. (Boston, 1919), 4:42–43; CFM, Autobiographical Sketch, Mercer-Hunter Papers.

46. CFM to James Monroe, February 24, 1812, CFM Letters, UVA.

6

The General

On June 1, 1812, as Mercer was preparing for his western venture, a clerk in the taper-lit House of Representatives droned out James Madison's war message. Three days later the House voted for war, 79 to 49; the Senate concurred two weeks later. But it was not a unified nation that went to war. Of the forty Federalist congressmen and senators voting on the message, not one, North or South, cast his ballot with the majority. As in the 1790s, the conservatives opposed war with England because they believed Britain was fighting their fight. Although France under Emperor Napoleon was neither revolutionary nor popular with the Republicans, American conservatives attributed Madison's call for war to partiality for the French. The war, editorialized one Virginia Federalist paper, was not only "a great national calamity," but unnecessary, as "the points of controversy" could "have been easily adjusted without it."[1]

Because of their desire to avoid war with Britain, a nation they deeply admired, Federalists were willing to explain away any outrage that country wished to inflict upon the United States. Conversely, they tended to focus on French attacks on American commerce in speeches that added to the discomfort of the administration because many of the charges behind them were essentially true. Where Federalist rhetoric ventured, Mercer was sure to be found. "Soothed by the late [French] imperial opiate," he fumed, "these exclusive patriots have already lost all sense of the many spoliations" inflicted on the United States by "the tyrant of Europe." Stumping the state against this policy, he told his audiences what Madison was only too slowly learning to be true: "France has in fact made no pause in her hostility."[2]

Mercer resolutely maintained this position as the United States slowly edged toward war with Britain. On January 9, 1812, Mercer and the Federalists voted against a Virginia House resolution approving of Madison's diplomacy. Two days later he tried to amend another resolution that said "peace, as we now have it, is disgraceful, and war is honorable," by inserting the words "with [both] Great Britain and France" after the word "peace." It lost, 141 to 25, approximating the margin by which the first resolution carried.[3]

Even so, Mercer was caught off guard by Madison's call for war. He had expected only posturing from the administration. "They have not the spirit to urge, or the firmness to insist upon such an ultimatum," he had assured his uncle. Before long, however, Mercer was speaking out against Madison's war message. He told a Richmond audience that the president's call was based on three incorrect notions: "1st. That France has paused in her career of hostility toward us. 2ndly. That the proofs of this pause . . . have been presented to Great Britain in a shape so unquestionable as to entitle us to demand of her a revocation of her orders of Council. 3rdly. That this demand ought, now, to be maintained by actual war."[4]

There was much truth in Mercer's speech. Madison gave the Federalists fuel by noting in his war message that the Berlin and Milan decrees had been revoked. But even as the message was being read, Napoleon was going to war with Russia to maintain the continental embargo ordered in those decrees. Yet Mercer, in all his speeches assailing French seizures of American property, steadfastly refused to mention the approximately nine thousand American citizens impressed into the Royal Navy. Nor did he pause to consider the implications of allowing a nation many Americans remembered as their mother country to continue to violate and ignore American sovereignty.[5]

Nevertheless, just before Madison's war message—and at the same time that his bank bill was working its way through the House—Mercer "tendered his services" as an officer to his "personal friend" James Monroe. Because of the pressure of his duties at the Deparatment of State, the secretary was spending a great deal of time at his Loudoun County property instead of returning to Albemarle. That home, conveniently for Mercer, was in Aldie, just a few minutes' walk from his own house. The association between the two men, by now a decade old, became closer, and Mercer thought he had every reason to expect a commission. He also believed that Monroe owed him a political favor.[6]

Mercer had mixed reasons for requesting a commission. Some

were altruistic, for he was a patriot. Regardless of his stand on the war, he knew the conflict with England would be a difficult one, and he sincerely wished to aid his country. But he must have realized that a military position was politically advantageous, especially for a Federalist. For years Federalists had been dodging the claim that they were monarchists disloyal to the great republican experiment. Now the war he had so long dreaded provided him with the opportunity to demonstrate that he loved his country as much as any man. Moreover, in Virginia, a military title was carried through life. For a man whose meager property holdings did not provide him with status, an officer's rank was a claim to power and prestige.[7]

But the administration was not granting commissions to Federalists in 1812, and certainly not to one who for two years had heaped abuse on Madison in the president's home state. Instead of passing Mercer's request along to the entire Virginia representation in Congress for approval, Monroe tendered the nomination to a caucus of hostile Virginia Republicans. The result, not surprisingly, was a resounding rejection. To make matters worse, Mercer heard about the fate of his nomination not from Monroe but from "a friend who was jealous of [his] reputation." The consequence was not only a denial of a commission but a temporary breach in the friendship between Monroe and Mercer.[8]

The breach did not last long. Mercer vented his outrage in a letter to Federalist John Lewis, who showed the letter to Monroe. The secretary quickly fired off a missive to Mercer professing anew his friendship. It was only lack of time, Monroe disingenuously insisted, that led to such an expedient. Four days later Mercer replied and apologized, saying that he "should have felt no doubt of your friendly intentions toward me." There the matter rested, although still he had no commission.[9]

If the news crushed Mercer's hopes, it pleased his family and his friends. An unsuspecting John Fenton, then in the last month of his life, informed Monroe that he "had not heard my Brother express anything like a wish for employment in the army." Garnett's friend John Randolph, who had become increasingly close to Charles Fenton, was both surprised and outraged to hear of his application to Monroe. He had suspected "that friend Mercer's opinion of [war] was not very different from ours." Like most of the Quids, Randolph was opposed to the war, fearing it would augment the powers of the national government. Mercer had no such fears, of course, but as he wished to retain this new friendship he paid an extended fence-mending visit to Roanoke, where the two men spent long hours talking politics.[10]

Randolph's behavior toward Mercer was affable, but in May 1812 Mercer left to prepare for his western expedition. He made time for a final trip to Washington, in a last attempt to convince the administration to grant him a commission. Garnett correctly perceived the situation to be hopeless. "The Government did not think proper to accept his Services," he chortled to Randolph, "at which I heartily rejoice, so that unless he goes out as a Militia man, he is not likely to draw his sword in this war."[11]

Yet Mercer missed the first weeks of the Marshall expedition. In the few months since the beginning of the war he had come to believe that a true Federalist resurgence was finally possible. If his party was ever going to regain power the time was now, and Virginia would have to take the lead. The war was extremely unpopular in much of the state. Opposition was naturally concentrated in the Federalist areas of the Northern Neck, the Shenandoah Valley, and the western counties, but it was also growing in the Tidewater, the Quid stronghold. And Virginia Republicans were in a state of chaos. Although widely admired, Madison was not the man, many believed, to lead the nation in time of war.[12]

Mercer was correct in his assessment of the Republican situation. When the 1812 congressional caucus met, Madison was renominated without opposition, although the New York legislature confounded the administration by nominating Lieutenant Governor De Witt Clinton. Clinton's candidacy not only destroyed the Virginia–New York axis that had been crucial to the success of the Republican party since the election of 1800, it also opened the door to a Federalist alliance. Clinton, who was much more sympathetic to commercial concerns than southern Republicans, was actively courting Federalist support. For their part, the Federalists prayed that the war, Madison's disastrous early campaigns, and splits in the Republican party would produce a conservative triumph. Mercer was especially pleased when former Secretary of State Robert Smith published an "extraordinary attack on his late chief." Perhaps, he thought, "the spectators of the exhibition will be so thoroughly disgusted as to drive all the performers from the stage and break up the company."[13]

To drive the Republicans from the stage, Mercer suggested a tactic that was for Federalists both highly unusual and completely new: an open-door political convention complete with ballyhoo

and bombast. The caucus system traditionally was used to nominate presidential candidates as well as state slates of presidential
electors. Mercer conceived of a meeting so open that it would
forever smash the label of elitism and encourage greater participation in the state party. Mercer was, a doubting John Randolph
snorted, "the Chief instrument in producing this Opposition."[14]

The first step toward a convention began on a steamy August 22
at the Leesburg courthouse in Loudoun County. For weeks notices
had been posted calling for a general meeting to name deputies to
meet with other delegates in Staunton on September 21, where a
ticket of electors was to be named. On the day of the Leesburg
meeting, Federalists were pleased to discover a "respectable" crowd
in attendance. Burr Powell was called to the chair. To no one's
surprise, Mercer and William Noland were chosen as the delegates
from the Loudoun district. A committee of correspondence was
then set up to "give notice of the approaching Election of Electors,"
and Mercer, Noland, and W. Bradley Tyler were authorized to prepare and publish an address "explanatory of the views of this
meeting."[15]

In mid-September Mercer's address, dated August 28, was published in various Federalists papers, one of which carried the revealing name of *Staunton Republican Farmer.* The long essay
began by trying to explain the complexity of the General Ticket
Law while denouncing it as an aristocratic scheme to tell a free
people "for whom we shall vote." The only response to such despotism, Mercer argued, was a democratic convention to unify the
opposition to Madison and the war. He then moved to an indict-
ment of the administration's policies, including the war itself, the
call for war while unprepared, and the ancient Federalist cry,
French influence in the government. "Having surrendered to [Na-
poleon] the right of chusing for us an enemy," he roared, "may not
our liberty and independence hereafter follow?" Mercer was silent,
however, on what the Federalists would do should they return to
office. Not only did he stop short of calling for an immediate end to
the war, he tried to appeal to Republicans critical of Madison's
handling of the crisis by condemning him as both "rash and im-
provident" and "timid and irresolute." All Mercer would promise
was the restoration of an honorable peace and a return to "commerce and prosperity."[16]

The publication of the speech, which was written less by committee than by Mercer, was the prelude to two weeks of hectic
preconvention activity. In addition to the long speech, Mercer

wrote two short essays for Virginia newspapers and "rode 170 miles & made two public speeches" to drum up support for his project. He even made a serious attempt to achieve a formal union with the Quids by inviting John Randolph to join him in Staunton and having his name placed on the Federalist electoral ticket. Randolph drolly replied that he did not wish "to suffer" that honor and declined.[17]

On Monday, September 21, Mercer joined twenty-nine men from sixteen counties in Staunton. The turnout was lower than Mercer had hoped; Virginia had ninety-nine counties. But he put his disappointment aside and brought the convention, meeting in the old Mason's Hall, to order. In a democratic flourish, he urged "that the doors be thrown open." A second motion called for a committee to draft a memorial to the legislature demanding the repeal of the General Ticket Law; Mercer and six others were so appointed. A final motion was made "to remonstrate to the Congress . . . against [their] frequent private sessions," as Congress had voted for war behind closed doors. The convention then adjourned for the day to wait for more delegates to arrive.[18]

The next day the convention moved across the road to the larger Methodist Meeting House. At ten, after two more delegates arrived, the group was called to order. The committees appointed to draft the two protests, their point evidently having been made, were "discharged" from further consideration. Two crucial motions were then made. The first resolved that a committee be composed of one delegate from each district present to name an electoral ticket under the banner of "PEACE, UNION and COMMERCE." The second was to create a committee to inform those chosen of their nomination and to solicit active support for the ticket. Mercer was placed on both committees.[19]

On Wednesday, the third day of the convention, Mercer read the electoral ticket report, which, along with three resolutions with blanks left for national nominations, was passed. The third resolution allowed for the nomination of "other Federal characters" at a later date should the other states demand different candidates. It was the first time the term *Federalist* was used in conjunction with the Staunton meeting. The true nature of the convention was then made clear by a motion to fill the first blank with the name of Federalist sachem Rufus King of New York. A second motion was made to fill the vice-presidential blank with that of William R. Davie of North Carolina.[20]

Then Mercer became oddly coy. Before the nominations could be voted on, he stood and received permission to speak. He would, he said, "cheerfully support" any candidate the group might wish to name, but he felt himself "inhibited by the Constitution of the United States, from restraining, by any such previous nomination, the free deliberation and decision of the Virginia College of Electors." He wished to "withdraw from the Convention." Mercer did tarry long enough to read the letter he had written to those named as electors. It was agreed to—as was his peculiar request—and with no more business to attend to, the group adjourned.[21]

Mercer's sudden attempt to distance himself from the convention he had toiled so hard to create struck Virginia Federalists as strange, even perverse. Yet it reflected his growing political sophistication. For all its originality and progressive rhetoric, the convention was not a success. The hoped-for Quid alliance did not materialize, and less than a quarter of the Virginia counties chose to participate. Mercer undoubtedly was also displeased with the choice of King, whom he much admired but whom he knew was not likely to appeal to moderate southern Republicans. So when the twenty-five-man electoral ticket was presented by Mercer's convention committee, his name was not on it. Burr Powell instead represented Loudoun on the platform of "PEACE, UNION AND COMMERCE, AND NO FOREIGN ALLIANCE."[22]

Worse still for the fortunes of Federalism, the national party was deeply split over the question of a candidate. Just as the Staunton meeting was breaking up, a Federalist national convention was taking place in New York behind closed doors. Sixty men from eleven states attended, but, significantly, none from Virginia. The New York convention displayed none of the democratic trappings of Mercer's gathering. Its deliberations were kept secret even after it adjourned. Most of the party leaders were willing to accept Clinton's overtures, an idea unacceptable to Rufus King, who wished to retain the purity of Federalism (and the nomination). In the end the majority voted for Clinton, the candidate probably preferred by the pragmatic Mercer. The Staunton convention allowed for a different nominee, but because the meeting was such a disappointment, Virginians chose not to meet again to ratify the New York convention. King remained the Virginia nominee, Clinton the national.[23]

The situation was made even more uncomfortable for Virginia Federalists when the Staunton convention came under a blistering attack for its alleged treason. One letter to the state's foremost Republican paper labeled the gathering "an association of Tories, who presume to insult Americans and Patriots by calling themselves Federalists." A second missive wondered whether "they expect to gull the people by this sort of [democratic] language?" It even taunted the Virginia party by noting the activities of the reactionary New England branch, "who seek [the union's] 'speedy and awful dissolution,' because they cannot mount into the seats of power." The continual use of the term *union* at Staunton had not worked its desired effect.[24]

Virginia Republicans were not fooled by Mercer's last-minute attempt to dissociate himself from the convention. They, or at least Thomas Ritchie, knew who had been behind it. Did not the organizer of the "Staunton Convention apply for a Commission in the army of the U.S. and was he not disappointed?" crowed one Republican. "Has he not now taken up arms against that very war?" The charge was less than subtle and more than demagogic, for Mercer was not engaged in treasonous activity but merely exercising his political rights. Yet the charges made him aware that he would have to tread lightly as long as the nation was in peril.[25]

Despite these burdens and attacks, the electoral ticket pledged to King and Davie made a respectable showing. It won the Eastern Shore handily and carried most of the northwest with a total vote of about 20,700, or 27 percent. This was up from John Adams's 1800 vote, the last time the Federalists had done well in Virginia, and no doubt they would have done better had it not been for the General Ticket Law, which at the very least discouraged Federalist turnout. Outside of Virginia, most Federalists supported Clinton over King. The election was a victory for the state organization and little else.[26]

Mercer, however, was paying less than close attention to the outcome and was not even in the East to notice the attacks on his character. Following the convention's adjournment, he immediately rode west and set to work with Marshall on the Kanawha. Possessing a sharply focused mind, he tended to concentrate fully on one subject at a time, shutting out all others. He forgot politics in his concern with internal improvements. On his way west, he spent "some days at Point Pleasant with the Virginia troops." While there he noticed that most of the men lacked even blankets, a fate he nastily if correctly attributed to the Republican philosophy of states' rights.[27]

In early December Mercer hardened himself against the expected abuse and returned to Richmond for the next session of the legislature. On December 15 he introduced a resolution he had written while descending the New River to create a "Fund for Internal Improvement." Under his plan, a fund to be used only for river improvement and "public highways" would be devised from shares held by the state in the Little River Turnpike, the Potomac, James River, and Appomattox canal companies, the Bank of Virginia, and the Farmers' Bank. The dividends from these shares were to be administered by a "corporate body," the president and Board of Public Works.[28]

The House of Delegates was generally friendly to Mercer's plan; almost all the members recognized the need to make economic overtures to the discontented western counties. But the legislators were also aware, as Thomas Ritchie was all too fond of reminding them, that placing all surplus money in one inviolate fund could endanger the war effort. In an attempt to salvage his plan, on January 2, 1813, Mercer introduced "some amendments" to his own resolution, providing that as long as the conflict continued the fund would be "subject to such appropriations as may be deemed expedient by the General Assembly."[29]

Mercer's amendments were designed not only to save his fund but to demonstrate his support for the war. Indeed, ever since his withdrawal from the Staunton convention he had been hard at work on his political rehabilitation. In this he had the aid of many moderate Republicans who admired his abilities and thought him unfairly abused by Ritchie. One of them was Wilson Cary Nicholas, who told Mercer that because the state had so few men who wished to serve, he thought it "a national calamity that a man both as able and willing as you are shou'd lessen his ability by bringing upon himself any portion of public odium." Nicholas urged Mercer to lessen his attacks on Madison now that the election was past. "It can now do no good," he suggested, "to expose the folly and weakness . . . of men that are to direct our measures."[30]

Mercer's chance to improve his political fortunes came long before either he or Nicholas thought possible. In early February word reached Richmond that a British fleet under Sir George Cockburn had appeared in the Chesapeake. The American army was hard-pressed to defend Washington, and Madison informed Governor James Barbour that the weak and ill-prepared Virginia militia must handle the state's defense.[31]

Because nearly one-third of Virginia had voted for a peace ticket only three months before, Barbour tried to garner Federalist support during the crisis. He invited Mercer, the chief Federalist in the House, and John Campbell, the Federalist leader of the Senate, to accompany him to Norfolk as aides-de-camp in his capacity as state commander in chief. Mercer leaped to accept. To the rare applause of the *Enquirer* Major Charles Fenton Mercer proudly rode out of Richmond to do battle with the British. The internal improvement resolutions were all but forgotten.[32]

The trio arrived in Norfolk late in the evening of February 10. The British fleet had not moved, and the three men occupied themselves with checking fortifications and seeing to the needs of the civilians who had fled their homes and taken refuge within the American lines. With little more to do, Barbour decided that Mercer's sharp pen could be of better use to the state than his untrained sword. The governor thought the federal government should bear the cost of calling out and equipping the militia. Mercer and Campbell were quietly sent back to Richmond, and on February 25 the two men secretly mounted the Washington stage "on confidential business."[33] While they were there, word arrived from Richmond that upon Barbour's return to the capital the legislature had created a regiment of regular army "for the defence of the State." On the recommendation of the governor, Mercer was promoted in rank to lieutenant colonel and made second in command of the regiment. He had been in the service but one month.[34]

For more than two months Mercer remained in Washington. Campbell returned to Virginia on business and left his colleague to prepare a long and detailed report on what the state had already spent in its own defense. Not surprisingly, Mercer's argument was based on a broad interpretation of the Constitution. He claimed that the government was liable for payment under the clauses that provided for the common defense and gave the central government the power to raise and support armies. "It is very hard to get from these patriots payment for services already performed," Mercer grumbled. "I mean to stick to them, however," he promised an unsympathetic Garnett.[35]

At the same time Mercer badgered the War Department, the Richmond papers published news of Mercer's reelection to the House of Delegates. His vote tallied just below the total of veteran William Noland, but he decisively defeated three challengers, an impressive achievement considering his inability to campaign. He must have felt sure that his recent course was the correct one when he read that John Randolph, an outspoken foe of the conflict, was defeated in his bid to return to Congress. Mercer considered this to be the "worst" news he had heard of late, although he admitted it would be "the most acceptable to the great men" of Washington.[36]

Randolph's attempt to swim against the Republican tide demonstrated anew the enormous difference between conservatives like
Mercer and the reactionary Quids. More and more Virginians such
as Randolph and Garnett found themselves philosophically at odds
with the Republicans in Washington. The war had done what
Mercer alone could not: it brought the Quids into an alliance with
the Federalists. But it was not an alliance that could be sustained or
would provide the basis for future cooperation. The man described
by Ritchie as "literally and locally on the same side of the House
with the Federalists" was in fact only allied with the older
Federalists of New England. Mercer and Campbell, the leading
Federalists in the state, no longer wished to be identified with
Randolph. "I am content to abandon the field to more youthful &
sanguine champions," Randolph moaned to Mercer. Mercer was
willing to be that young champion.[37]

In late April, however, the young champion again found himself
without a military post. While preparing his paper for the secretary
of war, Mercer finally realized the implications of his own nationalist arguments. He insisted that as one of the duties of the
federal government was to raise troops, the government had a
constitutional obligation to reimburse Virginia for her militia debt.
If this was true, the state army had no legal right to exist. To his
credit, ideological purity was more important to him than the
position that had saved his political life. He hoped to "put down"
the regiment "altho' it [would] terminate" his military career. "I
have an abhorrence of State armies," he told Garnett. "They con-
stitute the first step toward disunion."[38]

On April 30 Mercer left Georgetown and rode south. The claims
against the government were still unsettled, although he believed
his presence in the capital would not "render any farther service"
to the state's case. The problem of the state regiment was more
important to him now. At Monroe's urging, he forwarded a written
argument to Barbour, who agreed and called a special session of the
legislature to deal with the question. On May 24, on a motion of
Mercer's, the state army was disbanded by a vote of 182 to 2. He
was again a private citizen.[39]

Because of Mercer's admirable performance in Washington and
his usefulness as a Federalist leader, Barbour wished to keep him
involved in the war effort. He suggested that Mercer might consider serving as a recruiter for the federal army. Because it required
travel into areas under attack, the job sounded horribly active and
risky, and so Mercer was all for it. By mid-July he proudly reported to the governor that he had raised a troop of cavalry in

Loudoun County. He was currently searching for reinforcements for General John Armstrong, a job, he bragged, that allowed him "in three entire days twelve hours repose to recruit the fatigue of 130 miles hard travel, two addresses to the militia and six hours of writing."[40]

Yet Mercer had not given up the idea of military service, and very likely had accepted the role of recruiter in hopes of obtaining a commission in the federal army. In early October, Garnett reported to a disapproving Randolph that he had read in an Alexandria paper that Mercer had frequently been seen wandering about Congress and "eyeing from its Galleries, with longing looks, the great autocrat of the Dutch," Rufus King.[41]

Nothing came of either his recruiting or his less than subtle overtures to King, and so in December of 1813 Mercer returned to Richmond for the next legislative session. The focus of discussion, not surprisingly, was the pitiful condition of state finances. In this Mercer saw the opportunity to advance his latest cause, internal improvements, in a way that would seem to be supporting the war effort. On the ninth he introduced a resolution calling upon Barbour to detail what money had been spent since the last session on the war effort, specifically that amount which was not being contested with the federal government. Washington had imposed a direct tax on the states to pay for the war, although it was up to the states to decide how they would pay the tax. Philip P. Barbour, the chairman of the finance committee, urged that Virginia continue to rely on bank loans to pay for both. But Mercer argued that it was "absolutely impractical" for the state to borrow, given the pathetic state of her treasury, and he introduced a substitute to Barbour's report that called for the levying of a state tax.[42]

The House found Mercer's substitute to be sounder than Barbour's report, and on February 10 it passed his tax bill, 105 to 53. The act increased current taxes by 33 percent on all subjects then taxed, primarily slaves and land, although the tax on the latter had been almost nonexistent. No further loans were taken during the war. Mercer had taken a tremendous chance sponsoring a tax bill since Federalists, who believed the war indefensible, considered taxes to pay for it equally so. Indeed, he later thanked his constituents for their support. They "generously permitted me," he noted, "to enlarge the old and invest new taxes." What his supporters could not have known was that Mercer was as interested in building an economic base for his schemes as he was in aiding the war effort.[43]

At the same time, Mercer introduced a bill that augmented the capital and extended the charter of the Bank of Virginia, which had been severely weakened by numerous war loans to the state. Moderate Republicans, cognizant of the state's growing inability to support its militia, voted for the bill. Even the normally antibank Joseph Cabell supported the act in the Senate, thereby bringing himself "under the lash of [Jefferson's] censure." But Mercer's bills only further confounded the Quids. "I am half-vexed with the federalists in our assembly," Randolph shrieked at Garnett. "They *unite* with the rank Jacobins on many important questions affecting both measures & men."[44]

The real reason for Mercer's burst of activity emerged on the last day of the session. With the state's finances approaching solvency, he worked to force the attention of the House back to internal improvements. The Marshall expedition report never had been presented to the legislature, and now Mercer wrote a resolution calling for its endorsement. Not wishing to appear too obvious, he prevailed upon another delegate to introduce it. The resolution endorsed the ideas implicit in the expedition, ordered the report of the commissioners to be published, retained 250 copies for the House of Delegates, and submitted the rest to Congress and the governors of "various states and territories." The resolution passed, although Mercer's role did not remain hidden. Both Republican and Federalist newspapers identified the document as his.[45]

Mercer's legislative efforts, whatever their real intent, did not go unnoticed by influential state Republicans. During the previous December a new militia bill had been passed with an eye to Virginia's claims, for it specifically designated the recruits as being in the service of the federal government. With the end of the session, Mercer was "called" into the militia as a major of the Fifth Virginia Regiment. Barbour thought his talents could be put to better use elsewhere and suggested that he take Mercer's place. But the Federalist frantically "insisted on being immediately ordered to Norfolk," where it was believed, erroneously, that Admiral Thomas Cochrane had arrived.[46]

Upon arriving in Norfolk Mercer was greeted with the news of Napoleon's imminent collapse. A local Federalist paper, reflecting Mercer's attitude and that of his party everywhere, rejoiced. It was "confident that the fall of Bonaparte will terminate the quarrel between England and America." Virginia Republicans knew better. With the French army "broken down," Joseph Cabell groaned, "Britain is to rule the Globe." Soon the seasoned veterans who had defeated France would arrive in America to do battle with the weak United States.[47]

Mercer had little leisure to celebrate Napoleon's banishment. He was placed in command of an elite corps of four companies of riflemen and light infantry. His first real test as a leader came on April 10, when the term of service for his troops expired. The new recruits had not yet arrived, and it was up to Mercer to convince his men to remain until they could be replaced. His address had the desired effect, for most of them were in place when the fresh soldiers reached Camp Nimmo.[48]

Mercer's efforts were rewarded by General Moses Porter, when the veteran commander arrived in early May to replace the sickly Richard Parker. Mercer was given control of all rifle companies not then under his command, as well as a squadron of cavalry. With his men, he was ordered to inspect the army posts along a marshy thirty-mile stretch of beach and to keep a sharp eye on the British fleet in Lynnhaven Bay. Should the English land in force, Mercer was instructed to slow their march inland and, if possible, capture any marauding parties from the fleet.[49]

Mercer remained at this difficult task throughout the hot summer months. The recruits, who never served long enough to become inured to the malarial swampland they patrolled, were a constant source of trouble. Hundreds had to be released from duty when they became too sick to serve, many of them dying before they could reach home. In all, three thousand soldiers who never met the enemy on the field died and were buried at Norfolk. They were quietly interred at night by the yellow light of flickering torches, Mercer sighed, "in order to avoid depressing the spirits of the survivors." Finally, he too fell sick. He was immediately placed aboard a ship in the harbor and transported to the healthier climate of Richmond. There he slowly recovered.[50]

As Mercer was recovering, word arrived of the burning of Washington in late August by a British force under Major-General Robert Ross and George Cockburn. Madison was forced to flee the capital, the sky glowing orange behind him. Virginia was in a state of panic, and as confused and frightened troops poured into Richmond the militia was hastily reorganized to defend the state capital. Barbour offered the position of adjutant general to Mercer, who gracefully urged the governor to grant the post to an officer of greater experience. Barbour then suggested that his talents could be well used as inspector general, which he accepted. His duties, which officially began on August 31, were to devise and report a plan to the governor on the defense of Richmond and Petersburg, using only thirteen thousand men.[51]

Within a week Mercer's report was completed and approved. He then rode out to scout defensible positions for the army to occupy should the British army move south. But the English instead moved north into Maryland and from there sailed south for New Orleans and Andrew Jackson. On November 9 Mercer resigned his post and returned to the House of Delegates. There he met a response much different from that of two sessions past. Instead of abuse, he heard nothing but praise. He was named chairman of the Committee on Finance, the most powerful of the five standing committees. From that post, which made him one of the six most influential members of the House, he promptly recommended a second tax increase. The Virginia banks were complaining about the declining financial situation of the state, and John T. Brooke, a wealthy bank stockholder, bluntly informed the new chairman, "Taxes must be increased."[52]

Accordingly, Mercer requested that Barbour provide the House with a statement of how much money the state had spent in defense aside from that detailed in the governor's report of the previous session. With the report in his hands, Mercer introduced legislation one month later to increase taxes by not less than $200,000, an amount, significantly, greater than the sum owed to the two Virginia banks. This tax, unlike the first, did not simply increase the rates on present taxes but assessed new items, placing some of the burden on small farmers and urban artisans.[53]

On December 22 the House passed Mercer's tax bill by an overwhelming vote of 127 to 25. Most Federalists followed his lead; only four cast their ballots against the bill. The remaining negative votes came from the traditional Quid strongholds. But most Republicans were impressed with the way the new finance chairman had taken control. "Our revenue will be swelled by the new taxes," Cabell gushed to Jefferson, "to a million of Dollars."[54]

Despite all that he had accomplished, Mercer was again unhappy. State finances were once more sound, but he knew that despite his groundwork his internal improvement project would be ignored as long as the war continued. Most of all, he secretly longed to return to "the State army." In the early days of 1815 he hit upon the answer to his quandary. As temporary chairman of the Committee on Defense, he drafted a bill creating an additional army of ten thousand men. The bill provided for six general officers to be chosen by a joint ballot by the combined houses. As in the earlier militia bill, recruits were to be considered federal soldiers. Almost without debate, and even without a final draft, the measure passed both houses just before midnight on January 17.[55]

The next day, just as the sun was slipping away, the officers were elected, and with a show of "great hesitation" Mercer allowed himself to be nominated. Two major generals were chosen first, one of the posts going to hotheaded Armistead T. Mason, who had served with Mercer in Norfolk. Four brigadier generals were elected next. John Hartwell Cocke was picked first, then Mercer was named and elected. It was a signal honor, and he knew it, but privately he was chagrined that Robert B. Taylor was named a major general instead of him. What did he care, he sniffed, if the legislature preferred "a miserable dealer in slaves, a Captain of Cavalry who was always too unwell to attend a muster," a man who had even served as "a clerk in my own mill."[56]

In less than a month news reached Richmond that peace had been signed with England on Christmas Eve. The war was over. On February 20 the regiment was disbanded, and General Charles Fenton Mercer reluctantly returned to civilian life. With the session in Richmond finished, he rode north to Aldie. There he received word that the young man he had tapped to replace retiring William Noland in the assembly was seriously ill. Arriving at Noland's home, where the young man lay, Mercer recognized the signs of malaria. There was nothing to do but sit with the boy, who died three days later. In the interim one of Mercer's new slaves, Jack, who accompanied him as a servant, also fell ill. When Jack appeared better, Mercer rode on to Leesburg, but when he got there he slumped out of the saddle, exhausted.[57]

For three weeks Mercer lay near death, his doctors holding out no hope that he would recover. His weight dropped until he was but a skeleton, and he passed in and out of consciousness. It was during this time, when his mind was most "impaired," that he underwent a profound religious experience. "When the world was receding from me," he told his sister, "the cross of Christ appeared before me." When he awoke he called for an Episcopal prayer book and made a formal confession of faith.[58] By March 20, after being fettered to his bed for thirty days, Mercer was finally able to sit up in a chair. He was still in great pain and faced several more weeks of convalescence, but he would live. His two doctors considered his recovery "astonishing" and thought him out of danger. "I indulge that hope myself," he wrote laughingly, "and am seconding their efforts by every means in my power."[59]

Mercer's religious experience did not noticeably affect his personality or behavior. He remained as stubbornly pessimistic about life as ever, and in his political thinking his view of the meek changed not a whit. He had been a religious man from his "earliest youth" and had long served as a vestryman in the Shelburne parish in Loudoun. A religious rebirth required a constant reliving of the experience by professing it to others, but Virginia gentlemen lived by the staid Episcopal ritual and frowned upon the extravagances of Baptist camp meetings. Most southern whites did not attend services regularly, and the distance between Mercer's home and his church in Leesburg was great enough that Mercer was no exception. He had no way to sustain his new-found faith.[60]

When Mercer regained consciousness, he discovered that he had been elected to a sixth term in the House. His election came as no surprise, but he was pleased to hear that his constituents had voted for him even though his death was rumored on the very day they returned him to office. Elsewhere in Virginia his party did equally well, achieving a new record in votes cast. The Republican vote also rose, however, and the Federalist percentage fell below its 1812 share.[61]

By mid-April Mercer was up and writing to Wilson Cary Nicholas, the new governor. The peace of Ghent, he insisted, had saved the United States from "bankruptcy, disunion, and civil war, combined with foreign invasion; in fines, from national dishonor and ruin." He might have added that it had also saved his political career and thrust him into the forefront of Virginia politics. That the war he had so long dreaded had made him a powerful man was an irony he probably did not savor, yet it was so. Moreover, the war had allowed Mercer to set the economic groundwork for two of his favorite schemes: internal improvements and public education. With his service behind him, the one-month general would return to the influential Finance Committee for two of the most fruitful and creative legislative sessions of his political life.[62]

Notes

ABBREVIATIONS

ACS	American Colonization Society
CFM	Charles Fenton Mercer
COCC	Chesapeake and Ohio Canal Company
DAB	*Dictionary of American Biography*, ed. Allen Johnson and Dumas Malone, 21 vols., 1928–1936.
JQA	John Quincy Adams
JSH	*Journal of Southern History*
LC	Library of Congress

NJHS   New Jersey Historical Society
NYHS   New-York Historical Society
PRO, FO Great Britain, Public Record Office, Foreign Office
UVA   University of Virginia
VHS   Virginia Historical Society
VMHB   *Virginia Magazine of History and Biography*
VSL   Virginia State Library
WMQ   *William and Mary Quarterly*

1. Ralph Ketcham, *James Madison, A Biography* (New York, 1971), 527–28; Roger H. Brown, *The Republic in Peril: 1812* (New York, 1971), 165; *Alexandria Gazette*, September 25, 1812.

2. CFM to John Francis Mercer, October 12, 1810, Mercer Family Papers, VHS; CFM, undated speech, CFM Papers, NYHS.

3. *Journal of the House of Delegates of the Commonwealth of Virginia* (Richmond, 1911), 71, 75.

4. CFM to John Francis Mercer, October 12, 1810, Mercer Family Papers; CFM, speech in Richmond, 1813, CFM Papers, NYHS.

5. George Dangerfield, *The Era of Good Feelings* (New York, 1952), 49; Samuel Flagg Bemis, *John Quincy Adams*, 2 vols. (New York, 1950–56), 1: 140.

6. CFM, Autobiographical Sketch, Mercer-Hunter Papers, VSL; Harry Ammon, *James Monroe: The Quest for National Identity* (New York, 1971), 291.

7. On this point see Daniel P. Jordan, *Political Leadership in Jefferson's Virginia* (Charlottesville, 1983), 50, and Rhys Isaac, *The Transformation of Virginia, 1740–1790* (Chapel Hill, 1982), 109.

8. CFM to James Monroe, February 24, 1812, CFM Letters, UVA. It was not until late 1814 that Madison thought it safe to grant commissions to Federalists. See Ammon, *Monroe*, 542.

9. CFM to James Monroe, February 24, 1812, CFM Letters, UVA.

10. John Randolph to James M. Garnett, September 22, 1811; James M. Garnett to John Randolph, June 2, 1812, both in John Randolph Papers, LC; John Fenton Mercer to James Monroe, January 24, 1812, Mason Family Papers, Gunston Hall Archives; John Randolph to CFM, June 15, 1812, CFM papers, NYHS.

11. James M. Garnett to John Randolph, August 11, 1812, Randolph Papers, LC.

12. Myron F. Wehtje, "Opposition to the War of 1812," *VMHB* 78 (January 1970): 66, 79; Irving Brant, *James Madison: Commander in Chief, 1812–1836* (New York, 1961), 23.

13. John S. Murdock, "The First National Nominating Convention," *AHR* 1 (July 1896): 680; John Niven, *Martin Van Buren: The Romantic Age of American Politics* (New York, 1983), 34; Jordan, *Political Leadership*, 17–18; John S. Pancake, "The 'Invisibles': A Chapter in the Opposition to President Madison," *JSH* 21 (February 1955): 36; CFM to John Francis Mercer, July 30, 1811, Mercer Family Papers.

14. John Randolph to James M. Garnett, September 15, 1812, Randolph Papers, LC.

15. *Staunton Republican Farmer*, September 10, 17, 1812; *Alexandria Gazette*, September 5, 1812.

16. *Staunton Republican Farmer*, September 17, 1812.

17. John Randolph to James M. Garnett, September 15, 1812, Randolph Papers, LC.

18. *Staunton Republican Farmer*, October 1, 1812.

19. Ibid; *Martinsburg Gazette*, October 23, 1812.

20. *Staunton Republican Farmer*, October 1, 1812.

21. Ibid.

22. *Alexandria Gazette*, September 30, 1812; *Martinsburg Gazette*, October 23, 1812.

23. David H. Fischer, *The Revolution of American Conservatism: The Federalist Party in the Era of Jeffersonian Democracy* (New York, 1965), 87–88; Niven, *Van Buren*, 34–35.

24. *Richmond Enquirer*, October 16, 8, 1812.

25. Ibid., October 9, 1812.

26. James H. Broussard, *The Southern Federalists, 1800–1816* (Baton Rouge, 1978), 147; Ketcham, *Madison*, 545.

27. James M. Garnett to John Randolph, December 1, 1812, Randolph Papers, LC; Charles Fenton Mercer, *An Exposition of the Weakness and Inefficiency of the Government of the United States of North America* (N.p., 1845), 253.

28. CFM, Autobiographical Sketch, Mercer-Hunter Papers; CFM to Charles James Faulkner, December 14, 1832, Faulkner Family Papers, VHS; *Richmond Enquirer*, December 19, 1812; *Journal of the House*, 56–57.

29. *Richmond Enquirer*, December 19, 1812, January 2, 1813.

30. Wilson Cary Nicholas to CFM, January 30, 1813, Wilson Cary Nicholas Papers, LC.

31. William Sharp to House Speaker, February 4, 1813, in *Journal of the House*, 135.

32. CFM, Autobiographical Sketch, Mercer-Hunter Papers; *Richmond Enquirer*, February 9, 1813; William W. Hening, general orders, February 6, 1813, in H. W. Flourney, ed., *Calendar of Virginia and Other Manuscripts*, 11 vols. (1875–92; rpt. New York, 1968), 10:188; CFM to Claiborne W. Gooch, September 26, 1823, Gooch Papers, VHS.

33. *Richmond Enquirer*, February 16, 1813; CFM, Autobiographical Sketch, Mercer-Hunter Papers; James Barbour to Legislature, May 22, 1813, in *Journal of the House* (special 1813 session), 14; John Campbell to David Campbell, February 24, 1813, Campbell Family Papers, Duke University Library.

34. CFM, Autobiographical Sketch, Mercer-Hunter Papers; *Richmond Enquirer*, March 16, 1813; James Barbour to the General Assembly, March 1813; Acceptances by Officers of Appointments in the Corps, 1813, both in Flourney, ed., *Calendar of Virginia State Papers*, 10:217, 297.

35. C. Johnson to James Barbour, March 23, 1824, in Flourney, ed., *Calendar of Virginia State Papers*, 10:507; CFM and John Campbell to James Armstrong, March 19, 1813, in *Journal of the House*, 14–19; CFM to James M. Garnett, April 29, 1813, in James Mercer Garnett, ed., *Biographical Sketch of Hon. Charles Fenton Mercer, 1778–1858* (Richmond, 1911), 39.

36. *Richmond Enquirer*, April 20, 1813; Daniel P. Jordan, "John Randolph of Roanoke and the Art of Winning Elections in Jeffersonian Virginia," *VMHB* 86 (January 1951): 399–400; CFM to James M. Garnett, April 29, 1813, in Garnett, ed., *Biographical Sketch*, 39.

37. Brown, *Republic in Peril*, 147, 150, 154; *Richmond Enquirer*, April 9, 1813; John Randolph to CFM, March 11, 1813, John Randolph Papers, VSL.

38. CFM, Autobiographical Sketch, Mercer-Hunter Papers; CFM to James M. Garnett, April 29, 1813, in Garnett, ed., *Biographical Sketch*, 40.

39. CFM to James Barbour, April 30, 1813, in *Journal of the House*, 29; CFM, Autobiographical Sketch, Mercer-Hunter Papers; *Journal of the House*, 31, 36.

40. CFM to James Barbour, July 18, 1813, in Flourney, ed., *Calendar of Virginia State Papers*, 10:261.

41. James M. Garnett to John Randolph, October 5, 1813, Randolph Papers, LC.

42. *Richmond Enquirer*, December 9, 1813; *Journal of the House*, 95; CFM, Autobiographical Sketch, Mercer-Hunter Papers.

43. *Norfolk and Portsmouth Herald*, February 10, 1814; Charles Fenton Mercer,

ed., *The Farewell Address of the Hon. C. F. Mercer to His Constituents* (N.p., 1839), 3.

44. Joseph Cabell to Thomas Jefferson, January 23, 1814, Cabel Papers, LC; John Randolph to James M. Garnett, February 14, 1814, Randolph Papers, LC.

45. *Richmond Enquirer*, March 5, 1814; CFM to Wilson Cary Nicholas, April 14, 1815, Nicholas Papers; *Norfolk and Portsmouth Herald*, February 25, 1814.

46. *Journal of the House*, 56–57; CFM, Autobiographical Sketch, Mercer-Hunter Papers; *Norfolk Gazette*, April 6, 1814.

47. *Norfolk and Portsmouth Herald*, April 1, June 14, 1814; Joseph C. Cabell to Wilson Cary Nicholas, January 30, 1814, Nicholas Papers.

48. CFM, Autobiographical Sketch, Mercer-Hunter Papers.

49. CFM to Richard E. Parker, May 1, 1814, in *Norfolk Gazette*, May 7, 1814; CFM, Autobiographical Sketch, Mercer-Hunter Papers.

50. John Randolph to CFM, August 4, 1814, General Manuscripts, Princeton University Library; CFM, Autobiographical Sketch, Mercer-Hunter Papers.

51. CFM, Autobiographical Sketch, Mercer-Hunter Papers; *Norfolk and Portsmouth Herald*, September 6, 1814.

52. CFM to John H. Cocke, September 29, 1814, Cocke Collection, UVA; CFM, Autobiographical Sketch, Mercer-Hunter Papers; Joseph Cabell to Thomas Jefferson, September 17, 1814, Cabell Papers; John T. Brooke to CFM, October 24, 1814, CFM Papers, Duke University Library.

53. *Richmond Enquirer*, November 12, 26, 1814.

54. Ibid., December 22, 1814; Norman Risjord, "The Virginia Federalists," *JSH* 33 (November 1967): 510; Joseph Cabell to Thomas Jefferson, December 27, 1814, Cabell Papers.

55. *Richmond Enquirer*, January 18, 1815; John Campbell to David Campbell, December 10, 1814, Campbell Family Papers; CFM, Autobiographical Sketch, Mercer-Hunter Papers.

56. *Richmond Enquirer*, January 21, 1815; *Virginia Argus* (Richmond), January 21, 1815; CFM to Wilson Cary Nicholas, April 14, 1815, Nicholas Papers; John Campbell to David Campbell, January 21, 1815, Campbell Family Papers; CFM to unknown, March 10, 1857, CFM Papers, Yale University Library.

57. *Richmond Enquirer*, February 22, 1815; CFM, Autobiographical Sketch, Mercer-Hunter Papers; CFM to the Public, December 30, 1817, in Charles Fenton Mercer, ed., *Controversy between Armistead Thompson Mason and Charles Fenton Mercer* (Washington, D.C., 1818), 32; CFM to Mary Eleanor Garnett, March 20, 1815 (misdated 1814), Garnett Papers, Duke University Library.

58. CFM to John H. Hobart, March 24, 1815, in Garnett, ed., *Biographical Sketch*, 38–39; CFM to Timothy Pickering, February 27, 1827, Pickering Papers, LC; CFM to Mary Eleanor Garnett, March 20, 1815, Garnett Papers.

59. CFM to Wilson Cary Nicholas, April 14, 1815, Nicholas Papers; CFM to Mary Eleanor Garnett, March 20, 1815, Garnett Papers.

60. CFM to the Public, December 30, 1817, in Mercer, ed., *Controversy*, 32; William Meade, *Old Churches, Ministers and Families of Virginia*, 2 vols. (Philadelphia, 1897), 2:277; Clement Eaton, *The Growth of Southern Civilization, 1790–1860* (New York, 1961), 13–14; Eugene D. Genovese, *Roll, Jordan, Roll: The World the Slaves Made* (New York, 1972), 184.

61. CFM, Autobiographical Sketch, Mercer-Hunter Papers; *Virginia Argus* (Richmond), April 15, 1815; *Richmond Enquirer*, April 19, 1815; Broussard, *Southern Federalists*, 172.

62. CFM to Wilson Cary Nicholas, April 14, 1865, Nicholas Papers.

7

Pauperism Black

When the House of Delegates convened in early December, Mercer's health had not yet completely returned. But it was to be perhaps the "most laborious" year of his political life, for his zeal for internal improvements and banking had never waned during the war years. Mercer was immediately reappointed chairman of the Finance Committee, a post that consumed much time but also granted him much power.[1]

As soon as word reached Virginia that the war was over, Mercer decided to reintroduce the resolutions on internal improvements that he had first brought before the House in December 1812. He chose to renew the resolutions in their original form, but he did work to secure the support of Governor Wilson Cary Nicholas. If the plan appeared to be bipartisan, it would have a greater chance of passing. He also urged Nicholas to lobby "the Richmond papers, and especially, the Enquirer." Mercer believed that Ritchie's arguments against such vast expenditures during wartime had "occasioned my failure on the former occasion."[2]

Mercer was successful in gaining the support of the moderate Nicholas. When the legislature met on December 4 to receive the governor's annual message, it heard him call "in the most forcible manner, to take up the subject of internal improvements." Nicholas reminded the legislators of the Marshall expedition and Mercer's resolutions, saying that such a plan "would confer incalculable benefits, political and commercial," upon the commonwealth.[3]

Armed with this endorsement, Mercer wisely decided to strike fast. Three days later, he moved to refer the part of the governor's message that "relates to Internal Improvement" to the Committee on Roads and Canals. Like all delegates who chaired one of the five standing committees, he was expected to serve on other committees as well. Not surprisingly, this was one of them.[4]

On December 30 Mercer released his committee's report. Like that of 1812, the report called for the creation of a fund for internal improvement to consist of all the stock held by the state in the two central banks as well as "all future acquisitions from the same source." The capital of the fund would fund two-fifths of a project when the remaining three-fifths of the necessary construction costs had been supplied by private investors. The report was, Ritchie blandly observed, "an almost literal transcript" of the earlier report.[5]

At the heart of the fund report was the Board of Public Works. This body would be composed of members chosen annually by the legislature, but to protect underrepresented western interests, they were to be chosen from specified sections of the state. The intent was to centralize Virginia's haphazard programs for improvement by meeting before the legislature did and deciding which projects—both those being planned and those already under construction—merited state assistance. Finally, the board would employ a civil engineer to provide technical advice, a scarce commodity in the agrarian commonwealth.[6]

The single greatest obstacle to industrial development in Virginia was its lack of an adequate system of transportation. A program of internal improvements would aid the entire Virginia economy, but it would aid the merchants, commercial farmers, and budding industrialists most of all. By making the shipment of produce and raw materials to market less expensive, canals and roads would induce industrial growth in urban centers like Richmond and Petersburg. Such economoic rationalization would turn the state into "a unit in action," Mercer thought, and so "the more efficient she will be."[7]

Support for such a program came primarily from the Federalist party, which was strongest in the western counties, the region most likely to benefit from improved transportation, but the party was also strong in the eastern hub of Richmond, where the incipient manufacturers and capitalists were located. They supported the bill because it would, in Mercer's words, allow them to better receive raw materials and then "with small expense diffuse" finished goods "to all who consume."[8]

Opposition to the plan was especially strong in the slave-heavy eastern counties. Residents of the Tidewater already had easy access to water transportation for their export staples and were not anxious to vote for an extensive system that would not directly benefit them and might require a tax increase. But in late 1815 this opposition remained largely muted. The western counties had recently renewed their cry for increased representation in the legis-lature. The planters were loath to give up any of their power by yielding the calls for a new state constitutional convention, and so they were not inclined to provoke further western hostility by actively opposing Mercer's proposition.[9]

The eastern districts, however, found their voices when faced with another of Mercer's banking bills in the same month, a mea-sure that was an interlocking part of his system of transportation. With the war over, Virginia banks was again in economic chaos. Both state banks had made loans to the state, but the claims against the federal government, now in excess of $1 million, re-mained unsettled. Besides, the state had accrued large sums of money from increased taxes and profits from the stock of the Farmers' Bank. The job of reducing the tax rate and providing some semblance of organization to state finances fell to the Finance Committee.[10]

The two Virginia "mother" banks, like every other bank outside of New England, had been forced to suspend specie payment by early 1815. With no hard money moving out of the states, the federal government had been forced to default repeatedly, and the nation made do with unsupported paper money. This situation made a second National Bank inevitable, though it would not be created soon enough to suit Mercer. Because his fund required three-fifths private funding for a project before the state could act, it was crucial for investors to be able to obtain capital. But the shaky state banks were unlikely to loan large sums of money until they were repaid by the state.[11]

Mercer hoped to restore state solvency by discounting real paper, thereby increasing the importation of specie "in the course of commerce." He also wished to fix a date by which the stubborn Virginia banks would be forced to resume specie payment "to their mercantile customers." Finally, he was prepared to "import, if necessary, by the purchase of bills, the current coin of the United States, or gold or silver bullion, from wherever it can be had."[12]

Stabilizing Virginia's economy would not only aid local transpor-tation projects, it would increase the likelihood of outside invest-ment in both internal improvements and state manufactures. Even if state banking returned to a sound basis, the chances of local investment were not great. Precapitalist Tidewater planters, who were unlikely to invest in such projects, had all their ready capital tied up in slaves. Urban merchants and small manufacturers had more cash on hand, but their wealth could not compare to that of the New England merchants who had been pouring their capital into industrial ventures since the embargo. It was critical, Mercer thought, to show northern industrialists that Virginia was economically sound. He was thus anxious to demonstrate that the common "prejudice" that "the policy of Virginia is essentially hostile to commerce, and to the rights of commercial men," was wrong.[13]

But the cause of Virginia industrialization required more than the stabilization of the two state banks. Still more branches must be created. The Piedmont and the Shenandoah Valley had only two chartered facilities, in Lynchburg and Winchester, and the trans-Allegheny and the upper Potomac had no chartered banks, although a number of unchartered banks had emerged to fill the needs of the latter. Two of these were in Loudoun County. Mercer hoped to tie all these financial goals into one comprehensive bill. On December 15 he moved that all of the petitions submitted calling for new banks be discharged from the Grievance Committee and referred to a select committee "with leave to report thereon by bill." The resolution passed with no great difficulty, and on his authority as chairman of the Finance Committee Mercer appointed a group of seventeen men. The delegate from Loudoun headed the committee.[14]

Less than a month later, on January 6, 1816, Mercer's select committee presented its voluminous report. It audaciously proposed the creation of fifteen new banks as branches of the two mother banks and mandated that all of the new banks would pay in specie, the same form in which taxes would continue to be paid. The report was met with astonishment in the House and hostility from the Republican press, but, undaunted, Mercer presented it on January 22.[15]

The bill immediately ran into trouble. Ironically, some of the opposition—and some of the much needed support—came from unexpected quarters. John Brockenbrough, president of the Bank of Virginia and an ardent Republican, reported to Mercer that his stockholders endorsed the creation of new branches. But the Farmers' Bank was not so encouraging. Even though Mercer's 1812 creation had been serving the state on a politically nonpartisan basis, it had come under the control of the Richmond Junto. Mercer had anticipated this turn of events, but he had not guessed that his child would turn against him so soon. Yet it did on January 4, when Benjamin Hatcher informed him that the stockholders had decided it was "inexpedient" to create more branches.[16]

Other opposition was not so surprising. Traditionally antibank Republicans viewed the bill with horror; those who had supported Mercer's bank bills during the crisis of war were not likely to do so in the calm of peace. Many of them had been willing to allow for the creation of the Farmers' Bank when specie was pouring out of the state, but now they were more inclined to wait out the chaos. In the nation's capital Madison was ignoring Republican principles by allowing for the creation of the Second Bank of the United States, which was expected to help right the economy. Moderate Republicans were therefore more likely to follow the lead of Jefferson, who attacked the "deluded citizens [who] are clamoring for more banks, more banks."[17]

The assault on the bill turned into a personal attack on Mercer, something he had not been subjected to since 1812. Ugly rumors circulated that he wished only to certify the unauthorized banks in his district because he and his friends had invested in them. He truthfully argued that he had dissuaded his partisans from investing in these banks. He was simply working to aid his constituents while carrying out traditional party policies and achieving his long-range goals. But the rumors persisted.[18]

By the time the House resolved itself into a committee of the whole of February 6 to consider the legislation, Mercer knew that his bill was in serious trouble. He even ran into difficulty with the partisan public printer, who not only intentionally delayed printing Mercer's bill and report but, when forced to do so, printed the report in impossibly tiny type. When the bill finally reached the floor, Robert Scott of Tidewater York County made a motion to postpone further consideration until April 1, a move tantamount to killing the bill. Mercer and the Federalists "vehemently opposed" Scott's motion, but the opponents of the act, sure of their number, smugly made no reply but to call for a vote. The outcome was a count of 109 to 62 in support of Scott. The Republicans voted 93 to 33 to table; the Federalists, whose desire to support their historic agenda overcame their unhappiness in voting for banks that would come under Republican control, were almost unanimously against the motion.[19]

The Republicans were kinder toward Mercer's first bill. Their willingness to agree to internal improvements surely stemmed from the realization that two blows in one session to western economic aspirations would fuel the fire of constitutional reform. When the House discussed Mercer's transportation bill at almost the same moment the majority party was killing his bank bill, very few Republicans rose to voice their opposition. The dogmatic John S. Barbour did make the requisite if halfhearted attempt to have the bill postponed but received little support. After "a long and luminous" appeal from Mercer the bill passed. The Federalists overwhelmingly supported it by 32 to 1; the Republicans split in favor, 77 to 50.[20]

On February 2 the Senate announced its acquiescence after making several minor amendments that were readily agreed to by the House. Two weeks later, the pain of having his magnificent bank bill killed was eased considerably when Mercer found that he had been elected as one of the ten members of the Board of Public Works. His elation was dampened when he discovered that he would be serving with Thomas Jefferson, who had made his program less cohesive by taking the lead in killing the accompanying bank bill. But Mercer was pleased that the fund attracted the attention of important New England Federalists such as Daniel Webster.[21]

In a final indignity, Mercer was asked at the end of the session to be present at a public banquet attended by delegates from both parties. In honor of his election to the board, Mercer was asked to speak first. But the report of the dinner in the city's leading paper said he spoke last. It was "the meaness" of Ritchie that led to such persecution, Mercer peevishly told his uncle: "I have received many thanks for having introduced [the bill], I mean, from my fellow [Federalist] members, for our democratic presses, acknowedge no public service out of their ranks."[22]

Mercifully, the session was nearly at an end. Mercer, still not completely over his illness and bloodied anew by his latest battle with the Republicans, began to consider abandoning politics for an extended trip abroad. Yet an offhand remark was not only to keep him in the legislature but was to provide him with a new cause, linked to his economic program. Late one night in February, he fell into in a political discussion with two of his colleagues, both of whom shared his apartment. Suddenly Federalist Philip Doddridge, waxing voluble in the grip of alcohol, blurted out that Thomas Jefferson was "a consummate hypocrite." General Dabney Minor, a Republican, who was also "much intoxicated," demanded to know what evidence Doddridge had for such a claim. The former replied that Jefferson had recommended the colonization of free blacks in his famous *Notes*, but when asked to implement such a policy several times by the Virginia legislature, he had "coldly evaded their application." There, in stunned silence, the conversation ended.[23]

The next day, cloth-headed but sober, Mercer asked Doddridge to explain his remark. In reply, Doddridge told the younger man that several times around the turn of the century, when he had been serving in the Virginia Senate, the legislature had discussed the colonization of insurgent slaves. The matter had been dealt with behind closed doors, and members had been sworn to secrecy, but if Mercer was interested, he might consult the secret journals and the correspondence between then Governor James Monroe and President Jefferson that had resulted from the discussions. Curious, Mercer called on the clerk of the Senate, who "incautiously" showed him the journals.[24]

The journals revealed that following the discovery of Gabriel's conspiracy of 1800 and the Easter conspiracy of 1802 the Virginia Assembly had authorized Monroe to sell or remove outside of the United States all slaves convicted of complicity in the plots, thereby reviving the once popular idea of colonization. The legislature had also requested that Monroe consult with Jefferson on the possibility of obtaining land in the far West for such a purpose. But the resolution was vague in its wording, and Monroe carefully explained to Jefferson that the measure was intended as an alternative to the death penalty and was not meant to propose a colony for free blacks. He also suggested that Jefferson interpret the mandate broadly and consider areas besides the western territories.[25]

Jefferson would not consider the West; that was to be the province of white yeomen. He accordingly instructed Rufus King, the American minister in London, to contact the founders of the Sierra Leone colony in Africa, which had been created as a home for the American slaves who had fled into British lines during the Revolution. But William Wilberforce and Henry Thornton replied that the colony was in serious financial trouble and would probably have to be taken over by the British government. They were in no position to welcome unruly slaves from the United States. There the matter, which remained a secret, rested for well over a decade.[26]

Mercer was fascinated by the idea of colonization and not just as a penal colony for rebellious slaves. Considering himself under no restriction of secrecy, he told all who would listen of the secret correspondence. But with the session all but over, it was too late to take any significant action, and he promised himself that if he were reelected to the House, he would renew the resolutions at the following session. Several days later, on February 29, 1816, the legislature adjourned.[27]

Although his age placed him in a generation that was not as hostile to slavery as men of the revolutionary period, Mercer believed that slavery was the "blackest of all blots, and foulest of all deformities." Indeed, he viewed slavery in much the same way as the Enlightenment Virginians—like his father—whom he so much admired. But also like many of those men, he had not the faintest idea what to do about the problem. He adhered to the popular cant that slavery had been "fastened upon them" by England, and though he joined "in the expression of deep conviction, that slavery is wrong," there seemed to be no solution to it. Most of all, Mercer, who had recently bought another house "servant," echoed the popular sentiment "that freeing the slaves now would do more harm than good."[28]

If Mercer could or would do no more than wring his hands over the issue of slavery, he believed that there was something far worse: the large and rapidly growing number of free blacks in the upper South. If anything, "the state of the free colored person" was even more "degrading and deplorable" than that of the slaves. The problem, as he saw it, was that "an everlasting mark [of color]" held down the condition of the free black. It was not that the free black was a danger to slavery; it was that his skin made him a part of a permanent lower class and thus a danger to an industrializing society. As much as banking and internal improvements, colonization would come to be an integral part of Mercer's increasingly cohesive economic system.[29]

As the idea formed in Mercer's mind, it became clear to him that colonization could act "as a drain for pauperism in Virginia." Especially because free blacks were "every day polluting and corrupting public morals" in the state, he believed that the old resolutions would receive support. Thinking of "the spirit of which certain British economists have done the removal of Irish, Scotch and English paupers," Mercer decided that colonization was "certainly a cheaper remedy of pauperism" than to "maintain them at home." Besides, he asserted, "more than half the [free black] females are prostitutes and [half] of the males rogues."[30]

Despite such rhetoric, colonization was not founded upon racism. Mercer was clearly racist in his thinking but no more so than all but the most enlightened men of his time (including many

abolitionists). He simply and accurately recognized the power of
racism and believed that it would present a permanent barrier to
black improvement. Mercer could try to improve or control lower-
class whites—he was then working on a plan for public education
that would do just that—but racism would keep free blacks a
perpetual, and hence a highly dangerous and discontented, lower
class. Indeed, Mercer used identical phraseology when discussing
lower-class whites. Class, not race, was the clue to colonization.[31]

But if colonization was not fueled by racism, neither was it
designed to achieve abolition. In promoting his rationale for colonization, Mercer was completely blunt. Colonization had, he
wrote, "in truth, nothing, whatever, to do with domestic slavery."
He had no desire to abolish slavery, for though he thought it an
abominable system, abolition would only release into society more
of that dangerous class he wished to remove. Neither did he believe
that colonization would hasten the end of slavery by making masters more likely to manumit their slaves. Nor was it designed to
strengthen slavery by removing a caste dangerous to the planters.
Mercer would not raise a finger either to destroy or protect slavery
(other than to participate in it); he simply saw free blacks as a
danger to his vision of the future American society.[32]

Such ideas were swirling through Mercer's head when the Virginia legislature adjourned. He remained in Richmond on private
business until March 8, when he boarded the stage for Aldie. He
was still seriously considering an extended tour abroad, but in mid-
April word arrived that he had been reelected to the House of
Delegates despite his failure to campaign or even to attend the
election. He then abandoned the thought of going to Europe. The
idea of gaining support for colonization in the Virginia legislature
had come to dominate his mind.[33]

Instead of traveling to Europe for his health, Mercer decided
upon a short but leisurely summer visit to Saratoga. On his way he
paused briefly in Washington, where he stopped to hear the debates
in the House of Representatives. While in the gallery he stumbled
upon two old friends, Francis Scott Key of Georgetown and Elias B.
Caldwell, an old schoolmate from New Jersey, who was then a clerk
at the Supreme Court. Mercer told both men of his plan to reintroduce the secret resolutions in the next session of the legislature, and both were enthusiastic. Key, a young Federalist with a
minor talent at putting new words to old songs, said he would
consider returning to Maryland and obtaining a seat in the legislature with an eye toward introducing a similar resolution.[34]

Elias Caldwell was no less interested in Mercer's ideas, although he informed the Virginian that because of financial obligations to his family he could not return to his home state of New Jersey. He could, however, write to his numerous friends and family in that state, and especially to his sister Esther's husband, Robert Finley. Caldwell obviously told Mercer the name of his brother-in-law, although when Mercer repeated the story a year later he garbled it, saying that "Fidley" was Caldwell's uncle. But the connection was clear; Caldwell told Mercer that he contacted Finley, and Mercer noted that it was through Caldwell and Finley that "our object, was set on foot in New Jersey."[35]

It was at this point that control of the delicate issue began to slip from Mercer's grasp. To his dismay, Robert Finley did more than just try and raise the wind for the project in the North. The son of an immigrant Scottish merchant, Finley had entered the College of New Jersey at the age of eleven in 1783. There he dedicated his life to serve the Presbyterian church. After his ordination, his first post was in the small town of Basking Ridge, not far from Princeton. He became a trustee of the college in 1807. In 1815 he was named director of Princeton's new theological seminary.[36]

Yet Finley remained spiritually unfulfilled. He thought about how much many others had accomplished in life at an earlier age, and he began to look about for a benevolent cause with which to identify. He was ripe for a project like colonization when he heard about it from Caldwell in April 1816. While Caldwell was writing to his friends and family in New Jersey, Mercer was still in Washington. He suffered a serious relapse and was "very sick," and evidently he infected Key. The two men spent several weeks together in the same room in John Randolph's Georgetown mess while they recovered. There the two conservatives spent many of their hours discussing colonization.[37]

By April 29 the two men had recovered sufficiently that Key hosted a large party at his home, where Mercer proudly revealed his plan to a larger group. John Randolph, Jeremiah Mason, Rufus King, Thomas Swann, and Littleton W. Tazewell were among those present, and most of them, he fumed, "laughed at it, as an extravagent, or ridiculous project." The argumentative and arrogant Mercer refused to be dissuaded and no doubt was still trying to convince Mason of the plan's feasibility when the two men, joined by Daniel Webster, left town the next day on the Baltimore steamer.[38]

On his way north Mercer stopped at Baltimore, Philadelphia, and

New York, telling all who would listen of his ideas. He previously had concluded that although all who had voted on the earlier Virginia resolutions had taken vows of secrecy, his inebriated innocence in hearing the story released him from any such oath. While on the road he "penned" new resolutions that were "shewn to many persons" and "everywhere approved."[39]

In early June Mercer left New York and hurried south. The Federalist party had scheduled a large barbecue for June 15, and as the leader of the party in the House Mercer could not miss it. Such expensive festivities had long been a mainstay of the Republican party, especially in Virginia, where the lesser classes expected to be wined and dined by the party leaders. It was not easy for the Federalists to overcome their distaste for these lavish affairs, but they were essential if the party were to gain widespread support. Mercer put aside his disgust and attended the "Barbacue" at which the principal attraction was Charles C. Pinckney, the party's two-time presidential nominee. He then returned to northern Virginia, where he mentioned his plan to Bushrod Washington at Mount Vernon.[40]

In early August Mercer again left Virginia and traveled north to the cool climate of Canada. By the first of October he had regained his strength enough to return to Richmond. On October 9, however, he stopped in Princeton to dine with Samuel Stanhope Smith, the former president of his alma mater. The daybook Mercer was then keeping makes no mention of Finley, although it does note that he brought up "the enterprise which then engrossed [his] thoughts" in an attempt "to learn what aid might be anticipated" from the northern states. At this time Finley was associated with the college, and though Finley had already heard of the scheme from Caldwell the previous spring, it is not unlikely that he heard of it again from Smith.[41]

By November Mercer was back in Richmond. During this month Finley, without Mercer's knowledge or approval, first "unveiled his scheme" to a small group of townspeople, businessmen, students, and professors at Princeton. In the scheme Finley discussed, the ideas of Mercer had undergone considerable evolution. Instead of having several states request the president to remove free blacks to Africa, Finley sought to create a national colonization society that would be located in Washington so that it could better lobby the federal Congress for funds. It would turn out, however, to be a plan Mercer could accept.[42]

At the same time Mercer pressed ahead with his own plan. On

December 14 he submitted to the Virginia House a resolution requesting the federal government to obtain territory in Africa or "elsewhere"—this word was inserted without his consent—to serve as an asylum for free blacks who chose to emigrate. The legislature considered this resolution without any knowledge of the society preparing to form in Washington, although by now Key was informing Mercer all actions in the capital. Mercer, apparently, did not want the touchy Virginians to hear about any developments to the north.[43]

Because of the delicate subject matter, the Virginia legislature, not unlike the General Assembly of 1801, dealt with the resolution in a secret session. But debate lasted only one full day, and when the vote was taken, Mercer's idea was endorsed by an overwhelming vote of 137 to 9. On December 15 the injunction of secrecy was removed, and the resolution was sent to the Senate. There it passed on December 20 "with but one dissenting voice."[44]

At that very moment the organization that was to become the American Colonization Society was being formed in Washington by Caldwell, Key, and Finley. Needing a more prominent name than any of theirs to head their organization, Caldwell and Key prevailed on conservative Supreme Court Justice Bushrod Washington to act as president. Washington, who had already heard of the plan from Mercer, of course carried his famous uncle's name, but in addition he was Mercer's godfather.[45]

The first meeting of the group, without Mercer but, as the Virginian later boasted, "founded" on his "Virginia resolution," took place on December 21. The attraction of Washington's name clearly worked, for in attendance were such well-known political figures as Henry Clay, William H. Crawford, and John Taylor of Caroline. Richard Rush, another schoolmate of Mercer's, was there, as was the doubting Randolph of Roanoke. Daniel Webster's dark visage was visible in the back of the hall. Finley was also present, although he was not mentioned by either the Washington or Richmond papers.[46]

Two weeks later, John Randolph, with as little enthusiasm as possible, read the society's request for federal aid to the House of Representatives. The document was referred to the Slave Trade Committee. Despite the famous names connected with the petition, the southern-dominated committee was not overly receptive to the idea; it urged instead cooperation with the British at Sierra Leone, an honor the English had declined more than a decade before.[47]

Following the organization of the national society, Finley returned to New Jersey, where he succeeded in creating a state colonization society auxiliary to the Washington group. At his home in Basking Ridge, Finley fired off letter after letter in support of colonization. It was there, on February 14, 1817, that he sat down to write his famous letter to John Mumford, selling the ideas he had so recently heard in Washington. But he had little opportunity to write any others; shortly thereafter he accepted the position of president of the University of Georgia, where he contracted a fever and died on October 3, 1817.[48]

Except for Princeton circles, there was never any doubt who revived the idea. Margaret Mercer, the Maryland cousin of the Virginian, who became an important colonizationist herself, wrote in 1817: "There is a glorious scheme in contemplation & indeed going into execution to make a colony of free blacks in Africa," adding that "it originated with [Charles] Fenton Mercer." Mercer, however, never attempted to take credit for reviving the idea (aside from denying Finley its paternity), probably because the scheme was not his own but merely one that he had stumbled upon drunkenly. He did allow himself the reflection that the "history of its origin is not a little curious," and he was always proud that the 1816 resolutions of his "Native State" took "the lead" in colonization.[49]

Throughout his long life Mercer neither worked for abolition nor believed that colonization would bring about the gradual end of slavery. Yet the interpretation that has prevailed is that colonization was a religiously inspired, benevolent, mildly emancipationist movement, and it has prevailed because of the kindly if unimportant Finley. "I know this scheme is from God," Finley said.[50] But the truth, as Monroe's son-in-law George Hay observed, is that Charles Fenton Mercer was "the father of the Colonization Society and all of their projects." And the scheme came not from God but from a much less exalted place.[51]

Notes

ABBREVIATIONS

ACS   American Colonization Society
CFM   Charles Fenton Mercer
COCC   Chesapeake and Ohio Canal Company
DAB   *Dictionary of American Biography*, ed. Allen Johnson and Dumas Malone, 21 vols., 1928–1936.

JQA   John Quincy Adams
JSH   *Journal of Southern History*
LC   Library of Congress
NJHS   New Jersey Historical Society
NYHS   New-York Historical Society
PRO, FO Great Britain, Public Record Office, Foreign Office
UVA   University of Virginia
VHS   Virginia Historical Society
VMHB   *Virginia Magazine of History and Biography*
VSL   Virginia State Library
WMQ   *William and Mary Quarterly*

1. CFM, Autobiographical Sketch, Mercer-Hunter Papers, VSL.

2. CFM to Claiborne W. Gooch, September 26, 1823, Gooch Papers, VHS; CFM to Wilson Cary Nicholas, April 14, 1815, Nicholas Papers, LC.

3. *Richmond Enquirer*, December 5, 1815.

4. Ibid., December 9, 1815.

5. CFM, Autobiographical Sketch, Mercer-Hunter Papers; *Richmond Enquirer*, December 30, 1815.

6. CFM, Autobiographical Sketch, Mercer-Hunter Papers; Carter Goodrich, "The Virginia System of Mixed Enterprise: A Study of State Planning of Internal Improvements," *Political Science Quarterly* 64 (September 1949): 362; Philip M. Rice, "The Virginia Board of Public Works, 1816–1842" (M.A. thesis, University of North Carolina, 1947), 38–44.

7. Wiley E. Hodge, "Pro-Governmentalism in Virginia, 1789–1836," *Journal of Politics* 25 (May 1971): 344; Charles Fenton Mercer, *An Exposition of the Weakness and Inefficiency of the Government of the United States of North America* (N.p., 1845), 357.

8. James H. Broussard, *The Southern Federalists, 1800–1816* (Baton Rouge, 1978), 353; Mercer, *Exposition*, 359.

9. Virginius Dabney, *Virginia: The New Dominion* (New York, 1971), 213.

10. CFM, Autobiographical Sketch, Mercer-Hunter Papers.

11. Harrison, Jr. "Oligarchs and Democrats—The Richmond Junto," *VMHB* 78 (April 1970): 194–95; Virginia Moore, *The Madisons: A Biography* (New York, 1979), 359; Glyndon G. Van Deusen, *The Life of Henry Clay* (Boston, 1937), 111.

12. Charles Fenton Mercer, *Report on Banks* (Richmond, 1816), 15.

13. Ibid., 4.

14. *Richmond Enquirer*, July 15, 1825, December 16, 1815.

15. *Journal of the House of Delegates of the Commonwealth of Virginia* (Richmond, 1911), 131; *Richmond Enquirer*, January 6, 1816.

16. Benjamin Hatcher to CFM, January 4, 1816, in Mercer, *Report on Banks*, 16; Harry Ammon, "The Richmond Junto," *VMHB* 61 (October 1953): 401, n. 20; John Brockenbrough to CFM, January 2, 1816, in Mercer, *Report on Banks*, 16.

17. Thomas Jefferson to Charles Yancey, January 6, 1816, in Paul L. Ford, ed., *The Works of Thomas Jefferson*, 12 vols. (New York, 1904–5), 11:497.

18. *Richmond Enquirer*, July 15, 1825.

19. Ibid., July 19, 1825, February 8, 1816; *Norfolk and Portsmouth Herald*, February 12, 1815; Broussard, *Southern Federalists*, 340, n. 16.

20. *Richmond Enquirer*, January 20, 1816; CFM to Claiborne W. Gooch, September 26, 1823, Gooch Papers; Norman Risjord, "The Virginia Federalists," *JSH* 33 (November 1967): 513.

21. *Richmond Enquirer*, February 6, 15, 1816; *Norfolk and Portsmouth Herald*, February 9, 1816; *Journal of the House*, 184; Daniel Webster to CFM, May 13, 1816,

in Harold D. Moser et al., eds., *The Papers of Daniel Webster*, 7 vols. to date (Hanover, N.H., 1974–86), 1:418.

22. CFM to John Francis Mercer, March 4, 1816, Mercer Family Papers, VHS.

23. Charles Fenton Mercer, *An Address to the American Colonization Society at Their 36th Annual Meeting* (Geneva [Switzerland], 1854), 2–3; CFM to John H. Cocke, April 19, 1818, Cocke Collection, UVA.

24. Mercer, *Address*, 3.

25. Dumas Malone, *Jefferson and His Time*, 6 vols. (Boston, 1948–81),4: 253. jFor the Jefferson-Monroe correspondence see Philip Slaughter, *The Virginian History of African Colonization* (Richmond, 1855), 2–6.

26. Betty Fladeland, *Men and Brothers: Anglo-American Antislavery Cooperation* (Urbana, 1972), 90.

27. Mercer, *Address*, 2–3. For a discussion of the historiography of colonization, the incorrect belief that Robert Finley revived the idea, and the question of the date of his famous Mumford letter, see Douglas R. Egerton, " 'Its Origin Is Not a Little Curious': A New Look at the American Colonization Society," *Journal of the Early Republic* 5 (Winter 1985): 464–65, 477, and n. 1.

28. CFM to Mary Eleanor Garnett, March 20, 1814, James Mercer Garnett Papers, Duke University Library; Mercer, *Exposition*, 167, 171, 173, 284.

29. Mercer, *Exposition*, 170, 169.

30. CFM to Alexander Stevenson, November 3, 1823, Benjamin Bland Papers, VHS; CFM to William Gaston, January 1, 1828, Gaston Papers, University of North Carolina, Chapel Hill.

31. Two historians who believe that racism was behind colonization are Merton L. Dillon, "The Failure of the American Abolitionists," *JSH* 25 (May 1959): 166, and Charles I. Foster, "The Colonization of Free Negroes in Liberia, 1816–1835," *Journal of Negro History* 38 (January 1935): 47. The latter cites Mercer as an example of a racist thinker.

32. Mercer, *Address*, 9.

33. CFM Diary, February 28–March 8, 1816, CFM Papers, NJHS; CFM to John Francis Mercer, March 4, 1816, Mercer Family Papers; John Campbell to David Campbell, March 8, 1816, Campbell Family Papers, Duke University Library; *Richmond Enquirer*, April 20, 1816.

34. Mercer, *Address*, 3; CFM, Autobiographical Sketch, Mercer-Hunter Papers; CFM to John H. Cocke, April 19, 1818, Cocke Collection.

35. Mercer, *Address*, 3; *DAB*, 6:391; CFM to John H. Cocke, April 19, 1818, Cocke Collection.

36. P. J. Staudenraus, *The African Colonization Movement* (New York, 1961), 15–16; *DAB*, 6:391.

37. CFM Diary, April 16–28, 1816, CFM Papers, NJHS; John Randolph to James M. Garnett, April 16, 1816, John Randolph Papers, LC.

38. CFM Diary, April 29–30, 1816, CFM Papers, NFHS; CFM to John H. Cocke, April 19, 1818, Cocke Collection; Daniel Webster to John Randolph, April 30, 1816, in Moser et al., eds., *Papers of Webster*, 1:197–98.

39. CFM, speech of 1833, in *African Repository*, 9:266, CFM, Autobiographical Sketch, Mercer-Hunter Papers; *North American Review* 35 (1832): 126; CFM to John H. Cocke, April 19, 1818, Cocke Collection.

40. David H. Fischer, *The Revolution of American Conservatism: The Federalist Party in the Era of Jeffersonian Democracy* (New York, 1965), 100; CFM Diary, June 1–July 29, 1816, CFM Papers, NJHS.

41. CFM Diary, August 10–November 3, 1816, CFM Papers, NJHS; Mercer, *Address*, 3.

42. Henry N. Sherwood, "The Formation of the American Colonization Society," *Journal of Negro History* 11 (July 1917): 218.

43. CFM, Autobiographical Sketch, Mercer-Hunter Papers; Mercer, *Address,* 4; CFM, speech of 1833, in *African Repository,* 9:266.

44. *Richmond Enquirer,* January 9, 1817; Mathew Carey, *Letters on the Colonization Society Addressed to the Hon. C. F. Mercer* (Philadelphia, 1832), 7; CFM, Autobiographical Sketch, Mercer-Hunter Papers; CFM, speech of January 1, 1818, in *First Annual Report* [of the American Colonization Society] (Washington, D.C., 1818), 15; Charles Fenton Mercer, ed., *Slave Trade,* House Committee Report 348, Serial 201, Vol. 3 (Washington, D.C., 1830), 20–21.

45. Isaac Brown, *Biography of Rev. Robert Finley* (1857; rpt. New York, 1969), 132; CFM to John H. Cocke, April 19, 1818, Cocke Collection.

46. Mercer, *Address,* 4; *National Intelligencer,* December 23, 24, 1816; *Richmond Enquirer,* December 31, 1816.

47. Mercer, ed., *Slave Trade,* 33–34.

48. Brown, *Biography of Finley,* 124; *DAB,* 6:391.

49. Caspar Morris, *Memoir of Miss Margaret Mercer* (Philadelphia, 1848), 110; Margaret Mercer to John Gordon, 1817, Mercer Family Papers; Mercer, *Address,* 2; CFM to John H. Cocke, April 19, 1818, Cocke Collection.

50. See, for example, Staudenraus, *African Colonization,* 17.

51. Diary, April 29, 1819, in Charles Francis Adams, ed., *Memoirs of John Quincy Adams, Comprising Parts of His Diary from 1795 to 1848,* 12 vols. (Philadelphia, 1874–77), 4:354.

8

Pauperism White

Content that his colonization venture was safely under way, Mercer was finally able to devote his full attention to a topic that had held great interest for him ever since his travels in France: public education. It was a subject, he admitted, that was critical to his economic program, for it was one of "the three great objects" that he had "at heart[:] Colonization, Internal Improvement and public education." In Mercer's mind these interlocking objects, fully as much as banking, were necessary for ushering in "the revolution [he] so much desire[d] to occur."[1]

That Mercer was as anxious to create a system of public education in 1816 as he was in 1806, when he spoke to the Washington Society, reflected the continuing influence of Europe on his mind. Such an interest was unusual in Virginia, for nothing like a standardized system of education existed anywhere in the South. Several New England states, which benefited from compact settlement, had begun to institute centralized and largely state-financed schools, but even these were not as innovative as what Mercer had in mind. Virginia's system of education, if its haphazard arrangement could be so dignified, was especially backward. Following the Revolution, a number of local private elementary schools, called district schools, had been started. Their curriculum was determined by those who funded them. In areas where no funding was available, there were no schools.[2]

At the same time, a large number of academies, or "classical schools," sprang up about the state to provide education for children who had completed primary instruction, although they often also included some elementary subject matter. Between 1800 and 1860 almost 250 of these schools were incorporated by the General Assembly; incorporation was the state's only legal relationship with these academies. These schools provided the education most commonly received by Virginia children, and they were completely supported by tuition fees paid by the parents of those attending. The fees were generally low, but still high enough to be prohibitive for many families.[3]

Finally, three colleges had appeared in Virginia by 1817: William and Mary, Hampden-Sydney, and Washington. They were far below the quality standards of the school attended by Mercer, and critics such as Thomas Jefferson regarded the latter two as little better than grammar schools. Even the older and more established College of William and Mary, the school attended by James and George Mercer, averaged only fifty students a year. At best 150 young men attended the three institutions each year during this period. Many leading Virginians realized there was a serious need for educational reform at all levels.[4]

The first real attempt at reform in this period, not surprisingly given Mercer's long interest in education, was a product of his fertile mind. This was the law of February 2, 1810, which established the state Literary Fund from the allocation of "escheates, penalties and forfeitures, and all rights accruing the State as derelict." Though not yet a member of the House, Mercer had drawn up the bill and convinced fellow Federalist William Noland to introduce it. The fund was devised so that the General Assembly could draw from it as it saw fit to provide educational facilities for the poor children of the state.[5]

But the fund received too little money to do any good, and most Virginians turned to more traditional schemes for financing education. One of these appears in an 1814 letter of Thomas Jefferson to his favorite nephew, Peter Carr. The former president, enjoying his well-earned retirement and meditating on the future of education in the commonwealth, suggested that the legislature divide every county in the state into wards five miles square to form educational districts. This was essentially a revival of his 1779 plan, although redesigned to provide "three years' instruction" to "future citizens." This idea was no more than a sketch for Carr, who well knew his uncle's views on elementary education, and said nothing about the practical aspects of creating a statewide school system. No method of funding was prescribed, for Jefferson always contended that primary schools could be devised without appropriations from the Literary Fund, and the reference to "future citizens" casts doubt upon whether girls were meant to be included. In all events, Carr mailed the letter to Thomas Ritchie, and it was published in the *Richmond Enquirer* and became the accepted Republican model.[6]

Despite the limitations of Jefferson plan, it focused attention on the issue. The governor's next yearly address to the combined houses of the legislature mentioned the sorry state of public education. Although Governor Nicholas was Jefferson's ally, he agreed with Mercer that the Literary Fund should be used for its intended purpose. He therefore accompanied his Literary Fund report with an urgent request for "speedy . . . farther appropriations in aid of the Literary Fund."[7]

One of those listening to the governor's plea was Mercer, who was continuing as chairman of the House Finance Committee for the 1815–16 session. He now believed that he had the necessary mandate to recommend that the fund be increased by $1,210,550, which could be attained through the repayment of the Virginia war loan he had attempted to negotiate from the federal government. With this increase, the fund would total an impressive $3,115,894. Gaining this money, Mercer knew, would be difficult, but it was only the first step in a much more ambitious plan he was formulating.[8]

The heavily Republican House responded favorably to Mercer's recommendation and appropriated the funds in February 1816. Mercer believed that the House made the appropriation because it would make repayment by the government more likely. Republican Senator Joseph Cabell thought that the publication of Jefferson's letter had led to the "passage of that resolution." Both views may be correct, but certainly the Republican patriarch's interest in the question must have helped sway the younger members of his party. In any case, the state finally had the means to take a significant step in public education, and the House requested the president and directors of the Literary Fund to present a plan for all educational levels at the next General Assembly. But the House, as the committee of the whole, also ordered that the Literary Fund report be sent to Mercer's Finance Committee with instructions to "bring in a bill or bills." A certain amount of cooperation between the two assemblages was assumed, for there seems to have been no anticipation that the fund directors' advice would differ fundamentally from the committee plan.[9]

When the Virginia legislature met in the fall of 1816, Nicholas dutifully called again for a system of education for "those whose parents are unable to defray the expense of it." But when the directors of the fund produced the report called for in the previous session, the majority of the paper was devoted to the establishment of a university, and only five paragraphs at the end pertained to elementary schools. Yet it reflected Jefferson's thinking on public education. The plan provided for a highly decentralized system in which each county would be divided into townships containing an unspecified number of "housekeepers." The housekeepers in each township would choose seven men as trustees, and they in turn would fix the site, appoint a teacher, and devise the curriculum. Children whose parents could not pay tuition would receive three years of free education, and those who could afford to would go on to the academies. The schools would be restricted to boys. The university, not the public schools, was clearly the heart of the fund report.[10]

This report, however, was only a recommendation; the Finance Committee would draw up the bills. Mercer's bill was not expected to differ seriously from the basic themes laid down by Jefferson and the directors. Several Republicans had been in touch with him throughout 1816, and Cabell had shown Jefferson's letter to him before its publication. Cabell was the former president's protégé and legislative liaison in the Virginia Senate, and with the backing of Jefferson and his own distinguished family background Cabell had become quite the leading light since the days when he and Mercer had first tangled over the Lynchburg bank bill. The Republican had reason to believe that he was privy to government machinations in Richmond. He confidently informed his mentor that Mercer "appears quite pleased with your view on the subject." The normally astute Cabell was gravely in error, yet he foolishly promised Jefferson that he would do "anything in [his] power to promote" Mercer's bill when it appeared.[11]

In the midst of this profound misunderstanding Mercer rose on February 8, 1817, to introduce his bill. As usual, he had plans of his own. Despite his affiliation with the minority party, he was, at the age of thirty-eight, a formidable figure in the legislature. The Federalist party was firmly under his control, and many moderate Republicans admired him and were willing to follow his lead, at least to an extent. He had also come to fancy himself, with perhaps too much certitude, a political tactician.

Instead of accepting the Jeffersonian format, Mercer presented the legislature with a bill that turned the fund report on its head. Instead of the university-oriented plan of the directors, Mercer's bill provided that the fund would "be immediately applied to the establishment of a [primary] school in each township" and that only "after the accomplishment of these objects, the surplus that may remain, be applied to found and support the University of Virginia."[12]

Mercer's measure was sweeping in scope, and in a time of short bills it ran fifteen pages. It proposed a system of public education administered by a board of education and financed by the Literary Fund. Primary schools were to be established first, "free of any charge whatever" for "all free white" children. Following that was a system of academies, forty-eight for boys and three for girls. If the money held out, four colleges were to be built throughout the state and a university was to be established in a central location.[13]

Surprisingly, as Thomas Ritchie noted, this "most important" act "excited very little attention" at first. It was ten days before Linn Banks of Madison made a motion to postpone further consideration of the bill until March 20, a delay tantamount to killing it. Mercer argued eloquently against the motion, and it was defeated. Mercer then forced the bill, without amendments, onto the floor for consideration. It passed, 66 to 49, with the Federalists in favor, 14 to 2. The Republicans split slightly in favor. Then, in an unwise effort to stress its main focus, the act was retitled to place the word "primary" before the word "university" in its name. After its passage by the House, the measure was sent to the Senate, where it was referred to the committee chaired by Cabell. There it ran into trouble.[14]

The bill contained several features that disturbed Virginians, even some of those who supported the notion of state-funded elementary education. Hostility toward the bill originated from two interlocking problems—regional tensions and political partisanship. Sectional animosity in Virginia had long been fierce, based on religious, economic, and political considerations, for the independent-minded western counties resented their reduced representation compared with the Tidewater. The education bill brought these tensions to the surface. The wealthy lowland planters tended to educate their children privately (Mercer was a product of that system). They balked at the prospect of paying for an educational system they would probably not use. Mercer countered this objection with an argument "also founded on the unequal operation of moral and physical causes upon different portions" of the same state. "When war and invasion threaten," he asked pointedly, "shall the inhabitants of the mountains say to those of the sea-coast, Fight your own battles?"[15]

Tensions also arose over the proposed location of the university.

Jefferson had long dreamed of establishing one within view of his hilltop estate, but Mercer's bill specifically provided for the university to be established near "the geographical center of the commonwealth." Sharp Republicans quickly perceived Mercer's political objectives for choosing a central location. Mercer had no knowledge about Jefferson's desires, and he hoped that the former president would not "befriend [a Charlottesville site] since he had been a pupil of William and Mary, an apparently rival institution." But the Federalist leader erred badly and was tempting disaster, for the eastern districts were overrepresented in the legislature, especially in the Senate.[16]

The issue was not simply the location of the university; it was a question of political power, and it directly involved Mercer. The west had long demanded that the state capital be moved to a more central location and, failing that, insisted on a constitutional convention to redistribute apportionment. A reform meeting had been held in Staunton the previous summer, and only his illness had kept Mercer, who had been elected as a delegate, from attending. He had obvious incentives in giving more power to the Federalist west, and following his lead, the House finally passed a measure allowing for a popular referendum on the question of a convention. The Federalists strongly favored the bill, 21 to 4, and the Republicans split against it. But the keen political mind of Joseph Cabell correctly recognized that the question of placement of a university was a sectional Federalist plot in a state power grab. "Staunton wants the seat of Government," he warned Jefferson, and "any brilliant [educational] establishment at the Eastern foot of the Ridge will shake those claims."[17]

Mercer's past record of supporting the west raised questions and suspicions from easterners and became a serious blunder when he securely tied power politics and education together. By serving as the chief eastern spokesman for western rights, Mercer had turned the university into a partisan issue and confirmed what Cabell and his supporters already suspected: the placement of the university was merely a ploy for the west to gain political power. The irony was that using the university to secure western rights was only a subplot in Mercer's larger scheme, for he actually cared very little about any university.[18]

If some regional tensions lurked behind the question of the university site, region and politics were not two separate issues. Jefferson regarded the western Shenandoah Valley as a "Tory" district, and he was almost obsessed with fears of what mischief the

Federalist Presbyterians who lived there, with their disturbingly northern business habits, might be up to. Under no circumstances would he or Cabell, who shared this view, allow the university—or the capital—to be placed there.[19]

The university, and hence the primary education system that topped it, became entwined with political issues in other and more potent ways. The matter of the convention was one example, albeit one tinged with regionalism. The issue of state banking was potentially dangerous, for the stubborn Federalist leader insisted on grounding the Literary Fund with new fund banks to hold the money set aside for education, which were made part of the new bank bill that he introduced in January 1817. Mercer moved to establish three banks spread evenly around the state. The one in Richmond was to be the largest with a capital of $1. million, although the measure was primarily intended to please "every neglected [western] county in the state."[20]

Mercer had obviously not forgotten his desire to provide banking for the west and ready capital for investors in his internal improvement plans. But it was a foolish blunder to complicate his educational plans with other legislation, for notwithstanding the willingness of the Republicans to charter the Farmers' Bank, Mercer was not far wrong in his claim that the Jeffersonians "were crying out against all banks as an evil." It was the misfortune of the education bill that it, and the question of a state convention, became involved with this volatile and partisan issue. He should have known better inasmuch as his bank bill of the previous session had been such a spectacular failure.[21]

The political climate in Virginia respecting banks had, however, changed slightly since the previous session. The refusal of the legislature to agree to Mercer's previous bill had led to howls of protest from the western counties that could not be easily ignored. But the Bank of Virginia and the Farmers' Bank, both firmly under the control of eastern capital and the Republican Richmond Junto, were still wary of banks that would aid western Federalist counties. At the very least, they were not inclined to support as all-encompassing a bill as Mercer's. Moreover, there was a subtle connection between banking and the drive for a constitutional convention in that the same groups supported both movements. This connection was absolutely clear to Cabell. It was the "Federalists of the West" who wanted a convention, he reported to Jefferson, although this desire "originated among Bank Stockholders." Viewing these demands as tantamount to extortion,

Cabell compared the entire question to the hated Federalist Hartford Convention. The issues of education, western representation, and banking were now one.[22]

The new bank bill only served to incite those Republicans who might have been willing to support Mercer's education bill. "What!" shrieked one observer in the *Richmond Enquirer*, "Shall we do nothing without a bank? Shall we educate our children by a bank? Pray, Sir, where will this mania stop?" But Mercer and his supporters foolishly paid these warnings no heed, and the new bank bill, with the fund banks included, passed the House on January 10 in a close vote and with the Federalists voting in favor 21 to 6. The delegate from Loudoun serenely voted aye.[23]

Joseph Cabell, as usual, was quietly watching these developments from the upper chamber and passing the information along to Jefferson. Sending a copy of the new bank bill to a disapproving Monticello, the Republican added: "I think it will be much altered in the Senate, and perhaps will fail entirely in the end." His prophecy was accurate, if for no other reason than that he took the lead in "hewing down" the bill and eliminating the fund banks. This action came on February 9, and it should have served as a warning for Mercer. Perhaps the Federalist leader was counting on the general desire in Virginia to see the Literary Fund used. Perhaps also Mercer's political sense had been dulled by his burning desire to get a banking bill passed.[24]

This was where Mercer made his fatal error. There was no consensus on how the newly acquired money should be spent, as he could have seen from the fund report he had so carefully ignored. It was this lack of consensus on emphasis that shed the most light on the fundamental differences the two parties in Virginia. The regional and political problems reflected in the education bill doubtless drew opposition to the act, but they were factors that operated on a partisan basis. Mercer's emphasis on primary education and his insistence on a highly centralized system reflected political philosophy in which the fundamental variance between the two parties was most pronounced. Indeed, although it explained the Republican opposition to the measure, it demonstrated much more about the Federalist penchant for the act.

There was a fundamental difference in political philosophy between Mercer and the Federalists and Cabell and the Jeffersonians. Jefferson did not believe that education fell under the scope of government, and he was rigidly antagonistic to the central authority implied in such a belief. "If it is believed that these elementary schools will be better managed by the Governor" than "by the parents within each ward," he lectured Cabell, "it is a belief against all experience." Jefferson went on to deal with the rhetorical question on which all other debate rested: "What has destroyed liberty and the rights of man in every Government which has ever existed under the sun? The generalizing and concentrating all cares and powers into one body."[25]

This feeling was standard for Virginia Republicans, and it surfaced often in Ritchie's newspaper, the most influential journal in the state. On February 18 an anonymous letter attacked the centralizing aspects of the bill, specifically the board of education, which was depicted as "a vast and most expensive engine for forming and fashioning the opinions, principles and habits of every future generation." The obligatory comparisons were made with the dreaded European systems, those "violent opponents of liberal principles and the rights of man." Two days later a similar letter assailing the board appeared in the same publication. "Their capacity for evil [will] be increased by the powers they may assume over Public Education! Give them this moral lever," the author brayed, "and he who rules the legislature, will rule the people." Here was true fear.[26]

Mercer, being a Federalist, naturally did not share the Republican view about the dangers of the state becoming too powerful. He ridiculed such fears as groundless, and he impugned those "individuals of no small influence in society, who think that popular education is not a proper subject of political government." Such minds, he believed, "suppose a coercion, which is not proposed; is unnecessary, as experience demonstrates; and is nowhere attempted in America." Indeed, the Federalists' inability to make political headway during the war had only convinced him of what he had long suspected, that "an influence, purely federal[ist]," would never control the Virginia legislature as long as "the rabble are counted."[27]

If Mercer had given up on his party's chances for success, he was nonetheless not being completely honest. A coercion was intended, although it was a coercion far more subtle than any the Republicans feared. He knew that his party had not only permanently lost the great political battles of the new republic, but that it was now facing a rapidly expanding franchise that threatened to destroy the society dear to the Federalists. He would blunt the expanding suffrage, which remained limited in Virginia, through subtle devices, one of which was mass education. To Mercer the

Republican party, a "set of clod-hoppers," was rapidly extending the general suffrage "to embrace all the idle, worthless, ignorant and corrupt mass of population," and unless some action were taken this "popular filth" would swamp the nation by its "ebullition of dregs and froth." His long contemplated system of education was designed to control the common man, not to liberate him. It was a method of discipline and management, and it was grounded in a much deeper fear than any the Republicans could imagine.[28]

Evidence of that thrust surfaced in the way the bill was to be carried out. Despite the recent increase in the Literary Fund, it would be impossible to provide for all three educational levels. Mercer's bill was careful to make the central focus explicit: "The board shall regard the primary schools as its foundation; and in its gradual execution . . . no money shall be drawn from the revenue of that fund for the establishment of the university, or any academy or college, so long as it is possible that such an application of the fund may leave any primary school unprovided for."[29]

Cabell's nimble mind also grasped this reality. He reported to Jefferson that "I fear it will be difficult" to "procure money for the [university]." He lamented that "the prevailing opinion seems to be to establish schools first and colleges afterward." Cabell, of course, harbored no fears about the common man. An elitist in many ways, he nonetheless was at peace with the Republican doctrine that the yeomen and poor whites were essentially wise and needed no taming. He cared not a whit for primary schools; they could be set up as local authorities saw fit. His only concern reflected Jefferson's: the need to create a secular university rivaling those of New England.[30]

It is clear that other Federalists shared Mercer's views. A Federalist Norfolk paper, editorializing on the "greatest features" of the education bill, stated "that no Academies &c. are to be established, by the aid of the Literary Fund, until primary schools are provided for." Virginians were again witness to an unusual but increasingly popular sight. The Federalists, routinely excoriated as the party of reactionaries, elitists, and monarchists, were now championing an issue that allied them with the middle and lower classes, who certainly desired free schools. The situation gave Mercer another opportunity to sound progressive, and rhetoric was crucial in passing his essentially conservative legislation. When the Republicans, for example, complained that if Mercer's bill passed, taxes would have to be raised to support the huge system, he responded with blazing rhetoric that "the sons of opulence" should "not complain that the children of poverty are taught at their expense."[31]

This unnatural alliance should not be accepted without substantial qualification. Like his colonization venture, Mercer's bill was a measure for, not of, the lower classes. He did not see as much of a need to provide an education for Virginians as he did to impose one upon them in the name of social stability. As he had said a decade before, laws could only do so much; they could "only punish." Education could "prevent crimes," control the "great mass of people," and guard against the "worst of all associations, ignorance and general suffrage."[32]

Although active, Mercer's reformist impulse was anything but optimistic. His fears were based on the grim assumption that industrialization would make class division more severe. What he had seen in Birmingham had taught him that these "ills yet to come" would only serve to "expedite the division of property" and multiply "the number of the indigent, even more rapidly, than that of the wealthy." For Mercer, education would not only control the "corrupt mass" but "draw the extremes of society nearer together, and . . . multiply that [middle] class between them."[33]

Suggestive of the way Mercer's social views were woven into his education scheme, which was admittedly based in part on the Napoleonic system he had heard so much about over a decade before, was his effort to institute military indoctrination into primary schools. "In lieu of those childish games and amusements," Mercer pleasantly suggested, "which answer at present no other useful purpose than that of healthful exercise, military instruction might be early introduced." Military training for young children not only would create the disciplined soldier of the future, it would teach obedience and docility. It could, he noted, inculcate "habits of industry, among the children of the poor," and instill "the spirit of the laws into [the] infant mind." It would turn individuals into a compliant mass machine, which in an industrializing society would have many benefits.[34]

These benefits could also serve Virginia Republicans, who included some of the most wealthy and powerful men in the nation. But they were benefits that the agrarian-oriented Republicans did not ask for because their fears were of a far different nature. Cabell's motivation was alien to such thinking. And Jefferson's fears, like Cabell's, were aimed not at the lower classes but at the Federalists. As a result, Jefferson loathed Mercer's primary school system, but he more truly feared Federalist influence at the institutional level he considered more important: the university. He saw his university not as an institute of academic freedom but as a vehicle to crush dangerous Federalist ideas. It would indoctrinate loyalty to Republicanism and save Virginia "from the tax of toryism, fanaticism, and [the] indifferentism of their own State" that college students—like Charles Fenton Mercer—received in the North.[35]

By February 19 the education bill was under consideration in the Senate. Cabell wrote to Jefferson, telling him to prepare for the worst because he could not "predict its fate." The Republican senator added that the measure came "at a most inauspicious period, when the members are impatient to break up and go home." Cabell also mentioned with barely concealed pleasure that the bill "for taking the sense of the people as to the expedience of calling a convention was rejected in the Senate."[36]

It may have been part of Mercer's plan to introduce his bill so late in the session; if he was not yet the sophisticated tactician he fancied himself, he was becoming more politically astute. The two sections of the state were about evenly matched in the House, but the Tidewater dominated in the Senate, and Mercer delayed the vote until enough Republican senators had begun to drift home. Indeed, an angry Ritchie complained that the bill was discussed "when the [Senate] had dwindled into a sort of Rump Parliament."[37]

On February 20 the measure reached the floor. Speaker Chapman Johnson reported several amendments to the bill, which were agreed to by a desperate House. One of these was to move the location of the university to the east. No doubt this was painful for the western districts to accept, but Mercer urged approval in the hope that this concession would save the primary schools. Then Cabell calmly rose to offer another amendment, which "went to suspend the execution of every part of the law, except what relates to a Board of Public Instruction, and to laying off the counties into townships." No other part of the act would go into effect unless sanctioned by the next legislature. The bill was so amended after "considerable debate," although no record mentions a vote. In one deft move, the wiley Cabell had gutted the bill. The board remained, but the huge system of primary schools had disappeared. It could be revived if passed again in the next session, but as Cabell well knew, rumor held that Mercer intended to run for a seat in

Congress, and with his tremendous energy gone the bill had no chance. Thomas Ritchie, often lauded as a supporter of public education, rejoiced.[38]

There was nothing left but the final vote, meaningless now. The vote was a tie, 7 to 7, and so in a final indignity, the gutted act was rejected. Significantly, Cabell voted in favor of the bill, a sign that it was popular with his constituents. Mercer was reduced to spending the remainder of the session pressing for another Virginia war claim against the federal government, no doubt intended to bolster the Literary Fund, which he now knew would soon be raided for appropriations for a university. But the House had dwindled to a bare quorum and soon adjourned.[39]

For the rest of his life Charles Fenton Mercer held that it was "reckless party spirit" that killed his "beautiful and efficient system." He refused to admit, even to himself, that he had made a relatively nonpartisan issue partisan in nature by tying it to several highly political questions. Jefferson certainly hoped that the legislature would allocate all available funds to a university, but there were doubtless enough Republicans willing to allow Mercer's almost ignored bill to pass had he not excited their ancient hatreds. Deeper political motives were operating as well that explain the actions of Jefferson and Cabell. They feared not the common man but the Federalist party, and unfortunately this fear left Virginia with a seriously stunted system of education. Faith in the lower classes, in their view, was a substitute for positive action in their behalf, and there was some merit in Mercer's charge that the Republicans were content to leave "the mass of voters . . . not enlightened." Mercer lacked the faith of the Jeffersonians, but it was his dislike of the present and his fear of the future that led him to demonstrate that the party that had so little faith in democracy could also be the progressive party. Were it up to him, public education in Virginia would not have "gone to the tombs of all the Capulets."[40]

Notes

ABBREVIATIONS

ACS	American Colonization Society
CFM	Charles Fenton Mercer
COCC	Chesapeake and Ohio Canal Company
DAB	*Dictionary of American Biography*, ed. Allen Johnson and Dumas Malone, 21 vols., 1928–1936.

JQA   John Quincy Adams
JSH   *Journal of Southern History*
LC   Library of Congress
NJHS   New Jersey Historical Society
NYHS   New-York Historical Society
PRO, FO Great Britain, Public Record Office, Foreign Office
UVA   University of Virginia
VHS   Virginia Historical Society
VMHB   *Virginia Magazine of History and Biography*
VSL   Virginia State Library
WMQ   *William and Mary Quarterly*

1. CFM to John H. Cocke, September 16, 1825, Cocke Collection, UVA. Some historians, especially Norman Risjord, "The Virginia Federalists," *JSH* 33 (November 1967): 516–17, and Linda K. Kerber, *Federalists in Dissent: Imagery and Ideology in Jeffersonian America* (Ithaca, 1970), 110, use Mercer's education bill to demonstrate that some Federalists were progressive. The thesis of this chapter is at odds with that interpretation.

2. Bernard Bailyn, *Education in the Forming of American Society: Needs and Opportunities for Study* (Chapel Hill, 1960), 45; Virginius Dabney, *Virginia: The New Dominion* (New York, 1971), 56–57; Edward J. Knight, *The Evolution of Public Education in Virginia* (Washington, D.C., 1916), 4.

3. Cornelius J. Heatwole, *A History of Education in Virginia* (New York, 1916), 124–28.

4. Alfred J. Morrison, *The Beginnings of Public Education in Virginia, 1776–1860* (Richmond, 1917), 8.

5. CFM to Claiborne W. Gooch, September 26, 1823, Gooch Papers, VHS; CFM to Timothy Pickering, February 28, 1827, Pickering Papers, LC; *Richmond Enquirer,* April 16, 1830.

6. *Journal of the House of Delegates of the Commonwealth of Virginia* (Richmond, 1911), p. 51; Thomas Jefferson to Peter Carr, September 7, 1814, in Nathaniel F. Cabell, ed., *Early History of the University of Virginia, as Contained in the Letters of Thomas Jefferson and Joseph C. Cabell* (Richmond, 1856), 385; *Richmond Enquirer,* February 17, 1816; Joseph C. Cabell to Scott, December 13, 1817, Cabell Papers, LC.

7. Address of Gov. Wilson C. Nicholas to Senate and House, December 4, 1815, *Journal of the House,* 7; Literary Fund report, December 19, 1815, ibid., 54.

8. *Journal of the House,* 194; CFM to Bushrod Washington, February 25, 1816, CFM Papers, NYHS; CFM, Autobiographical Sketch, Mercer-Hunter Papers, VSL.

9. CFM to Claiborne W. Gooch, September 26, 1823, Gooch Papers; Joseph C. Cabell to Thomas Jefferson, February 21, 1816, Cabell Papers; *Journal of the House,* 199; *Virginia Argus* (Richmond), January 20, 1816.

10. Address of Gov. Wilson C. Nicholas to Senate and House, November 11, 1816, *Journal of the House,* 8, 17–18; *Sundry Documents on the Subject of a System of Public Education for the State of Virginia* (Richmond, 1817), 22.

11. *The National Cyclopedia of American Biography,* 61 vols. (New York, 1906), 22:139–40; Joseph C. Cabell to Thomas Jefferson, January 24, 1816, Cabell Papers.

12. *Sundry Documents,* 33.

13. Ibid., 35–49; CFM, Autobiographical Sketch, Mercer-Hunter Papers. Ironically, Mercer's bill is better remembered than he is. For a historiographical discussion of the act, see Douglas Egerton, "To the Tombs of the Capulets: Charles Fenton Mercer and Public Education in Virginia, 1816–1817," *VMHB* 93 (April 1985): 155, n. 1.

14. *Richmond Enquirer,* February 18, 20, 1817; *Norfolk and Portsmouth Herald,*

February 24, 1817; *Journal of the House*, 214–15; Risjord, "Virginia Federalists," 516; *Journal of the Senate of the Commonwealth of Virginia* (Richmond, 1817); 65.

15. Charles Fenton Mercer, *A Discourse on Popular Education* (Princeton, 1826), 62.

16. *Sundry Documents*, 47; CFM to Timothy Pickering, February 28, 1827, Pickering Papers, LC.

17. *Richmond, Enquirer*, July 15, 1825, January 30, 1817; Risjord, "Virginia Federalists," 515; Joseph C. Cabell to Thomas Jefferson, February 26, 1816, Cabell Papers.

18. Charles Fenton Mercer, *An Exposition of the Weakness and Inefficiency of the Government of the United States of North America* (N.p., 1845). Ironically, Mercer's bill gave him the reputation of a supporter of university education, and prominent Republicans approached him to help raise funds for Central College. See James Madison to CFM, August 1817, James Madison Letters, Manuscript Division, UVA.

19. Dumas Malone, *Jefferson and His Time*, 6 vols. (Boston, 1948–81), 6:249; Joseph C. Cabell to Thomas Jefferson, February 26, 1816, Cabell Papers.

20. *Richmond Enquirer*, January 2, 1817; *Alexandria Herald*, January 13, 17, 1817.

21. Mercer, *Exposition*, 155; *Richmond Enquirer*, May 20, 1825.

22. Joseph C. Cabell to Thomas Jefferson, August 4, 1816, Cabell Papers.

23. *Richmond Enquirer*, January 4, 1817; *Alexandria Herald*, January 10, 1817; James H. Broussard, *The Southern Federalists, 1800–1816* (Baton Rouge, 1978), 341.

24. Joseph C. Cabell to Thomas Jefferson, January 12, February 9, 1817, Cabell Papers; *Richmond Enquirer*, February 6, 1817; *Norfolk and Portsmouth Herald*, February 3, 1817.

25. Thomas Jefferson to John Taylor, July 21, 1816, in Paul L. Ford, ed., *The Works of Thomas Jefferson*, 12 vols. (New York, 1904–5), 12:21–27; *Richmond Enquirer*, February 18, 1817; Thomas Jefferson to Joseph C. Cabell, February 2, 1816, in Cabell, ed., *Early History*, 54–55.

26. *Richmond Enquirer*, February 18, 20, 1817.

27. CFM to Timothy Pickering, February 28, 1827, Pickering Papers; Mercer, *Discourse on Popular Education*, 35; CFM to John Francis Mercer, October 12, 1810, Mercer Family Papers, VHS; Mercer, *Exposition*, 76.

28. Michel Foucault, *Discipline and Punish: The Birth of the Prison*, trans. Alan Sheridan (New York, 1979), 147, 149, 156–61, 166; David H. Fischer, *The Revolution of American Conservatism: The Federalist Party in the Era of Jeffersonian Democracy* (New York, 1965), 49; Mercer, *Exposition*, 247, 39.

29. *Sundry Documents*, 36–37.

30. Joseph C. Cabell to Thomas Jefferson, January 12, 1817, Cabell Papers; Wiley E. Hodge, "Pro-Governmentalism in Virginia, 1789–1836," *Journal of Politics* 25 (May 1971): 339; Thomas Jefferson to Charles Yancey, January 6, 1816, in Ford, ed., *Works of Jefferson*, 11:493–97.

31. *Norfolk and Portsmouth Herald*, February 19, 1817; Charles F. Arrowood, *Thomas Jefferson and Education in a Republic* (New York, 1930), 34; Mercer, *Discourse on Popular Education*, 62.

32. Charles Fenton Mercer, *An Oration Delivered in the Episcopal Church on the Twenty-second of February, 1806* (Alexandria, 1806), 27; Mercer, *Exposition*, 167.

33. Mercer, *Oration*, 26; John Marshall to CFM, April 7, 1827, Chamberlain Papers, Boston Public Library; Mercer *Discourse on Popular Education*, 38.

34. Mercer, *Discourse on Popular Education*, 70, 77; Herbert G. Gutman, *Work, Culture and Society in Industrializing America: Essays in American Working-Class and Social History* (New York, 1977), 53; Foucault, *Discipline and Punish*, 165–66; Mercer, *Oration*, 27.

35. Leonard W. Levy, *Jefferson and Civil Liberties: The Darker Side* (Cambridge, Mass., 1963), 153; Neil McDowell Shawen, "Thomas Jefferson and a 'National' University: The Hidden Agenda for Virginia," *VMHB* 92 (July 1984): 334; *Virginia Patriot* (Richmond), February 26, 1817; Thomas Jefferson to Charles Yancey, January 6, 1816, in Ford, ed., *Works of Jefferson*, 11:493–97.

36. *Norfolk and Portsmouth Herald*, February 17, 1816; *Richmond Enquirer*, February 13, 1817; Joseph C. Cabell to Thomas Jefferson, February 19, 1817, in Cabell, ed., *Early History*, 74.

37. *Richmond Enquirer*, February 28, 1817.

38. *Journal of the Senate*, 67; *Richmond Enquirer*, February 22, 28, 1817.

39. *Alexandria Gazette*, February 25, 1817; *Journal of the House*, 201. Malone, *Jefferson*, 6:253, n. 7, argues that Cabell was not against public education and "voted for [Mercer's] bill." That is true, but only after he had effectively gutted it.

40. Mercer, *Exposition*, 162, 265, 161.

9

The Coward

The rumors Joseph Cabell had heard were true. After seven terms in the House of Delegates, Charles Fenton Mercer was preparing to run for Congress. If his education bill were to succeed, he would have to continue to serve in the state legislature, but ambition had always burned within Mercer, and his recent acclaim in Virginia only made the flame burn brighter. He probably knew that public education was for the time dead in Virginia; he now looked to the national arena for the success of his increasingly cohesive legislative schemes. And Joseph Lewis, the Federalist congressman from his district, had announced his retirement. No better opportunity was likely to appear.

A seat in Congress would further tax his meager financial resources. To combat this "want of money," this "most unpleasant family disease," Mercer made one last effort in land speculation. To raise the necessary capital he rented his mill to William Noland for ten years at $2,000 a year. He also sold the last of his western land, 2,395 acres, to Benjamin Rush for $8,000. This money was used to purchase a large estate in Maryland, which was in turn sold and the profit invested in gold. With that he bade "goodbye to all farther speculation," an occupation the aristocrat found "most unpleasant and degrading," but also one that preserved him from "absolute ruin." Yet Mercer's concept of ruin revealed the limits of a patrician's perspective; only a handful of Loudoun residents paid more taxes, and his farm remained in his possession and would be worked by his two families of human property.[1]

As the most prominent Federalist in the state, he could easily win the nomination of his party. Indeed, there was no caucus; when Mercer announced his candidacy the other aspirants faded away. The Republican nominee, Armistead T. Mason, was just as obvious and was a formidable opponent. Mason was born in Loudoun County in 1787, the son of United States Senator Stevens T. Mason. A graduate of William and Mary, he served as a colonel in the Virginia volunteers in the war and for a time was stationed with Mercer at Norfolk. In the last days of the conflict he was elected a major general. In early 1816 he was elevated to a seat in the United States Senate, but in March 1817 he resigned that post to become a candidate for the House. As the owner of thirty-five slaves, Mason was the wealthiest man in the county.[2]

Unfortunately, there was much bad blood between the two men. In a state where personalities were nearly as important as issues, the contest was bound to be brutal. At the time of his election to the Senate, Mason believed that Mercer had indulged "in language personally disrespectful and injurious to me." He demanded an explanation. The clear implication was that if Mercer either refused to explain his words or provide an adequate answer, he would be called out. It was a nice point of etiquette, for only gentlemen fought duels.[3]

Word of Mason's demand reached Mercer in the early days of April 1816. Mercer was then in Georgetown recovering from his relapse and discussing colonization with Key, but he put aside his other affairs long enough to prepare an appropriate response. He discussed the matter with Littleton W. Tazewell and John Randolph as well as with Key, all of whom were friendly with Garnett. After several sleepless nights Mercer came to the conclusion that he would respond to Mason's charge but would neither "give, nor accept a challenge" should the matter come to that.[4]

A flurry of letters ensued in which Randolph and Richard M. Johnson acted as intermediaries. Throughout the correspondence Mercer studiously avoided the issue by insisting that he had been absent from the House during Mason's confirmation. Mason finally accepted this hollow explanation, though his final letter, dated April 20, hinted that he still believed the charge to be essentially true. Given Mercer's taste for invective and his habit of using the Federalist bloc to elect the least objectionable Republican, the hot-tempered Mason was probably correct. There the matter rested for almost a year, settled but not healed.[5]

The climate was bound to be tense when the voters of Fairfax, Loudoun, and Prince William counties went to the polls in April 1817. Each county held a separate poll on different days so that the candidates could attend so the result would not be known until the several sheriffs met later to tally the returns. The number of election days also gave each candidate time to canvass votes in the different counties, a task many aristocrats found distasteful but few could afford to ignore. Mercer was willing to engage in electioneering, but only to a point. "I never was at a caucus, a faro bank, or a cock fight," he later boasted.[6]

When election day arrived, the freeholders gathered at the county courthouse. As their names were called out, each one stepped forward and stated the man of his choice. It was at this point in the Loudoun election that Mercer's problems began in earnest. As the candidates watched the polling, they were allowed to protest any voter they suspected of not meeting the property qualification. When John M. McCarty, Mason's cousin and brother-in-law, stepped forward and voted for Mercer, the Republican candidate immediately protested McCarty's vote. Mason was outraged that a near relation would vote for his opponent, but he had good reason to fear McCarty's influence. In an open poll, gentlemen of consequence were likely to influence the choice of their social inferiors. McCarty was then required to take an oath that he met the qualification, a calculated insult. McCarty "instantly" applied to Mason "such epithets and such language" that all spectators expected Mason to respond with a challenge. But Mason, "to the astonishment of all," let the matter drop.[7]

The election returns slowly trickled in. On April 15 it was reported that Mason was ahead, but three days later the tide turned and the Loudoun County results put Mercer out in front by 147 votes. Finally, on May 6 the complete returns were posted. Mercer was elected by a slim margin as one of ten new representatives to the House. Other Federalists, however, did not fare as well. The Virginia Republicans gained four seats.[8]

But even before the final tally was printed, Mason let it be known that he would contest the election. The Republican was certain that nearly one hundred bad votes had been given to Mercer in Loudoun County alone. Mason also took the unusual view that had the voters of Fairfax—which he carried—known how close the election was more would have turned out. Mason even traveled to numerous Virginia taverns taking his own poll and seeking evidence of irregularities. Washington's leading newspaper confidently predicted that "General Mason will be returned upon a canvass before Congress."[9]

Mercer received formal notice on September 8 that Mason intended to petition Congress to seat him instead of Mercer. Mason had concluded that Mercer had nearly three hundred bad votes on his poll, although when pressed, Mason could not name even a dozen. It was a preposterous charge, for just over two thousand votes had been cast in the district. Yet as Mercer had won by a margin of but seventy-two it was not a charge he could afford to ignore. Strangely, Mercer admitted that some of his urban supporters, who owned little land but hotly resisted their legal disfranchisement, lacked the property qualification to vote. He simply insisted that "my adversary has unquestionably as many bad votes on his poll, as I."[10]

In desperation, Mercer announced that he would contest those votes Mason had received that were misspelled; the Republican made it his "duty" to do so. Mercer insisted that Mason also intended to dispute misspelled votes, although he could produce no evidence to support such a charge. This allowed Mason to take the high road by printing circulars to the effect that Mercer wished to deny legal votes on a technicality. On October 2 Mercer was forced to place a card in the Leesburg paper saying that he "never meant to rely on such a ground of exception, but for my own protection."[11]

In this situation, Garnett reported to Randolph, Mercer could "think of little else, at present, but his contested election with Mason." Garnett understood his cousin well, for he noted that the morose conservative "seems to derive the greater part of his enjoyment . . . from occupying some situation to render the public service." Unfortunately for Mercer, Randolph's melancholy attempt at comforting his friend compared politicians to gamblers and suggested that he was better off losing.[12]

Since college Mercer had dreamed of and worked for this day. His view of the world demanded a life in politics, but now his sole reason for life seemed to be slipping away. The situation made him physically ill, although he was well enough in body; his sickness was purely moral. His sensibilities told him that his ambition was wrong, that his recent behavior was poor, that there was indeed some small amount of fraud involved in his election. "You congratulate me," he told his uncle, "on what I have been constantly deploring." Virginia and "the General Assembly," he moaned, should have been enough "for my ambition. I have been forced into Congress."[13]

His self-pity and Mason's unrelenting attacks blurred Mercer's judgment. Had he kept his wits about him and quietly waited for Congress to convene, all would have been well. But following a speech of Mason's on October 8 he did an amazingly foolish thing:

he publicly called Mason "a blackguard and a bully." Seven days later, Mason pronounced Mercer to be "an infamous liar and scoundrel." When this mudslinging failed to achieve the desired result, Mason wrote to Mercer, saying that nothing but the critical state of his wife's health prevented him "from taking immediate steps to punish you." Soon, he promised, she would be well, and he would then resign his commission and meet Mercer on the field of honor. Gerrard Alexander was named as his second.[14]

Mason's invitation to shoot him provided Mercer with a horrible dilemma. In a moment of confusion and passion Mercer used the two words calculated to spark a duel. Deep down, he almost wished to fight. Despite his good birth and family name, Virginia political society increasingly doubted that farmer Mercer (and his industrial visions) was one of them, a suspicion strengthened by his recent bills for education and colonization. A duel, like his overeducation and military title, would serve as a claim to deference and power. To fight Mason would be at once an affirmation of cherished cultural values and an expression of renewed loyalty to his class. And to refuse a challenge after using such intemperate language would not only damage his standing among the upper class, it would injure his image among his social inferiors, the voters.[15]

But having uttered the words, Mercer immediately began to back away. To fight Mason was not only a violation of his religious principles but a quick road to the grave. He wished to express fealty to southern culture, but he could not; he no longer believed in it. For several days he held Mason at bay by insisting that his letter was illegible and needed to be revised. Finally, on November 21, Mercer sat down before breakfast and wrote a reply. He informed Mason that he could not "violate [his] solemn vows to God for the applause of the world." "As a man, and more especially a Virginian," Mercer wrote, "I ought not to accept your professed challenge: as a christian, I cannot." Nevertheless, Mercer began to carry a pistol beneath his cloak.[16]

Mercer's refusal, which was printed in several Virginia papers only further outraged Mason. The Republican immediately fired back, hitting Mercer in a tender spot. "After laboring for years to cheat the world into the belief that he is a hero in spirit," Mason roared, "he abandons at once a character which all his arts can no longer enable him to maintain." Mason renewed his challenge and proclaimed "to the world that [Mercer] is a consummate hypocrite, and a most contemptible coward!"[17]

Despite this latest provocation, however, Mercer still had many supporters, some of whom were Republicans. Benjamin Watkins Leigh urged Mercer to be proud of his refusal. "To act according to your own ideas of duty, in defiance of the opinions of the world, ought surely to give you no pain." Leigh informed Mercer that "the judgement of men of honor" was against Mason, although he warned Mercer that the same men refused to excuse him for his harsh language. Even so, Mercer was aware that many Virginians were opposed to duels in principle but would fight when publicly branded with cowardice. He was not even sure that he had the full support of the Federalist party.[18]

Leigh's letter did little good, and as he waited for Congress to sit and decide his political future, Mercer was more miserable than ever. The "defence of my late conduct," he confided to Hobart, was "the most trying event of my whole life." He was branded a hypocrite and a coward, but to give the lie to the second was to confirm the first. "To be thus persecuted, is a trial which has required all my piety to sustain, without sinking beneath it."[19]

The challenge forced Mercer to examine his "troubled" and unhappy life. The conclusions he reached did not please him. He reproached himself for his lust for fame, power, and position. "I have sinned in coming here," he moaned, "for I have left a theatre of action on which I was of some use, to enter upon one where, in all human probability, I shall be of none." If only he had not "strayed from the true source of Christian consolation," if only he had conquered his "zeal" to rise in the political world! How could he ever "overcome those moral prejudices which my late conduct will inspire?"[20]

Yet the fact was that he had left state politics. He had sought higher office, and should Congress rule in his favor, a seat in the House of Representatives was his. There was no choice but to prepare his case, and this he did from Rufus King's Georgetown mess. Poring over old Virginia journals in search of supporting documents, Mercer began to believe he would be seated after all. Benjamin Watkins Leigh, his friend since early 1813, provided him with a detailed explanation of the election laws of 1785, 1786, and 1792, all of which pointed to Mercer's political vindication. At the age of thirty-eight, Mercer was on the verge of a new phase of his career.[21]

Ironically, the party Mercer had done so much to salvage was not to continue on with him. Despite his best efforts, and the efforts of those like him, the Federalists were a vanishing breed. Their demise has suggested to some that the southern Federalists had been kept alive by a fear of Napoleon and that with him banished their prime reason for existence was gone. There was some truth to this, for Mercer loathed Napoleon and did everything he could to keep the United States out of a war that would aid him. Mercer and the Federalists had indeed, in the words of Republican Philip Nicholas, "obtained success to their prayers for the overthrow of Bonaparte."[22]

But after 1803 Napoleon never presented a direct threat to the Americas. Instead, it was what France stood for that so terrorized conservatives, and this fear remained long after the sale of Louisiana. France symbolized what Mercer saw in the eyes of the men of Birmingham and what he knew was in the hearts of the men of America. And so to the class consciousness that Mercer had exhibited as a student was added the fear of class conflict. Europe and the age of revolution, both social and industrial, had forever smashed the safe world of Marlborough. The "world, which I endeavor to serve," he told Hobart, "is not lovely in my view."[23]

The death of Federalism came not with the end of Napoleon but from an inability to adjust to the expansion of the franchise. Despite their glittering rhetoric, Mercer and other young Federalists had been unable to broaden their political base beyond the urban business class and the upward-looking western yeomen. The reactionary northern wing had sealed the fate of the party with the Hartford Convention. Against this political suicide the young men of the party and their progressive rhetoric were no match.

Even so, Mercer's "seven year apprenticeship" was extremely useful. It allowed him to develop and test his program of aiding the infant industrial order, despite working in an agrarian state with a leadership hostile to his way of thinking. All of Mercer's later schemes—banking, internal improvements, public education, and especially colonization—were programs he had first experimented with in Richmond. He had not yet bound them together in a completely cohesive fashion, nor had he devised an attractive name for his program. Nonetheless, at the state level were laid the foundations of the American System, the basis for the National Republican and Whig parties. Mercer never claimed paternity of the system, for many of his ideas were adapted from economic theorist Mathew Carey, and other young Federalists such as John Quincy Adams had supported various aspects of the program on a local level. But Mercer had gone farther than any other in putting forth the several pieces, and he had done it at a time when many of those who would later be associated with the program were its sharpest critics.[24]

Mercer's seven terms also allowed him to experiment with a progressive, even reformist, brand of Federalism. The old Federalism had bluntly appealed to the better sort, and it wanted nothing to do with electioneering, open conventions, and legislation for free public education. But he worked hard to drag his party in that direction. His programs were never of the lower classes, but designed for them, although through the careful use of rhetoric he was often able to make it sound as if they were. It was a reformist conservatism, but it was not especially attractive, and despite its rhetoric and the means it used to attain its ends, it was neither progressive nor optimistic. It was designed to perpetuate, if not actually foster, inequality. But by adopting the voice of democracy it helped transform the old conservatism. The conservatism of James Mercer had been based on family status as well as wealth, but the son's public attacks on the former and his presentation of new routes to the latter helped lay the groundwork for a new conservatism in which class was based primarily on wealth.[25]

But, burdened by its very name, the new Federalism could not survive. The party was indelibly tainted by the ghost of Hamilton and by the secessionist impulses of the reactionary Hartford men. What conservatives like Mercer needed was a new, untained vehicle, a party that could sell its ideas to an unsuspecting electorate. The realization of this goal would not come until late in Mercer's career, but its early stages would come soon, for in 1817, when Charles Fenton Mercer finally took his seat in the Fifteenth Congress, he would take it as a Republican. And the next years, as John Randolph had long predicted, would see the United States "once more under the rule of federalism, christened over again & swaddled in moderation."[26]

Notes

ABBREVIATIONS
ACS   American Colonization Society
CFM   Charles Fenton Mercer
COCC   Chesapeake and Ohio Canal Company
DAB   *Dictionary of American Biography,* ed. Allen Johnson and Dumas Malone, 21 vols., 1928–1936.

JQA   John Quincy Adams
JSH   *Journal of Southern History*
LC   Library of Congress
NJHS   New Jersey Historical Society
NYHS   New-York Historical Society
PRO, FO   Great Britain, Public Record Office, Foreign Office
UVA   University of Virginia
VHS   Virginia Historial Society
VMHB   *Virginia Magazine of History and Biography*
VSL   Virginia State Library
WMQ   *William and Mary Quarterly*

1. CFM Diary, April 1, 1816, CFM Papers, NJHS; Census Records, 1820, reel 137, p. 153, National Archives; Loudoun County Personal Property Tax, 1818, VSL; CFM to John Francis Mercer, July 25, 1817, Mercer Family Papers, VHS.

2. *The National Cyclopedia of American Biography*, 61 vols. (New York, 1906), 4:550; *Richmond Enquirer*, February 9, 1819; Loudoun County Personal Property Tax, 1818, VSL.

3. John C. Vinson, "Electioneering in the South, 1800–1840," *Georgia Review* 10 (Fall 1956): 270; Armistead T. Mason to CFM, April 5, 1816, in Charles Fenton Mercer, ed., *Controversy between Armistead Thompson Mason and Charles Fenton Mercer* (Washington, D.C., 1818), 33–34.

4. CFM Diary, April 6, 1816, CFM Papers, NJHS; CFM to James M. Garnett, April 29, 1813, in James Mercer Garnett, ed., *Biographical Sketch of Hon. Charles Fenton Mercer, 1778–1858* (Richmond, 1911), 39; CFM to the Public, December 5, 1817, in Mercer, ed., *Controversy*, 26.

5. CFM to Armistead T. Mason, April 6, 1816; Mason to CFM, April 12, 1816; CFM to Mason, April 16, 1816; Mason to CFM, April 20, 1816, all in Mercer, ed., *Controversy*, 34–36.

6. Anthony F. Upton, "The Road to Power in Virginia in the Early Nineteenth Century," *VMHB* 62 (July 1954): 260–62; *National Intelligencer*, April 25, 1817; Daniel P. Jordan, *Political Leadership in Jefferson's Virginia* (Charlottesville, 1983), 197.

7. Armistead T. Mason to the Public, September 26, 1817, in Mercer, ed., *Controversy*, 3; Rhys Isaac, *The Transformation of Virginia, 1740–1790* (Chapel Hill, 1982), 111; JQA Diary, February 6, 1819, in Charles Francis Adams, ed., *Memoirs of John Quincy Adams, Comprising Parts of His Diary from 1795 to 1848*, 12 vols. (Philadelphia, 1874–77), 4:246; John M. McCarty to the Public, September 30, 1818, in John M. McCarty, ed., *A View of the Whole Ground: Being the Whole Correspondence between Mr. John M. McCarty and General A. T. Mason* (Washington, D.C., 1818), 1.

8. *Richmond Enquirer*, April 15, 18, May 6, 1817.

9. *National Intelligencer*, April 24, 25, 1817; Jordan, *Political Leadership*, 262, n.

10. CFM to the Public, October 2, 1817, in Mercer, ed., *Controversy*, 7; Armistead T. Mason to CFM, September 1, 1817, Mason Family Papers, Gunston Hall Archives; CFM to John Francis Mercer, July 25, 1817, Mercer Family Papers; J. R. Pole, "Representation and Authority in Virginia from the Revolution to Reform," *JHS* 24 (February 1958): 31.

11. CFM to Armistead T. Mason, September 27, 1817, in Mercer, ed., *Controversy*, 10; Printed Letter, September 27, 1817, Mason Family Papers; CFM to the Public, October 2, 1817, in Mercer, ed., *Controversy*, 10.

12. James M. Garnett to John Randolph, October 3, 1817, John Randolph Papers, LC; John Randolph to CFM, December 15, 1817, General Manuscripts, Princeton University Library.

13. CFM to John Francis Mercer, July 25, 1817, Mercer Family Papers.

14. CFM to the People of Loudoun, October 18, 1817; Armistead T. Mason to the Public, October 25, 1817; Mason to CFM, November 19, 1817, all in Mercer, ed., *Controversy*, 17–18; *Virginia Herald*, May 14, 1817.

15. Bertram Wyatt-Brown, *Southern Honor: Ethics and Behavior in the Old South* (New York, 1982), 353; Drew Gilpin Faust, *James Henry Hammond and the Old South: A Design for Mastery* (Baton Rouge, 1982), 51.

16. CFM to Armistead T. Mason, November 21, 1817; CFM to the Public, December 30, 1817, both in Mercer, ed., *Controversy*, 19–20, 27.

17. Armistead T. Mason to the Public, December 4, 1817, ibid., 23.

18. Benjamin Watkins Leigh to CFM, December 5, 1817, CFM Papers, NJHS; Virginius Dabney, *Virginia: The New Dominion* (New York, 1971), 131; CFM to the Public, December 30, 1817, in Mercer, ed., *Controversy*, 26.

19. CFM to John H. Hobart, January 2, 1818, in John McVicar, ed., *The Early Life and Professional Years of Bishop Hobart* (Oxford, 1838), 456.

20. CFM to John H. Hobart, January 4, 1818, ibid., 457–58.

21. Benjamin Watkins Leigh to CFM, December 5, 1817, CFM Papers, NJHS.

22. The thesis is that of James H. Broussard, *The Southern Federalists, 1800–1816* (Baton Rouge, 1978), 402; Philip Nicholas to Wilson Cary Nicholas, July 13, 1814, Nicholas Papers, LC.

23. CFM to John H. Hobart, January 2, 1818, in McVicar, ed., *Early Life*, 456.

24. Charles Fenton Mercer, ed., *The Farewell Address of the Hon. C. F. Mercer to His Constituents* (N.p., 1839), 5. Samuel Flagg Bemis, *John Quincy Adams*, 2 vols. (New York, 1950–56), 1:127, claims that Adams was "the real father of the American System," although he is able to cite only one bill for internal improvements of 1807. In fact, many young Federalists supported such a program on the state level; no single man is deserving of that title.

25. Lee Benson, *The Concept of Jacksonian Democracy: New York as a Test Case* (Princeton, 1961), 86–88, rejects any ties between the Federalist and Whig parties, saying that their similar view of a positive state is not enough. The difference, he believes, is that the Federalists held "an elitist, paternalistic, antidemocratic concept of the Good Society," whereas the Whigs believed in a "well-rounded economy beneficial to all." Such a view does not take the rhetoric or program of the later Federalists into account.

26. John Quincy Adams, *The Lives of James Madison and James Monroe* (Buffalo, 1850), 315–16; John Randolph to James M. Garnett, September 4, 1806, John Randolph Papers, LC.

PART THREE

*Washington City
1817–1840*

10

The Republican

The nation's capital in 1817 was a forlorn place. Designed with an eye to the future, it presented an awkward attempt to ape the splendor of European cities. Its broad boulevards were unpaved and overgrown with weeds and grass and lined with but a few smoky clusters of buildings. Much of the area was swamplike, and the smell of fever was always in the air. The city, and especially the executive mansion, still displayed the scars of British vandalism. Yet Washington reflected the energetic young nation in its growth and expansion. Rebuilding was under way, with scaffolding about even in the middle of town. The social life was also more elegant and formal than in the past. For Mercer, the city was the axis of the world; it had been his dream of the past twenty years.[1]

While awaiting the verdict of Congress on his election, Mercer moved into the Georgetown mess of Rufus King. He had first met the Federalist leader in London, when the New Yorker had stayed on as Jefferson's minister. King was also a longtime friend and correspondent of John Henry Hobart. More to the point, the spacious Union Tavern, with its ballroom, private parlors, and sculptured gardens, separated from Washington by a narrow cow trail, was inhabited only by Federalists of the better sort; Mercer was more at ease there than in the rougher hotels clustered about Pennsylvania Avenue.[2]

Notwithstanding his choice of residence, Mercer was determined to give up the Federalist party. It was dying fast; in the previous House there had been sixty-seven Federalists; but in the new House, counting Mercer, there would be only forty. The party had taken a beating not only in New York and Virginia but even in its old stronghold of Massachusetts. Most of the new western states sent no Federalists to Congress.[3]

145

The party had seen hard times before, especially after the debacle of 1804, but Mercer was now convinced that it would never
recover. Despite his best efforts, the party was hopelessly tainted
by the Hartford Convention, even in states like Virginia, where
Federalists had been loyal to the war effort. Mercer admitted as
much in his maiden speech in Congress when he mentioned the
"disloyalty" of Massachusetts. Even more telling was a second
comment. The "Federalists suffered themselves to be outwitted in
yielding the popular title [of Republican] to their opponents," he
sighed, "a prominent cause, I have no doubt, of their ultimate
discomfiture." The first comment won him a kind but firm rebuke
from arch-Federalist Timothy Pickering, but none would come
forward to give his second statement the lie.[4]

The election of James Monroe to the presidency also made Mercer's defection easier. The fifty-nine-year-old Monroe, six feet odd
and strikingly handsome in his knee-length pantaloons and white-
topped boots of an earlier time, was a Republican Mercer could
admire. More formal and consciously aristocratic than Jefferson,
Monroe was also far less intelligent and, most important, less
dogmatically attached to the Republican agrarian agenda. Monroe
was even willing to grant the coveted post of secretary of state to
John Quincy Adams, a former Federalist, thereby recognizing not
only Adams's considerable diplomatic skills but also the importance of the growing commercial branch of the Republican party.[5]

For years Mercer had admired Monroe not only as a man—
Mercer was personally friendly with many Republicans, even
Cabell—but also as a politician. Monroe's moderation would make
him "a democratic antidote for the poison of democracy." "There is
no one," he thought, "so capable of uniting the honest men of both
parties as Col: Monroe." The "evidence of independence, wisdom
and firmness, which his public confidence has recently furnished,
assures to him, the confidence, at least, of all the Federalists."[6]

With their adoption of a second Bank of the United States and
their increasing interest in manufactures and tariffs, the Republicans had crept toward Mercer as much as he had crept toward
them. This the Old Republicans recognized, and they were as
hostile to Monroe as the Old Federalists were to Mercer. Ritchie
and the Richmond Junto, contrary to their usual practice, withheld
their comment on the presidential election until after the congressional caucus had nominated Monroe. John Randolph, with his
customary caustic exaggeration, informed Garnett: "The only
friends that [Monroe] has are the Hartford Convention Men."[7]

Most of all, democracy was winning. The common wisdom of the older Federalists that those who owned the nation ought to rule it could no longer be stated openly. For Mercer to carry out his plans he would have to sound progressive and look progressive, and no better vehicle existed than James Monroe's Republican party. The "sovereigns, who indulge in dirt and rudeness, are voters, and none dare thwart them," Mercer wrote privately. Men like himself could no longer "prevent noise, singing, rudeness, and throngs in the streets and grounds, because the blackguards who disturb the community are voters."[8]

With Mercer in Washington were a group of exceptional men, who would play an integral part in the new Republican's political career. Foremost among them was John Quincy Adams, just returned from Europe to serve as Monroe's secretary of state. At fifty-one, Adams was just more than a decade older than Mercer, yet the two men were very much alike and after several false starts would become close friends. Balding, short, rotund, and perpetually frowning, Adams even resembled the Virginia conservative. (The slim youth of Princeton had long since given way to a plump participant in the good life.) Adams was even more learned than Mercer, but the Virginian was a superior politician, and Adams would discover that he needed men like Mercer more than they needed him.[9]

Of nearly equal importance was House Speaker Henry Clay of Kentucky. The dashing "Harry of the West," only a year older than Mercer, had turned Congress into a rival of the president as the initiator of policy. It was he who appointed House members to the various standing committees, which had become crucial administrative agencies. Unfortunately for Mercer, Clay had coveted the top spot in Monroe's cabinet, and when it went to Adams he developed a savage hostility to the administration. Moreover, Clay had his doubts about Mercer because of the young man's "regard for his bitter enemy," John Randolph. But like Mercer, Clay was prepared immediately to turn on the agrarian agenda; Monroe's preferred course was to be a more hesitant abandonment.[10]

Perhaps the most popular man in Washington next to Monroe was William H. Crawford of Georgia, continuing as secretary of the treasury. A native Virginian, Crawford was a huge, handsome man with a magnetic personality. That he was a duelist who had killed one man and wounded another was distasteful to Mercer, but his following was great, especially in the Old Dominion. He had nearly received enough votes in the 1816 caucus to succeed Madison and was already spoken of as a presidential candidate in 1824. Despite his reputation as a strict Republican, Crawford was willing to compromise his principles. And because he was nominally a colonizationist, Mercer thought him a man worth watching.[11]

Finally, the gaunt figure of John C. Calhoun of South Carolina drew Mercer's attention. Unusually tall with striking gray-blue eyes, the intelligent if introverted secretary of war was, like Adams and Clay, an unabashed nationalist. Indeed, it was Calhoun who had introduced the legislation for the second bank, and he was also a warm supporter of internal improvements. That Calhoun, like Clay, Crawford, and Mercer, was a slaveholder raised no eyebrows in a city where a small army of several thousand blacks slowly repaired the damaged buildings.[12]

Congress sat on December 1, 1817. Mercer was allowed to take his seat on a provisional basis until the disputed election could be decided. He was a part of the twenty-three-man Virginia delegation, second in size only to that of New York. With him in the House were William Henry Harrison, John Tyler, and Henry Clay, who was promptly reelected Speaker. Mercer noticed uneasily that he was also serving with Richard M. Johnson, who had achieved minor fame by allegedly killing the Indian chief Tecumseh but was familiar to Mercer as Mason's intermediary. Mercer was placed on the Committee on Public Lands.[13]

Little activity took place in Congress before the first of the year, but on January 6 George Strother of Virginia presented a petition in behalf of Mason, contesting the election "and praying to be admitted to a seat in the House, in the place of the said Charles F. Mercer." The petition was referred to the Committee of Elections, as were various accompanying "depositions and documents" that Clay laid before the House. Two weeks later, on January 19, the Committee of Elections was discharged from further consideration of Mason's petition. No explanation was given for this action but the outcome was clear: Mercer's seat was safe, at least for the present term.[14]

With his spot in Congress secure, Mercer finally felt he could answer Mason's charges. The thought of releasing their correspondence disgusted him, yet because the Virginia General Assembly, "after seven years of faithful and requited service, seems to have disregarded my feelings," he believed that politically he had no other choice. Two thousand copies of their letters dating back to their first quarrel were printed, although for two months they sat piled in a corner of his room until he finally forced himself to distribute them. Half a dozen were sent to John Francis Mercer to be given to his Maryland neighbors; the rest were distributed in Virginia and among such important Washington officials as John Quincy Adams.[15]

The correspondence caused a sensation in the capital and focused attention on the new congressman. The pamphlet did not, however, place Mercer in a completely positive light. Mercer clearly had used words likely to spark a challenge. Congressman David Daggett believed that "the perusal of it will give no real pleasure to either of the parties."[16]

Worse still, the pamphlet outraged Mason anew, and again Mercer's alleged cowardice was dragged into the public eye. Mason crowed that at the last moment Mercer, "who had until then been relied upon as the champion of his party, gave way." The Federalists, he insisted, were "mortified and chagrined" and hoped that his quarrel with McCarty would flare up and "would wipe off the dishonor of the dastardly conduct of Mr. Mercer, who after all his vaporing, had so woefully disappointed" his party.[17]

In short, as Louis McLane, another new congressman, observed, Mercer had "unluckily marked his entrance" into Washington society "with rather an embarrassing circumstance." Christians were not expected to fight duels. But many believed that his religion was not a justifiable "refuge," for a "mind so thoroughly impressed" with religion "would never give occasion for a challenge." Mercer had certainly done so. If "these scruples could be shifted while the injury was doing, they should not be obeyed when reparation was demanded, otherwise a man may add hypocrisy to injury." That he was continuing to receive advice from Randolph did him little good in any quarter.[18]

But having released his correspondence, Mercer was silent. If he heard his situation discussed in the halls and messes of the city, he bore this indignity in silence. Four months later a frustrated Mason fired another broadside ostensibly directed at his brother-in-law. "I wish [McCarty] to know," he roared, "that I do not, in imitation of the example of Mr. Mercer, wish any of my friends to fight my battles for me." Wisely, Mercer still made no reply and tried to hide his mortification in the society of his new and glamorous acquaintances, especially that of Winfield Scott.[19]

There was little time for self-pity. Like all new congressmen, Mercer had to prepare for his maiden speech, an event of great importance for it could make or break his reputation among the senior members. He found just the topic in the case of John Anderson, a revolutionary war veteran from Kentucky. Anderson had visited Washington to argue a legal claim and to serve as an agent for several friends, all of whom had incurred losses in the Michigan territory during the War of 1812. The Kentuckian foolishly tried to accomplish his purpose by offering a bribe to Lewis Williams, chairman of the Committee on Claims, who promptly reported him. Clay then ordered Anderson seized, and the House prepared to debate not only what punishment he deserved but whether Congress had the power to hold and punish.[20]

On Friday, January 9, 1818, Mercer rose unsteadily to address the second question. In a high-pitched voice and speaking without notes, he elegantly though not powerfully laid out his position. The House had the right to hold Anderson, he insisted, for it had the right under English common law, which was implicit in the Constitution. This argument was in keeping with standard Federalist dogma, which held that the Revolution had been a break only with the crown, not with British legal tradition. "Do we look for the monuments of our own history no farther back than the glorious era of '76," he wondered. "Are we ashamed of the achievements of our British ancestors?"[21]

The reason why Mercer was drawn to the case quickly became clear. Hidden within the question was the doctrine of states' rights and strict construction. "It cannot be justly inferred," Mercer ventured in a classic exposition of implied powers, "that the enumeration of these privileges excludes the constitutional exercise of all others." He pointed to the establishment of the first Bank of the United States, thereby obliquely noting the constitutional question inherent in the recent creation of the second bank. "Precedents established in good times," he claimed, remained in others. The House had this power and more; what it chose as punishment for Anderson was not his concern.[22]

Perhaps because the men of Washington had begun to take sides on the question of Mercer's religion and honor, the reaction to his speech was mixed. Louis McLane, a Federalist of lower-class origins who had already formed a distinct dislike—founded, it seems, on jealousy of Mercer's reputation—of the egotistical patrician, reported gleefully that Mercer disappointed "the expectations of everybody." He "aimed to imitate Randolph," McLane believed, "but his whole speech was the merest compound of bombast and folly I ever listened to." McLane had a point. Mercer's speeches were logical and flawlessly organized. Aware that his audience consisted of some of the finest orators in the land, however, he labored mightily to make his words ever more informative and important. As a result, his speeches grew ever longer.[23]

On January 15 the question of whether Anderson should have been brought before the House for a reprimand was voted upon. By now the "farcical comic tragedy" had assumed major proportions; the case had even inspired two songs. Based on the doctrine of implied powers, it was decided that Congress indeed had the authority by a decisive margin of 118 to 45, with Mercer in the majority. McLane, who argued the same side, estimated that "three fourths of the members, before the debate was begun, would have voted to free Anderson." Mercer had reason to be pleased.[24]

A second issue that session presented a much more treacherous trial for Mercer: the question of internal improvements. Monroe had been wrestling with the troublesome question of whether the federal government had the power to construct roads and canals in the states, and his illogical conclusion was a novel combination of loose and strict construction. He decided that Congress had the power to appropriate funds for internal improvements but lacked the authority to construct such projects under the commerce clause. Monroe unveiled this "settled conviction," an attempt to appease both wings of his expanding party, before Congress in his first annual message of December 2, 1817.[25]

Mercer naturally disagreed with this view, but there was no question that the sentiment in favor of internal improvements, so strong only a few years before, was fading. New York was losing interest in a federal scheme in proportion to the work completed on the state-financed Erie Canal. And much of the South, aside from lack of interest in such an economic program, opposed national intervention into such areas for the reason John Randolph suggested: a federal government that could dig a canal could also emancipate the slaves.[26]

To get around Monroe's constitutional scruples, Senator James Barbour introduced a resolution for an amendment that would explicitly grant Congress that right. But when the House discussed the resolution and Henry St. George Tucker's committee report on Monroe's message—which argued that no amendment was necessary—the debate degenerated into a shouting match. Clay, spoiling for a fight with the administration, came down from the Speaker's chair and joined the melee. He suspected that a majority of the House disagreed with Monroe, and he intended to prove it. Mercer threw himself into the fray, suggesting that Monroe's having stated his position "was no reason for dispensing with a full consideration and discussion." The executive's opinion, he reminded Congress, was not the last word on constitutionality.[27]

Late in the evening on March 6, Clay began a long and vicious attack on Monroe that would last until the next day. The speech dealt primarily with the issue of internal improvements, but from first word to last breath Clay's speech was highly personal. He ridiculed Monroe's "late tour" of the North, in which the people "rise en masse, as the audience at the Theatre Francais or Covent Garden, upon the entrance of the Sovereign." He could make such criticisms honestly, he lied, because he had desired no position in the cabinet. But many of his charges rang true. Madison and Monroe had accepted some extensions of power and sovereignty over the states, such as the second bank, while turning their backs on others.[28]

Clay's vitriol put Mercer in a difficult position. He was as warm an advocate of internal improvements as any man in the House, but his political future in his district and his personal relationship with Monroe rested on his ability to support Clay's position without endorsing his speech. This Mercer did on March 9, when he delivered his second major address. "I never, at any period of my life," he began, "entertained a sentiment of personal hostility" toward Monroe. Yet to "apply to the Constitution the plainest dictates of common sense" meant that he would respectfully have to disagree with his chief. A national system of canals was crucial for all "our happiness," and such benefits should not be sacrificed upon the altar of states' rights. "What paralyzed the efforts of the National Government during the late war?" he queried. "States rights again. It is horrible!" he shouted. "We do not mean to prostrate the jurisdiction of the States over their own soil. We only deny that it is exclusive."[29]

Mercer was successful in separating his course from Clay's, and the Georgetown *National Messenger* heralded it as an "able speech." But his constitutional arguments were in vain. On March 14, after a final plea from Mercer, the House voted not on the Tucker committee resolution but on a series of substitutes. Following Monroe's tortured reasoning, Congress decided that it had the constitutional mandate to "appropriate" money for internal improvements. A resolution endorsing the power to construct roads and canals with that appropriated money failed.[30]

With that, Mercer's first year in the national light ground mercifully to a halt. But as he was to discover, another tempest was already blowing up that would again ally him with Clay against Monroe. It would also gain him the wrath of a new and dangerous antagonist, for the issue was Andrew Jackson's invasion of Spanish Florida, an action that Monroe had long been convinced was necessary to force Spain to adhere to Pinckney's Treaty.[31]

Monroe had several reasons to chastise Spanish Florida. A so-called Negro fort just below the border had become a magnet for runaway slaves, and the region was a haven for Seminole Indians who raided into Georgia. The president also hoped that a temporary invasion would force Spain to turn Florida over to the United States, and when Jackson suggested that he seize Florida Monroe made no attempt to check the general. In March 1818, the Hero of New Orleans and some one thousand men crashed into Florida, where they defeated the Seminoles, occupied the town of St. Marks, executed two British citizens, captured Pensacola, and deposed the Spanish governor. With that, the general considered his work done and marched home.[32]

Jackson, however, had been a little too thorough and noisy in his methods. In the face of Spanish outrage Monroe floundered, unwilling to admit his true intent, and Clay saw an opportunity not only to discredit the administration but to ruin the career of a possible western rival. Calhoun too wished to see Jackson punished, in part because he also saw the popular general as a political rival, but mostly because as secretary of war he wished to see his orders obeyed.[33]

Congress as a whole was no less hostile to Jackson and the administration, and for a wide range of reasons. Many, like Mercer, were outraged by the invasion's clear violation of Congress's constitutional war-making powers. The Old Republicans saw the expedition as another example of Monroe's expansion of federal authority. To ignore the invasion, moaned John Tyler, would be to legitimize "all the roads asked for, all the National Banks which can be asked for." Even Clay honestly believed that if the raid had Monroe's authority it made Congress's war-making authority "a dead letter."[34]

The administration realized that it faced a hostile and powerful coalition, and Monroe and Adams knew that they could expect another tirade from Clay. Mercer recognized that he was again in a difficult spot. Once more he differed with Monroe, yet he did not wish to appear to be working with the Speaker. It was even whispered to Adams that Clay was "now using C. F. Mercer for his purpose." The secretary, however, for all his lack of political acumen, had come to knew Mercer. That the independent Virginian would be anybody's pawn, he decided, was unlikely.[35]

The starting gun was fired on January 20, when Clay rose to introduce four resolutions censuring Jackson and the administration. All of Washington turned out to see the fireworks. The Senate adjourned to hear Clay, and the gallery was full of foreign ministers; Margaret Bayard Smith, a senator's wife, pushed her way onto the floor, where she found four "genteel and fashionable" ladies "under the protection" of Mercer.[36] Then all fell silent as Clay came down from his chair, inviting the gallery to admire him. He began by insisting that he harbored no "unfriendliness" to either Monroe or Jackson; he "would never form any systematic opposition to his administration, or to that of any other." Then Clay struck. He compared Jackson to Napoleon and the execution of the two British subjects to "the execution of the unfortunate member of the Bourbon house." "Bonaparte, with his grenadiers, entered the palace of St. Cloud, and dispersing, with the bayonet the deputies of the people." It could happen again, he warned, adding slyly that he was "far from intimating that Gen. Jackson cherished" any such designs. He "thanked God" that Jackson did not, but he "thanked him still more that he could not, if he would, overturn the liberties of the Republic."[37]

Mercer would not echo such extravagence. He had no wish to endorse personal attacks on the president. Yet he agreed essentially with the Speaker. Even for a man who believed in the doctrine of a powerful state, the invasion was in violation of the Constitution. Accordingly, five days later Mercer rose to introduce a resolution calling for information on the subject, specifically the "military orders" that pertained to the destruction of the "Negro Fort." Jackson's supporters were immediately on their feet in an attempt to shout him down. The Virginian calmly replied that he intended "to show, by the papers called for, that the United States were the aggressors in the war which ensued with the Seminole Indians." The resolution was finally put to a vote, whereupon it was discovered that the House lacked a quorum. The next day Mercer renewed his resolution, and it was agreed to.[38]

On January 26 Mercer delivered his major address on the Seminole War. He again began by noting his esteem for Monroe, "the friend of my early youth." But Clay's resolutions had to be supported, he argued, and for three crucial reasons. The first was that there was no justification for war because the Seminoles, who lived "beyond the limits of the United States," had done nothing to provoke military action. The second and more important reason was that the action was blatantly unconstitutional. The "hostile invasion of that territory is as much an act of war against Spain as against the Indians themselves," Mercer reasoned, and as it was "unauthorised by any act of Congress, it involves a similar violation of the constitution." Finally, justice required that Jackson be condemned for his treatment of the Spanish governor and the two British citizens. In his classical style, Mercer spent the next hour citing Vattel and every other available precedent to demonstrate that Jackson openly violated national and international law in deposing the governor and executing Alexander Arbuthnot and Robert Ambrister.[39]

Having savaged the general's character, Mercer sat down. The politician in him was very proud of his speech; he had spent several days preparing it, and with the proper citations carefully noted he had it published. Ironically, it was delivered to an almost empty chamber. The debate over the Seminole War, every congressman knew, would be long, and few were interested in hearing all of the speeches, especially those given for home consumption. And even in a day of lengthy orations, Mercer was already acquiring a reputation for long-windedness. Only fifteen members were in their seats, and six of them were members of his mess who were simply being polite. Among them was Louis McLane, who, despite his dislike for the diminutive Mercer, had recently moved into the Union Tavern. "Our ears," he complained, "have intermittently dinned with the noise of ranting speakers and pygmy statesmen."[40]

Even as Congress was debating, however, opinion in Washington was slowly turning in Jackson's favor. In late November Adams had released his dispatch on the war, which audaciously defended the general on the grounds that he had acted defensively. Jackson had been "impelled" by the "necessities of self-defense, to the steps of which the Spanish Government complains." Not only did the secretary refuse to apologize to Madrid, he insisted that Spain pay the cost of the invasion, which had been made necessary by her inability properly to control Florida. Adams tore away the legal and moral high ground the administration's critics needed to support their arguments. The classical citations of Mercer and the biting rhetoric of Clay were to no avail; their legal case, superior though it was, was lost.[41]

On February 8 Clay's four resolutions came to a vote. Adams's dispatch had done its work, for all four were decided in the Old

Hero's favor, three of them by large margins. Only the resolution frowning on the establishment of a civil government in Florida without the authority of Congress was defeated in a close vote of 83 to 87. On all four resolutions Mercer sided against Jackson and in the minority.[42]

Mercer emerged from the debates still free of the political fissure between Clay and the administration. He had remained ideologically consistent while winning the notice of the powerful Speaker and without greatly antagonizing either Monroe or Adams. He had, however, made a dangerous enemy in Andrew Jackson, who was not quick to forget his antagonists. Mercer had not only criticized Jackson's actions, he had criticized the general's military prowess. All of this was carefully remembered by a man who threatened to "punish" those who had attacked him in Congress. "I wish to god Mr. Mercer was before St Marks to make us a good dry encampment below it," Jackson roared, "which he said in his speech on the seminole question I might have easily done."[43]

With the Seminole issue behind him, Mercer looked ahead to his reelection; the contest was only two months away. In the distance he saw the disquieting figure of Armistead Mason, who was again seeking office and again attacking him in the press. Mason had again fallen out with McCarthy, which he blamed on the Federalist party. Having failed to pressure Mercer into fighting him, he insisted, "they are now seeking to involve me with somebody else, in the hope that my life will fall sacrifice." But the truth, as Adams observed, was that Mason had never reconciled himself to his defeat and was "raving to fight a duel ever since he had lost his election."[44]

McCarty did not fancy a duel and was trying his best to avoid a fight with his hotheaded cousin. He responded to Mason's latest challenge by suggesting that they both sit on a keg of gunpowder, each holding a torch. Either might touch the powder and kill them both. When that offer was refused, McCarty ventured that they might hold hands and jump off the capitol building. This too was rejected "as not according with established usages" and "calculated to establish a dangerous precedent."[45]

In hope of discouraging Mason, McCarty next proposed that they fight with muskets loaded with three balls each at a distance of three paces. But he accepted. The two men met just after dawn on February 6 above Georgetown at a spot on the bank of the Potomac where the trees thinned out. Each was accompanied by two friends and a surgeon. When the handkerchief was dropped, both brought their muskets up to their sides and fired simultaneously without aiming. Mason's balls glanced off the butt end of McCarty's musket and grazed his arm. The tall and corpulent Mason made a better target. McCarty's balls shattered his arm—he was standing sideways—and drove bone splinters into his chest in three places. Mason, who had finally gotten his wish, was dead on his feet.[46]

Washington was horrified by this latest demonstration of gallantry. Every sorry aspect of the duel was dragged through the press, and every story mentioned Mercer and his refusal to fight. Between the lines could be discovered a curious paradox. Southerners—and the capital was a southern town—loathed dueling, but they loathed these almost monthly tragedies less than they did cowardice and abdication of honor and duty. Many thought Mercer had started these events moving, yet it was McCarty who had fought and Mason who lay dead. When it was reported that Mason left a bereaved mother, a young wife, and a small child, the gloomy Mercer had new cause for misery. "Taken in all of its circumstances," Daniel Webster sadly remarked, "it was the bloodiest affair I have heard of."[47]

Mercer was even more despondent when the duel, now billed as the "murder" of Mason, was hauled before Congress. David Morril of New Hampshire moved a resolution to strike from any muster rolls the names of the seconds, all of whom were in the military, for "aiding or abetting the late duel." The motion, Mercer was relieved to discover, was quietly tabled.[48]

Mercer wished the issue would go away, and he refused to speak of it or further defend his actions. His old friend Hobart, however, rode to his rescue by having the last word in print. Let "it be known, and published throughout the land," Hobart wrote in a religious journal, "to his honour . . . as he was called *coward* and *hypocrite*, he had the *courage*, as well as the *principle*, to fear God rather than man." Hobart did not mention Mercer by name, but there was no need to.[49]

Congress soon adjourned, and Mercer was glad to leave Washington, although it meant that he would have to return to electioneering and face a handful of hostile Masonites. All in all, however, his first term in Congress had been a good one, and he knew it. He had quietly slipped out of his dying party and had been accepted by the new breed of Republicans. He had won the praise of Henry Clay while maintaining important personal and political ties with James Monroe. His chief tormentor and political rival was dead, and not before his time, in Mercer's opinion. In April he was reelected without opposition. Finally, Mercer was using his seat in Congress to aid the American Colonization Society, which through his good offices was on the verge of its greatest political success.[50]

Notes

ABBREVIATIONS

ACS   American Colonization Society
CFM   Charles Fenton Mercer
COCC   Chesapeake and Ohio Canal Company
DAB   *Dictionary of American Biography*, ed. Allen Johnson and Dumas Malone, 21 vols., 1928–1936.
JQA   John Quincy Adams
JSH   *Journal of Southern History*
LC   Library of Congress
NJHS   New Jersey Historical Society
NYHS   New-York Historical Society
PRO, FO Great Britain, Public Record Office, Foreign Office
UVA   University of Virginia
VHS   Virginia Historical Society
VMHB   *Virginia Magazine of History and Biography*
VSL   Virginia State Library
WMQ   *William and Mary Quarterly*

1. Nathan Sargent, *Public Men and Events in the United States*, 2 vols. (1875; rpt. New York, 1970), 1:54–55; Louis McLane to Catherine McLane, December 5, 1817, Louis McLane Papers, University of Delaware.

2. Rufus King to John H. Hobart, August 9, 1805, in Arthur Lowndes, ed., *The Correspondence of John Henry Hobart*, 6 vols. (New York, 1912), 4:525; *National Intelligencer*, October 9, 1824.

3. John A. Munroe, *Louis McLane: Federalist and Jacksonian* (New Brunswick, N.J., 1973), 67.

4. *Annals of Congress* (Washington, D.C., 1817), 15th Cong., 1st sess., 642; Timothy Pickering to CFM, February 24, 1819, CFM Papers, Harvard University Library.

5. Harry Ammon, *James Monroe: The Quest for National Identity* (New York, 1971), 357, 361, 367–68; George Dangerfield, *The Era of Good Feelings* (New York, 1952), 97.

6. CFM to John Francis Mercer, July 30, 1811, October 12, 1810, both in Mercer Family Papers, VHS.

7. Harry Ammon, "The Richmond Junto," *VMHB* 61 (October 1953): 405; John Randolph to James M. Garnett, September 10, 1823, John Randolph Papers, LC.

8. Charles Fenton Mercer, *An Exposition of the Weakness and Inefficiency of the Government of the United States of North America* (N.p., 1845), 65.

9. Dangerfield, *Era of Good Feelings*, 9–10.

10. Robert V. Remini, *Andrew Jackson*, 3 vols. (New York, 1977–84), 1: 341–42; Henry Clay to CFM, October 19, 1835, Henry Clay Papers, Kentucky Historical Society.

11. Samuel Flagg Bemis, *John Quincy Adams*, 2 vols. (New York, 1950–56), 1:251–52; Chase C. Mooney, *William H. Crawford, 1772–1834* (Lexington, 1974), 188; CFM to John Hartwell Cocke, March 25, 1825, Cocke Collection, UVA.

12. Charles M. Wiltse, *John C. Calhoun: Nationalist, 1782–1828* (New York, 1944), see esp. 108–36 for Calhoun's support for the bank and internal improvements.

13. *Annals of Congress*, 15th Cong., 1st sess., 397–400.

14. Ibid., 565–66, 790; *National Intelligencer*, January 9, 1818. For unknown reasons, the Mercer-Mason case is not included in M. St. Clair Clarke and David A. Hall, *Cases of Contested Elections in Congress* (Washington, D.C., 1834).

15. CFM to John Francis Mercer, March 24, 1818, Mercer Family Papers; CFM to John Quincy Adams (Printed Circular), January 19, 1818, Adams Family Papers, Massachusetts Historical Society.

16. David Daggett to Jeremiah Mason, February 10, 1818, in G. S. Hillard, ed., *Memoir and Correspondence of Jeremiah Mason* (Cambridge, Mass., 1873), 190.

17. Armistead T. Mason to the Public, January 31, 1818, in John M. McCarty, ed., *A View of the Whole Ground: Being the Whole Correspondence between Mr. John M. McCarty and General A. T. Mason* (Washington, D.C., 1818), 9–10.

18. Bertram Wyatt-Brown, *Southern Honor: Ethics and Behavior in the Old South* (New York: 1982), 354; Louis McLane to John Milligan, January 3, 1818, McLane Papers.

19. Armistead T. Mason to Thomas F. Tebbs, May 11, 1818, in McCarty, ed., *View of the Whole Ground*, 14–15; Winfield Scott to CFM, May 28, 1819, CFM Papers, NJHS.

20. *National Intelligencer*, January 8, 9, 1818; *National Messenger*, January 14, 1818; CFM, Autobiographical Sketch, Mercer-Hunter Papers, VSL.

21. *Annals of Congress*, 15th Cong., 1st sess., 636–39. The description of Mercer's speaking style comes from the diary of colonizationist John H. B. Latrobe, in John E. Semmes, *John H. B. Latrobe and His Times, 1803–1891* (Baltimore, 1917), 368–69.

22. *Annals of Congress*, 15th Cong., 1st sess., 640–42.

23. Louis McLane to Catherine McLane, n.d., McLane Papers.

24. *Annals of Congress*, 15th Cong., 1st sess., 776–77; *National Messenger*, February 11, 1818; Louis McLane to Catherine McLane, January 15, 1818, McLane Papers.

25. *Annals of Congress*, 15th Cong., 1st sess., 17–18. Even friendly biographer Ammon calls the essay "a baffling production" (*Monroe*, 390).

26. *Richmond Enquirer*, March 20, 1818; Dangerfield, *Era of Good Feelings*, 323.

27. Henry Clay to Martin Hardin, February 22, 1818, in James F. Hopkins et al., eds., *The Papers of Clay*, 8 vols. to date (Lexington, Ky., 1959–85), 2:439; *Annals of Congress*, 15th Cong., 1st sess., 22, 1114–15.

28. *Annals of Congress*, 15th Cong., 1st sess., 1116–80.

29. CFM, Autobiographical Sketch, Mercer-Hunter Papers; *Annals of Congress*, 15th Cong., 1st sess., 1180–1318.

30. *National Intelligencer*, March 13, 1818; *National Messenger*, March 13, 1818; *Annals of Congress*, 15th Cong., 1st sess., 1384–89.

31. Ammon, *Monroe*, 414–16.

32. James Monroe to Andrew Jackson, July 19, 1818, in Stanislaus M. Hamilton, ed., *The Writings of James Monroe*, 7 vols. (New York, 1898–1903), 6:54–61, provides a detailed list of objectives and reasons for the invasion.

33. Glyndon G. Van Deusen, *The Life of Henry Clay* (Boston, 1937), 126–27; Bemis, *Adams*, 1:315.

34. *National Messenger*, March 13, 1818; John Tyler to Henry Curtis, January 18, 1819, John Tyler Papers, LC; Henry Clay to Charles Tait, June 25, 1818, in Hopkins et al., eds., *Papers of Clay*, 2:580.

35. JQA Diary, January 5, 1819, in Charles Francis Adams, ed., *Memoirs of John Quincy Adams, Comprising Parts of His Diary from 1795 to 1848*, 12 vols. (Philadelphia, 1874–77), 4:212.

36. *National Messenger*, January 29, 1819; Gaillard Hunt, ed., *The First Forty Years of Washington Society* (New York, 1906), 145.

37. *Annals of Congress*, 15th Cong., 2d sess., 631–55.

38. Ibid., 786–87.

39. Ibid., 797; Charles Fenton Mercer, *Speech of the Hon. Mr. Mercer, in the House of Representatives on the Seminole War* (Washington, D.C., 1819), 4, 8, 18–33.

40. CFM, Autobiographical Sketch, Mercer-Hunter Papers; Louis McLane to Catherine McLane, January 26, 1819, McLane Papers.

41. JQA to George W. Erving, November 28, 1818; JQA to Don Louis de Onis, November 30, 1818, both in *American State Papers, Foreign Relations*, 6 vols. (Washington, D.C., 1832–59), 4:539–46.

42. *Annals of Congress*, 15th Cong., 2d sess., 1135–38.

43. Andrew Jackson to James C. Bronaugh, February 12, 1820, in John Spencer Bassett, ed., *Correspondence of Andrew Jackson*, 6 vols. (Washington, D.C., 1926–33), 3:13–15.

44. Armistead T. Mason to the Public, December 23, 1817, in McCarty, ed., *View of the Whole Ground*, 6; JQA Diary, February 6, 1819, in Adams, ed., *Memoirs*, 4:246.

45. *Alexandria Gazette*, February 8, 1819; Rufus King to Charles King, February 9, 1819, in Charles R. King, ed., *The Life and Correspondence of Rufus King*, 6 vols. (1894; rpt. New York, 1971), 6:209–11; *National Messenger*, February 22, 1819.

46. Rufus King to Charles R. King, February 6, 19, 1819, in King, ed., *Correspondence of King*, 6:204–5, 209–11; *Richmond Enquirer*, March 23, 1819; JQA Diary, February 6, 1819, in Adams, ed., *Memoirs*, 4:246.

47. *National Intelligencer*, February 8, 1819; *National Messenger*, February 22, 1819; Daniel Webster to Timothy Farrar, February 7, 1819, in Harold D. Moser et al., eds., *The Papers of Daniel Webster*, 7 vols. to date (Hanover, N.H., 1974–86), 1:242–43.

48. *National Intelligencer*, February 9, 1819; *National Messenger*, February 8, 1819; JQA, Diary of February 6, 1819, in Adams, ed., *Memoirs*, 4:246.

49. John H. Hobart, "Christian Courage," *Christian Journal*, May 1819, in John McVicar, ed., *The Early Life and Professional Years of Bishop Hobart* (Oxford, 1838), 40.

50. Richmond *Enquirer*, April 2, 13, May 4, 1819.

11

The African Cosmogonist

Despite his seemingly endless problems with Mason and his hectic first term in Congress, Mercer never forgot the question of African colonization. Since the foundation of the American Colonization Society, he had almost literally run it from his mess in Georgetown. He conducted a large share of its correspondence, wrote its voluminous second and third annual reports, franked more than eight thousand pieces of mail, and chaired the meetings of its board of managers. Bushrod Washington, its figurehead president, played a very small role in the organization but received most of the attention. That was fine with Mercer. Tired of the poisonous abuse heaped upon him by his native state, he "desired . . . to keep [his] name out of view."[1]

Because Congress met only a few months out of the year, Mercer used his considerable leisure time to raise funds for the organization. During his return from the North in the autumn of 1816 he had been told by Robert Oliver, a wealthy Baltimore merchant, that he would donate ten thousand dollars to the society once it was organized. Mercer hurried back to Baltimore following his election to Congress, but when pressed, the once expansive merchant became less so, and he contributed far less money than originally promised.[2]

Mercer quietly labored to create auxiliary societies to support the one in Washington in the hope that a network of such organizations across the South would not only provide public aid and "approbation, but to collect us, we trust, sufficient sums to give existence to our colony." At some point the "public confidence" would be so great and "the disposition of our free people of Colour to go there" would be so strong that the state and federal govern-

161

ments would "relieve us from farther contributions, except through the medium of taxation."[3]

The local societies were also designed to spread word of the true intent of the organization throughout the South and to demonstrate that it was not a danger to slavery. But when Mercer traveled through northern Virginia in the summer of 1817, he encountered "marked hostility." A passionate speech in Fredericksburg resulted in the creation of "a most respectable Society," although when Mercer left town its opponents got the upper hand and the organization crumbled within days. By the time he reached Richmond he was discouraged and harassed by questions about the society's finances. He did not try to form a society in Richmond, but he was so well known as the national colonization leader that newly created auxiliaries in Georgia reported directly to him.[4]

Because of these setbacks, Mercer struggled to make his rationale for colonization clear. Speaking in Washington in early 1818, he told his audience that free blacks were but "a banditte, consisting of this degraded, idle, and vicious population, who sally forth from their coverts" and "plunder the rich proprietors of the valleys." They were an increasingly dangerous class, for their social and economic improvement was blocked. "The rapid increase of the free people of colour," Mercer insisted, "if it has not endangered our peace, has impaired the value of [our] private property."[5]

The society desperately needed money to finance an expedition to Africa to scout areas as possible colony sites. Samuel Mills and Ebenezer Burgess had agreed to lead the mission, which would first go to England in search of aid. The journey was estimated to cost five thousand dollars, and the society had raised only half that amount. Placing their faith in providence, the optimistic pair set sail, confident that the society would be able to collect the money to bring them back. They reached the coast of Africa by March 1818, where Mills soon fell sick and died of fever.[6]

Just as the two men were nearing Africa, the society's board of managers requested that Mercer and Key travel at their own expense to Philadelphia, New York, and Boston to help finance the mission. Mercer accepted, and as soon as Congress adjourned he and Key hastened to Baltimore. Robert Purviance, a wealthy member of the local society, introduced him to the city's first citizens. But it took fully two months for Mercer to raise $4,700, enough to cover the cost of the mission but far less than he had hoped. By the end of July, Mercer was exhausted and demoralized, and he traveled no farther north.[7]

Mercer's Baltimore venture appeared wildly successful compared to the fate of both Virginia's and the society's resolutions to Congress. The latter had been presented to Congress with as little zeal as possible by John Randolph and was referred to the Committee on the Slave Trade. In February 1817, the committee reported that not only was the expense too great, but that logic insisted that blacks be removed from beyond any possible area of white expansion. This meant Africa, and the report urged cooperation with Britain, which had already declined the favor. The Virginia resolutions fared no better. Following the removal of the injunction of secrecy in the House of Delegates, the Monroe-Jefferson correspondence was to have been published, but in the bustle of his move to Washington Mercer misplaced the copies that were before the House. By the time he applied to the Senate for its copies during the following session, many Virginians had been scared away from the scheme. In a new atmosphere the concept was reviewed, with Monroe's son-in-law George Hay leading the growing opposition to the plan. When the vote was taken, only two senators voted to grant the House their copies. A second attempt at a later session met with the same result.[8]

It appeared likely that the society might simply fade away as a result of southern hostility and northern indifference. Yet Mercer persisted. Without aid he wrote the enormous annual reports—huge collections of speeches, statistics, and testimonials—to serve as propaganda. The third report was read to a nearly empty hall. Fewer than twenty persons attended the annual meeting, "so little interest did the members of the Society or the public then take in African Colonization."[9]

By the time Burgess returned from Africa the society had less than three thousand dollars in its coffers. The annual receipts from membership dues were the only source of income, and they were far too little to launch any plan for colonization. Unless the organization could somehow tap into the federal treasury, Mercer sadly observed, the society would "be incapable of rendering such aid to the emigration of the people of colour, as would provide for colonizing their annual increase."[10]

It was at this unhappy stage that providence arrived in the large person of William H. Crawford. The secretary of the treasury had read a story in a Georgia newspaper about the public sale of more than fifty Africans, who had recently been removed from a captured slave ship. Under an 1817 Georgia law, the Africans were to be sold into slavery, and the proceeds would go to the state. The law contained a provision, however, that required the governor to deliver the Africans to the American Colonization Society, provided the society would pay all the expenses incurred by the state. In April 1818, Crawford passed this startling news along to the board of managers.[11]

Crawford's bombshell "astonished" Mercer. Together with Crawford, he recommended to the board of managers that the society send an agent to Georgia to arrest the sale of the Africans. It was questionable whether the society would be able to pay whatever costs the state should decide upon and whether the agent would arrive in time. If so, the agent was to implore the state to turn over to the society the proceeds from the sale of the human cargo "for its benevolent use."[12]

News of the Georgia sale also sent Mercer to investigate the federal law of 1807 that outlawed American participation in the international slave trade. He immediately discerned the problem. The law levied heavy penalties on persons engaged in the trade, but it placed any Africans who might be captured at the disposal of the legislature of the state into which they were brought. The southern states could not afford to send the Africans back, but they were not inclined to set them free. Instead, they sold the Africans into slavery and kept the profits for themselves. This loophole in the law, Mercer complained to Adams, allowed for the continuance of "a trade forbidden to the citizen, for the benefit of the State."[13]

Mercer realized that the loophole also provided the society with an excellent opportunity to dip into the national treasury, although it would have to be done very carefully, for the South was united in not wanting the society to receive any federal money. Federal aid, in the southern view, was the first step toward emancipation. Still it occurred to Mercer that if he could frame a bill that would plug the loophole in the 1807 law in a way that would also aid captured Africans, he could obtain federal funds without seeming to do so. He discussed the matter first with Monroe and then with John Floyd, a Virginia member of the House Committee on the Slave Trade, although he was careful only to say that he wished to make the law "consistent with the avowed policy of the United States."[14]

Accordingly, on January 4, 1819, Mercer rose to introduce two resolutions. He had made a discovery that "demanded" the attention of Congress. At least twenty vessels had recently been fitted out in American harbors for the "obvious purpose" of carrying on the slave trade. Such a trade, he charged, was allowed to thrive because the states derived financial rewards from it. He requested that the secretary of the navy inform Congress as to what steps were being taken to subdue the detestable traffic. Finally, he slyly requested that Secretary of the Treasury Crawford report to Congress the number of ships and Africans recently captured and how they had been disposed of by the states.[15]

The resolutions were agreed to, but not without some difficulty that demonstrated the notorious southern dislike of discussing any topic even remotely connected with its peculiar institution. George Strother of Virginia moved to amend the resolution so that the report would name the ports from which the ships had sailed; he wished to demonstrate that the "ignominy of this trade" belonged "to the whole country." Fellow Virginian John Floyd amended it further by calling for the "names of the places" where the vessels were owned, an attempt to place the blame on Yankee merchants. Mercer was annoyed by these distractions but did not dare object to any of the amendments, so they all were agreed to.[16]

Mercer already possessed most of this information. He requested it only to raise the wind in Congress for the bill he was preparing and to serve notice to his touchy southern brethren that such an act would be introduced. With the help of Samuel Mills he had, in fact, already written an anonymous report on the illegal slave trade to be submitted by his society in conjunction with his bill.[17]

Just over a week later, on January 13, Henry Middleton of South Carolina, the chairman of the Slave Trade Committee, reported Mercer's bill, which was accompanied by the society's second annual report as well as by its memorial on the trade. All three were written by Mercer, who silently watched Middleton from his seat. He was not a member of the Slave Trade Committee, and doubtless he thought it wiser to have a representative from South Carolina introduce the measure. He did not wish the measure to appear to come from the society. The act was twice read and, along with the annual report and the memorial, was ordered to be printed. The three items, Mercer thought contentedly, made "together a very large document."[18]

The bill that Congress heard on that day was mundane in many ways. Most of it was devoted to closing the loopholes in the act of 1807, which had allowed states to benefit from the illegal traffic. The bill authorized the president to order the navy to cruise the coasts of the United States and Africa and to seize and bring into port all "vessels of the United States, wheresoever found, which may have taken on board, or which may be intended for the purpose of taking on board" any African in violation of the act of 1807.

As an incentive, the proceeds of the captured ship would be divided equally between the officers and the crew who brought it into port. Significantly, however, the slaves on board would be turned over to a federal marshal, and their disposal was left to the president. In short, the fate of the captives was transferred from the state to the federal government.[19]

To Mercer and the society, the most important part of the bill was section two, which made it the duty of the president to make arrangements "for the safekeeping" and "removal beyond the limits of the United States, of all such negroes" who were illegally brought into the country. It also instructed the president to appoint a person "residing upon the coast of Africa, as agent" for "receiving the negroes," who would be sent back to their native country. The bill authorized the appropriation of one hundred thousand dollars "to carry this law into effect."[20]

As the House awaited the return of the bill from the printer, the first stirrings of a tempest that would almost destroy the Union blew up in Congress. For years the residents of the Missouri territory, mostly transplanted southerners, had been petitioning Congress for statehood. Clay presented a bill that resulted in an enabling act, and in early February the measure was taken up in the committee of the whole. But James Tallmadge of New York rose to introduce two amendments. The first prohibited the further introduction of slaves into Missouri; the second provided that all slave children born in the region after it became a state would be freed upon reaching age twenty-five. Southerners were aghast, but before the question could be taken the House adjourned.[21]

Tallmadge was adamant in his refusal to let the matter drop, and three days later he brought his amendments to a vote. The first, which prohibited the further introduction of slaves into Missouri, passed by a vote of 87 to 76. The second amendment also passed, although by a smaller margin of 82 to 78. The entire Virginia delegation, including the man some contemporaries hailed as the "American Wilberforce," voted against the amendments. Missouri was one of the two issues during Mercer's long career on which the delegation was unanimous. Any other course would be political suicide for so new a congressman because most Virginians agreed with Thomas Ritchie, who bitterly denounced the amendments as a "galling injustice."[22]

With Congress in an uproar over the Tallmadge amendments, Mercer began to fear that his slave trade bill would be lost. In their outrage over the Missouri question, it was possible that southern men would refuse to pass any measure that even obliquely attacked their way of life. And to make matters worse, John Floyd, the Virginian who was expected to assist the measure on the floor of the House, was suddenly forced to return home by an illness in his family.[23]

The bill was scheduled to be taken up on March 1. With so little time left in the session, Henry Middleton, who had introduced the measure, urged Mercer to "abandon" it. Middleton had never completely supported the measure, although like most congressmen he harbored only mild objections to the first section; he thought little about the second. He told Mercer that with the Missouri question in the air his bill would never get through both houses and that there was opposition to the clause that divided the booty between the naval officers and their men. But Mercer would not be dissuaded. He determined to act as floor manager for the bill in the House and "procure friends for it in the Senate," an audacious move for a first-term representative.[24]

On March 1 the bill was taken up by the committee of the whole. As Middleton predicted, the sections on bounties for the officers and crews came under attack from Virginians George Strother and Hugh Nelson, who thought the penalties too light. Both men were careful to explain that their opposition was not caused by an unwillingness to destroy the hated trade. Mercer deftly parried these and other attacks and explained every aspect of the bill in great detail. Finally, the committee approved the bill and ordered it to be placed before the entire House on the following day.[25]

When the bill was brought up again the next morning, Nelson and Strother again attacked it. As on the previous day, Middleton was no help, and Mercer was again on his feet defending the bill. The clause dealing with the return of the Africans was not brought up; the House accepted it for what it was purported to be, an act to extinguish the illegal trade and to aid those innocents caught in its web. With little further fanfare, the act was passed and sent to the Senate.[26]

The House then immediately turned to the Senate's version of the Missouri enabling act. The South was outvoted by the more populous North in the House, but in the Senate the two sides were equal. There Charles Tait of Georgia, on the recommendation of Crawford and Calhoun, dropped the Tallmadge amendments and returned the act to the lower chamber for concurrence. Tallmadge then moved to postpone the bill, but the House refused to take that step. The angry body again insisted on its amendments, and the bill was returned to the Senate, which at that moment was considering Mercer's slave trade act.[27]

The clauses dealing with how the booty should be divided met with even greater opposition in the Senate than in the House. But the act was defended by James Burrill of Rhode Island, and within hours the House received a message that the slave trade bill had passed the Senate and gone to the president. To everyone's surprise but his own, Mercer had almost single-handedly gotten his bill passed.[28]

Moments later, a second message arrived from the Senate insisting on the amendment removing the restriction on slavery in Missouri. The question was then put as to whether the House would hold to the Tallmadge resolutions and passed by a vote of 78 to 66. Again, Mercer and the Virginians voted as a bloc to allow Missouri to enter the Union as a slave state. The next day, March 3, a wary Fifteenth Congress adjourned with Missouri's fate undecided. That afternoon, however, Monroe signed Mercer's slave trade bill into law.[29]

To Mercer's great surprise, the Missouri question worked to his advantage. Many southern congressmen continued to believe that slavery was profoundly wrong. They would not allow the North to dictate their rights to them, yet neither did they wish to be seen as defenders of the institution; the cautious and qualified opposition of Strother and Nelson to the slave trade bill demonstrated their position. They could soothe their troubled consciences by supporting Mercer's bill. The leading Washington paper, the *National Intelligencer,* cited the bill's authorship by a Virginian as "proof" that southerners who voted against the Tallmadge amendments also wished "to check the increase of slavery." Even Thomas Ritchie, who could rarely say a kind word about Mercer, considered the bill "perhaps the most interesting to the national character of any act passed during the present session."[30]

Easily the happiest of all was the American Colonization Society. The day after Congress adjourned, the board of managers met and appointed a delegation to visit President Monroe. Bushrod Washington, Key, and Walter Jones were to offer the services of the society in carrying the act into effect. With the bill law, the society no longer needed to maintain a discreet distance. The bill, Mercer now admitted to a Virginia colonizationist, had been drafted "in conformity" with the needs and desires of the society. "It admits of such a construction, in its operation," he added, "as to succeed the accomplishment of our views."[31]

Within a week the committee members paid Monroe a visit and explained the act to him. They innocently insisted that it allowed for the purchase of land in Africa for the establishment of a colony. Using an argument devised by Mercer, they reasoned that the measure placed liberated slaves under the care of the federal government, required their prompt return to Africa, and provided money for that purpose. Surely the money was meant to be spent in part on a colony to serve as a base from which the Africans could reach their final destination. Monroe allowed that he "did not conceive himself fully authorized under the late law" to purchase land, but if the society would buy the land, he would appoint and pay an agent to live there. More than that, he would "defray all expenses of transporting the captured negroes & making provisions for their reception there."[32]

Half convincing the president of their interpretation was one thing, getting it past the less malleable secretary of state was something else again as the society discovered on March 12, when Monroe casually mentioned to Adams that he wished to have a cabinet meeting on the matter. The government could not buy the land desired by the society, Monroe reasoned, although he now took the position that it was only because not enough money had been appropriated. Perhaps, he mused, Congress would appropriate more. When Adams recovered, he calmly told the president that he was certain Congress had not intended to provide money for the purchase of territory. But Monroe was insistent. The Virginia legislature had recommended such a step in 1816, he maintained, and he agreed that free blacks were a "very dangerous people." They lived, he lectured Adams, "by pilfering," and he was determined to help the society in this endeavor.[33]

Adams was amazed but said nothing else. He did, however, find his voice when he walked across the street to his office and found Key and Jones waiting for him. Jones tried the same interpretation on the secretary that they had used on the president, telling him that the bill "contained a clear authority" to purchase land in Africa. Such a purchase was constitutional, he insisted, citing the Louisiana Purchase as evidence. Adams listened politely but replied that the act "had no reference to the settlement of a colony." Louisiana, he reminded his guests, was contiguous to the United States; land in Africa for free blacks would mean the creation of a colonial government subordinate to the United States. Congress had voted only to suppress an illegal traffic, he lectured, and to derive such an interpretation from the bill "was an Indian Cosmogony."[34]

Four days later Monroe and his cabinet met. The president relied greatly on the advice of his cabinet, and though he reserved the final decision for himself, he routinely laid before the members all subjects of great importance, especially those pertaining to foreign affairs. Monroe began by discussing the interpretation given him by the society, saying that it would not do to permit the slaves returned to Africa to starve. Adams again insisted that Congress never intended to appropriate money for the purchase of land and that the Constitution allowed for no colonial system. Throughout the discussion Crawford sat quietly. It was finally decided, or so Adams thought, that the president had no authority to purchase land in Africa and certainly none to pay for the return of free blacks born in America.[35]

For Adams only one question remained to be settled: the legal position of the captured Africans living in Georgia. Late in the month Adams met with Crawford and Attorney General William Wirt. This time the treasury secretary spoke up. He believed the act was "retrospective" and that under it Monroe might return to Africa the slaves advertised for sale even though they had been imported before the passage of the bill. Again Adams refused to budge. Although he was a proponent of loose construction, Adams cared little for either Crawford or the American Colonization Society, and he argued that if that was what the bill intended, it should have said so. Wirt agreed, and Crawford, seeing that he was outvoted, reluctantly conceded that the society should apply for the Africans, which the law of Georgia allowed it to do.[36]

But the matter was not ended. With Congress adjourned, Monroe returned to his Oak Hill plantation in Aldie, where he was building a larger house. There the president was but a ten-minute walk from the persuasive Charles Fenton Mercer. During the months of adjournments Mercer convinced Monroe that the society did not wish to create a colonial empire. It simply wished to purchase land to use as a portal through which captured Africans could pass on their way back home. It might, of course, Mercer added, be necessary to create a "society" in Africa to protect and feed the slaves when they arrived. His logic appeared impeccable, and as he had written the bill, Monroe was inclined to accept it. Monroe at length guaranteed his young friend that he would "act with the advice of the Society." By early April Mercer promised a fellow colonizationist that Monroe was "willing to go, to any length to aid us, in forming a colony of our free people of colour," short of an outright purchase of land. Even so, Mercer thought it best "not to excite the jealousy of enemies" by "making known our intimacy with the Administration."[37]

By the time the Sixteenth Congress convened the following December, Monroe had been thoroughly convinced that it was his duty to supply "for recaptured Africans" a "secure station" in their homeland. The president was wise enough to understand that such an interpretation would win him few friends, and he warned Mercer that an appropriation would be forthcoming "on condition that no eclat should be given to the Act and his construction of it."[38]

On December 9 the president stopped by Adams's office to inform the secretary that he was going to appoint an agent to Africa after all. The agent, yet unnamed, was to be furnished with a credit of twenty-five thousand dollars on the London House of Baring to be spent on the support of the returned captives. The incredulous Adams, who had thought the matter settled, bluntly wondered "if it was clear that the Executive was authorized to incur this expense by the act." Monroe allowed that he now thought so, but he promised Adams that the issue would be discussed one final time at the next day's cabinet meeting.[39]

When Adams arrived at the White House, he found that much had changed since the spring. Monroe was adamant about providing the society with funds, and if Congress disagreed it could pass an explanatory act. Adams sputtered that such a course placed the supporters of the administration in a difficult position. But the secretary was alone in his arguments. Crawford now openly argued the society's case, and he brought Wirt over to his side. Finally, Monroe agreed to send a special message to Congress detailing his position. Congress could then do what it liked. The society, Adams sniffed, had "the ear of the President" and so "got their fingers into the purse." For all of "their members, and auxiliary societies and newspaper puffs, they have no funds," he observed. Adams now realized the hidden intent of Mercer's bill.[40]

A week later, several days after sending Congress his annual message, Monroe dispatched a special note on the bill. He admitted that some doubt existed as to the intent of the legislation, submitted his understanding of the act, and suggested that if Congress disagreed it should amend the bill at a future date. The message was read to a preoccupied House and ordered to be referred to the

Slave Trade Committee. There Mercer, starting his second term and now a committee member, "took care" to see that it went no further. Monroe, he shamefacedly observed, had opted for an interpretation, "which though liberal, was not more just than indispensably necessary to the due execution of the act."[41]

Monroe's decision left Adams greatly annoyed. The president's construction, the secretary fumed, was not only illogical but contrary to his advice. Adams admitted that the president had given Congress fair warning. Yet Adams—and Monroe—would have been horrified if he knew that Eli Ayres, one of the colonial agents, intended to use the money advanced by Monroe to buy territory in Africa. (Most of Liberia was purchased at gunpoint for less than three hundred dollars.) For just a small part of the sum appropriated, Mercer later conceded, Monroe unknowingly accomplished "the actual establishment, which Virginia had so long desired, in conformity with her renewed resolution of 1816."[42]

In keeping with his promise, Monroe appointed Samuel Bacon and John Bankson, the two men suggested by the society, as chief agents of the federal government. On February 20, 1820, these men and eighty-six settlers sailed out of New York harbor aboard the *Elizabeth*. As Mercer had been promised almost a year earlier, the United States sloop of war *Cyane* accompanied her as convoy.[43]

The entire expedition was funded by the federal government, which made little attempt to hide the fact that it was a colonization venture. Bacon hired free black colonists ostensibly to serve as laborers and carpenters. Of the eighty-six blacks, only a third were men; the rest were their wives and children. None were Africans removed from illegal slavers, and the navy made no arrangement for their return voyage. Appropriately, the society responded to this largess by naming the capital of Liberia, as the colony came to be called, after the president: Monrovia.[44]

All of this proved too much for many of Monroe's southern critics, who saw his tenure in office as a slow and awkward but steady move away from the agrarian principles most Virginians honored. Mercer, who had reason to be pleased by the president's latest turn toward economic nationalism, thought such criticism hypocrisy. "Monroe is *condemned* for discovering *constitutional* motives for the *applauded acts* of his predecessors," he fumed to colonizationist John Hartwell Cocke.[45]

But in truth it was Mercer, not Monroe, who set the society on its way in Africa. He wrote the act of 1819 and unrelentingly argued the society's interpretation to Monroe, as he later admitted when he wrote that Liberia "owed its success to the legislation of Congress quite as much, if not more than, to the American Colonization Society." Indeed, he was so obviously at the center of the issue that in the summer of 1819 he received a letter from a free black, asking to be sent to Africa. None of this political maneuvering, however, could disguise the real purpose of colonization—it was a plan for, not of, free blacks, who resolutely claimed the right of American citizenship. It was to be the bane of the society's existence that black Americans refused to be convinced that Mercer and the others were really their friends. A few slaves even refused to accept manumission if as a condition they were to be sent to Liberia.[46]

Regardless of the hostility of free blacks, Mercer had engineered a considerable victory for the society. He was triumphant, and he had good reason to be. But Mercer's victory would not last long, for even as the winds carried the *Elizabeth* to Africa the explosive issue of slavery blew back into Congress in the next stage of the Missouri question. Before the issue was settled, Mercer would be on his way to becoming even more of an outsider in his native state.[47]

Notes

ABBREVIATIONS

ACS	American Colonization Society
CFM	Charles Fenton Mercer
COCC	Chesapeake and Ohio Canal Company
DAB	*Dictionary of American Biography*, ed. Allen Johnson and Dumas Malone, 21 vols., 1928–1936.
JQA	John Quincy Adams
JSH	*Journal of Southern History*
LC	Library of Congress
NJHS	New Jersey Historical Society
NYHS	New-York Historical Society
PRO, FO	Great Britain, Public Record Office, Foreign Office
UVA	University of Virginia
VHS	Virginia Historical Society
VMHB	*Virginia Magazine of History and Biography*
VSL	Virginia State Library
WMQ	*William and Mary Quarterly*

1. CFM, Autobiographical Sketch, Mercer-Hunter Papers, VSL; James M. Boyd to Ralph R. Gurley, January 10, 1827; Board of Managers, Minutes, December 11, 1818,

both in ACS Papers, LC; Richard Peters to CFM, January 25, 1819, CFM Papers, NYHS; CFM to Ralph R. Gurley, October 9, 1827, ACS Papers.

2. Charles Fenton Mercer, *An Address to the American Colonization Society at their 36th Annual Meeting* (Geneva [Switzerland], 1854), 3.

3. CFM to John Hartwell Cocke, April 2, 1819, Cocke Collection, UVA: P. J. Staudenraus, *The African Colonization Movement* (New York, 1961), 69.

4. Mercer, *Address*, 4; John Brockenbrough to William Meade, June 8, 1819, in John Johns, *A Memoir of the Life of William Meade* (Baltimore, 1867), 122; William Turner to CFM, December 28, 1819, Peter Force Papers, LC.

5. CFM, Speech of January 1818, in *First Annual Report* (Washington, D.C., 1818), 15–16.

6. Charles Fenton Mercer, *Colonization of Free People of Color*, House Committee Report 101, Serial 160 (Washington, D.C., 1827), 10.

7. Board of Managers, Minutes, February 5, 1818, ACS Papers; CFM, Speech of 1833, in *African Repository*, 10:266; Mercer, *Address*, 4–5.

8. *Annals of Congress* (Washington, D.C., 1817), 14th Cong., 2d sess., 481, 639, 939–41; Charles Fenton Mercer, ed., *Slave Trade*, House Committee Report 348, Serial 201, Vol. 3 (Washington, D.C., 1830), 33–34; Mercer, *Address*, p. 4; JQA Diary, April 29, 1819, in Charles Francis Adams, ed., *Memoirs of John Quincy Adams Comprising Parts of His Diary from 1795 to 1848*, 12 vols. (Philadelphia, 1874–77), 4:354–55; *Richmond Enquirer*, January 28, 1819.

9. *African Repository*, 10:266; Mercer, *Address*, 2.

10. Mercer, in *Third Annual Report* (Washington, D.C., 1820), 33; Mercer, *Address*, 4–5.

11. Mercer, *Address*, 5; Mercer, in *Third Annual Report*, 10–11; Chase C. Mooney, *William H. Crawford, 1772–1834* (Lexington, Ky., 1974), 189; Mathew Carey, *Letters on the Colonization Society Addressed to the Hon. C. F. Mercer* (Philadelphia, 1832), 9–11.

12. Mercer, *Address*, 5; CFM to John Hartwell Cocke, April 19, 1818, Cocke Collection.

13. Mercer, *Address*, 5–6; CFM to JQA, May 25, 1826, Adams Family Papers, Massachusetts Historical Society.

14. CFM, Autobiographical Sketch, Mercer-Hunter Papers; Mercer, *Address*, 6.

15. *Annals of Congress* (Washington, D.C., 1819), 15th Cong., 2d sess., 442; Mercer, ed., *Slave Trade*, 57; *Richmond Enquirer*, January 9, 1819.

16. *Annals of Congress*, 15th Cong., 2d sess., 443; *National Messenger*, January 6, 1819.

17. Minutes of Annual Meeting, January 12, 1819, ACS Papers.

18. *Richmond Enquirer*, January 19, 1819; Louis Filler, *The Crusade against Slavery, 1830–1860* (New York, 1960), 20; Mercer, *Address*, 6.

19. *Annals of Congress*, 15th Cong., 2d sess., 2544.

20. Ibid., 2545; CFM, Autobiographical Sketch, Mercer-Hunter Papers.

21. Glyndon G. Van Deusen, *The Life of Henry Clay* (Boston, 1937), 134; *Annals of Congress*, 15th Cong., 2d sess., 1166.

22. *Annals of Congress*, 15th Cong., 2d sess., 1214–15; *National Intelligencer*, February 17, 1819; *African Repository*, 10:265; *Richmond Enquirer*, February 25, 1819.

23. Mercer, *Address*, 6; CFM, Speech of 1833, in *African Repository*, 10:266.

24. Mercer, *Address*, 6; CFM, Autobiographical Sketch, Mercer-Hunter Papers.

25. Mercer, *Address*, 6; *Annals of Congress*, 15th Cong., 2d sess., 1430–31; *National Intelligencer*, March 3, 1819; *National Messenger*, March 5, 1819; *Richmond Enquirer*, March 6, 1819.

26. *Annals of Congress* (Washington, D.C., 1820), 16th Cong., 1st sess., 812; Ibid., 15th Cong., 2d sess., 1433. No breakdown of the vote was provided.

27. Ibid., 15th Cong., 2d sess., 1433, 1435; Charles M. Wiltse, *John C. Calhoun: Nationalist, 1782–1828* (New York, 1944), 192.

28. *African Repository,* 10:266; *Annals of Congress,* 15th Cong., 2d sess., 1435.

29. *Annals of Congress,* 15th Cong., 2d sess., 1436–38; *National Intelligencer,* March 3, 1819.

30. *National Intelligencer,* March 12, 1819; *Richmond Enquirer,* March 6, 1819.

31. Board of Managers, Minutes, March 4, 1819, ACS Papers; CFM to John Hartwell Cocke, April 2, 1819, Cocke Collection. Betty Fladeland, *Men and Brothers: Anglo-American Antislavery Cooperation* (Urbana, 1972), 94–95, writes that the society "saw their opening" for federal funds in Mercer's bill. In fact, it was written with the society's needs in mind.

32. Charles Fenton Mercer, *To the August Assembly Convened in the City of Paris, to Confer on Restoring the Peace of Europe, the Memorial of the American Society for Colonizing in Africa the free people of colour of the United States* (London, 1856), 5; Board of Managers, Minutes, March 31, 1819, ACS Papers.

33. JQA Diary, March 12, 1819, in Adams, ed., *Memoirs,* 4:292–93.

34. Ibid., 293–94. The State Department stood on the site of the present Treasury building.

35. Samuel Flagg Bemis, *John Quincy Adams,* 2 vols. (New York, 1950–56), 1:254; JQA Diary, March 16, 1819, in Adams, ed., *Memoirs,* 4:298–99.

36. Adams, ed., *Memoirs,* April 2, 1819, 4:321–22; Mooney, *Crawford,* 189.

37. Harry Ammon, *James Monroe: The Quest for National Identity* (New York, 1971), 408; CFM to JQA, May 25, 1826, Adams Family Papers, Massachusetts Historical Society; CFM to John Hartwell Cocke, April 2, 1819, Cocke Collection.

38. CFM, Autobiographical Sketch, Mercer-Hunter Papers.

39. JQA Diary, December 9, 1819, in Adams, ed., *Memoirs,* 4:473–74.

40. Ibid., December 16, 10, 1819, pp. 479, 475–77.

41. *Annals of Congress,* 16th Cong., 1st sess., 30–31; *National Intelligencer,* December 21, 1819; CFM to John Clayton, July 4, 1854, John Clayton Papers, LC; Mercer, *Address,* 7.

42. JQA Diary, February 2, 1831, January 8, 1820, in Adams, ed., *Memoirs,* 8:309, 4:496; Staundenraus, *African Colonization,* 65; Mercer, *Address,* 19.

43. *African Colonization: An Enquiry into the Origin, Plan, & Prospects of the American Colonization Society* (Fredericksburg, 1829), 6; Fladeland, *Men and Brothers,* 96; CFM to John Hartwell Cocke, April 2, 1819, Cocke Collection.

44. Staundenraus, *African Colonization,* 57–58; CFM, Autobiographical Sketch, Mercer-Hunter Papers.

45. George Dangerfield, *The Era of Good Feelings* (New York, 1952), 101; CFM to John Hartwell Cocke, March 25, 1825, Cocke Collection.

46. CFM, Autobiographical Sketch, Mercer-Hunter Papers; Louis R. Mehlinger, "The Attitude of the Free Negro toward African Colonization," *Journal of Negro History* 1 (July 1916): 276–301; Alexander Waugh to CFM, June 2, 1819, Peter Force Papers, LC. Letter written in behalf of George Bowling; Eugene D. Genovese, *Roll, Jordan, Roll: The World the Slaves Made* (New York, 1972), 126.

47. *Annals of Congress,* 16th Cong., 1st sess., 734–36.

12

Between Two Fires

The American Colonization Society was finally seeing results, and Mercer had good reason to be pleased. But had he known what lay ahead, the pessimistic Virginian would have had new cause to be gloomy. For even as Monroe was granting the society its funds, the issue of Missouri was again before Congress. Before the issue was resolved, Charles Fenton Mercer would be forced into a very difficult position, caught between the growing abolitionist movement of the North, a faction he needed for his crusade against the slave trade, and the growing southern movement to defend slavery as positive good. The dilemma, he remembered later, placed him "between two fires."[1]

The trouble began on December 15, 1819, when John Taylor of New York, now leading the restrictionist forces in the absence of Tallmadge, rose to suggest that the bill enabling Missouri to enter the Union be postponed until a committee could be formed to look into prohibiting slavery in the territories west of the Mississippi. Mercer was the first man to respond. The territory of Missouri, he insisted, already possessed the requisite population to be admitted as a state, and to delay consideration for as long as Taylor wished was "an infraction of its rights." He suggested a much shorter postponement, to which the House agreed.[2]

Mercer's compromise gave both sides time to marshal their forces. For the next three months, every aspect of slavery was probed and discussed and scrutinized by Congress. Southern men previously untainted by the toil of deep thought were forced to examine their way of life, and some began to turn to a concept foreign to minds such as Mercer's. Like Mercer, most southerners were willing to grant that Congress had the right to prohibit slav-

ery in unorganized territories. But Missouri was organized, and
that led to their votes against restriction. But on January 20,
Nathaniel Macon of North Carolina, one of the last of the revolutionary generation, rose to invite his northern friends to return
with him to his plantation and witness for themselves the happy
life of his black children. With this, the positive good theory of
slavery was formally announced.[3]

Macon's interpretation presented a serious problem for Mercer.
Although a slaveholder himself, the Virginian continued to view
the institution as a moral blot; he would never endorse such a
theory. But to vote for Missouri could make it appear that he did,
which would seriously damage the American Colonization Society
in the North. It would be possible, if dangerous, for him, given the
small number of slaves and the large number of Quakers and
antislavery Methodists in his northern county, to follow his heart
and vote for restriction. But that path would place him in opposition to his entire state, and although that day would come, he was
not yet ready for it. It would also place him in opposition to Monroe
and other moderate Republicans, who believed that restriction was
a Federalist plot to regain national power.[4]

Again the slave trade held the answer to Mercer's dilemma. As a
colonizationist he opposed the trade because it brought into the
nation more of that group he was trying so hard to export. But he
was also outraged by the cruelties of the middle passage, and he
was sincere in wishing to see the trade crushed. A new crusade to
destroy it would put him in an alliance with the rising northern
antislavery groups. He could thus back the admission of Missouri
and retain his position in mainstream southern politics while not
damaging the position of the society in the North. Accordingly, on
December 23, and again five days later, Mercer rose to complain
that the government had still not done enough to suppress the
traffic.[5]

Such timid complaints, however, would not be enough. He
would have to do better, and so again he was miserable. He began to
drink. He could not even find relief at his mess, for Louis McLane
was constantly irritated with him. McLane's jealousy of Mercer
had not abated, and he deeply resented this "conceited little blad-
der" for his breeding and education. He was especially outraged by
Senator James Bayard's daughter Caroline's "fullsome affection" for
Mercer, her complete inability to conceal it, and his utter lack of
interest. Even Randolph found him "suspicious" and "unap-

proachable" and could not bear to be around his "wounded spirit." "So morbid a sensibility I have never known," he sighed to Garnett.[6]

The situation became more complex on December 30, when the Maine enabling bill came before the House. Southern men were unwilling to allow another northern state to enter the Union, especially if Missouri's inclusion was to be again postponed. Clay even went so far as to suggest that it was "just to make the admission of Missouri the condition of that of Maine." This blackmail, however, could not be enforced in the House, where the Maine bill was passed and sent to the Senate on January 3.[7]

But in the Senate Clay's demand was supported by the evenly matched southern forces. The impasse mandated a compromise, which was forthcoming from Senator Jesse Thomas of Illinois, an opponent of the Tallmadge amendment. On February 3 he suggested that Missouri be admitted as a slave state and that the rest of the Louisiana Purchase north of Missouri's southern border be forever free. Maine would be separated from the Missouri bill, although it would be admitted at the same time. Thomas's proposal was not really a compromise; it created not a consensus but two blocs of majorities. Yet moderates like Mercer were immediately drawn to it.[8]

On March 2, 1820, word arrived in the House that the Senate had removed the clause restricting slavery in Missouri and replaced it with one that excluded slavery from all the territories, save Missouri, north of 36° 30' north latitude. It was now up to the House to complete the compromise. Several speeches followed the message, most calling for conciliation. James Stevens of Connecticut spoke briefly. Mercer was next; "with great earnestness" he pleaded for compromise. Suddenly, his knees buckled and he made an uncertain grab for the edge of his desk. But it was too late. As his startled colleagues watched, Mercer, who routinely drove himself to a state of exhaustion, landed in a heap on the floor.[9]

As those seated around Mercer did their best to revive him, someone kept his wits enough to call for a vote on the main question. Already Mercer's long and classical speeches were becoming legendary, and men on both sides unfriendly to compromise had seized the opportunity to grab a bite of dinner. The Missouri bill, without the restriction, was promptly passed by a close 90 to 87. A groggy Mercer was awake enough to vote with the majority. The clause prohibiting slavery in the territory north of Missouri was then put to a vote and passed, 134 to 42. Mercer and four other Virginians were again in the majority; the seventeen other members of their delegation voted nay.[10]

The crisis over Missouri appeared to be at an end, although several red-faced northern men had to explain their absence from the floor. Henry Edwards of Connecticut, who would have voted for restriction, protested that he had not eaten and thought it safe to slip out while the gusty Mercer was speaking. This explanation did not much please his critics, and the *Hartford Courant* thought it reflected badly on Edwards. "Mark here, Reader: The fainting Mercer, like a true son of Virginia, remained at his post, and voted for Southern slavery and supremacy" while "our representative could not forgo one single meal to prevent the extension of slavery."[11]

With that ordeal behind him, Mercer gladly turned again to the slave trade. During a brief, and obviously necessary, respite at Aldie, he drafted a report for the Slave Trade Committee, of which he was now a member. But he did not advocate a new bill. The cost of his 1819 bill had already led some to suggest its repeal; another act would never pass a now suspicious Congress. Instead, the report was designed to attain "the utter abolition of the traffic" in "the only practicable mode, by the universal denunciation of the Slave trade, as piracy." The plan was simple, yet for all its brevity, brilliant. The problem of insurgent Latin American privateers turned pirates dated back to the Madison administration. But present laws were ineffective, and a new and stronger bill was then before the Senate. Mercer realized that when the bill reached the House he could amend it so that it covered slavers as well as privateers. This was a crucial, if subtle, point because pirates were at all times liable for search and punishment by any nation. Such a classification would make the exchange of the right of visit and search with Great Britain unnecessary, an interpretation he confirmed by consulting Justices Washington and Marshall.[12]

Not surprisingly, since it was less than a decade after the war with England, Mercer thought it unwise to reveal the subtleties of his plan. Saying that he wished to classify slavers as pirates was enough. His chance came on May 8, when the chairman of the Slave Trade Committee was absent. He rose and reported an amendment to the piracy act, which held that any American citizen engaged in the slave trade, even on a foreign vessel, "shall be adjudged a pirate" and "shall suffer death."[13]

Mercer was far from finished. The next day he returned to the question of the slave trade, this time stressing the need for international cooperation. The American flag, he told Congress, had been used less as a cover for slavers since his bill of the previous year, but the trade continued unabated. It was unreasonable for Americans to think that the trade could be suppressed merely by guarding American shores. "And humiliating as must be the confession," cried the Virginian, "there are, in our own bosom, individuals who are ever ready to afford an asylum to the vicious agents." Coming from a southern man, this was an amazing admission, especially following months of northern abuse and vilification. He then introduced a complex web of three resolutions. The first called upon the president to negotiate with governments friendly to the United States "on the means of effecting an entire and immediate abolition of the African slave trade." The second requested that Monroe negotiate a formal declaration with the leading maritime powers recognizing the permanent independence and neutrality of Liberia. The third requested Monroe to instruct the navy "to afford every aid" to the efforts of the American Colonization Society "upon the western coast of Africa."[14]

As anticipated, Mercer's efforts met with a cold reception from his southern colleagues. But they also attracted hostility from an unexpected quarter: the secretary of state. Adams had not yet gotten over his unhappiness with Monroe's interpretation of Mercer's 1819 slave trade bill. More to the point, Adams was fiercely protective of American maritime rights in relation to Britain, and Mercer's amendment to the piracy act gave him fresh reason to dislike the congressman from Loudoun. Shortly thereafter, when the two men found themselves face to face in Monroe's drawing room, they fell into a violent shouting match.[15]

On Friday, May 20, Mercer's three resolutions and his amendment to the piracy bill were brought up. Weldon Edwards of North Carolina promptly moved to table the resolutions, but a division was called for. Edwards's motion was put to a vote on the first resolution, which dealt with the slave trade. Like Edwards, the Virginia delegation had heard enough talk of slavery for one session; Missouri no longer helped but hindered Mercer's plans. Although it was not tabled, most of the Virginians voted to lay it down. The second resolution also survived, but the third was tabled. It was then moved that the first resolution be postponed until the next session, and this too failed. A motion to postpone the second resolution, however, was successful. Then, with little debate, the House passed the piracy law, including Mercer's amendment, and sent it to the Senate.[16]

The Senate considered the piracy bill the next day. The hostile lower South bloc immediately made motions to strike out Mercer's amendment but received only six votes. Most border senators were evidently not yet hostile to every bill that touched upon their peculiar institution, especially if it was drawn by a southern hand. The act was passed by a large majority and signed into law by Monroe two days later.[17]

On May 15, the day the piracy bill was signed into law, the upper chamber took up Mercer's first resolution. William Smith of South Carolina argued for postponement, but James Burrill of Rhode Island, who had fought for Mercer's law of the previous year, urged its consideration. Rufus King lectured Smith that southern men should be proud to vote for the resolution because "it had origi-nated with an individual from [their] part of the Union." John Walker of Alabama disagreed and called for a vote on postpone-ment, which failed, 10 to 15. It was then suggested by Walter Lowrie of Pennsylvania that the Senate suspend the rule against reading a bill twice on the same day because it was the last day of the session. But the motion, and hence the resolution, was lost on a tie vote, and the Senate adjourned for the year.[18]

On balance, the session was more of a victory for Mercer than a defeat. The slave trade was now considered piracy and carried the penalty of death, an event aided by the desire of at least some southerners to demonstrate anew their refusal to defend slavery as an abstract principle. And his society had emerged from the storm in good condition; because of Mercer's skillful maneuvering nei-ther North nor South had been given new cause to turn against it. He had probably not expected all three of his resolutions to pass. His third resolution, which called for naval aid for the colony, was so outrageous that it was almost certainly designed to draw fire away from the crucial first resolution—and the piracy act.

With the adjournment of Congress, a much debilitated Mercer left the capital. He may not have been aware as he rode through the dung-ridden streets toward his uncle's Maryland home that a con-gressional caucus was being held to renominate James Monroe for president. The Federalist party did not present a candidate. It had, Adams observed, "become almost merged in the republican party." Indeed, considering the principles of the new breed of Republicans, the two parties were "so mingled that their individuality was entirely lost." That, as far as Mercer was concerned, was all to the good.[19]

By the end of June, Mercer had almost completely regained his health. Nursed by his spinster cousin Margaret, a teacher and an ardent colonizationist, the dour Virginian was "nearly fully restored" by the time Calhoun saw him late in the month. Never was good health more needed. By the time he returned to Washington, he would discover that the failure of his first resolution to pass had not meant that it had no effect on foreign policy. He would also discover that the storm over Missouri had returned.[20]

Since the end of the Napoleonic Wars, Viscount Castlereagh, the British foreign minister, had sought to convince the European powers and the United States to join with England in crushing the international slave trade. Monroe had continually rebuffed such overtures because he would not concede the right of search, a grant absolutely vital to ending the traffic. (The president was blissfully unaware that Mercer's amendment had essentially conceded that right.) Castlereagh, however, took advantage of Mercer's resolutions to approach the administration again. On October 26, 1820, Stratford Canning, the British minister in Washington, strode into the State Department and discussed the subject with Adams for over two hours. The granite-faced secretary was unmoved. He bluntly told Canning that in light of Britain's late behavior, the requirement of the right of search "was an objection to the plan itself."[21]

Charles Fenton Mercer, then in secret contact with Canning, was not willing to give up. On December 4 he rose innocently to introduce yet another resolution, this one calling for the president to lay before the House any correspondence between the United States and any of the governments of Europe "in relation to the African slave trade." The connection was made more obvious on December 20, when Adams arrived at his office to find the handsome British minister again waiting to see him. Canning, Adams discovered, had been "instructed" to approach the administration now that this "important question" had been revived by Mercer. Holding his temper in check, Adams replied that the president's position was unchanged.[22]

It was at this time that the problem of Missouri again appeared before Congress. During the previous summer, Missouri had produced a constitution that it now presented to Congress preliminary to the recognition of the state government. Northern congressmen objected to the document because it barred entry to free blacks and mulattoes. Since free blacks were considered citizens of some New England states, this provision was in violation of the constitutional clause that guaranteed to citizens of each state the rights and privileges of citizens in every other state. Antislavery forces were given another opportunity to deny Missouri statehood, and when the matter came before the House on December 13 the constitution was rejected, 79 to 93. The Virginia delegation again voted as a bloc for admission.[23]

Monroe was dismayed by this latest development, just as he was dismayed by Mercer's endless resolutions on the slave trade; he was dismayed by any event that might injure his cherished reputation as president of all the people. Nonetheless, on January 5, 1821, Monroe produced the information Mercer requested. That there was so little demonstrated that the administration was firm on the question of visit and search.[24]

Just over a month later, the stubborn Mercer issued his reply to Monroe in the guise of his committee report. It approvingly noted the piracy law of 1820, but as Britain clearly required a formal concession from the executive branch as well, it added that the trade could be abolished only by a grant "by the maritime Powers, to each other's ships of war, of a qualified right of search." The best place to capture the slavers, it observed, was on the coast of Africa, a place the American navy seldom reached. The committee urged the president "to enter into such arrangements" with "one or more of the maritime Powers of Europe." Word for word, it was his first resolution of the previous session.[25]

No further action was taken on the resolution, however, for the entire legislative session was again devoted to the questions of slavery and Missouri. Several attempts at compromise failed, and finally Clay engineered the selection of a special committee composed of members of both houses. The result was a vaguely worded resolution stating that nothing in the Missouri constitution was to be understood as being in violation of the federal Constitution. This bare-faced lie proved to be the answer and was adopted by the House on February 26. The entire Virginia delegation save John Randolph voted with the majority. As the foremost apostle of states' rights, Randolph would not vote for any measure that did not admit Missouri unconditionally.[26]

Four months later Missouri formally agreed to Clay's compromise resolution, contemptuously adding that Congress had no power to bind the state. Monroe happily agreed that this response was acceptable, and on August 10, 1821, an executive proclamation admitted Missouri into the more or less happy Union. The president and his secretary of state were now free to form a response to Mercer's latest call for negotiations.[27]

The protracted debate over Missouri and the accompanying argument over the morality of slavery, however, made Mercer more than ever an outsider in his region. The second Missouri debate moved the South one step closer to the defense of slavery as a positive good. It also sent many of the younger, more nationalistic southern Republicans, lulled by two decades of Virginia rule, scurrying back to strict construction and states' rights. The Congress of 1820–21, unlike that of the previous two sessions, was less inclined to accept Mercer's ideas on colonization and the slave trade. The South was changing. He never would.[28]

Worse still, by the time Mercer returned to Washington the following fall, a new element had appeared to complicate further action on the slave trade. Political divisions were now appearing with an eye to the next presidential election. Federalists, both those who kept their identity and those who had left the party, favored the national conservatism of either Adams or Clay. The growing states'-rights wing of the bloated Republican party, calling themselves Radicals, clustered around the standard of the jovial secretary of the treasury. Mercer liked Crawford but could not tolerate his followers. And though he was closer to the economic nationalism of Adams, Mercer would never support the secretary as long as the two differed on the slave trade.[29]

Mercer discovered that the question of succession, still three years away, was the leading topic even in his mess. In addition to the usual residents, King and Harrison Gray Otis, the Union Tavern was now the home of two new members, James Buchanan and Martin Van Buren. The latter, serving his first term as New York's junior senator, found the company of the educated, urbane Federalists who dominated the mess preferable to that of his own party. It seemed to him that the only "straight-line" Republican in the mess was Mercer. Louis McLane was also back, still hating the Virginian. Were it not for the "contemptible little Mercer," McLane complained, the "mess would do very well."[30]

Despite the new problems swirling up about him, politically and socially, Mercer thought only of the issue that had long dominated his mind. On January 15, 1822, he made a motion to instruct the Committee on the Slave Trade—of which he was now the leading member—to investigate whether the current laws were adequate to suppress the trade. Should it be found that they were not, the committee was to suggest "adequate remedies." On this subject, Monroe wished to explain to his friend the complexities involved, but Mercer was undaunted.[31]

Two months later, on April 12, Mercer responded to his own motion by releasing his report under the guise of the Slave Trade Committee. He pronounced that the traffic would never be crushed by "separate and disunited efforts." International cooperation was again recommended although Mercer stopped short of accepting Castlereagh's concept of mixed tribunals. Any American captured would be tried in American courts. But he did urge granting the right of visit and search to other powers, and this meant Great Britain. "Your committee cannot doubt that the people of America have the intelligence to distinguish between the right of searching a neutral on the high seas, in time of war," he continued, "and that of mutual, restricted, and peaceful concession by treaty." The report concluded with a request that the president enter into negotiations with other maritime powers. It was the third time in three years that Mercer had introduced exactly the same resolution.[32]

British officials were heartened when news of the latest resolution reached their shores, although a crisis in the government delayed any official action. Foreign Minister Castlereagh had worked himself into a state of nervous collapse over the issue. In early August he committed suicide by cutting his throat from ear to ear with a small penknife. His successor, George Canning, was no less of a crusader against the trade. On October 11 he directed his cousin Stratford, the minister in Washington, to urge Adams again to adopt the course recommended by the Slave Trade Committee.[33]

Mercer carefully watched all this maneuvering; he was preparing another all-out effort in behalf of an international agreement on the trade. To this end he contacted William Wilberforce in London, in hope he would rally support for cooperative action. He was again quietly feeding information to Stratford Canning, with whom he had become quite cozy. Canning informed his cousin on February 8, 1823, that he believed the mood in Congress to be "far more favourable than any that appeared last year" on the subject of an agreement on the trade.[34]

The British minister yet again presented himself at the office of the American secretary of state. Canning repeated his government's "invitation" to form a convention on the slave trade and suggested slyly that "the American cabinet"—he did not need to mention colonizationist Crawford by name—perhaps favored cooperation. Only the State Department, he bluntly told Adams, stood in the way of the mutual concession of the right of visit and search.

Given the mood of Congress and the nation, he hinted, Adams might be wise to devise some counterproposal.[35]

Mercer was not about to leave the issue in the hands of the hostile Adams. He was in constant touch with Monroe, who, nearing the end of his second term, was suddenly much more willing to make a major concession on the issue than was his secretary. To increase the pressure, on February 10 Mercer introduced his resolution for the fourth time in as many years. He brought it up so late in the session, he told Canning, to prevent it from being sent to the Senate for confirmation. The chances of it passing that body, where the South enjoyed equal power, were slim, and he deemed that a consideration of more importance than whatever weight a joint recommendation might bring. The resolution was then published by Mercer as a one-page pamphlet.[36]

Two weeks later, Mercer brought his resolution up for consideration, supporting it with a long speech that demonstrated more than ever the interlocking nature of colonization and the slave trade. The nation, he warned, must not "be insensible of the danger" of being inundated with "new floods of black population." It was a danger "greatly enhanced by the rapid increase" of a "third caste, midway between the slave and the white population of the South." Even as he spoke, Mercer bawled, "new views of the malignity of this growing evil crowd upon [his] imagination." When he finished, numerous congressmen were on their feet shouting amendments, some to postpone, others to qualify the right of search. But all were defeated, and Mercer's resolution passed by an overwhelming vote of 131 to 9. All nine opposing votes were from the South.[37]

To Adams, the message could not have been any louder if it had been blown from trumpets. Although he would not admit it, even in the privacy of his extraordinary diary, he desperately wanted to be president. His position had become untenable in Congress, just as it was becoming unpopular in the nation. Those who were supporting it, he was convinced, were doing so for political reasons. His final change of heart came after a long talk with Mercer, who had just returned from a society meeting. There too, his resolution had carried by a large majority, and Mercer proudly provided the names of those who were for it. Adams thought the list "remarkable," for it was a "union of Crawfordites, federalists, Clintonians, and . . . Calhounites." Such an odd mixture, Adams told himself, "would have something else in view" besides the slave trade. "It was a warning to me."[38]

Accordingly, on March 31 and again on June 24, Adams sat down at his desk to draft an alternative to the British paper. He still could not bring himself to agree to granting America's traditional enemy the right of search and instead fell back on Mercer's amendment to the 1820 piracy act. Then he had opposed the amendment, but it now appeared to be the best compromise. He forwarded the pertinent clauses from the law to Canning and suggested that Britain adopt a similar law. Adams was quick, however, to disagree with Mercer's interpretation, and he wished it made clear that such a law was not a grant but "a substitute for that of conceding a mutual right of search."39

While this proposal was making its way across the Atlantic, an event was taking place that would alter the course of both the upcoming election and the negotiations with Britain. As he journeyed south from Washington, William Crawford was taken ill, perhaps with erysipelas. A local physican was summoned, who overdosed the patient with lobelia. The huge treasury secretary was left sightless and paralyzed from the waist down. His handlers labored diligently to hide the severity of their candidate's affliction, and the Georgian was still given the best chance for election when Congress convened for its regular session on December 1, 1823. By this time, the question of succession eclipsed almost every other topic. Mercer knew that he would have to make a decision. He held no influence over the outcome, but pressure to take a position in the four-sided contest was becoming great, and Mercer, like Adams, was beginning to understand that the slave trade issue was hopelessly bound to the election.40

Strangely enough, Mercer's decision was not easy. Adams should have been his logical choice, for the secretary had built a solid base of support among former Federalists, manufacturers, merchants, and northeastern financial men. Moreover, Adams was a nationalist who supported the use of federal funds for internal improvements. Yet Mercer, as much as he might agree with the secretary on most issues, had done nothing but fight with Adams over the slave trade and the society. "Adams is no friend of the colonization Society," he told John Hartwell Cocke.41

A more likely choice was Henry Clay, the Speaker of the House. Like Adams, Clay was a nationalist, and by 1823 he was hard at work piercing together his American System, an interlocking program made up of legislation Mercer had supported for more than a decade. Clay had reversed himself on the bank, was a colonizationist, and supported federal funds for internal improvements; indeed, Clay and Mercer had compiled an amazingly similar voting record. But Mercer's superior political acumen led him to suspect what the Kentucky hotspur did not: Clay would not finish in the top three in the electoral college and would be "excluded" from "all chance of being brought into our house."[42]

Jackson, of course, was not worthy of consideration. That left Crawford, who was reputed to be regaining his strength. The Georgian was the candidate of the Old Republicans, although their choice of him was strangely inappropriate. In 1811 he had introduced a bill for continuing the old bank charter for another two decades, he supported moderate tariffs, and he was inclined to believe that Congress had the right to build roads and canals. He was a colonizationist, although Mercer was forced to admit that Crawford had never attended another meeting after the society's second annual convention. But there was no other choice, and in any case Mercer would "not assail Mr Crawford, on account of the cunning and malignity of his adherents." Indeed, that Mercer's ancient enemies were supporting Crawford said more about their lack of choice than his.[43]

Crawford's handlers hoped to use the congressional caucus, the established form of nominating a Republican candidate, to reduce the field. But supporters of the other three candidates knew that the February 14 meeting would be stacked in Crawford's favor, and early in the month more than half the members of Congress signed a statement declaring that they would not attend. The caucus was a pathetic affair; only sixty-eight members of Congress attended. As expected, Crawford was nominated by an overwhelming sixty-four votes. Mercer, who did not attend, well understood what this meant. The field would be so scattered that no candidate would be able to achieve a majority in the electoral college, and thus "we have Crawford, Adams, and Jackson for the three candidates, who are likely to come before this House." Mercer's prediction was correct; only his order was wrong.[44]

Just before the caucus met, Mercer moved a resolution in Congress, calling on the president to turn over any "correspondence or negotiation which he may have instituted with any foreign Government" on the slave trade since his resolution of the previous year. This was not an honest attempt to gain information, for he well knew that negotiations with Britain had finally reached fruition. Instead, he desired to gain House support for Adams's final product, which he correctly suspected would not be met with unanimous praise in the Senate.[45]

The convention was signed on March 13. Adams, looking ahead

to the election, had almost completely capitulated to Mercer's House report of April 1822. The document stipulated that both nations regarded those involved in the trade as pirates and that the two navies would work together to crush the traffic through a reciprocal allowance of visit and search of each other's merchant ships. Unlike in Castlereagh's original proposal, mixed tribunals would not be used, and captured ships would be sent to their home country for trial. The convention also held that no crew member was ever to be removed from a captured vessel and that the officer of the capturing ship would be held responsible for any misuse of the right of search. As soon as the convention was signed, Parliament passed a law making the slave trade piracy.[46]

Adams had tarried far too long; the shadow of the election hung over the affair. Early in May Mercer attended a wedding ball, where he encountered Adams. The two men found that everything had changed with the political winds. Rufus King, who backed Adams, was as enthusiastic about the convention as was Mercer. But James Barbour, a Crawford man, "seemed very cooly disposed toward it." As long as it appeared that Adams would fight any treaty with England, his opponents were all for it. Ironically, now that Adams had completed such a treaty, the Crawfordites were completely against it. They simply could not allow him another diplomatic triumph. Mercer made his first tentative overture to Adams, bluntly telling the secretary that he had objected to much of his past handling of the issue. Now he was more than "satisfied."[47]

Mercer was not about to sit by and watch the issue to which he had devoted the last five years die without a struggle. Together with Ralph Gurley, the society's secretary, he produced as propaganda the largest report the group ever printed. The president aided the effort by sending endless additional documents to the Senate. Monroe even asked Crawford to use his influence among his supporters to get the agreement passed. To his astonishment, Crawford not only refused but insisted that he had not approved the draft convention when it was before the cabinet. Monroe was angered by the still incapacitated secretary's refusal to control his followers, though he kindly attributed Crawford's assertion to a loss of memory brought on by his illness.[48]

But the opponents of the convention discovered that they lacked the votes to kill it outright. King reported to Adams that the Crawfordites would instead try to modify it to make it almost useless, a sentiment Henry Addington, the new British minister in Washington, reported to George Canning. When Monroe heard this news he was astonished, and he took the problem to his cabinet. Calhoun thought that while the convention was before the Senate, it might be wise to have Mercer make another call for information, which "would operate as an admonition to some of the Senators." Adams suggested that the Senate should be left to act without coercion, but that if the convention was rejected, the administration could lay all of the documentation before the House in answer to Mercer's previous call.[49]

On Friday, May 21, the Senate took up the subject behind closed doors. A minor amendment allowing the United States to renounce the convention on six months' notice was agreed to. The next morning, the convention was read a third time. Nathaniel Macon of North Carolina moved for postponement, which was defeated. Josiah Johnston of Louisiana then urged that Britain not be allowed the right of search on the coast of America, and this clause was struck out by a vote of 23 to 20 under the two-thirds rule. Finally, after a furious debate and unusual pressure from Monroe, the Senate ratified the convention, 29 to 13. Of the eight men who voted against ratification, at least six, including Van Buren, were Crawfordites. The Jackson faction, including John Eaton, Thomas Hart Benton, and the old general himself, all voted aye.[50]

Also on the floor were Mercer and Addington, who saw defeat in the last amendment. Undaunted, Mercer immediately requested permission to publish the secret proceedings in the Washington papers. Addington detained the British packet until the printed journal could accompany the ratified document. As they waited for the journals to arrive, the two men discussed how it would be met in England. The British minister was now "in better humour with the treaty" than before and thought it would be accepted. Addington's calming words eased Mercer's "fears for its fate."[51]

As a precaution, Mercer determined to write to his friend Stratford Canning, now back in England, urging ratification of the modified treaty. The published documents, he believed, would not reveal the true opposition to the convention. Mercer read his long letter to both Addington and Monroe, who approved this blunt missive; the president badly desired one last diplomatic triumph before leaving office. The letter and its contents, however, were hardly a secret. Mercer also read the entire letter to William Plumer, a congressman from New Hampshire, and doubtless to others as well. Plumer promptly told Adams of the letter.[52]

The letter was dated May 23, and it probably accompanied the convention on the British packet. In it, Mercer openly admitted that the treaty was "battered and mutilated," but he nonetheless urged its acceptance. He told Canning that "the opposition to the treaty is the work of a single faction, prompted by the hope of prejudicing the public mind against one of the candidates for the Presidency." It was true that he leaned toward Crawford, the candidate to be aided by rejection, and that Adams, the candidate to be injured, "you know to be no favorite of mine," but he correctly insisted that he was the exception. Moreover, Mercer urged immediate acceptance, saying that if Crawford was elected, the treaty would not be renewed, and that if Adams was elected, he might revert to his old opposition to the right of visit and search. Finally, Mercer demonstrated a sophisticated knowledge of foreign affairs by observing that rejection would be a French triumph over Anglo-American disagreement, as well as a signal to Russia that further Franco-British resistance to the Holy Alliance was unlikely. George Canning, at the same time, received a similar analysis from Addington.[53]

Three days later, on the evening of May 27, Adams walked up to the Capitol in search of Mercer. The two men briefly discussed his letter to Canning, Mercer repeating that the opposition to the convention was "merely personal, pointed against" Adams, and that opposition to it would probably be even greater at the next session. The secretary replied that regardless of ratification, Monroe intended again to refer the issue to a select committee, which would not bring it up until after the election. The committee could then recommend a modification of the treaty or a second attempt at ratification in case of failure. Adams loudly let slip that he was present when Crawford favored the concession of search. Mercer colored and stammered that although he had always considered Adams an enemy of international cooperation and colonization, he was not "intimate" with Crawford. Adams quickly promised that he "should be happy to co-operate" with Mercer on the issue in the future. Mercer replied that he was satisfied; he had moved another step closer to Adams.[54]

The news from Britain was bad. In early August Richard Rush informed Adams that he had spoken to George Canning and that the government could not accept the second amendment. Mercer's appeal was laid before the council, and Canning hinted that he well understood the opposition to the treaty. The removal of the right of search on the coast of America, however, formed an "insuperable bar" to English consent. It "cannot but appear to imply the existence on one side," Canning noted innocently, "of a just ground either of suspicion or misconduct" on the part of Britain. Formal notification of the document's rejection came on August 27.[55]

By then Congress had adjourned and the nation was deeply embroiled in the last days of the campaign. As fall approached, the temperature in the capital turned tense. Washington ladies began to organize their parties on an Adams, Jackson, or Crawford basis. When the electioneering smoke finally cleared—Congress allowed the states more than a month to conduct their elections—it was discovered that Jackson had outpolled his rivals in the popular vote. The general led in the electoral count as well, with ninety-nine votes compared to eighty-four for Adams, forty-one for Crawford, and thirty-seven for Clay. Virginia gave its twenty-four votes to Crawford, although the election showed the Richmond Junto to be badly damaged. Because of their desire for internal improvements, the western districts supported Adams. But as Mercer predicted a year before, Jackson fell short of a majority, and the House would decide between the top three candidates.[56]

The situation gave considerable influence to Speaker of the House Henry Clay, whose name would not be under consideration. Despite his past spats with Adams, Clay's logical choice was obvious. Their economic views were almost identical, and it would be easier for Clay to succeed a northeastern man than Jackson or the still incapacitated Crawford. On January 2, at a public dinner for the visiting Marquis de Lafayette, a speech by Mercer "enchained the attention" of all but Clay and Adams, who agreed to hold a private conversation in the near future. A week later, Clay called on Adams, and for three hours they discussed the election. Clay stated that he would soon come out for Adams. Probably no formal deal was made, but then none had to be.[57]

Clay well knew what his future held when Mercer and McLane invited him, along with Jackson and Adams, to a dinner at their mess. Yet he greatly enjoyed the power he temporarily wielded. When he found a vacant chair between Jackson and Adams he took it, saying: "Since you are both so near the chair, but neither can occupy it, I will slip in between you." "Banquo yet lives," retorted the old general.[58]

On February 9, 1825, the House met. The crucial New York delegation was tied, 17 to 17, and both sides thus fell upon the weak and wavering Stephen Van Rensselaer. As a member of the Union Tavern mess, Van Rensselaer was thought by Van Buren to be securely in the Crawford camp. During the day the Magician, as well as McLane and a vacillating Mercer, who put aside their mutual dislike long enough to cooperate, urged Van Rensselaer to hold firm. But Clay and Webster got to him last, and when the New Yorker emerged from the Speaker's room he cast his ballot for Adams. The effect was electric. The galleries rocked with both applause and hissing, and the House had to pause before Clay calmly pronounced Adams the winner.[59]

With the election decided, Mercer made one last attempt to renew his resolution on the slave trade, first submitted five years before. In 1823 it had carried overwhelmingly. But when he brought it up two days before Adams's inauguration, the House refused even to consider it. It was an ominous sign for both Mercer and the incoming administration.[60]

The years that Mercer devoted to the slave trade had not been wasted. Despite their inability to come to an agreement, both the United States and Britain had proclaimed the slave trade piracy and a capital crime. And if the American Colonization Society was damaged by the heat of the Missouri debates—and the injury was slight—it was hardly because he had not done everything in his power to protect it. Yet the failure of the two nations to reach an accord was serious, and it allowed the international trade to exist for another half-century. Mercer was correct in placing much of the blame on Canning, for the British foreign secretary should have realized that American hostility to granting the right of search in its waters was natural in light of England's behavior just a decade before. The United States, as Mercer argued, was capable of searching its own coasts; the English navy could have made good use of its right of search on the African shore.[61]

Adams also carried a share of the blame. The secretary, as Mercer later observed, "laid the foundation of the rejection of the convention." Adams opposed giving England the necessary right until it was too late. He changed his position, probably for political reasons, only when the election was close. And by suddenly supporting the idea he allowed Van Buren and the Crawfordites—who were far from innocent—to return to their natural position of frowning upon any discussion that touched on slavery. Still, in a few years Mercer had obtained federal funds for his society, and he had done more than any American since 1807 to crush the international slave trade. It was time to turn his "attention to another object after years of zealous labor in this interesting enterprise."[62]

Notes

ABBREVIATIONS

ACS   American Colonization Society
CFM   Charles Fenton Mercer
COCC   Chesapeake and Ohio Canal Company
DAB   *Dictionary of American Biography*, ed. Allen Johnson and Dumas Ma-
        lone, 21 vols., 1928–1936.
JQA   John Quincy Adams
JSH   *Journal of Southern History*
LC   Library of Congress
NJHS   New Jersey Historical Society
NYHS   New-York Historical Society
PRO, FO Great Britain, Public Record Office, Foreign Office
UVA   University of Virginia
VHS   Virginia Historical Society
VMHB   *Virginia Magazine of History and Biography*
VSL   Virginia State Library
WMQ   *William and Mary Quarterly*

1. Charles Fenton Mercer, *To the August Assembly Convened in Paris, to Confer on Restoring the Peace of Europe, the Memorial of the American Society for Colonizing in Africa the free people of colour of the United States* (London, 1856), 6.

2. *Annals of Congress* (Washington, D.C., 1820), 16th Cong., 1st sess., 734–36; *Richmond Enquirer*, December 21, 1819.

3. Charles M. Wiltse, *John C. Calhoun: Nationalist, 1782–1828* (New York, 1944), 196; Glover Moore, *The Missouri Controversy, 1819–1821* (Lexington, Ky., 1953), 63; *Annals of Congress*, 16th Cong., 1st sess., 226.

4. Patricia Hickin, "Gentle Agitator: Samuel M. Janney and the Antislavery Movement in Virginia, 1842–1851," *JSH* 37 (May 1971): 166, n. 181; John Tyler to Henry Curtis, February 5, 1820, John Tyler Papers, LC.

5. *Annals of Congress*, 16th Cong., 1st sess., 788, 812–13.

6. Louis McLane to Catherine McLane, March 9, 1818, Louis McLane Papers, University of Delaware; John A. Munroe, *Louis McLane: Federalist and Jacksonian* (New Brunswick, N.J., 1973), 98; John Randolph to James M. Garnett, January 29, 1820, John Randolph Papers, LC.

7. *National Intelligencer*, December 30, 1819; *Annals of Congress*, 16th Cong., 1st sess., 849. No breakdown of the vote is provided.

8. *National Messenger*, March 1, 1820.

9. *National Intelligencer*, March 4, 1820; *Annals of Congress*, 16th Cong., 1st sess., 1586; *Richmond Enquirer*, March 7, 1820.

10. *Annals of Congress*, 16th Cong., 1st sess., 1586–88; *National Messenger*, March 3, 1820.

11. Moore, *Missouri Controversy*, 104–5.

12. Francis Scott Key to William Meade, March 7, 1820, Key Letters, LC; CFM, Autobiographical Sketch, Mercer-Hunter Papers, VSL; CFM to John Hartwell Cocke, March 25, 1825, Cocke Collection, UVA.

13. *Annals of Congress*, 16th Cong., 1st sess., 2207–11; CFM, Autobiographical Sketch, Mercer-Hunter Papers; Charles Fenton Mercer, ed., *Slave Trade*, House Committee Report 348, Serial 201, Vol. 3 (Washington, D.C., 1830), 91.

14. Mercer, *To the August Assembly*, 4–5; Mercer, in *Third Annual Report* (Washington, D.C., 1820), 12–13; *Annals of Congress*, 16th Cong., 1st sess., 2216.

15. JQA Diary, January 4, 1839, in Charles Francis Adams, ed., *Memoirs of John*

Quincy Adams Comprising Parts of His Diary from 1795 to 1848, 12 vols. (Philadelphia, 1874–77), 10:88.

16. *Annals of Congress*, 16th Cong., 1st sess., 2236–37; *National Intelligencer*, May 13, 1820; *Richmond Enquirer*, May 16, 1820.

17. *Richmond Enquirer*, May 19, 1820; *Annals of Congress*, 16th Cong., 1st sess., 693–94; *National Intelligencer*, May 16, 1820; Mercer, ed., *Slave Trade*, 91–92.

18. CFM, Autobiographical Sketch, Mercer-Hunter Papers; *Annal of Congress*, 16th Cong., 1st sess., 697–700; *National Intelligencer*, May 16, 1820.

19. John Quincy Adams, *The Lives of James Madison and James Monroe* (Buffalo, 1850), 340.

20. John C. Calhoun to James Monroe, June 24, 1820, in Edwin M. Hemphill et al., eds., *The Papers of John C. Calhoun*, 16 vols. to date (Columbia, S.C., 1959–84), 5:217–19.

21. JQA Diary, October 26, 1820, in Adams, ed., *Memoirs*, 5:191–92.

22. *Annals of Congress*, 16th Cong., 2d sess., 476; CFM to Stratford Canning, May 23, 1824, PRO, FO, 352/9; *National Intelligencer*, December 5, 1820; Stratford Canning to JQA, December 20, 1820, in Mercer, ed., *Slave Trade*, 106–7; JQA Diary, December 18, 1820, in Adams, ed., *Memoirs*, 5:214.

23. *Annals of Congress*, 16th Cong., 2d sess., 669–70; *National Messenger*, December 13, 1820.

24. *Annals of Congress*, 16th Cong., 2d sess., 743.

25. Ibid., 1064–71.

26. *National Messenger*, February 28, 1821; *Annals of Congress*, 16th Cong., 2d sess., 1239–40.

27. *National Intelligencer*, August 11, 1821.

28. Moore, *Missouri Controversy*, 119, 347–48.

29. Adams, *Lives of Madison and Monroe*, 350.

30. Henry Warfield to Henry Clay, May 30, 1822, in James F. Hopkins et al., eds., *The Papers of Henry Clay*, 8 vols. to date (Lexington, Ky., 1959–85), 3:210; John Niven, *Martin Van Buren: The Romantic Age of American Politics* (New York, 1983), 117; Louis McLane to Catherine McLane, March 18, 1822, McLane Papers.

31. *Annals of Congress* (Washington, D.C., 1822), 17th Cong., 1st sess., 718–19; James Monroe to CFM, February 1, 1822, CFM Papers, NJHS.

32. *Annals of Congress*, 17th Cong., 1st sess., 1535–38. Adams wrote that Canning had told him that Mercer was "all for" exchanging the right of search. See JQA Diary, June 4, 1823, in Adams, ed., *Memoirs*, 6:140.

33. Samuel Flagg Bemis, *John Quincy Adams*, 2 vols. (New York, 1950–56), 1:426.

34. CFM to Rufus King, April 22, 1825, CFM Papers, NYHS; William Wilberforce to Richard Rush, November 5, 1823, Richard Rush Papers, LC; Stratford Canning to George Canning, February 8, 1823, PRO, FO (copy in Series 5, 175, LC).

35. Stratford Canning to JQA, January 29, 1823, PRO, FO.

36. *Annals of Congress*, 17th Cong., 2d sess., 928; *Resolution Submitted by Mr. Mercer*, February 10, 1823 (N.p., n.d.); Stratford Canning to George Canning, March 10, 1823, PRO, FO (copy in Series 5, 175, LC).

37. Stratford Canning to George Canning, March 10, 1823, PRO, FO (copy in Series 5, 175, LC); *Annals of Congress*, 17th Cong., 2d sess., 1147–55.

38. JQA Diary, June 4, 5, 1823, in Adams, ed., *Memoirs*, 6:150, 140–41.

39. JQA to Stratford Canning, March 31, 1823, in *American State Papers, Foreign Relations*, 6 vols. (Washington, D.C., 1832–59), 5:328; JQA to Stratford Canning, June 24, 1823, PRO, FO, 352/8. Bemis, *Adams*, 1:428, gives Adams far too much credit by claiming it was his idea to make the trade piracy under international law. Betty Fladeland, *Men and Brothers: Anglo-American Antislavery Cooperation* (Urbana, 1972), 154, n. 30, correctly notes that Mercer "was far ahead of Adams in this."

40. Robert V. Remini, *Martin Van Buren and the Making of the Democratic Party* (New York, 1970), 43; George Dangerfield, *The Era of Good Feelings* (New York, 1952), 295; Adams, *Lives of Madison and Monroe*, 426–28.

41. William Nisbet Chambers, *Old Bullion Benton, Senator from the New West: Thomas Hart Benton, 1782–1858* (1956; rpt. New York, 1970), 118; CFM to John Hartwell Cocke, March 25, 1825, Cocke Collection.

42. CFM to William Gaston, May 6, 1824, Gaston Papers, University of North Carolina, Chapel Hill.

43. Charles Fenton Mercer, *An Address to the American Colonization Society at their 36th Annual Meeting* (Geneva [Switzerland], 1854), 2; CFM to William Gaston, May 6, 1824, Gaston Papers; *National Intelligencer*, February 14, 1824.

44. Niven, *Van Buren*, 14; *National Intelligencer*, February 11, 16, 1824; CFM to William Gaston, May 6, 1824, Gaston Papers.

45. *Annals of Congress* (Washington, D.C., 1824), 18th Cong., 1st sess., 1204.

46. Convention, March 13, 1824, *American State Papers, Foreign Relations*, 5:319–24; Act of Parliament, March 31, 1824, in *Register of Debates in Congress* (Washington, D.C., 1824), 18th Cong., 2d sess., 18–19.

47. JQA Diary, May 7, 1824, in Adams, ed., *Memoirs*, 6:322–23.

48. P. J. Staudenraus, *The African Colonization Movement* (New York, 1961), 79; James Monroe to the Senate, Executive Session, May 8, 1824, *American State Papers, Foreign Relations*, 5:341, 360. Chase C. Mooney, *William H. Crawford, 1772–1834* (Lexington, Ky., 1953), 191, attributes Crawford's strange claim to illness, not to politics. My view is the latter.

49. CFM to Stratford Canning, May 23, 1824, PRO, FO, 352/9; JQA Diary, May 12, 14, 18, 1824, in Adams, ed., *Memoirs*, 6:328–29, 338; Henry Addington to George Canning, May 21, 1824, PRO, FO (copy in Series 5, 185, LC).

50. Henry Addington to George Canning, May 29, 1824, PRO, FO (copy in Series 5, 185, LC); Senate session, May 21, 1824, *American State Papers, Foreign Relations*, 5:361–62; *Register of Debates*, 18th Cong., 2d sess., 22.

51. CFM to Stratford Canning, May 23, 1824, PRO, FO, 352/9; CFM to Rufus King, May 25, 1824 (misdated 1825), CFM Papers, NYHS.

52. Mercer, *Address*, 21; CFM, Autobiographical Sketch, Mercer-Hunter Papers; CFM to Stratford Canning, May 25, 1824 (misdated 1825), PRO, FO, 352/9; JQA Diary, May 26, 1824, in Adams, ed., *Memoirs*, 6:357.

53. CFM to Stratford Canning, May 23, 1824, PRO, FO, 352/9; Henry Addington to George Canning, May 21, 1824, PRO, FO (copy in Series 5, 185, LC).

54. JQA Diary, May 27, 1824, in Adams, ed., *Memoirs*, 6:359–63.

55. Richard Rush to JQA, August 9, 1824, *American State Papers, Foreign Relations*, 5:364; CFM, Autobiographical Sketch, Mercer-Hunter Papers; George Canning to Richard Rush, August 27, 1824, in *Register of Debates*, 18th Cong., 2d sess., 24.

56. Glyndon G. Van Deusen, *The Life of Henry Clay*, (Boston, 1937), 188; John C. Fitzpatrick, ed., *The Autobiography of Martin Van Buren* (1920; rpt. New York, 1969), 146–47; *Register of Debates*, 18th Cong., 2d sess., 526; Harry Ammon, "The Richmond Junto," *VMHB* 61 (October 1953): 414.

57. Van Deusen, *Clay*, 185–86; Bemis, *Adams*, 2:39–40; Nathan Sergent, *Public Men and Events in the United States*, 2 vols. (1875; rpt. New York, 1970), 1:92.

58. Louis McLane to Catherine McLane, January 13, 1825, McLane Papers.

59. *Register of Debates*, 18th Cong., 2d sess., 527; Munroe, *McLane*, p. 183; *National Intelligencer*, February 10, 1825.

60. Mercer, *To the August Assembly*, 13; *Register of Debates*, 18th Cong., 2d sess., 697, 736.

61. Mercer, *To the August Assembly*, 13–14.

62. Mercer, *Address*, 20; CFM, Autobiographical Sketch, Mercer-Hunter Papers.

13

Rare Chance for Capitalists

Even before the last days of the battle over the slave trade convention, Mercer had turned his interests and energies to a new
endeavor: creating a canal between the Chesapeake and the Ohio
Valley. In some ways, his latest labor was a link to the old conservatism of his father, for the Ohio Company had envisioned a similar
trade route. But in more important ways it was simply a continuation at the national level of his efforts in behalf of internal
improvements while in the Virginia House. Indeed, the canal to the
West, a crucial part of the emerging American System, was almost
the perfect symbol for the fate of National Republicanism.

As the Ohio Company had understood, the Potomac was an
excellent route to the riches of the West. Geographically, it was the
shortest, and with the creation of the national capital on its banks,
it was also the most potentially lucrative. But the Ohio Company
was short of funds. A second attempt by the Potomac Company to
dredge the river without the aid of federal funds also failed. In
February 1823, a third effort was made, when the company obtained a new act of incorporation from Virginia under the title of
the Potomac Canal Company. Although the act did not require
federal approval, it did demand confirmation by the state of Maryland, and when it failed there it became inoperative in Virginia.[1]

Mercer watched this activity with keen interest. For a decade he
had dreamed of such a project, and the failure of the Potomac
Company presented him with a perfect opportunity. During the
same month in 1823 that the company requested a new act of
incorporation, he appeared uninvited at its board meeting and
presented a resolution stating that "the rights of the company
should be surrendered" to yet a fourth company upon liberal compensation. The new effort would be built on the charter of the old.

When Maryland refused to act, the company, facing failure and financial ruin, reluctantly passed Mercer's resolution.[2]

Such a project, Mercer well knew, would require federal assistance and thus tremendous public support. As a first step, he called for a public meeting to be held in Leesburg on August 25, 1823. There a central committee, chosen in advance, invited delegates from Pennsylvania, the district cities, Virginia, and Maryland to attend a larger convention in Washington set for November 6 and to devise a practical plan for a canal connecting the Chesapeake with the Ohio River. Mercer, William Mason, and three others were chosen as delegates to represent the Leesburg group.[3]

Mercer almost failed to attend his own convention. Just days before it was set to begin, as he was riding with Monroe on the president's farm, Mercer's horse bucked suddenly and threw the seasoned rider down a rocky slope. Miraculously, no bones were broken, and though in great pain, he gingerly mounted up five days later and rode toward Washington, where the convention was set to meet in the Supreme Court chamber.[4]

Nearly two hundred delegates from Maryland, Virginia, Pennsylvania, and Ohio had squeezed into the tiny chamber when Mercer finally arrived. Among them were the colonization junto of Caldwell, Jones, and Joseph Kent; Key was absent because of sickness. At noon on November 6 Mercer called the meeting to order. In accord with his growing desire to keep his name out of view, he moved that Kent act as chairman of the convention. He then put forth several resolutions. He urged that provisions be made to obtain the support of the state of Pennsylvania and the federal government. It would be necessary to rely on the latter for initial funding, and he recommended asking for an enormous loan of $2,750,000, to be repaid in four annual installments. Finally, he urged that a central committee of thirteen be appointed to advise on what specific measures should be adopted. The convention, essentially a democratic prop to gain crucial attention for his scheme, agreed.[5]

The next morning, several more delegates arrived. Mercer again addressed the convention, arguing that attempts to dredge the Potomac should be abandoned. Instead, he proposed a canal that would reach the point of "highest constant steam boat navigation" on the Ohio. A joint-stock company, the system of mixed enterprise long a favorite of his, should be formed to attain this goal. To stress the national nature of the undertaking, he suggested the grandiose name Union Canal. (It was later discovered that a short canal in Pennsylvania already bore this name.) He then moved that the resolutions be referred to a select committee of fifteen, which he would head. The convention again roared approval.[6]

To prepare the convention—and the nation because the proceedings were being reported in detail by the Washington press—for his spectacular scheme, Mercer launched into a long history of his dream. The delegates were told that their purpose was in accordance with the expectations of "more than half a century," which were, he offered expansively, "the most sanguine hopes, of more than a million of the American people." He admitted that his exact plans for the western section of the canal were vague but that such a connection was the greatest dream of his "hero," George Washington. Typically, Mercer then burdened his audience with an endless and detailed exposition on the canals of England, Holland, France, China, and Russia. The Union Canal, he concluded, would be greater than any of these and would provide for the "lasting happiness" of all Americans.[7]

Along with his lavish optimism, Mercer had to play the role of the hardheaded businessman. Many of the delegates, warmed by Mercer's patriotic fervor, generously wished to increase the compensation awarded to the old Potomac Company. (The indemnity Mercer had offered the company at its February meeting was less than that suggested by the Virginia legislature.) He well knew what financial difficulties his canal faced, and he had no wish to throw good money after bad. He had offered to assume the Potomac Company's charter only for expedience and was prepared to fall back on the "resort to a legal remedy" should the company resist his overture. He would pay no more.[8]

Saturday, November 8, was the last day of the convention. A bleary-eyed Mercer presented the resolutions that he and the select committee had worked almost through the night preparing. Six standing committees were to be created, one for each of the four states represented, one to memorialize Congress, and one to serve as a central committee. With a few minor modifications, the resolutions were adopted by the convention. Then, with the sun low in the fall sky, the convention adjourned. When Kent read the names of the members of the committees, no one was surprised that Mercer was chairman of the central committee.[9]

That evening the citizens of Washington gave a public dinner for the delegates at Brown's Hotel. About one hundred of the delegates attended, along with Adams and Calhoun, both then members of

Monroe's cabinet. No written toasts were prepared, but after the cloth was removed, numerous spontaneous sentiments were offered. Calhoun rose and proposed: "Canal navigation, may it receive the patronage and support of the nation." Adams characteristically mumbled that internal improvements were the "first duty" of the government. To Mercer's delight, he was toasted as "the eloquent and enlightened advocate of the best interests and true glory of his country." Flush with victory, Mercer allowed himself to be happy and decided to make a roaring good evening of it, and the press reported that the toasts were interspersed with the lusty singing of "a number of excellent songs." Something of a Puritan, Adams left following his toast.[10]

The next day, fatigued but cheery, Mercer called on Monroe. In the past, internal improvements had foundered on the president's few remaining Old Republican principles, and so Mercer had carefully structured his plan in accordance with Monroe's avowed policy. He read the resolutions to the president, and because no federal construction was required Monroe "entirely approved" of them. Monroe then read Mercer his essay on the subject, which the two men had disagreed on several years before, to demonstrate that he was willing to aid such a project if it met with his principles.[11]

Less than a month later, on December 2, Monroe virtually endorsed the project in his annual message. The president asserted that a connection of the Chesapeake and the Ohio waters would be of great benefit to the nation, and he reiterated his belief that Congress had the right to appropriate money for such a national project. He suggested a congressional report and commission to examine the idea of such a canal. Mercer was overjoyed. He wrote that Monroe "thus embraced . . . entire purpose of the Washington convention." It was true that on the surface Monroe adhered to his principles, but by applauding the expenditure of funds for the project he had made another in a long series of steps away from the agrarian agenda. Monroe's latest abandonment was made even more explicit when Mercer was named to chair the committee Monroe recommended.[12]

With Monroe's latest support for the emerging American System securely on public record, Mercer turned his tremendous energy to the states. His determination propelled the project, for even before the four state committees could act, he wrote and submitted bills for the incorporation of the Chesapeake and Ohio Canal Company to the legislatures of Virginia, Maryland, and Pennsylvania. The long and identical acts, which read more like contracts than legislation, held that building could not begin until the company had received the assent of each of the three states, the Potomac Company (which was to receive compensation of one dollar per share), and Congress.[13]

This phase of Mercer's program flew along at great speed. On December 30, 1823, the act was introduced in the Virginia legislature. Although it was only an act of incorporation, it met with considerable opposition from many Tidewater Republicans, who were unwilling to endorse such an agenda. But a majority of the legislature saw no harm in passing the act, and in less than a month, on January 27, the bill emerged from Senate. It passed only after a formal declaration that the clause requiring the assent of Congress could not be construed as an admission "of the much contested power of the Federal Government, to institute a System of Internal Improvement."[14]

At this point, Mercer's plans hit a snag. Just five days before, the Maryland House passed the bill of incorporation by a vote of 43 to 23. But the act was held up in the Senate, ironically, by Baltimore business interests, who feared that the city would be seriously injured if the canal should terminate in the District of Columbia. The bill did not emerge from the Maryland Senate, until the following December, and then with a peevish amendment stating that by confirming Virginia's act Maryland was not denying the constitutional power of the United States "to legislate on the subject of roads and canals."[15]

Pennsylvania continued to lag behind, but with the support of two states Mercer was prepared to bring the issue before the national stage. In late 1824 he introduced a bill requesting ratification of the acts of Maryland and Virginia and incorporation of the company in the District of Columbia and, he was careful to add, only there. Privately, Mercer pressed Monroe again to bestow his approval in his upcoming annual address. Although still supporting the canal, Calhoun urged the president to refrain from any further communications until after the report of the Board of Engineers had been completed. But Monroe would not be dissuaded. In his message he told Congress "that there is good cause to believe, that this great national object may be fully accomplished."[16]

With Monroe's public endorsement, Mercer moved to take up his bill on February 5, 1825. The motion was opposed by John Cocke of Tennessee but carried. The act was then taken up and read, and Mercer urged that it be engrossed for a third reading on the following Monday. Cocke again objected and insisted that the House was ill prepared to vote on the measure, which most likely would require the expenditure of large sums of money. Mercer broke in to reply that the bill was merely one of incorporation and "involved no appropriation of money whatever." Cocke was forced to admit that this was true, but he correctly contended that if the bill was passed Mercer would soon be back with additional legislation that would require funding. Mercer again interrupted, and the noisy debate ended only when it was moved to table the bill.[17]

In the meantime, Mercer received unexpected aid in the early release of the federal surveys and the accompanying Board of Engineers report, which Monroe hurried to Congress on February 14. The report made no cost estimates for the complete project, but it "confirmed the practicability of the contemplated" undertaking. But detractors such as John Cocke were not appeased; the canal's southern critics were less flexible in their states' rights philosophy than was the Virginia president. Cocke was again on his feet, prating that the report was based on "a principle to which he could never consent, as it interfered with the rights of the states, and had never been confided to Congress by the people."[18]

But Cocke was in the minority and for the same reason that the Tidewater Republicans were in the minority on the Virginia bill: Mercer's simple act of incorporation did not openly infringe on traditional Republican dogma. On February 24 Marcer discharged his bill from the committee of the whole, and the next day an enthusiastic Clay brought it to a vote. Hoping to force the remaining Old Republicans to stick to their ideals, Cocke refused to allow a voice vote. But the bill passed by an overwhelming 116 to 34, with a majority of Virginians voting yea.[19]

The Chesapeake and Ohio Canal bill crossed Monroe's desk on March 3, 1825, his last full day in office, and he signed it with a flourish. In doing so, he was delivering his final blow to the arcadia that he had spent the last eight years abandoning. He did so timidly and made younger, brighter men like Mercer come to him as much as he came to them, but Mercer preferred it that way. The president's tortured papers and long protests made his capitulation to the nation's business interests less obvious. Those interests were yet in an infant—and hence minority—state, and modern conservatism found it unwise to give them its open and unqualified support. Mercer would rather compromise with the ever-compromising Monroe, for that way he got most of what he wanted.[20]

But the period of shadowy support for the business community was at an end, for the next day was the inauguration of John Quincy Adams. At nine o'clock that morning, Mercer found himself in the midst of a mob at the door of the Capitol. The ladies were allowed in to sit, but he and other members of Congress had literally to fight their way into the House chamber. There Monroe sat beside the members of the Supreme Court. Just after noon, Adams, dressed in a plain black suit, arrived and made his way to the Speaker's chair. After taking his oath, he spoke for forty minutes, calling for a grand design of internal improvements but alluding only briefly to the slave trade and mentioning colonization not at all. Mercer was "a disappointed spectator." The new president "is no friend of the colonization Society," he grumbled. "There is no internal improvement; not the union of all the waters of the Globe, [that] is half so important to Virginia, as the removal of the coloured race from her bosom."[21]

Despite his unhappiness with Adams's inaugural speech, Mercer immediately began to edge closer to the new administration. This move was made easier when it became apparent that Adams had no intention of stopping the expenditures for Liberia. Adams wrote later that he allowed them to continue because he "did not feel at liberty to reverse the decision of Mr. Monroe." But politics was also involved. Adams's political skills were undeveloped, but he was capable of making pragmatic decisions. As a minority president, he could ill afford to alienate any large interest group, and as colonizationists tended to support other aspects of the American System, it was only logical that he should encourage their support.[22]

Mercer's move toward Adams was also made easier because he was less involved with colonization in 1825 than he had been two years before. When the society's board of managers requested that he undertake a speaking tour of the Northeast at their expense, he turned down the request. His work in behalf of the canal required so much time, he gruffly informed Ralph Gurley, the society's secretary, that he would not be able to frank all of the mail Gurley sent him. Mercer was unable to succeed "in any great purpose," he confided to Charles James Faulkner, "without increasing devotion to them, which is a state of mind utterly incompatible with much attention to more than one object at a time."[23]

Mercer found his opportunity to make a formal declaration for Adams on the night of April 13 at a public dinner held in the president's behalf at Clagett's Hotel in Alexandria. The steamboat *Surprise* carried Adams, Secretary of the Navy Samuel Southard, Attorney General William Wirt, and Mercer, the most vocal congressional supporter of internal improvements, downriver to the sound of saluting cannon. After the meal, Mercer rose and delivered an impromptu toast, commending Adams on the reappointment of Federalist sachem Rufus King as minister to Britain. Adams was surprised but pleased by this unexpected endorsement. If the new president would "not put down our african Colony or counteract our efforts on behalf of their remaining brethren in America," Mercer informed King, "he shall have the cooperation of one Virginia representative in aid of his administration."[24]

Mercer saw the president's appointment of King, whom the Virginian greatly admired, as a sign of good faith. Adams needed all the allies he could get, and his gestures toward former Federalists were logical and welcome to Mercer. This group, Adams wrote, had abandoned their party but "remained true to their instincts" and would flock to his program. It was a dangerous if necessary move, Adams realized, for it would rekindle the "fires of party." Mercer had no doubts as to the nature of the president's opposition: "Andrew Jackson appeared under the Jeffersonian Democratic auspices, and the champion of their policies and measures."[25]

Meanwhile, Mercer's canal suffered several critical setbacks. The Pennsylvania legislature waited until the end of the session to consider his bill of incorporation, so late that it was postponed. Backers of the project pointed out that the bill was "conclusive" in that planning for the eastern section could continue. Yet it was a bad omen, for the lack of a western terminus would cripple support for the canal in the other states.[26]

Hostility to the project was also growing in Virginia, in part brought on by fear of Adams's nationalistic program of liberty with power and in part by the ever-present distrust of Mercer among the Old Republicans. "Can you have the patience to endure this," Mercer screeched at colonizationist John Hartwell Cocke. "I, whom she has treated, as a stepmother, have not and will not while I breath my native air, and can raise a hand or voice in behalf on my native soil."[27]

Mercer received his first good news in several months when on May 16 the stockholders of the Potomac Company met at Semmes' Tavern and formally voted themselves out of existence. They unanimously agreed to accept Virginia's act of incorporation because the December 1823 bill was void without this assent. They also surrendered their charter to the Chesapeake and Ohio Canal Company, along with all their property, rights and privileges. The last official act of the company was a resolution to inform Congressman Mercer of that decision.[28]

The next evening the central committee met at Brown's Hotel. The portly Virginian briefly apprised the group of his actions since the November convention, which demonstrated the truth of Mercer's boast that he was the central committee. He gave the members copies of the acts of the Virginia and Maryland legislatures, the federal law of March 3, and the resolutions of the now defunct Potomac Company. All that was left to do, he told them, was to expedite the appointment of commissioners to allow for the subscription of stock of the new company. To this end, Mercer promised to write to Adams and the governors of Virginia and Maryland.[29]

The chairman of the central committee obviously did not have to be told that it would also be necessary to keep up a constant drumbeat in his native state were the canal ever to receive public funds. His job even included keeping a detailed head count of the friends of the canal in the Virginia legislature. "The present moment is deemed best, or delay till another year objectionable," Mercer counseled Cocke, lest the fifty favorable votes he counted on should diminish with the already sinking fortunes of the Adams administration.[30]

In the administration, the president and Secretary of War James Barbour were zealous in their desire to aid the canal. Even before Mercer could write to Adams and ask for the three commissioners required by the act of Congress, Barbour informed his old friend that three military and one civil engineer had been placed at the disposal of the board of internal improvements to survey and examine the proposed route. Barbour sent a fifth engineer to New York to examine the locks of the Erie Canal to ascertain "the probable cost of the construction of the canal."[31]

In his first annual message, Adams fully endorsed the project and brought Congress up to date on its progress. The board of engineers had completed the surveys and was preparing a full report. The president had chosen three commissioners to act with a like number to be named by each of the states. Foreign monarchs, he continued, "are advancing with gigantic strides in the career of public improvement." But we, Adams lectured, "fold up our arms and proclaim to the world that we are palsied, by the will of our constituents." Mercer must have shuddered as he listened to the message. Conservatism could ill afford such blunt language.[32]

As he worried over Adams's lack of political acumen, good news arrived in the passage of Mercer's act of incorporation by the Pennsylvania legislature in early February 1826. It passed, however, with the proviso that exactly one-half of any federal funds obtained would be devoted to the western section of the canal. Mercer was annoyed by this unexpected outburst of independence, although Pennsylvania's compliance freed him to ask the aid of the general government. And he was no longer thinking of a loan. On April 3 he offered a memorial to the House, requesting that the books of the company be opened and that Congress subscribe to an unnamed amount of stock. The petition was sent to the Committee of Roads and Canals, where, despite Mercer's best efforts, it suffered a quiet death.[33]

More bad news was to follow. Just days after his second annual message, Adams released the commissioners' report to Congress. Although it did not question the feasibility of the canal, it estimated its total cost at the crippling sum of $22 million. The eastern section alone, a 186-mile stretch from Georgetown to Cumberland, Maryland, was set at just over $8 million; Mercer had envisioned the entire project at $10 million. But Barbour had quietly leaked these estimates to Mercer in October. The Virginian quickly called another meeting of the central committee, which issued the call for a second convention. He also prepared a letter jointly signed by thirty-one other members of Congress from ten states, demanding a second survey by two new engineers. Adams was more than happy to oblige.[34]

The winter of 1826 was unusually severe, and deep drifts of snow were blowing up against the Capitol when the delegates, chattering with cold, made their way into the House chamber for the noon opening of the December 6 convention. Despite the weather, the second convention was as impressive as the first. More than 160 delegates, including Clay, Barbour, and Treasury Secretary Richard Rush, as well as the usual colonization junto of Jones, Key, Caldwell, and Bushrod Washington, were in attendance. The second meeting was better organized than the first. Shortly after Governor Joseph Kent returned to the chair, Mercer presented his finished report. To give the delegates time to digest the massive document, the convention adjourned.[35]

The next afternoon Mercer reported the progress made by the central committee, of which, he proudly remarked, he was "almost the only acting member." He recommended that the convention petition Maryland, Virginia, and Congress for a subscription of

stock. The motion was agreed to. There followed a wave of meaningless resolutions from the floor, all of which demonstrated that
only Mercer truly understood the project. Finally, he rose to move
that the convention adjourn. It had served its purpose by making it
appear that there was a great public groundswell for the project
regardless of the cost.[36]

That such a project should be surrounded by the trappings of
democracy is not curious, for Mercer had almost pioneered the
convention as a political tool in 1812. Properly organized and
controlled, a convention did not have to be any more democratic
than the old closed-door Federalist caucuses; the way Mercer's
floor managers forced the confused delegates to withdraw their
resolutions was ample proof of that. His conventions galvanized
and directed public support. "Our Canal," he gushed to Monroe, "is
once more, in a fair way towards the commencement." The success
of the meeting, he beamed, "surmounted, the unexpected obstacle
thrown in our way, by the extraordinary estimates."[37]

But Mercer was overly optimistic, for his canal, like most of
Adams's agenda, was either ignored or served as a catalyst for the
opposition. The entire American System, which was the rock the
administration was built on, appeared to place the government at
the service of special interests: urban over rural, industrialist over
small producer, and rich over poor. The coalition emerging around
the president cloaked itself in the soothing title of National Republican, but to its enemies it was old Federalism reborn. In truth,
it was a continuation of the new Federalism practiced more than a
decade before by Mercer and others on the state level; if it was neo-
Federalism, it was only because the same term could have been
used to describe Mercer's state policies.[38]

The most visible part of the American System during the Adams
years was internal improvements. The huge system of roads and
canals called for by the president in his first annual address, however, would aid primarily those large producers—in the South up-
country staple growers, in the North, manufacturers—whose
output was greater than could be sold locally. In 1826 there were
few in this group. Administration men did not admit the group was
so small, and Mercer insisted that canals would equally benefit all
sectors of what he relentlessly argued was a classless society. "With
this easy and rapid distribution, a nation may manufacture at one
or two points for the whole nation, and with small expense diffuse
them to all who consume."[39]

Despite such assurances, the program roused opposition from

plain farmers all across the nation. The administration promised that the system would be financed from the nation's surplus revenue, but critics correctly pointed out that there was no surplus revenue, and the system would either add to their tax burden or be achieved by raising the price of western land. Congress refused to accede to Adams's request; the most it would do was to invest in shares for occasional projects. Even this truncated "Rail Road & Canal mania," Randolph complained to Garnett, would ruin and bankrupt the country.[40]

To lead the opposition, the Radicals, as the old backers of Crawford continued to style themselves, turned to Andrew Jackson, although not before making sure that he was hostile to Adams's program. To unseat Adams, the Jacksonians and their chief tactician, Van Buren, created the most effective campaign organization yet devised on the national scene. It was run by an eighteen-member central committee in Nashville, with a series of state and local committees fanned out north and east. There was even a sizable Jackson committee in Loudoun County.[41]

The secretary of state, who had shot one man in a duel and attempted to perform a similar surgery on John Randolph for bringing up his unfortunate understanding with Adams, had proven himself a fighter, and he was "damned" if he was going to sit idly by while Van Buren pieced together a new majority party. But Clay could only do so much without the president's support, and Adams remained stubbornly antiparty. In the House, the golden-voiced Webster did his best to push through the administration's programs, but Adams disliked and distrusted Webster's easy morals and made no attempt to sustain his efforts.[42]

The president's son had a superior sense of political reality, and Charles Francis Adams did his best to turn the loose National Republican coalition into a party. Throughout 1826 and 1827 he organized long sessions to discuss party strategy with Mercer and other "men of our side." One of these meetings found Mercer, who was seated next to his host, in a petulant mood; Adams concluded that he would be of little help to his father. But by June 1872, when Adams dined with Mercer and James Barbour at Analostan Island in the middle of the Potomac, he had more than reversed his opinion of the Virginia congressman.[43]

As a result Mercer became the primary spokesman for the administration in the South. Even without these conferences such a connection was inevitable since for nearly two decades he had been closely identified with the economic program that the coalition adopted as its own. Not surprisingly, Adams's supporters asked Mercer for aid in procuring political appointments. Such activity, however, also resulted, at least in his eyes, in the "continued and bitter persecution" of him in his home state. Because he did not relish being "farther hunted down" by the Jacksonians, he began to request that his friends burn his political letters.[44]

The attempts by the friends of Adams to organize did little good, and the off-year elections turned both houses of Congress over to the Jacksonians. As usual, Mercer faced no opposition, but he was mortified by the defeat of his old friend Alfred Powell. At least, Clay informed Webster, Mercer's seat was safe as long as he cared to have it.[45]

But the Adams men refused to give way easily. In January 1828, friends of the coalition in Virginia made a valiant attempt to win the state for the president. For five days, more than two hundred delegates attended a "monster" "Anti-Jackson Convention" in Richmond, organized by Mercer's friend Francis T. Brooke and the recently defeated Alfred Powell. Congress was still in session so Mercer declined to attend; only the Virginia constitutional convention would lead the conscientious representative to request a leave of absence from his constituents. The Richmond convention did, however, put Mercer's arguments from his Seminole War pamphlet to good use in the keynote address (even though Adams had defended the general's Florida invasion). Finally, the convention formally endorsed the ticket of Adams and Rush and named a slate of electors. Monroe was the Loudoun elector, although the former president wearily announced that he wished to remain netural, as befitting a past executive.[46]

This response from the man who had begun the program that Adams was embracing with such ardor was far from comforting. The canal campaign, meanwhile, continued. The commissioners appointed in June 1825 had opened books for the subscription of stock on the first day of the previous October. The state of Maryland and the corporation of Alexandria promptly bought nearly a million dollars worth of stock, although their purchase was conditional on a subscription by the federal government. It was understood that Mercer would presently introduce such a bill in the House, after which the commissioners would allow the formal organization of the company and the election of officers.[47]

These necessary preliminaries accomplished, Mercer rose on January 2 to introduce his bill. He requested that the republic purchase ten thousand shares of canal stock at a cost of $1 million.

The act demonstrated anew the interlocking nature of the American system, for the stock was to be purchased from the dividends that accrued to the government from its holdings in the Bank of the United States. In turn, the purchase allowed the treasury secretary to vote for the president and directors of the company. In addition to its dividends from the stock, the government would receive a proportion of the tolls collected commensurate to its share of stock.[48]

The chances for passage of Mercer's bill improved tremendously five days later with the release of the second survey report to the Committee on Roads and Canals. The paper, which was turned over to the entire House on March 15, again estimated the total cost at $22 million, not including land purchases and condemnations. The estimate for the crucial eastern section, however, was reduced from $8 million to well under $5 million.[49]

Considerable opposition to the bill still remained. New York had taxed itself greatly to complete the Erie Canal and was unwilling to use its own wealth to aid an enterprise that would produce competition. Urban workers feared that the program of internal improvements of which Mercer's canal was a conspicuous part would be financed by raising the price of western land, thus crowding the eastern labor pool and driving down already meager wages. The entire concept, which reeked of forced industrialization, deeply disturbed the agrarian souls of most Americans.[50]

But the second report was the deciding factor. On May 9 Mercer brought his bill to the floor. With little debate, the House approved the purchase of stock by a vote of 107 to 71. The Virginia delegation, again expressing disdain for an active government and the society envisioned by such a program, split two to one against the measure. Several days later, the bill passed the Senate.[51]

The next step was to elect the president and director of the company. As with the National Bank, the president had a great deal of influence in the choice, and Adams, despite his scorn of parties, was capable of making political decisions. On June 3 he met with Rush, and both agreed that the only suitable person was Mercer. The six directors would be chosen from each of the district cities and states involved. But the following day the treasury secretary returned, offering instead the name of Albert Gallatin from the key state of Pennsylvania. Adams exploded; he would "not listen to the mention of any other name" but Mercer's. It was "due to him, and could not without gross injustice be diverted from him," the president snapped. Besides, Adams was in serious trouble in Virginia;

Pennsylvania might be held in line by his support for the Philadelphia bank.[52]

To honor the yet unofficial president of the canal, a public dinner was given in Leesburg on June 10. The banquet was organized by John McCarty, the brother-in-law of the unfortunate Mason. The gathering was jovial, and "many good toasts were drunk," but depression had again seized Mercer, this time worse than ever. He gamely sat through the toasts to himself, Adams, colonization, and the tariff, then rose to address his friends. His constituents were essential to his success, he observed, speaking in the third person, "for however cherished at home, he is, abroad [in Virginia], the selected victim of an injustice." He caught himself and paused. "Forgive the painful allusion," he stammered, referring to his recent ugly newspaper war with Benjamin Watkins Leigh over a state constitutional convention. Again he faltered. With difficulty he brought himself under control to the point that he was able to raise his glass and stammer: "Popular education, a renewed prosperity to the county of Loudoun, and to the commonwealth of Virginia." He then mumbled something about looking ahead to "better times" and sat down. Even in his moment of triumph he could not be happy.[53]

A week later Secretary Rush bustled into the president's office to tell him that all was set for the next day's election. Mercer was to be president, and colonizationists Kent and Walter Smith were to be two of the directors. Adams's plan was formalized the following morning when the stockholders met in Washington's city hall. With his election final, Mercer took charge of the meeting. The total capitalization of the company, counting federal subscription, stood just under $4 million. Unlike Maryland, Virginia had not yet voted to purchase a single share of stock.[54]

A combination groundbreaking ceremony and political rally was set for Independence Day. Just before eight in the morning Adams met Mercer at the Union Hotel, where the directors, heads of departments, members of Congress, and foreign ministers had already congregated. At the top of the hour the procession moved down Bridge Street to the "excellent music" of a marine band. Amid the cheers of the crowd on the wharf they boarded the steamboat *Surprise,* which slowly moved up the Potomac. Those who could not find seats on any of the barges being towed lazily upriver followed along on the banks, slipping and falling over the smooth rocks. By the time the procession stopped just inside the Maryland border, the crowd numbered perhaps ten thousand. The throng pushed its way toward the president's party, leaving a hollow space for the ceremony; hundreds of boys hung from the umbrageous trees that bordered the river.[55]

Just at that moment the sun broke out from behind the clouds, and the crowd fell silent. The mayor of Georgetown stepped forward and handed Mercer the "consecrated instrument," a shovel. Mercer turned to Adams and held out the "humble instrument of rural labor, a symbol of the favorite occupation of our countrymen." May this shovel, he shouted, "prove the precursor, to our beloved country, of improved agriculture, of multiplied and diversified arts, of extended commerce and navigation."[56]

Adams took the shovel. Normally an appallingly poor public speaker, the president stepped forward and delivered a short address with unusual animation and energy. He began with the requisite classical allusions to demonstrate the precedence and tradition behind the project, then blossomed into a powerful political oration. Internal improvements, Adams argued, following Mercer's lead, would aid all segments of the economy and all classes in society, the farmer most of all. With that, Adams bent to his work. To his dismay, the shovel struck a root just below the surface. He tried again to no avail. Suddenly he threw off his coat and rolled up his sleeves, and this time he managed to raise a shovelful of earth. The audience was thrilled—here was the president as common man—and "a general shout burst forth." Adams then returned the shovel to Mercer, who took his turn digging. If he did not take off his coat, it was only because he did not wish to steal the president's glory, for it was precisely the symbolism he gloried in.[57]

Jacksonians were as unimpressed with the political spectacle as they were with the massive project. Mercer's performance at the groundbreaking was bitterly lampooned in song in the *Washington Columbian*, a Democratic paper. "Why Massa Charles Fenton Mercer," the slave dialect song began, "Massa Charles tell 'em dig grate long ditch. All same creek, full o' water, flote down kenne, make plente rich."[58]

Worse still, Mercer's victory was transient. Later in the month Mercer rode south as one of 170 delegates to the Charlottesville convention, designed to recommend a cohesive system of internal improvements to the state. Already there were Secretary of War Barbour, Monroe, Marshall, and Madison. As one of the central committee of thirteen, Mercer helped write eight resolutions, which suggested money for vitually every road, river, and canal in Virginia. The third resolution urged the state to purchase one-half million dollars worth of stock in the Chesapeake and Ohio Company. When the resolutions reached the floor, a motion was made to strike out the third. Mercer shouted for votes, but the motion carried in a close vote. Mercer, Monroe, and Francis T. Brooke all voted with the minority. "Reliance has always been had on the cooperation of Virginia," he admitted sadly. Stubbornly, he refused to concede defeat. The "late proceedings of the Charlottesville Convention do not discourage the hope of success in that quarter."[59]

Mercer's spirits continued to droop as the summer wore on and it became clear that Jackson would be victorious. Adams had long lost all hope of winning, although as late as October 1828 Clay still dreamed that the administration would be returned to office. Mercer was dismayed at the way the campaign was being run and at how poor a candidate Adams had turned out to be. The "late anti-Jackson convention," he complained to Monroe, had attacked the Hero as an ignorant military chieftain. It failed to convince Virginians to accept the American System. Mercer did not "believe the liberties of this country involved, in the issue of this contest," and he suspected that few others believed such an argument. And Adams, aside from the groundbreaking, was so unattractive to most of the country that Mercer almost wished he could choose "a third [candidate] of better qualifications."[60]

As the election returns slowly trickled in during the fall, Mercer knew he had guessed right. Jackson captured the West, Northwest, and South, receiving 178 electoral votes to Adams's meager 83. In the popular vote, Adams did better because of the heavy eastern majorities provided by the merchant, manufacturing, and landed groups. In Virginia, Adams carried the old Federalist districts of the upper Potomac—including Loudoun County—and the west, regions that did not share the Tidewater's notorious disdain for internal improvements or aid to manufactures.[61]

With the defeat of the American System at the hands of the people, the outgoing administration had nowhere to turn for support but abroad. It was decided that Richard Rush, the treasury secretary and vice-presidential candidate, would travel to Europe in the hope of obtaining subscribers and loans for the canal. His last annual report therefore was written with Europe in mind. "I intend to send it to London and Amsterdam," he informed Mercer, "where I will take care that it gets to the hands of the proper capitalists and bankers, hoping that it may prove no useless herald in advance of me." Rush also devoted much of his report to testifying "to the value" of the bank, which he suspected would come under fire from the new president.[62]

Well might Rush and Mercer be concerned. On March 4, 1929, nearly twenty thousand people poured into Washington to see their president take the oath of office, a mob scene that horrified conservatives. "I never saw any thing like it before," a disgusted Webster remarked. "Persons have come 500 miles to see Genl Jackson; & they really seem to think that the Country is rescued from some dreadful danger."[63]

John Quincy Adams, like his father, declined to attend the inaugural of his successor. The previous evening he had removed himself to Commodore David Porter's Meridian Hill home and placed a card in the paper saying that his "friends" might visit him there if they wished. "Very few, therefore, came out," Adams dryly observed. Indeed, only three came: Monroe's daughter Eliza Hay, squired by Mercer and colonizationist Richard Peters.[64]

Although Mercer surely did not realize it, his career was at its peak. He would rise no higher politically, and he would never again be as successful legislatively. Nor did he realize that his canal was a fitting symbol of the Adams years. Costly, ambitious, and overblown, the project was out of step with the gentle rhythms of the agrarian republic. Whether yeoman farmer or urban laborer, the public saw both the canal and the administration as serving only the interests of the wealthy. For all his talk about the canal serving the farmer, Adams was correctly perceived as turning the country over to the business community. His administration was, to borrow the words of an advertisement for property fronting the Chesapeake and Ohio Canal, a "rare chance for Capitalists." The chance, however, had passed.[65]

Notes

ABBREVIATIONS

ACS	American Colonization Society
CFM	Charles Fenton Mercer
COCC	Chesapeake and Ohio Canal Company
DAB	*Dictionary of American Biography*, ed. Allen Johnson and Dumas Malone, 21 vols., 1928–1936.
JQA	John Quincy Adams
JSH	*Journal of Southern History*
LC	Library of Congress
NJHS	New Jersey Historical Society

NYHS   New-York Historical Society
PRO, FO   Great Britain, Public Record Office, Foreign Office
UVA   University of Virginia
VHS   Virginia Historical Society
VMHB   *Virginia Magazine of History and Biography*
VSL   Virginia State Library
WMQ   *William and Mary Quarterly*

1. Walter S. Sanderlin, *The Great National Project: A History of the Chesapeake and Ohio Canal* (1946; rpt. New York, 1976), 46–51; Charles Fenton Mercer, *Chesapeake and Ohio Canal*, House Committee Report 414, Serial 262, Vol. 3 (Washington, 1834), 4.

2. Charles Fenton Mercer, *Speech of Mr. C. F. Mercer, on the Subject of the Chesapeake and Ohio Canal, Delivered in the Convention of Delegates* (Washington, D.C., 1823), 9; CFM to Claiborne W. Gooch, September 26, 1823, Gooch Papers, VHS.

3. CFM, Autobiographical Sketch, Mercer-Hunter Papers, VSL; Mercer, *Speech on the Chesapeake and Ohio Canal*, 4, 67.

4. CFM, Autobiographical Sketch, Mercer-Hunter Papers; *National Intelligencer*, November 4, 6, 1823.

5. *Proceedings of the Chesapeake and Ohio Canal Convention* (Washington, D.C., 1827), 3–6; *National Intelligencer*, November 7, 1823; *Alexanderia Gazette*, November 11, 1823; *Niles' Weekly Register*, November 15, 1823, pp. 173–74.

6. *Proceedings*, 6–12; *National Intelligencer*, November 8, 1823.

7. *National Intelligencer*, November 8, 1823; Mercer, *Speech*, 3–30.

8. Mercer, *Speech*, 9–10.

9. *Proceedings*, 12–17; *National Intelligencer*, November 10, 1823; *Niles' Weekly Register*, November 15, 1823, p. 175.

10. *National Intelligencer*, November 10, 1823; *Niles' Weekly Register*, November 15, 1823, p. 175.

11. CFM to Claiborne W. Gooch, September 26, 1823, Gooch Papers.

12. *Annals of Congress*, (Washington, D.C., 1824), 18th Cong., 1st sess., 21, 800; Mercer, *Speech on the Chesapeake and Ohio Canal*, 5.

13. Mercer, *Speech on the Chesapeake and Ohio Canal*, 5; *Acts of Virginia, Maryland, and Pennsylvania, and of the Congress of the United States, in Relation to the Chesapeake & Ohio Canal Company* (Washington, D.C., 1828), 2–15.

14. *National Intelligencer*, January 28, 1824; Charles Fenton Mercer, "Report of the Central Canal Committee," December 6, 1826, in *Proceedings*, 38.

15. *National Intelligencer*, January 28, February 11, 1824; *Acts*, 15–16; Mercer, "Report," in *Proceedings*, 39.

16. *Acts*, 16–17; Mercer, "Report," in *Proceedings*, 39; John C. Calhoun to James Monroe, September 11, 1824, in Edwin W. et al., eds., Hemphill (Washington, D.C., 1825), *The Papers of John C. Calhoun*, 16 vols. to date (Columbia, S.C., 1959–84), 9:309–10; *Register of Debates*, 18th Cong., 2d Sess., app., 5.

17. *National Intelligencer*, February 7, 1825; *Register of Debates*, 18th Cong., 2nd sess., 487.

18. Mercer, *Speech on the Chesapeake and Ohio Canal*, 6; *Register of Debates*, 18th Cong., 2nd sess., 590.

19. *Register of Debates*, 18th Cong., 2d sess., 681–83, 687; *National Intelligencer*, February 26, 1825.

20. *Register of Debates*, 18th Cong., 2d sess., app., 105.

21. *National Intelligencer*, extra ed., March 4, 1925; CFM to John Hartwell Cocke, March 25, 1825, Cocke Collection, UVA.

22. JQA Diary, February 2, 1831, in Charles Francis Adams, ed., *Memoirs of John*

Quincy Adams Comprising Parts of His Diary from 1795 to 1848, 12 vols. (Philadelphia, 1874–77, 8:309.

23. Board of Managers, Minutes, May 10, 1825; CFM to Ralph R. Gurley, May 31, 1828, both in ACS Papers, LC; CFM to Charles James Faulkner, December 22, 1832, Faulkner Family Papers, VHS.

24. *National Intelligencer*, April 16 1825; CFM to Rufus King, April 22, 1825, CFM Papers, NYHS.

25. John Quincy Adams, *Lives of James Madison and James Monroe*, (Buffalo, 1850), 431; Charles Fenton Mercer, *An Exposition of the Weakness and Inefficiency of the Government of the United States of North America* (N.p., 1845), 258.

26. *National Intelligencer*, March 31, 1825.

27. CFM to John Hartwell Cocke, March 25, 1825, Cocke Collection.

28. *National Intelligencer*, May 18, 1825; *Niles' Weekly Register*, June 4, 1825, p. 218; *Acts*, pp. 42–43; Mercer, "Report," in *Proceedings*, 39.

29. *Niles' Weekly Register*, June 4, 1825, p. 218; *National Intelligencer*, May 20, 1825.

30. CFM to John Hartwell Cocke, August 29, 1825, Cocke Collection.

31. CFM to JQA, May 19, 1825, Adams Family Papers, Massachusetts Historical Society; Richard Rush to CFM, November 20, 1828, Rush Papers, LC; James Barbour to CFM, May 9, 1925, in *Niles' Weekly Register*, June 4, 1825, p. 219.

32. *Register of Debates*, 19th Cong., 1st sess., 2–8.

33. *Acts*, 35–38; *Register of Debates*, 19th Cong., 1st sess., 2005.

34. *National Intelligencer*, December 8, 1826; General Bernard to Alexander Macomb, March 21, 1826, in *Proceedings*, 61; Mercer, *Speech on the Chesapeake and Ohio Canal*, 8.

35. *National Intelligencer*, December 7, 1826; *Proceedings*, 19–31; CFM, Autobiographical Sketch, Mercer-Hunter Papers, VSL. Mercer makes a rare error in his autobiography by placing the second convention in December 1827.

36. *Proceedings*, 31–36; CFM, Autobiographical Sketch, Mercer-Hunter Papers.

37. CFM to James Monroe, December 21, 1826, Monroe Papers, UVA.

38. George Dangerfield, *The Era of Good Feelings* (New York, 1952), applies the title "Neo-Federalist" to the National Republican party, saying that "the old Federalist emphasis on commercial capital had been replaced by a new emphasis on industrial capital," thereby ignoring a similar emphasis demonstrated by the later Federalists.

39. Robert F. Dalzell, Jr., *Daniel Webster and the Trial of American Nationalism, 1843–1852* (New York, 1972), 33; Mercer, *Exposition*, 359.

40. William Nisbet Chambers, *Old Bullion Benton, Senator from the New West: Thomas Hart Benton, 1782–1858* (1956; rpt. New York, 1970), 119; Samuel Flagg Bemis, *John Quincy Adams*, 2 vols. (New York, 1950–56), 14; John Randolph to James M. Garnett, November 24, 1832, Randolph Papers, LC.

41. Keith I. Polakoff, *Political Parties in American History* (New York, 1981), 112; *Richmond Enquirer*, January 5, 1828.

42. Robert V. Remini, *Martin Van Buren and the Making of the Democratic Party* (New York, 1970), 148; Bemis, *Adams*, 2:73; Robert V. Remini, *The Election of Andrew Jackson* (Philadelphia, 1963), 36.

43. Charles Francis Adams Diary, May 27, December 15, June 19, 1827, in L. H. Butterfield et al., eds., *Diary of Charles Francis Adams*, 6 vols. (Cambridge, Mass., 1964–74), 2:46, 93, 138. Analostan Island is now Theodore Roosevelt Island.

44. Philip Lightfoot to CFM, July 23, 1828, Mercer Family Papers, VHS; CFM to Timothy Pickering, February 8, 1827, Pickering Papers, LC. This recipient obviously did not carry out Mercer's request "to destroy this letter."

45. JQA Diary, May 1, 1827, in Adams, ed., *Memoirs*, 7:266; CFM to James Monroe, December 7, 1827, Monroe Papers, LC; Henry Clay to Daniel Webster,

April 20, 1827, in Charles M. Wiltse et al., eds. *The Papers of Daniel Webster,* 7 vols. to date, (Hanover, N.H., 1974–86), 2:193–94.

46. *Proceedings of the Anti-Jackson Convention Held at the Capitol in the City of Richmond* (Richmond, 1828), 15–19; *Richmond Enquirer,* January 10, 1828; Francis T. Brooke to Henry Clay, January 9, 1828, in James F. Hopkins et al., eds., *The Papers of Henry Clay,* 8 vols. to date (Lexington, Ky. 1959–85), 7:23–25; James Monroe to Francis T. Brooke, February 21, 1828, in Stanislaus M. Hamilton, ed., *The Writings of James Monroe,* 7 vols. (New York, 1898–1903), 7:153–54.

47. Mercer, *Speech on the Chesapeake and Ohio Canal,* 13–14.

48. *Register of Debates,* 20th Cong., 1st sess., 890–91; *Acts,* 48.

49. Mary W. M. Hargreaves, *The Presidency of John Quincy Adams* (Lawrence, 1985), 178; Mercer, *Speech on the Chesapeake and Ohio Canal,* 8.

50. John Niven, *Martin Van Buren: The Romantic Age of American Politics* (New York, 1983), 164; Dangerfield, *Era of Good Feelings,* 352.

51. CFM, Autobiographical Sketch, Mercer-Hunter Papers; *Register of Debates,* 20th Cong., 1st sess., 2639.

52. Daniel Walker Howe, *The Political Culture of the American Whigs* (Chicago, 1979), 46–47, draws the important distinction between Adams as an antiparty and political man; JQA Diary, June 3, 4, 1828, in Adams, ed., *Memoirs,* 8:23–24, 26–27.

53. *Niles' Weekly Register,* June 28, 1828.

54. JQA Diary, June 19, 1828, in Adams, ed., *Memoirs,* 8:37; *Niles' Weekly Register,* June 28, 1828; Mercer, *Speech on the Chesapeake and Ohio Canal,* 14.

55. JQA Diary, July 4, 1828, in Adams, ed., *Memoirs,* 8:49–50; *Niles's Weekly Register,* July 12, 1828, p. 326.

56. *National Intelligencer,* July 7, 1828; *Niles' Weekly Register,* July 12, 1828, p. 326.

57. JQA Diary, July 4, 1828, in Adams, ed., *Memoirs,* 8:50; Bemis, *Adams,* 2:102, writes that the canal speech "was the nearest to an outright political speech that he ever made in his life."

58. *Washington Columbian, District Advertiser,* July 4, 1828.

59. *National Intelligencer,* July 21, 25, 1928; CFM to Joseph Gales, August 25, 1828, COCC, National Archives.

60. Bemis, *Adams,* 2:112; Henry Clay to Robert P. Letcher, October 20, 1828, in Hopkins, ed., *Papers of Clay,* 7:510; CFM to James Monroe, February 2, 1828, Monroe Papers, LC.

61. Remini, *Van Buren,* 195; James H. Broussard, *The Southern Federalists, 1800–1816* (Baton Rouge, 1978), 193; Harry Ammon, "The Richmond Junto," *VMHB* 61 (October 1953): 410.

62. Richard Rush to CFM, December 8, 1828, Rush Papers, LC.

63. Daniel Webster to Achsah P. Webster, March 4, 1829, in Wiltse, ed., *Papers of Webster,* 2:405–6.

64. JQA Diary, March 4, 1829, in Adams, ed., *Memoirs,* 8:105.

65. *National Intelligencer,* February 28, 1825.

14

The Times Are Changed

There were some parts of his life that Charles Fenton Mercer would have been glad to relive; he often spoke of his college days in this way. One episode of which he later said little was his involvement in the Virginia constitutional convention of 1829–30. His reticence was not surprising, for although his efforts initially brought him some triumph, they ended in a staggering defeat, and the abuse heaped upon him during these days must have been painful to remember. Yet it is also ironic, for he played a central role in forcing the convention upon his reluctant state. Mercer's motivation provided perhaps the best example—as well as best illustrated the limits—of conservative reform. For if "he must swallow either arsenic or calomel," he observed, "he should prefer the calomel."[1]

Virginians had several reasons for desiring constitutional reform. Under the old 1776 document, written in part by James Mercer, the franchise was restricted to landholders, which disfranchised nearly half of the white males in the state. Moreover, the rapidly growing western counties were seriously underrepresented in the legislature. A wealthy freeholder could vote several times in the same election if he held land in more than one of the small Tidewater counties. And the oligarchical county court system, with its extensive command over local affairs, infringed freely on the lives of the people. Complaints about the document, favoring as it did east over west and rich over poor, awakened Mercer to the possibility of a political explosion and radical change should some meaningful reform not take place.[2]

The first impetus for reform, however, did not come from the conservatives. A letter of Jefferson's, dated April 19, 1824, appeared first in the *Richmond Enquirer* and then elsewhere around the

state. The former president firmly believed that every generation
had a natural right to decide its own political fate. The "basis of our
constitution," he wrote, "is in opposition to the principle of equal
political rights, refusing to all but freeholders any participation in
the natural right of self-government." Such a system, he thundered,
"is merely arbitrary, and an usurpation of the minority over the
majority." Upon what principle could anyone justify giving "every
citizen of Warwick as much weight in the government, as to
twenty-two equal citizens of Loudoun?"[3]

These were precisely Mercer's sentiments. Indeed, the congressman from Loudoun enthusiastically supported reapportionment, and for essentially the same reasons he had in 1816. Then he
had not taken the lead in the reform movement, but now he would.
The program he had pursued in the Virginia House had borne fruit
in the west. These counties, once Federalist and now National
Republican enclaves, were rapidly developing the kind of program
Mercer was now pursuing on the federal level. Especially on the
question of colonization the slave-poor western counties were willing to support him. "It is to ensure this triumph," he told John
Hartwell Cocke in March 1825, "that I wish to see a convention."[4]

Not surprisingly, the Tidewater was as hostile to reform as Mercer was enthusiastic. Many planters feared that if the west was
given political power commensurate with its population, it would
pursue a separate economic agenda. "Nearly all the funds for internal improvement, is expended above tide water," Abel Upshur
insisted, "& when that country comes to possess . . . a decided
preponderance in the Legislature, there will be nothing to prevent
our western brethren from taxing us ad libitum." Mercer, of course,
had exactly the opposite fear. The "undue preponderance of the
lowland counties" in the House of Delegates would prevent the
legislature from purchasing stock in his canal and thus "defeat all
our plans . . . for the Potomac."[5]

The changing economy of the western counties was reflected in
their political attitudes and entrepreneurial spirit. The abhorred
"doctrine of a liberal construction of the U.S. Constitution was
gaining ground rapidly in the West," someone reported to Daniel
Webster. His correspondent also noted: "Manufactures are said to
be springing up in that country." It should have surprised no one
that Mercer wished "to transfer the political power of the commonwealth from the wasted planes and fields of the lowlands" to the
"enterprizing spirit of the midlands."[6]

Hoping to capitalize on Jefferson's plea, Mercer turned to his now routine method of applying political pressure. He convened "a large and respectable meeting of the Freeholders of Loudoun" on June 14. The Leesburg meeting resolved that the constitution should be amended, and to that end the group voted to petition the General Assembly. Mercer and several others formed a committee both to prepare a memorial to the legislature and to "take such measures as they shall consider best to obtain the signatures of the Freeholders of this county to the same."[7]

Nothing came of Mercer's efforts. Undaunted, he tried a different tactic the following April at the Loudoun elections. Immediately preceding the voting—as usual, he ran unopposed—Mercer addressed the throng and submitted two resolutions. The first, which was unanimously agreed to, required the sheriff to take a poll to discover the views of the qualified voters of the county on a convention. The second resolved that in the event a majority was in favor of a convention, six deputies be authorized on behalf of the county to meet in Staunton on Monday, July 25. (Also as usual, this spontaneous democratic outpouring was very well organized.) At the close of the poll, Sheriff Ludwell Lee announced that the vote stood at 390 to 8 in favor. A voice from the "hustings" nominated Mercer to lead the Staunton delegation, and this too was unanimously adopted.[8]

Several days later Mercer appeared at the Prince William election. Again he addressed the crowd and argued in favor of a constitutional convention, and again his resolutions were overwhelmingly supported. A week later voters arriving at the Shenandoah courthouse were surprised to find Mercer on its steps, although they too were swayed by his oratory and supported a convention, 831 to 30. Two days later the indefatigable congressman read his resolutions to the Fairfax voters. Echoing Jefferson, an act Mercer must have found painful, he dealt particularly "upon the anomalous feature which gave to Warwick, and King and Queen, an equal influence in the Legislature with Frederick, Shenandoah, [and] Loudoun." He "boldly" declared his conviction that "the right of suffrage ought, and could safely be extended to all free white citizens" who—and this was an important qualification—had a "permanent interest in the State." Several vocal opponents notwithstanding, Mercer's resolutions passed by a vote of 114 to 65.[9]

It did not appear to bother Mercer that his victories came in just those populous counties underrepresented in the General Assembly. The "Convention I promised you eighteen months ago pro-

ceeds gloriously," he gushed to Rufus King. "I have fixed on the
21st. of July for the period of our preparatory meeting at Staunton
and have no doubt of its full attendance." The official invitations
appeared as cards in leading newspapers around the state, published by Mercer and nine others, the "Corresponding Committee
of Loudoun." Under the "authority" of the adopted resolutions, the
committee invited delegates from all counties "to co-operate with
us" in correcting the defects "of the state constitution." Mercer
then threw down the rhetorical gauntlet. Only those were invited
"who are willing to trust in the people."[10]

Mercer also made a halfhearted attempt to enlist newly elected
Governor John Tyler in his campaign. "You are probably opposed to
a Convention," he gamely ventured. "But it is well to consider,"
this reformer reasoned, that "if avoidable now, it will not soon be
otherwise, and if certain, those who oppose it from such motives
as you entertain would not act more wisely in concerting a temper-
ate and probably permanent reform." But Tyler's disingenous reply
merely "recognize[d] the right of the majority of the people to alter
or amend their government." When and if that day came, Tyler
allowed that he would be glad to work with Mercer for "reformation and amendment." What a majority was to do if the prepon-
derant minority refused to allow them to "amend their
government," Tyler declined to say.[11]

Tyler's laconic reply, Mercer was to discover, hid an unfortunate
truth: the old Enlightenment liberalism of Jefferson was vanishing
from Virginia. The Tidewater elite, never a truly progressive clan at
best, was slowly moving toward a reactionary pose. The Missouri
debates and a decade of nationalism under Monroe and Adams not
only sent this group scurrying back to their states' rights philosophy, it also hardened them against any reform that might endanger
their peculiar institution. Only 50,000 of Virginia's 450,000 slaves
lived west of the Blue Ridge, and the planters were understandably
leery of reapportionment. "I have no faith in CF Mercer," Abel
Upshur fumed. "I have always considered him a shallow politician,
& I now think him a dangerous one." The future secretary of state
was certain that the "principle object with the politicians of his
school, [is] to induce a gradual abolition of slavery, & that an
attempt of that sort will be made in the new convention, I do not
doubt."[12]

The response from Mercer's family members and planter friends
was neither supportive nor understanding of his motives. "Will any
thing but discord & anarchy grow out of it?" Garnett bleated at

Randolph. "Ought not the friends of the old Constitution to stand by her to the last?" As usual, Mercer and his southern opponents were speaking different languages. Precapitalist and antibourgeois in their attitudes, men such as Upshur, Garnett, and Randolph were incapable of understanding their friend's concerns.[13]

The worst was yet to come. On May 20 a long essay above the pseudonym "Mason of 76" appeared in the *Enquirer*. That the author was Mercer's old tormentor Benjamin Watkins Leigh was an open secret in Virginia. The essay named Mercer as the "prime mover" of the Loudoun resolutions and hinted that such activity was unwise; it awakened the hostility of his enemies, "and how many they are, he knows but too well." The present constitution, "Mason" insisted, was a small price to pay for stability and order, and such reforms as Mercer proposed were dangerous. Yet the author made a telling point. "But if the lovers of pure democracy . . . shall take Mr. Mercer for their ally and their leader in the work of reformation, I shall think the union strange." It was true: Mercer and the yeomen farmers and urban artisans, among whom could be found some of the most progressive reformers in the state, had very different motives for wanting political change. "Mason" correctly thought the alliance "a sure proof, that they are possessed with such ardour for the attainment of their ends, as renders them regardless of their means."[14]

Even before Mercer could reply, "Mason of 76" appeared in the next issue, more vicious than before. Leigh and the Republicans were frightened because it was the old Federalist counties and leaders who were in the forefront of the reform movement. Should these groups form a coalition with the eastern farmers, the Republicans' traditional constituents, Federalism in the guise of National Republicanism could make a spectacular rebirth in the state. To keep his disgruntled constituents in line, Leigh fell to time-tested demagogic imagery. "The only precedent" for the Staunton meeting, he sneered, "is the memorable Hartford Convention." For perpetrating such a crime, Mercer was "cut off from the common benefit of penitence: and, truly, he has done a deed, of which the bitterest tears of repentance could never wash away the remembrance."[15]

Mercer was far from repentant. He was also tired of being "singled out, as a subject of special and virulent animadversion." He had no choice but to defend himself in print. He hoped to vindicate both himself and his argument "that equal numbers of the free white citizens of the Commonwealth were entitled, no matter where they resided, to equal representation, or equal shares of political power." He was again careful, however, not to suggest that he was advocating universal white male suffrage. Reapportionment was his goal; a slight expansion of the franchise to those hardworking nonfreeholders he also thought wise, but it was a secondary concern. He was far too conservative to desire all restrictions removed. Mercer "very hastily" scrawled out a reply and forwarded it to his enemy Thomas Ritchie.[16]

In early June Mercer's reply appeared in Richmond and Washington newspapers under the signature "Freeman of 1825." Unlike Leigh's two pieces, Mercer's article dealt only with the constitutional question at hand; the "merits or demerits of Mr. Mercer is not more intimately involved in the proposed Staunton meeting, than the character of the arrogant writer." He repeated the charges he had made at the April elections, that the current system gave as much political power to "a declining village" as to "7000 in the most flourishing city," neglecting to mention that the flourishing cities were National Republican and colonizationist strongholds. He also urged the state to take action while Monroe and Marshall still lived. That both supported his economic program was another point he neglected to mention.[17]

Two days later another voice in defense of Mercer and reform arose in the Washington and Virginia press. Writing under the pseudonym of "A Friend of Equal Rights," the author, Mercer's old Federalist colleague Philip Doddridge, himself active in the reform movement, did his best to vindicate the congressman from Loudoun. Whatever his "aberrations" and "weaknesses" might be, the writer insisted in a peculiar acknowledgment of the occasional Republican hints about Mercer's sexuality, he still enjoyed tremendous support in the northern and western counties. It "has been the fashion" in Richmond, "A Friend" wrote, "ever since his difference with General Mason" to "abuse and decry him." But others "approve heartily of his conduct in taking the first steps toward effecting a convention."[18]

Mercer also received some much appreciated support from the leading Washington paper, the *National Intelligencer*, a National Republican daily. The paper, which published both the first "Mason" and Mercer's "Freeman" essay, editorialized: "Of Mr. Mercer's merits, in particular, we have formed an opinion not to be shaken by any denunciation which the collision of State politics . . . may draw down upon him from his adversaries."[19]

A week later a third "Mason" piece appeared in the *Enquirer.* The long essay began by naming Mercer as the author of the "Freeman" piece, a serious breach of tradition. It then degenerated into yet another vicious personal attack. Leigh ridiculed Mercer's emotionless political essay as "shrieks of agony." He suggested that it was common knowledge that Mercer's wish for reform "originated" in the legislature's "refusal to legitimate that spurned litter of unchartered banks" in 1816. Or perhaps, Leigh intimated, the cause was "his disappointment of a certain military honor, which he thought no more than his just due." Yet "Mason" hastened to add that he "by no means think him wicked, but only unsteady and unsafe." This was abusive talk, surely made bolder by Mercer's long-standing refusal to duel. A fourth "Mason" essay, published seven days later, finally dealt with constitutional and political issues.[20]

The war of words stunned the state. "It is virulent beyond any thing I have read for a long time," John Campbell commented, "and has produced a great excitement in our old Dominion." Not surprisingly, public reaction to the quarrel divided along political lines already established on the issue of reform. Campbell believed the west was firmly "on the side of Mercer in the personal controversy." He "will appear again," Campbell promised.[21]

Before Mercer could reply, a fifth, shorter "Mason" article appeared. Having tired for a time of personal abuse, Leigh resorted to race-baiting. Mercer, he incorrectly and perhaps knowingly charged, had called for a "universal extension" of the voting right. "I only know," Leigh screeched, "that this qualification, which he certainly did maintain, goes to the extent of giving the right of suffrage to free negroes."[22]

Amost two months after the first "Mason" piece appeared, Mercer released his second "Freeman." The long letter took up eight full-length columns and dealt primarily with the legal and moral correctness of the Staunton meeting. The "Constitution of Virginia," he observed, "unlike that of the United States, contains no provisions for its amendment. Away then with the resemblance between the Staunton Meeting and the Hartford convention." Having defended his meeting, he then adopted a peevish tone and defended his character point by point. He "candidly" acknowledged "the pain, with which I have found myself dragged into a personal controversy." This last section, however, embarrassed his friends. "Mercers last piece is too much of the *whining*" for "*my taste*," Campbell remarked to his brother. Leigh, Campbell added, was busy preparing "another *broadside*" at Mercer.[23]

In mid-July Leigh's final "Mason" essay appeared. He "was most heartily disposed to drop all further controversy with Mr. Mercer," he insisted, but was forced to respond. That "sentimental wrath, that whining for sympathy, is too much for me," this charmer wrote. "I long to get out of hearing of it." Once more Leigh eschewed all discussion of the constitutional issues. The entire piece was an attempt to demonstrate that Mercer's support for reform in 1816 was the result of the failure of his huge bank bill of that year. It was a brutal attack on Mercer. But it was also, and more profoundly, an attack on the northern economy and society with which Mercer was so closely identified—an economy that was reducing the South to colonial status and that Mercer wished to import to Virginia.[24]

The rancor that flowed from Leigh's pen aided as much as it hindered the cause of reform. So many of Leigh's arguments were preposterous that Mercer's petulance looked statesmanlike in comparison. Yet Leigh did land a telling blow. "Tempora mutantur," he quoted Mercer as writing, "leaving others to fill up the sentence, translate it, and make the application." It read: "The times are changed, and we are changed with the times." He, for one, Leigh promised, would never change. But he laughed that Mercer's great appeal to the farmers and artisans lapsed into Latin. Despite his best efforts, Mercer's democratic guise showed its true colors. He might be leading the fight for reform, but he would never be accepted as the reform leader.[25]

But there was little time for personal recrimination. Less than a week after Leigh's final attack, Mercer mounted up and rode for Staunton. Because of the divisive paper war, he was anxious to demonstrate that the meeting was open to all viewpoints. By prior arrangement, he met John Scott, a mildly antireform lawyer, at Woodstock. From there the two rode on together, Mercer listening intently to Scott's arguments against any extension of the franchise. When they finally reached town, they discovered over a hundred delegates already there. Every public house, and even most private homes, were "crowded to excess." At the edge of town sat the new Presbyterian church, where the meeting was to take place.[26]

On July 25, Mercer brought the meeting to order. Thirty-eight counties were represented, most of them from the west. Because several more delegates were expected, little was done until the next day. Then, with the doors open and the choir loft creaking from the weight of spectators, Mercer and Doddridge offered a resolution to form a central committee to report on "what measures" the meeting should "adopt for the attainment of [its] object." The motion was granted, and Mercer, Doddridge, and John Scott were named to head the committee. As with most Mercer conventions, the delegates were limited to ratifying—and drawing attention to—the program devised in advance.[27]

The central committee worked until late in the evening of Wednesday, July 27, finalizing the report. Even then, most of the work was done by a "subcommittee" of Mercer and six others. A series of specific resolutions was prepared, one of them recommending an extension of the franchise. Scott attempted to amend his resolution and was surprised to hear himself supported by Mercer. He was "very desirous to gratify" Scott, for he recognized that the resolutions would have to appeal not just to those attending the meeting but to the Tidewater as well. Mercer, however, "could not overcome" the rest of the committee, and the resolutions as written were approved by the larger central committee.[28]

The committee concluded its work and returned to the church; most of the delegates were drifting back to the building following their dinner. Mercer rose to read the report. It called for a constitutional convention and advised four key changes: the reduction of the House in size and its representatives subject to reapportionment "at stated periods"; the abolition of the council of state and the grant of more power to the governor; the grant of suffrage to all white, twenty-one-year-old males "capable of furnishing sufficient evidence of permanent interest with, and attachment to the community, in such a manner as to guard against the introduction of universal suffrage"; and that a method be devised for future amendments. The report, Mercer concluded, also urged that the independence of the judiciary should not be impaired. Finally, it resolved that a memorial be sent to the legislature requesting that a law be passed "for taking the sense of the people at the next Spring Election, on the question [of] Whether there shall be a Convention."[29]

Staunton was again quiet the next morning. The committee had issued 120 copies of the report, and the delegates were back in their rooms, digesting the material. But when the meeting reconvened late in the day, sparks flew. Daniel Sheffey of Augusta spoke out against any extension of the right of suffrage. Mercer, reversing his course of the previous day, jumped to his feet and gave an "animated" reply that lasted more than an hour. When he concluded, Sheffey regained the floor and tried to amend the resolution by striking out the words "whether freeholders or not." Mercer again defended the resolution, and Sheffey's motion was defeated by a vote of 86 to 17.[30]

The four resolutions were then put to a vote. The first, on reducing the size of the House, was adopted unanimously. The second, dealing with the franchise, passed by a vote of 86 to 17; Mercer's companion John Scott sided with the minority. With the only issue of any contention resolved, the remaining two points were passed by even larger margins. The meeting, despite Mercer's attempts to make it reflect a wide spectrum of thought—save that of the reactionary Tidewater—reflected only that of all but the most ardent reformers. The next day, Saturday, July 30, the convention adjourned to the usual public dinners and enthusiastic toasts. Mercer, Thomas Ritchie promised this readers, "was observed to take notes during the sitting" to be presented to the public as "a full and ample report." Such was in keeping with his long-held belief that public attention, properly handled and controlled, would help and not hinder the conservative cause.[31]

For two sessions the General Assembly contemptuously refused to issue a bill to discover the public's view on the matter. To an extent, Mercer enjoyed the rhetorical coup the assembly's refusal gave him, for it placed him and his party in the role of defenders of the rights of the people. Finally, the legislature caved in and agreed to a popular referendum at the April 1828 elections. Only persons then qualified to vote could participate. To the surprise of the Tidewater, which voted overwhelmingly against the question, the vote stood at 21,896 to 16,646 in favor of a convention. It had been two years since the Staunton meeting, but that gathering had stimulated and focused attention on the issue. After Staunton the convention was just a matter of time; Mercer's later boast that "from its proceedings resulted the Convention of the State in 1829" was not far wrong.[32]

Now the House of Delegates had to produce a bill organizing a convention. In early January 1829, the lower body passed the act by a vote of 123 to 81. The bill provided each district with a number of delegates in accordance with its population. Twenty-two counties received two delegates, three were granted three, and the four most populous counties, including Loudoun, were given four. But the Tidewater-dominated Senate, in a final act of self-preservation, amended the bill so that each of the twenty-four old senatorial districts would receive four delegates. Even before the convention sat, the chances of meaningful reform had vanished. Such a response, a proreform Richmond paper concluded, was not surprising. "Physicians are agreed that suicide is an act of insanity."[33]

Not unexpectedly, Mercer and Monroe were named as two of the Loudoun delegates. For the first time in his career, Mercer would have to be absent for a time from the House. Before leaving for Richmond, the conscientious representative asked for and received the permission of his constituents to attend. In early October he descended the Chesapeake by steamer, and as the ship was hurried along by a strong west wind he thought of how "wasted" and "stunted" the Tidewater appeared. "The march of desolation saddens this once beautiful country." Only his economic program, he concluded, would reverse this trend, and only reform could bring about his program.[34]

As Mercer steamed south, men from all over the state began to arrive in Richmond. It was an impressive group, with two former presidents and the chief justice of the Supreme Court in attendance. But young Hugh Blair Grigsby had already concluded that the main speakers would be Mercer, Doddridge, Littleton Tazewell, Chapman Johnson, and Leigh. The passage of time since the paper war had not dampened the feeling toward Mercer in the east. It was even whispered among his enemies that his real goal was "a seat in the Senate of *Uncle Sam*." Such an event, Edward Campbell concluded, would never occur. The "Easterners wil not agree to it, as they hate him as they do the D——l."[35]

When Mercer finally arrived, he found that his reputation had preceded him. Because of his role in making the convention a reality, young men on both sides of the issue who were unacquainted with him expected an imposing figure. They were disappointed. "The personal appearance of this gentleman was quite the reverse of my expectations," Grigsby confessed. "I had thought that he was large, but found him diminutive; thought his features prominent, but found them any thing else than prominent or strongly marked." Still, upon watching Mercer on the floor, the young man, despite his low opinion of reform, was impressed. "The talk, the dust, the sweat of the intellectual exertion cover him completely; he has the industry of the Law."[36]

Residing with Mercer in Richmond was his brother-in-law James M. Garnett. Although his former guardian took little part in the proceedings, Garnett had published a series of papers before the convention outlining his ideas. Far from encouraging reform, Garnett now wished to see the constitution revised to give even greater influence to the owners of land and slaves. These papers were so repugnant to the west that Garnett was savaged in the press by a " 'go the whole'; Jacksonite."[37]

Also in attendance was Garnett's alter ego, John Randolph. Years before, Mercer had concluded that his old friend was "nearly mad," and in the summer of 1826 Randolph horrified polite society by offering to shoot all his slaves—he said it would take him but two hours—if everyone else would shoot theirs. It was these "peculiar traits of malice," Mercer commented sadly to Monroe, "which have threatened, of late, to obliterate all the excellencies of his genius." Neither Garnett nor Randolph made any signal contribution in Richmond. Instead, the two reactionaries amused themselves by introducing resolutions "written in sport," recommending giving the vote to "vagabonds," "rabble," and "the profligate, and homeless."[38]

It was Monday, October 5, 1829, when the assembly finally convened in the decaying capitol. All of Richmond turned out to see the opening ceremony and the last gathering of the revolutionary generation. Madison, then seventy-eight and still powdering his hair, made his way through the crowd. With him was John Marshall, wearing the silk stockings and knee breeches of an earlier time. At a little past noon Madison rose and nominated the very ill Monroe as president of the convention. After being unanimously elected, Monroe was conducted to the chair by Madison and Marshall. Yet the scene also indicated that the real work of the convention did not lie in the hands of the ancients. To the left of the chair sat Madison and Marshall; on Monroe's right was Charles Fenton Mercer, calmly smoking his long clay pipe.[39]

The real work began two days later with the appointment of a central committee of twenty-four, one from each senatorial district. The committee, chosen by Monroe and presided over by Madison, was equally divided beween the pro- and antireform factions. As if to demonstrate their unanimity—or perhaps the moral superiority of their position—Mercer, Doddridge, and Alfred Powell sat far apart from the rest. Glowering at them from across the room were Leigh, Tyler, Randolph, and Littleton Tazewell.[40]

The animosity between Mercer and Leigh, wedged together in the tiny council chamber, came raging out. During one of Mercer's long speeches on the ideas of Locke, Leigh began to whisper across the table to Tazewell. Mercer immediately paused and asked for silence. Had he "the volubility of either," he sarcastically remarked, he "would have finished ere this." Leigh returned a bland smile and politely asked if Mercer "would permit the adjournment of the Committee forever."[41]

A second "collision" between the two men occurred less than a week later. While attempting to prove the superiority of a freehold franchise, Leigh impishly decided to use Mercer as an example. Mercer had stated that he was a landlord, Leigh observed. Since he "had the power to turn them, wife, children and all, out of doors, would not this gratitude show itself at the polls?" he mused. The "gentleman was disposed to make personal allusions," Mercer shot back, holding himself in check. Leigh innocently responded that he "certainly meant to impute no bad motive to the gentleman." The rest of the committee, though not approving of these breaches of protocol, found the exchanges fascinating. William Maxwell even judged the latest explosion, calling it in Leigh's favor. Both men, he thought, "excelled in language, particularly Leigh." But Mercer, although "a pretty fluent speaker," lacked "rigor" of "action."[42]

Young diarist Hugh Blair Grigsby, who also observed these exchanges, came to a smilar conclusion. Mercer "collects his statements with unparalled delyrum, and is ready in referring to any document of the living or dead, that may seemingly illustrate his subject," Grigsby marveled. "He is profound in his research, urgent in reasoning, eloquent in declamation, graceful in elocution, animated in delivery." But he had one flaw, fatal in a society that placed great stock in public speaking: "He lacks a voice." Even so, this verbal fencing did not damage Mercer among his supporters. Following one of their exchanges, Leigh was burned in effigy in Harrisonburg.[43]

On November 4, this animosity spilled over onto the floor of the House when Mercer delivered his primary address. Although most of the work was done in committee, each delegate made at least one long speech. In his, Mercer reiterated the points made at the Loudoun election and the Staunton meeting and again emphasized the issue of apportionment. But this time he did not slight the question of suffrage. "Should a freeholder be allowed to exercise the right of suffrage on fifty acres of land situated upon the summit of a barren mountain," he wondered, "while this right is withheld from the proprietor of a farm of twenty-four acres in some fertile valley?" Such a system of voting, he admitted, might be "open to all bidders for power; but if not an oligarchy, I have no conception of the import of the term." For three more hours, until eleven that evening, Mercer continued to pound away at the opposition.[44]

The next morning Mercer concluded his speech with a rude

blow at the two interests the planter society cherished most: slaves and land. Whatever the policy of the federal Constitution, he insisted, it was foolishness to count slaves for the basis of apportionment. Is "not the slave under our laws, as much an instrument in the hands of his master, as the wagon and team of the mountaineer?" It was true, he admitted, that the murder of a slave was a crime, but then the law also protected "the horse and the ox from wanton injury." It was also true that the three-fifths representation was based on precedent, although representation "in the House of Burgesses" preceded "the existence of counties, as the counties did the existence of slavery." With that, he concluded his speech of six hours and took his seat.[45]

Reaction to the speech was mixed. The west and proreform elements in the east thought Mercer's effort magnificent, and a Richmond National Republican paper, the *Constitutional Whig*, published the oration in full and pronounced it a "powerful argument." The Tidewater, not unexpectedly, was less than enamored, and Mercer made few new friends with his blunt assessment of the hidden motives of his enemies. Grigsby, despite his high opinion of Mercer as an intellect, was adamantly opposed to the white basis; "Mercer did not acquit himself to [his] satisfaction."[46]

Indeed, it was as if the reactionaries' rage was nourished by Mercer's very appearance on the floor. At about this time the latest example of their slander was brought to his attention. Richard Henderson, one of the delegates from Loudoun, showed Mercer a Warrenton paper containing an essay over the signature "Caution." The essay hinted that Mercer had promoted the convention to perpetuate his continuance as president of the Chesapeake and Ohio Canal. Henderson, who seemed to enjoy stirring up trouble, assured him that the author was John Scott. Mercer's enemies made their usual mistake. Unable to comprehend his larger agenda, they attributed his actions to personal ambition. Although such a statement normally required satisfaction, Mercer told Henderson that the attack would instead "preclude any farther intercourse" between himself and Scott. He also took the matter to Scott's friend John S. Barbour, telling him of the "wound" the essay caused.[47]

There the matter rested, although like the debate with Mason, only for a time. At all events, Mercer was too busy to feud with Scott. In early December the General Assembly convened in Richmond, and the convention had to leave the capitol and move to the First Baptist Church. Several days later Monroe, too ill to continue, left for Loudoun County, and Philip P. Barbour was appointed president in his place. Mercer returned to his committee work and fell back into a "good deal of squabbling" with Leigh.[48]

The squabbling took a more serious turn in late November. Delegates had tired of hearing their own long speeches, and with the two sides at an impasse it appeared that the convention would come to naught. John Tyler wearily counted the days until Christmas. Randolph suggested that the assembly break up and go home. Seizing the opportunity, Mercer moved to amend the report on suffrage by granting the vote to "housekeepers" and heads of families "who shall have been assessed with a part of the revenue of the Commonwealth," that is, taxpayers. Leigh was up and shouting objections, but Mercer "pressed the question." The amendment passed, with those in the minority declining to be named.[49]

But as the new constitution slowly emerged from the committees, it became evident that the "white basis" men were losing. The Tidewater position was simply too strong; the Senate had seen to that. But their strength was also owing to the weakness of the reform leaders. Conservative men by temperament, they lacked the fire of true reformers. "I think they all want nerve," fretted Edward Campbell. "Mercer is no hand at management at all," he continued. His attempts to put questions in such a way as to force the Tidewater to vote against their propositions routinely failed. "Leigh who is never off his guard and who is quick as lightening and who knows Mercer well, never fails to expose the trap." Nonetheless, Mercer stubbornly refused to quit, and he and Doddridge consistently voted for every reform measure save that of universal white male suffrage.[50]

The result was a staggering defeat for Mercer. The new constitution attempted to appease the Piedmont and Shenandoah regions by granting them somewhat greater representation in the legislature. But it not only rejected representation based on white population, it allowed the trans-Allegheny region fewer seats than it previously had. Thanks to Mercer, the document expanded the franchise slightly by giving the vote to men who owned land worth $25 or paid taxes in the county in which they rented. On the rainy evening of January 14, the convention approved the document by a vote of 55 to 40. Eastern men cast 54 of the 55 yes votes. Mercer voted against the document, and then, tired, disgusted, and defeated, requested leave to return to Washington.[51]

In a referendum the following April the new constitution was adopted by a count of 26,055 to 15,563. The Tidewater voted overwhelmingly in favor, and even Loudoun County went for the document, 505 to 128. The trans-Allegheny region, more populous than the Tidewater, voted the measure down by an overwhelming 7,230 to 1,195. In Doddridge's county the new constitution received not a single vote.[52]

But the nature of the reactionary mind was such that it was profoundly disturbed by any change, however slight, however inconsequential. Many eastern planters were as unhappy with the constitution as were residents of the west. Virginia, Randolph moaned to Garnett, "is ruined past redemption." Slaves would be "instigated to steal by the wretched 'House Keepers' who by the votes of Fenton Mercer and Madison and Monroe! were made voters," Randolph shrieked at a supposedly sympathetic Andrew Jackson. "We eastern folks were such asses as to swallow the vile compound for fear the next dose would contain arsenick."[53]

Although he did not know it, Randolph was paraphrasing Mercer, a pragmatic conservative who vastly preferred calomel to arsenic. And so to Mercer's mind, the entire episode was a colossal failure. He achieved neither the great political reform he sought nor the economic rewards of that reform. He revived anew an animosity toward himself such as he had not witnessed since the election of 1812. He even lost the friendship of John Randolph, although this was an acquaintance he no longer cherished; by 1830 Randolph had turned on almost all of his old friends. But Randolph's rage at Mercer was not madness, it was a rational fury toward a plantation-raised man who was doing his best to overturn the old Virginia. The Tidewater men, clever politicians all of them, had defeated Mercer and mild reform. They would be less successful against time.[54]

Notes

ABBREVIATIONS

ACS	American Colonization Society
CFM	Charles Fenton Mercer
COCC	Chesapeake and Ohio Canal Company
DAB	*Dictionary of American Biography,* ed. Allen Johnson and Dumas Malone, 21 vols., 1928–1936.
JQA	John Quincy Adams
JSH	*Journal of Southern History*
LC	Library of Congress
NJHS	New Jersey Historical Society

NYHS   New-York Historical Society
PRO, FO Great Britain, Public Record Office, Foreign Office
UVA   University of Virginia
VHS   Virginia Historical Society
VMHB   *Virginia Magazine of History and Biography*
VSL   Virginia State Library
WMQ   *William and Mary Quarterly*

1. *Proceedings and Debates of the Virginia State Convention of 1829–30* (Richmond, 1830), 449.

2. Dickson D. Bruce, Jr., *The Rhetoric of Conservatism: The Virginia Convention of 1829–30 and the Conservative Tradition in the South* (San Marino, 1982), 2–3; Virginius Dabney, *Virginia: The New Dominion* (New York, 1972), 213–14; J. R. Pole, "Representation and Authority in Virginia from the Revolution to Reform," *JSH* 24 (February 1958): 31.

3. *Niles' Weekly Register*, May 15, 1824, p. 179.

4. CFM to John Hartwell Cocke, March 25, 1825, Cocke Collection, UVA.

5. Abel P. Upshur to Francis Gilmer, July 7, 1825, Francis Gilmer Papers, UVA; CFM to John Hartwell Cocke, September 16, 1825, Cocke Collection.

6. John Lowell, Jr., to Daniel Webster, November 2, 1829, in Charles M. Wiltse et al., eds., *The Papers of Daniel Webster*, 7 vols. to date (Hanover, N.H., 1974–86), 2:430 (Lowell was writing from the convention); CFM to John Hartwell Cocke, March 25, 1825, Cocke Collection.

7. *Genius of Liberty* (Leesburg), June 21, 1824, reprinted in *Richmond Enquirer*, June 14, 1825.

8. *Richmond Enquirer*, April 29, 1825; CFM, Autobiographical Sketch, Mercer-Hunter Papers, VSL; *National Intelligencer*, April 14, 1825.

9. *National Intelligencer*, April 12, 1825; *Richmond Enquirer*, April 26, 29, 1825.

10. CFM to Rufus King, April 22, 1825, CFM Papers, NYHS; *Richmond Enquirer*, May 13, 1824.

11. CFM to John Tyler, December 2, 1826, Tyler Papers, LC; John Tyler to CFM, December 5, 1826, Thomas Jefferson Papers, UVA.

12. Harry Ammon, *James Monroe: The Quest for National Identity* (New York, 1971), 563–64; Norma Lois Peterson, *Littleton Waller Tazewell* (Charlottesville, 1983), 167; Abel P. Upshur to Francis Gilmer, July 7, 1825, Francis Gilmer Papers, UVA.

13. James M. Garnett to John Randolph, March 24, 1829, John Randolph Papers, LC.

14. *Richmond Enquirer*, May 20, 1825.

15. Joanne L. Gatewood, ed., "Richmond during the Virginia Constitutional Convention of 1829–1830: An Extract from the Diary of Thomas Green, October 1, 1829, to January 31, 1830," *VMHB* 84 (July 1976): 287; *Richmond Enquirer*, May 24, 1825.

16. CFM, Autobiographical Sketch, Mercer-Hunter Papers; CFM to John Scott, December 1838, CFM Papers, NJHS; CFM to Fitzhugh Lee, June 8, 1825, CFM Papers, UVA.

17. Marie Tyler McGraw, "The American Colonization Society in Virginia, 1816–1832: A Case Study in Southern Liberalism" (Ph.D. dissertation, George Washington University, 1980, rev.), 157; *Richmond Enquirer*, June 14, 1825.

18. *National Intelligencer*, June 16, 1825; *Richmond Enquirer*, June 17, 1825.

19. *National Intelligencer*, June 8, 1825.

20. *Richmond Enquirer*, June 21, 28, 1825; CFM to John Scott, December 1838, CFM Papers, NJHS.

21. John Campbell to James Campbell, July 9, 1825, Campbell Family Papers, Duke University Library.

22. *Richmond Enquirer*, July 5, 1825.

23. Ibid., July 15, 1825; John Campbell to James Campbell, July 9, 1825, Campbell Family Papers.

24. *Richmond Enquirer*, July 19, 1825.

25. Ibid.

26. CFM to John Scott, December 1838, CFM Papers, NJHS; *Richmond Enquirer*, August 9, 1825. The importance of the Staunton convention has been strangely ignored. Bruce, *Rhetoric of Conservatism*, 22, devotes but one paragraph to the meeting.

27. *Proceedings and Debates*, 701; *Richmond Enquirer*, August 2, 1825.

28. *Richmond Enquirer*, August 5, 1825; CFM to John Scott, December 1838, CFM Papers, NJHS.

29. *Richmond Enquirer*, August 2, 11, 1825.

30. Ibid., August 2, 5, 9, 1825.

31. Ibid., August 11, 9, 1825.

32. Lewis Summers to CFM, May 23, 1826, CFM Papers, NYHS; *Proceedings and Debates*, iii; CFM, Autobiographical Sketch, Mercer-Hunter Papers.

33. *Constitutional Whig* (Richmond), January 27, 6, 1829.

34. CFM, Autobiographical Sketch, Mercer-Hunter Papers; *Proceedings and Debates*, 204.

35. Hugh Blair Grigsby Diary, September 30, 1829, Grigsby Papers, VHS; Edward Campbell to David Campbell, December 17, 1829, Campbell Family Papers.

36. Hugh Blair Grigsby, Commonplace Book, Grigsby Papers.

37. *DAB*, 7:156; Grigsby Diary, October 9, 1829, Grigsby Papers; *Constitutional Whig* (Richmond), October 6, 1829.

38. CFM to William Gaston, May 6, 1824, Gaston Papers, University of North Carolina, Chapel Hill; Glyndon G. Van Deusen, *The Life of Henry Clay* (Boston, 1937), 223, n.32; CFM to James Monroe, February 2, 1838, Monroe Papers, LC; *Proceedings and Debates*, 444–45.

39. *Proceedings and Debates* 1–5; Grigsby Diary, October 5, 1829, Grigsby Papers.

40. *Proceedings and Debates*, 9–10; *Richmond Whig*, October 12, 1829; Grigsby Diary, October 8, 1829, Grigsby Papers.

41. Grigsby Diary, October 17, 1829.

42. Ibid., October 22, 23, 1829.

43. Grigsby, Commonplace Book, Grigsby Papers; *Constitutional Whig* (Richmond), November 21, 1829.

44. *Proceedings and Debates*, 174–77.

45. *Richmond Enquirer*, November 7, 1829; *Proceedings and Debates*, 185.

46. *Constitutional Whig* (Richmond), November 10, 1829; Grigsby Diary, November 5, 1829, Grigsby Papers.

47. CFM to John Scott, November 29, 1838; John S. Barbour to John Scott, December 15, 1838, both in John Scott, ed., *Judge Scott's Reply to Mr. Mercer* (N.p., 1839), 25–26.

48. Virginius Dabney, *Richmond: The Story of a City* (New York, 1976), 109; *Proceedings and Debates*, 588; Grigsby Diary, November 17, 1829, Grigsby Papers.

49. John Tyler to unknown, November 11, 1829, Tyler Papers, LC; *Proceedings and Debates*, 430, 441–42.

50. Edward Campbell to David Campbell, December 17, 1829, Campbell Family Papers. Bruce, *Rhetoric of Conservatism*, xvii, writes that many of the antireform arguments "could have come straight out of Federalist rhetoric, and it is not difficult to place them squarely in that older conservative tradition," thereby failing to note that the reform charge was led by former Federalists.

51. *Proceedings and Debates*, 896–902, 882–83; Gatewood, ed., "Richmond," 328; *Richmond Enquirer*, January 16, 1830; CFM, Autobiographical Sketch, Mercer-Hunter Papers.

52. *Proceedings and Debates*, 903; *Richmond Whig*, April 20, 1830; *Richmond Enquirer*, May 4, 1830.

53. John Randolph to James M. Garnett, April 1, 1829, Randolph Papers; John Randolph to Andrew Jackson, March 1, 1832, in John Spencer Bassett, ed., *Correspondence of Andrew Jackson*, 6 vols. (Washington, D.C., 1926–33), 4:413–14.

54. Robert Dawidoff, *The Education of John Randolph* (New York, 1979), 270.

15

Recreant to the Cause

Late in the afternoon of January 16, a weary and very cold Charles Fenton Mercer arrived in Washington, the first member of the Virginia convention to reach the nation's capital. Richmond was nearly out of his thoughts. His energies were required by the American Colonization Society, again on the verge of financial ruin. Over the next three years his persistent efforts to obtain federal funds for the society would play no small part in precipitating a crisis that would bring the republic to the verge of civil war and ultimately finish off Mercer's "African" society.[1]

For several years, the society had struggled to remain financially solvent. By 1830 the government had expended $264,000 supporting the two thousand "souls settled" in Liberia. Most of the money went for transportation and settlement of the first colonists who left America in 1819 under the care of agents appointed by Monroe. But the sums obtained under the 1819 law were not enough. The society was forced to fall back on its meager annual membership dues, donations from affluent Europeans and Americans—Mercer donated four hundred dollars to Liberia in one year alone—and "bequests of wealthy citizens."[2]

But the real problem facing the society was the growing hostility of the deep South. The same anger at the increasing economic hegemony of the North that was aimed at Mercer before the convention was, on the national level, aimed at Mercer's society. In 1828 Robert Turnbull of South Carolina produced a thick pamphlet entitled *The Crisis*, a detailed jeremiad that bitterly if correctly listed colonization as an integral part of the American System. It was advocates of this program, Turnbull charged, who desired a high tariff and internal improvements and were employing the "general welfare" interpretation of the Constitution to turn the state into a "firm, consolidated national government."[3]

Turnbull's harangue was quickly put to good use by Calhoun's henchman George McDuffie, another South Carolinian whom Mercer believed was "resolved" to crush his organization. That same year, McDuffie reported from the House Committee of Ways and Means a "bill to abolish the Agency of the United States on the Coast of Africa." Thankfully for the society, any such effort emanating from South Carolina was immediately suspect, even in the eyes of the rest of the South. The bill passed, but only after it was effectively gutted. The society continued to receive federal funds.[4]

In spite of, or perhaps because of, such attacks, Mercer reached the conclusion that the time had come for the society to ask the government openly for more money. He was astute enough to realize that such a request would carry more weight if it came from the states. Letters were accordingly sent to National Republicans in the New York legislature earnestly pressing them to "favour our views." Mercer's letters also traveled south, one reaching the influential cotton textile industrialist William Gaston of North Carolina. The nation, he pleaded, "will be released from crime as well as pauperism by African Colonization." Mercer hoped that Gaston agreed with him "that our money power extended to every such object, and you could elicit the expression of such a sentiment from your legislature."[5]

But many southern colonizationists found Mercer's latest efforts disturbing. One Virginian "respectfully" suggested that Mercer should instead use his influence "to prevent an application to Congress for aid." Without the support of the southern states, and especially the Old Dominion, colonization stood little chance. To ask Congress for money, this observer thought, "will effectually, and, I fear, for ever alienate Virginia." Mercer, of course, was well aware of this problem. A less obvious plan, he informed Ralph Gurley, "has as you full well know always been mine." But without increased funding the society was moribund. He knew that to ask Congress for aid was madness. Neither did he look forward to the inevitable and personal abuse such a request would bring. He simply had no choice.[6]

During the icy days of February Mercer labored to secure support for such a bill. Senator Theodore Frelinghuysen of New Jersey urged Mercer "to present a memorial" from the society along with a bill, to detail the financial needs of the group, and once more to explain the nature of the organization. Deeming the suggestion sound, he sequestered himself in his room and began to work at his writing table.[7]

Two months later, Mercer was ready to present his bill. He was confident of its passage, at least in the House. "To do so," he told Gurley, "we shall need prompt use of the report which accompanied and which will be voluminous." It was not an overstatement. The bill and his 293-page report, cleverly titled *Slave Trade,* were presented to the House on April 7. Stuffed with documents and commentary dating back to the first days of colonization, the report tried to blunt any southern attacks. "The Society has," it began, "at all times, recognized the constitutional and legitimate existence of Slavery." The only object of the group was to remove the "free colored population." His bill thus proposed the appropriation of twenty-five dollars "to defray the passage of every colored emigrant who may leave America, with intention to make a permanent settlement in Africa."[8]

Mercer could not possibly have made a more serious miscalculation. Virtually without support below the Potomac, the bill was immediately tabled. And southern reaction was swift and brutal. Mercer, James Henry Hammond editorialized in his South Carolina paper, was no true son of Virginia. "He is a bastard." "Tax us today for the transportation of our free negroes to Africa and tomorrow we will have to pay for the emancipation of our own slaves."[9]

The charge that funding colonization was the first step toward emancipation was made again and again throughout the South. As usual, Mercer and his opponents were talking past one another. The "object" of "Northern fanatics"—such was the description of Mercer—warned the pronullification *Charleston Mercury,* was to "colonize the free, and excite dissatisfaction in the bond. Then regulate slavery—inflame discontent to madness—render the property equally valueless and dangerous—and then abolish it entirely." Even South Carolina moderates such as Benjamin F. Perry observed that if the bill passed "we may well begin to calculate the value of this Union."[10]

Worse still, from the point of view of the society, was that what funds the group did get from the government were now in danger of being lost. Mercer's latest encounter with his planter brethren alerted Amos Kendall, the fourth auditor of the treasury, to the sums annually allotted to the society. The Kentucky editor had been brought to Washington to help Jackson in his quest for reform and retrenchment, and he was determined to carry out his chief's will. In an August letter to Navy Secretary John Branch, Kendall correctly observed that "a large portion of these expenditures is not justified by the language or object of the act of 1819." In an unintentional voicing of Adams's original position, he argued "that the terms of the act were hardly sufficient to authorize the establishment of a colony" for American-born free blacks.[11]

When in the following December Jackson forwarded his annual message to Congress, it included Branch's report, which endorsed the interpretation taken by the fourth auditor. Upon investigation, Branch discovered that only 252 of the several thousand colonists transported to Africa fell under the original guidelines of the act. "The terms of these acts are sufficiently defined to be readily intelligible," Branch continued. "It would seem that the authority given to the President was limited to the support of [captured] negroes or persons of color during their Stay in the United States, to their removal to the coast of Africa, and to delivering them to the care of an agent." No power was even implicitly vested in the executive to build a colony or to send free American blacks to Africa. (It was well that Jackson did not know that the society had bought land with the original funds.) In keeping with the language of the bill, Branch concluded, "it will in future be executed accordingly, and every effort made by the [Navy] Department to confine the application of this fund within the pale of its provisions."[12]

In vain Mercer protested. Kendall's letter, he charged, was "extraordinary considering the subordinate station of its writer." That both Monroe and Adams, as well as the "silent acquiescence of both Houses of Congress," had accepted his interpretation for more than a decade was "sufficient evidence" of the correctness of his view. Yet his harsh words betrayed something less than shocked innocence. The passage of ten years could not disguise the fact that men had not voted for a bill that even remotely implied Mercer's interpretation. He knew at the time that such explicit language would sink his bill, and so he opted for deception and placed his hopes on his ability to persuade Monroe of his views. Now he was found out.[13]

With no other recourse, the society leaders decided to pay a call on the president. Mercer would not do; Jackson still remembered the Virginian's criticism of his military prowess during the Seminole controversy. Instead the society sent Elliott Cresson, who meekly began to argue Mercer's interpretation. He got no farther. "Every word that Mr. Kendall had said was true," snapped the general. He could not help it that Monroe and Adams had "squandered the public money upon this establishment without law," but he would see to it that it stopped with him. Literally shaking with fear, Cresson fled from the old man's "abusive" language; never in his life had he been treated so "roughly."[14]

To these problems Mercer could find no solution. A year of constant setbacks for the society, coming hard on the heels of his failure at the convention, had taken their toll on him and left him wary and bewildered. On March 3, 1831, the last day of the session, Mercer struggled to his feet and meekly reintroduced his old resolution calling on the president to renew negotiations with the European powers "for the effectual abolition of the African slave trade, and its ultimate denunciation, as piracy " Almost to his surprise, the resolution passed by a vote of 118 to 32. All of the negative votes came from the South, seven of them from his own state. With that, Mercer rode for home.[15]

As a result of Mercer's long year of unfortunate actions, for the first time since 1817 he faced a real fight for reelection. His opponent was John Gibson, a Democrat from Prince William County. But the key to the election was colonization, not Jacksonism. Mercer lost in Prince William, and in Fairfax, the two Tidewater counties in his district. His margin of victory in Loudoun, however, with its few slaves and large Quaker population, was over 500 votes, and so he squeaked back into Congress by a bare 246 votes. Yet however bad life looked to Mercer during the steaming August of 1831, it was only to get worse.[16]

Even as Thomas Ritchie was reluctantly reporting Mercer's victory, news began to reach Loudoun of a slave uprising in the southern Virginia county of Southampton. Led by the messianic Nat Turner, the insurgents killed almost sixty whites before the revolt was crushed. It was the only uprising in Virginia history in which whites died. Turner remained at large, striking terror into residents of the state with the largest slave population, and Virginians responded with an orgy of brutality, perhaps murdering more than one hundred innocent blacks. Within forty-eight hours the rebellion was over, but reports of the ferocity formed a permanent scar on the heretofore outwardly serene southern psyche.[17]

The immediate result of the revolt was a dramatic shift in the attitude of both white and black Virginians toward colonization. Although no free blacks were implicated in the rebellion, the conspiracy reinforced the common white fear that free blacks lurked behind every act of slave disobedience. And free blacks, previously hostile to the idea of leaving the land of their birth, were suddenly anxious to escape the brutality and retribution of their white neighbors. In early December, more than 300 free blacks set sail from Norfolk for Liberia; 274 of them were from Southampton. Hoping to seize the advantage, Bushrod Washington took out a card in several Richmond papers, noting that twenty-five dollars would transmit one free black to Liberia. Contributions might be made either to the parent society or directly to "Gen. C. F. Mercer."[18]

Again Mercer seemed to have a chance. Hoping that the insurrection would shake the growing southern hostility to colonization, he tried in January 1832 to gain federal support for his scheme. He introduced a resolution that as soon as the national debt "shall have been discharged," the proceeds of the sale of the western lands should be applied "in the proportion of one moiety to popular education, and the other to the removal of such free people of colour as may desire to emigrate." (This classification excluded recently manumitted slaves.) He then moved that the resolution be referred to the committee of the whole, where it might stand a chance. Before he could finish, Clement Clay of Alabama was on his feet, demanding that the resolution be laid on the table. It was late in the day, and the House adjourned, but the next morning Mercer forced consideration. It was tabled by a vote of 124 to 54. Three other Virginians voted with Mercer, as did John Quincy Adams, now representing Massachusetts in the House. The fourteen other Virginians sided with the majority.[19]

With yet another crushing defeat on the national level, Mercer and the colonizationists focused their hopes on the debate over slavery then taking place in the Virginia House of Delegates. Hoping for an endorsement from the Old Dominion, which would carry much weight with the rest of the South, the society lobbied hard for a recommendation that the proceeds from the sale of public lands be used for colonization. Accordingly, the society solicited the constitutional advice of James Madison and Chief Justice John Marshall. The former president approved of the idea but hinted that such an "application" would require a constitutional amendment, a proposal Mercer knew could not "be carried." Marshall, true to his Federalist moorings, found no constitutional problem in using the proceeds from sale of land for colonization: "The lands are the property of the United States, and have heretofore been disposed of by the government, under the idea of absolute ownership."[20]

Mercer was determined to give the colonizationists in the Virginia legislature the best ammunition he could provide. Three days after his failure in the House, he obtained copies of Madison's and

Marshall's letters from Gurley and promptly mailed them to Charles James Faulkner, a young champion of his canal then leading the gradual abolition faction in the House of Delegates. He also fired off several of his pamphlets "to be distributed among the members" of the legislature, although he entertained "no hope" that the Tidewater-controlled body would "profit by these suggestions in relation to the proceeds of the public lands."[21]

Mercer was absolutely correct; several years of unrelenting abuse had persuaded him of this unhappy truth. On January 25, the House of Delegates voted down the report calling for immediate emancipation and colonization by a vote of 73 to 58. A meaningless preamble rejecting perpetual slavery and endorsing abolition at some future—and unnamed—date squeezed by in a close tally. Significantly, the Tidewater counties rejected even this meaningless absurdity. Of Mercer's district, the Loudoun delegates supported the emancipation proposal, while those of both Prince William and Fairfax repudiated even the preamble. "Our Legislature is the most remarkable of any in the Union for discussing propositions which prove by yielding no fruit so barren of everything but flowers of speech," Mercer huffed.[22]

Thus another step was taken toward the view of slavery as a positive good and thus another perplexity for Mercer. If the singular drama of the Turner revolt had not shaken Virginians from their complacency, nothing ever would. It did not matter that he had different reasons for colonization; their motives would have met his ends, and he was prepared to support emancipation if, and only if, it was coupled with his program for removing "our free coloured population." The few slaves he had inherited as a young man had passed away. He still thought slavery the "blackest of all blots," and he perceived this latest unfortunate turn as making him more than ever an outsider in his native state.[23]

It might seem odd that at this point Mercer turned his attention back to the national arena, but he was forced to do so. Early in the new year William Archer of Virginia stopped him in the halls of Congress and enthusiastically showed him a resolution he was preparing. Based on Madison's reasoning, the resolution called for a constitutional amendment to give Congress power to aid the society. Mercer was horrified. As a national conservative he believed that Congress already had this power. "But the result of an attempt to amend the Constitution the failure of which a rational doubt cannot be entertained," he told Gurley, would cripple the movement. "It is therefore the more important," he thought, that the society "immediately" again ask for aid before Archer could do any damage.[24]

On April 2, 1832, precisely two years since he had last requested federal funds, Mercer again laid a resolution before the House. The reaction of "a few intemperate members" to his earlier resolution had not convinced him that he had "overrated our strength in Congress." But instead of being a memorial from the society itself, this resolution was from "sundry subjects of Great Britain, residing in England, praying Congress to aid the American Colonization Society." Mercer had barely time to finish his presentation before his voice was drowned out by shouts and cries. James K. Polk bellowed that the resolution should be tabled. It "was a memorial signed by British subjects," he bawled, "praying for the abolition of slavery." Disposing of it quickly would "prevent similar annoyances in the future."[25]

William Drayton of South Carolina echoed Polk's charge. It should not even be read, he insisted, and he "should be very glad if the gentleman from Virginia would consent to withdraw the paper." At this Tristam Burges of Rhode Island demanded that it be read in full, which provoked further agony from Drayton. There were very few men "in the House," he snarled, "who were not acquainted with the peculiar notions of the gentleman from Virginia on the subject of colonization." Polk agreed, saying that if the memorial were read "a discussion would ensue, such as perhaps had never been witnessed in that Hall." But Burges persisted, noting that the South could not object to a memorial presented by a southern man. James Blair of South Carolina was up. He "did not regard that gentleman as a true representative of the Slaveholding States. He was a recreant to the cause." Blair was gaveled to order and instructed not to make personal remarks. Blair continued. When money from the western lands went to such a project, he shouted, "they from the South would meet it elsewhere. It would not be disputed in that House, but in the open field, where powder and cannon would be their orators." Northern men met this last with a burst of laughter.[26]

Through the storm Mercer stood and faced his tormentors. When the noise died down he tried again, saying he "had done no more than to obey the [1816] instructions" of his own legislature. But Blair again shouted him down. "Surely the House had already before it a sufficiency of subjects pregnant with angry discussion," he roared, "nor had any gentleman in that House had a greater agency in introducing such questions than the gentleman from

Virginia. His tariff question, and his internal improvement questions, and education questions, and colonization questions, were already shaking this Union to its foundation." The question of tabling the resolution was then put, and with no other choice, Mercer quietly withdrew the memorial and resumed his seat.[27]

Indeed, the House did face a sufficiency of impossible subjects, all of them—as Blair had so politely observed—tied together, and all of them a part of the American System. Yet one thing was certain: Andrew Jackson was slowly but methodically dismantling the program that the National Republicans had so carefully put into place. The latest evidence could be found in Jackson's annual message, which announced that the national debt would soon be liquidated. That happy fact presented an "opportunity" to modify the tariff downward so that it met only "the wants of the Government." A just reduction, the president affirmed, "is deemed to be one of the principal objects which demand the consideration of the present Congress."[28]

But the tariff was one of the central pillars of the American System. Protection was needed not only for the emerging industrial community but to raise funds for other aspects of the manufacturing program, for the tariff provided about 90 percent of the government's revenue. However they might feel about other issues, all National Republicans were good tariff men. Even in the South, where the tariff was generally met with hostility, members of the party supported the concept of protection; their only difference from the northern wing of the party was how high the tariff should be. And Mercer, although admitting that the tariff drove prices up for the consumer, was convinced that "the Locos oppose it; merely because moved by their opponents."[29]

Mercer's opponents, especially in the South, had great difficulty grasping the interlocking nature of the American System. They simply concluded that the tariff was unconstitutional. But for Mercer, the tariff played an integral role. Just after hearing the president's message he conferred with Adams, the chairman of the committee on manufactures. The New Englander hoped that the tariff would remain high enough so "that there might be about five millions [dollars] of revenue reserved annually for specific purposes of internal improvement." Mercer replied that he was "entirely in favor of it"—he was thinking also of colonization—but thought it "doubtful whether it could be carried through." Adams sadly agreed.[30]

As the tariff bill was pounded out during the spring of 1832, it became obvious that Mercer and Adams were right, although the latter saved as much as he could. But Adams also recognized the need to conciliate the South, and the final product brought the tariff back down to the general level of 1824. The bill swept away the minimum valuation system on woolens, and cheap wool was admitted duty free. Cotton, however, remained high, and the bill retained the principle of protection. Industrialists were not on the whole displeased, and after some grumbling Clay and Mercer, who thought the bill gave away too much, fell into line.[31]

On June 28 the bill came before the House. It passed handily by a vote of 132 to 65. Mercer was one of eleven Virginians who voted with the majority; the other nine members of the delegation voted against the measure. In a final and uncharacteristically skillful act of political wisdom, Adams moved to amend the title of the bill by inserting the words "to reduce the revenue of the United States collected by duties." Warren Davis of South Carolina moved to amend the title further by adding "and to protect domestic manufacturers." Adams briefly consented but then saw the trap. He refused, and the House adopted his title. Several weeks later the bill passed the Senate, and Jackson, announcing himself satisfied, signed it into law on July 14.[32]

The Jacksonian-controlled House then turned its attention to another aspect of the American System, Henry Clay's land bill. With the national debt nearing extinction, Clay had produced a bill and a long report that opposed "any considerable reduction" in western land prices. The manufacturing community opposed any reduction, fearing it would accomplish what eastern laborers hoped it would: allow for western migration and thus reduce the competition for jobs in urban areas. Yet both laborers and western farmers, Mercer observed caustically, held a far different perspective. They "advocate the recognition of settlement rights acquired by squatters and the reduction of the price of the public lands."[33]

With the tariff reduced, National Republicans had to find a new source of funds for other aspects of their program. Clay's bill indicated much consultation on that matter with the congressman from Loudoun; it contained verbatim portions of the resolution Mercer had submitted earlier in the session. It specified that 10 percent of the land revenues would be "applied to education, internal improvement, or colonization." Indeed, the bill contained virtually the entire American System—save the bank, which was then being considered in separate legislation—combined into one act.[34]

As long as the tariff preoccupied Congress Clay's peculiar bill had a chance. It passed the Senate on July 3 while that body was still fighting over the tariff and was sent to the House. There the Jacksonians had leisure to deal with it as they pleased. Richard Wilde of Georgia moved its postponement until the following December. Mercer was immediately on his feet shouting that the bill should be referred to the entire House for consideration. But the first motion received precedence and was carried by a close vote of 91 to 88. The Virginia delegation split 11 to 5 in favor; Mercer and Adams voted against postponement. "We are happy to see that this bill, so suspicious in its character and so startling in its importance," was tabled, editorialized Thomas Ritchie.[35]

But Wilde's actions did not go far enough to satisfy the Palmetto State; delay was not demise. And so in the presidential election of 1832, South Carolina, where only 10 percent of the population was qualified to vote, threw its vote away to Virginia Governor John Floyd, a Calhounite and ardent states' rights man. The election also returned to the legislature an overwhelming majority of nullifiers, who in turn summoned a state constitutional convention. On November 24, the convention declared the tariffs of 1828 and 1832 null and void within the state as of February 1, 1833. Appeals to the Supreme Court on the legality of nullification were outlawed, and Governor James Hamilton placed the republic on notice that attempts to coerce the state would be just cause for secession. Hamilton backed this threat by asking the legislature for troops. In a last act of defiance, medals were struck bearing the inscription: "John C. Calhoun, First President of the Southern Confederacy."[36]

The creation of these medals was a reasonable development, for at the heart of the web that the nullifiers had spun were the ideas first given a detailed presentation by Calhoun four years earlier in his *Exposition and Protest*. The concept was logical, but only on the surface. Calhoun held that because the states had ratified the federal Constitution in special conventions, they could reverse the process and by a second convention nullify any law they believed unconstitutional. Although the nullifiers were loath to admit it, the end result was that states, and not the Supreme Court, would be the final arbiter of a law's constitutionality. Not surprisingly, Mercer thought the concept chaotic and dangerous. "When such absurdities as these are uttered," he wrote, "where is the guarantee of any rational action or chance of existence in the government[?]"[37]

But if the South had grown embittered over the question of

tariffs, more complex issues lurked beneath South Carolina's rebellion. "I consider the Tariff act as the occasion, rather than the
real cause of the present unhappy state of things," Calhoun confided to Virgil Maxcy. Were the southern states unable to nullify
federal law, "they must be forced to rebel, or submit it to have their
paramount interests sacraficed, their domestick institutions sub-
ordinated by Colonization and other schemes, and themselves &
children reduced [to] wretchedness." Indeed, Calhoun saw the entire American System and the industrial society behind it as an
assault on Tidewater paternalism.[38]

The understanding that South Carolina's actions endangered
anew the National Republican program led public opinion in Virginia to split along regional and party lines. Benjamin Watkins
Leigh reluctantly admitted that if South Carolina rebelled "Eastern
Virginia will remain neutral and Western Virginia will take part
against them." And the editor of Richmond's leading anti-Jackson
paper, the Constitutional Whig, insisted that Virginia "is beginning
to discover and acknowledge, the true cause of Southern decline to
be in Slavery, and not in the Tariff—she will not adopt, but repudi-
ates, [the] theory of Nullification."[39]

Southern planter Andrew Jackson's response astounded Mercer
and the opposition. His annual message of December 4, 1832,
spoke in soothing tones to his native state and hinted at even
further tariff reductions; National Republicans met the message
with scorn, believing that the president would go to any lengths to
conciliate South Carolina. But six days later, after more complete
news from Charleston reached Washington, Jackson released his
proclamation—largely written by Secretary of State Edward
Livingston—to South Carolina. "I consider," the old general thundered, "the power to annul a law of the United States, assumed by
one State, incompatible with the existence of the Union." The
Constitution, he continued in a repudiation of the states' rights
compact theory, "forms a Government, not a league." Jackson
ended with a warning that none could safely dismiss. "Be not
deceived by names: disunion, by armed force, is treason. Are you
really ready to incur its guilt?"[40]

In answering Calhoun's theory, Jackson had adopted the National Republicans' concept of union. The president's southern
supporters were aghast. Ritchie called the proclamation "the great
error of the Administration." But Unionists flocked to Jackson's
standard, and for the first time in his life Mercer found himself in
agreement with the president. "Our country has reached a truly

awful crisis requiring from us all Great Moderation and equal firmness," Mercer advised one of his supporters. "To unlawful force I can concede nothing. The Union is not Union unless its legitimate authority can be sustained," he warned. "I would bear much and march firmly tho reluctantly to the threatened conflict."[41]

President Jackson, having issued a stern warning to South Carolina, decided in mid-January to back up the threat by requesting from Congress the authority to enforce federal law in that state. The president believed that as commander in chief he already possessed such powers; this maneuver was merely designed to demonstrate his resolve to the nullifiers. As with the December 10 proclamation, the so-called Force Bill message—South Carolina damned it as the "bloody bill"—met with nearly unanimous approval from the president's traditional foes. Indeed, when the message was placed before the House, Mercer promptly moved to have twenty-five thousand copies printed.[42]

To this about-face there was a curious corollary. If Jackson found new and unexpected support in the likes of Mercer, he antagonized many of his supporters. The southern wing of his party was even more horrified by his Force Bill message than by the December proclamation. Tidewater Virginians shuddered at the thought of marching into South Carolina to enforce the American System and all its distasteful branches. The Virginia legislature reaffirmed the resolutions of 1799 and denounced the December proclamation, all the while declaring nullification "illegitimate." It then sent Benjamin Watkins Leigh to South Carolina as a mediator. Mercer was infuriated perhaps the more so because his old enemy was involved. "The very mode in which Virginia sent down to her, added fresh insult to the thing," he growled, "and sent as it were an ambassador under the flag of sovereignty, to the court of . . . another sovereign."[43]

Further to confuse the situation, Henry Clay, recently defeated in the presidential contest, rose in the Senate on February 12 and announced his intention of introducing a new and lower tariff bill. Although he abhorred the Adams tariff of the previous year, Clay desired to beat the administration—which was preparing its own compromise tariff—to the punch and regain his old reputation as the great conciliator. Such a position might bring him greater southern support in future elections; as usual, Clay was prepared to sacrifice ideology for personal gain. Other party leaders, such as Adams, Webster, and Mercer, would not consent. "Mr. Calhoun and Mr. Clay have come together; and Mr. Clay and Mr. Webster are at variance upon the subject of the Tariff," Ritchie gloated. "What a strange jumble!"[44]

It was not difficult for Clay to forsake the tariff, for he was a man of elastic principles. But the next step must have been truly painful for the great nationalist. Late in the evening of February 20, the Force Bill came to a vote in the Senate. It passed by a vote of 32 to 1, the sole negative vote being proudly delivered by John Tyler of Virginia. William Rives, the other Virginia senator, voted aye, as did Webster. But Calhoun, now in the Senate and actually on the floor, declined to register a vote. Clay found it convenient to be elsewhere.[45]

Less than a week later, Clay's compromise tariff came down from the Senate. It passed handily by a vote of 119 to 85. Charles Fenton Mercer majestically voted against the measure, as did Adams and the entire Massachusetts delegation. But the south, on the whole, was pleased with the bill. "Every vote south of the Potomac," Thomas Ritchie pointedly remarked, "with the exception of Mr. Mercer, being in favor of it."[46]

The accusation that Mercer voted against his region, along with the view of the tariff of 1833 as "one of pacification," led Mercer to publish a long explanation of his vote in *Niles' Register*. He refused to vote for a lower tariff until the Force Bill was safely passed, which was by no means certain. More than that, the "testimony of so many men, representatives of the [north]eastern and middle States," whose "knowledge of the condition of the manufactures" he trusted, was opposed to the measure. The fact that "a great proportion of [them] voted against the bill in question,—occasioned in my mind no little hesitation to give it the sanction of my vote." If the plantation South needed further evidence that Mercer was no longer a part of it, this statement was it.[47]

The Force Bill came before the House a final time on the first day of March. After months of threats and counterthreats, the chamber was suddenly quiet. The bill was put to a vote and passed, 149 to 48. The Virginia delegation split, 14 to 7 in favor, with Mercer voting aye. A final yelp of indignation burst forth when Calhounite George McDuffie demanded that the bill be renamed "an act to subvert the sovereignty of the States of this Union." Annoyed and weary, the House made short work of dispensing with McDuffie's request.[48]

With the end of the session rapidly approaching, the House took up Clay's land distribution bill, postponed from the previous session. For several hours Mercer and Clement Clay of Alabama sparred over the measure. Clay argued that with the crisis in South Carolina winding down it was madness to press such a bill. "If anything is calculated," he argued, to produce a dissolution of the republic, "it is legislation upon this subject." Let an appropriation be made in aid of colonization, "and we shall hereafter hear it proposed to appropriate money to purchase and colonize our slaves." "Colonization and abolition," the Alabaman concluded, "are naturally and closely connected." Such arguments continued until almost midnight, when the bill was driven to a third reading. To Mercer's surprise, it passed by a vote of 96 to 40. Perhaps his specious argument that the bill was part of the comprehensive compromise package carried weight. But the South was not convinced; a majority of the Virginia delegation voted no, and South Carolina formed a bloc against the measure.[49]

Nor was Andrew Jackson convinced that he had been party to any such pact. On Saturday, March 2, the day before Congress adjourned, the president signed the Force Bill and then the tariff into law. Two days later, to the great "regret" of the American Colonization Society, Jackson celebrated his second inaugural with a pocket veto of the land distribution bill. It was not a piece of any compromise he had been party to; he may also have wished to conciliate South Carolina. If so, he succeeded. Later that month yet another South Carolina convention accepted the new tariff bill but pronounced the Force Bill "a monument to the corruption of the times" and in a final but far from meaningless act voted it "null and void." To this last spasm of treason Jackson pronounced himself satisfied, and so the crisis ended, at least for a time.[50]

For Mercer, the crisis was not yet complete. In early 1833 the American Colonization Society members gathered in the House chamber for their sixteenth annual meeting. Mercer presided over the subdued body, glumly staring down at Henry Clay from the Speaker's chair. Gurley rose to deliver his yearly report and recommendations, which were adopted by the body with little ado. Suddenly it became apparent that the lifeless prose contained a coup. The body, without realizing it, had voted to remove five members of the board, including Key and Walter Jones, in favor of a group of northern men. The delegates angrily voted to reinstate the former board, but the damage was done.[51]

Faced with the failure of the Virginia legislature to take any meaningful steps following the Turner rebellion, as well as growing disunionist sentiment from South Carolina, the northern minority whose "day-dream" it was to use the society as a first step toward abolition had decided to seize control of the society. They had come to the conclusion that the important politicians who ran the society "in truth neither designed nor wished [it to] effect any degree of emancipation." Hence, one charged Mercer, "when such a design was avowed by Mr Gurley's resolution, *you* & others opposed it." And so the great American Colonization Society committed suicide. Had it not, it would have died from natural causes brought on by the crises of the early 1830s. When the society next met, it was dominated by northern men. Key, Jones, and Mercer, then still a vice-president, were absent. The only representative of the southern states was John Marshall. Ironically, the truncated society had finally become what Mercer's critics had always believed it to be.[52]

In a final act of indignity, Mercer had to fight for his life in the April elections. His opponent in his recently gerrymandered district was Richard Mason of Fairfax, "a thorough-going State Rights man." At Leesburg, Mercer and Mason addressed the voters "from the hustings," both men "in neat and appropriate remarks" presenting "expositions of their political sentiments." Although Mercer carried Loudoun, it was by an embarrassing majority of only 236 votes. A week later the two men spoke on Mason's home ground of Fairfax. To the surprise of neither, the Tidewater county supported Mason. The election then went into the third and final contest, to be fought in Fauquier County, newly added to the district. "The chances," Ritchie gloated, "appear to be in favor of Mason."[53]

With the South turning inexorably toward the acceptance of slavery as a positive good, it appeared to Mercer that his defeat was merely a question of time. But Fauquier was in the Piedmont, not the Tidewater. When the votes were counted, it was discovered that the election had gone, however slightly, in his favor. He was returned to Congress for a ninth term but by a mortifying majority in his entire district of just 124 votes. Worse still, colonization was defunct. With Gurley and the northern men at the helm, it was no longer part of the American System, although Mercer would never bring himself publicly to admit that. Faced with the greatest rebellion in its history, Mercer's state had refused to take any significant action on slavery. And so the society split, forcing northern colonizationists, like many Americans, to make an agonizing decision. It was a decision that Mercer could not much longer avoid.[54]

Notes

ABBREVIATIONS

ACS   American Colonization Society
CFM   Charles Fenton Mercer
COCC   Chesapeake and Ohio Canal Company
DAB   *Dictionary of American Biography*, ed. Allen Johnson and Dumas
           Malone, 21 vols., 1928–1936.
JQA   John Quincy Adams
JSH   *Journal of Southern History*
LC   Library of Congress
NJHS   New Jersey Historical Society
NYHS   New-York Historical Society
PRO, FO   Great Britain, Public Record Office, Foreign Office
UVA   University of Virginia
VHS   Virginia Historical Society
VMHB   *Virginia Magazine of History and Biography*
VSL   Virginia State Library
WMQ   *William and Mary Quarterly*

1. *Richmond Whig*, January 21, 1830.

2. Mathew Carey, *Letters on the Colonization Society Addressed to the Hon. C. F. Mercer* (Philadelphia, 1832), 15–16; *Sixteenth Annual Report* (Washington, D.C., 1834), 7; Charles Fenton Mercer, *To the August Assembly Convened in Paris, to Confer on Restoring the Peace of Europe, the Memorial of the American Society for Colonizing in Africa the free people of colour of the United States* (London, 1856), 2.

3. P.J. Staudenraus, *The African Colonization Movement* (New York, 1961), 175.

4. CFM to Ralph R. Gurley, May 31, 1828, ACS Papers, LC; Charles Fenton Mercer, ed., *Slave Trade*, House Committee Report 348, Serial 201, Vol. 3 (Washington, D.C., 1830), 278–79.

5. CFM to Ralph R. Gurley, February 16, 1830, ACS Papers; CFM to William Gaston, January 1, 1828, William Gaston Papers, University of North Carolina, Chapel Hill.

6. William M. Atkinson to CFM, December 2, 1828; CFM to Ralph R. Gurley, December 7, 1828, both in ACS Papers.

7. CFM to Ralph R. Gurley, February 25, 1830, ibid.

8. CFM to Ralph R. Gurley, April 9, 1830, ibid; Mercer, ed., *Slave Trade*, 3–6.

9. Drew Gilpin Faust, *James Henry Hammond and the Old South: A Design for Mastery* (Baton Rouge, 1982), 47–48.

10. William W. Freehling, *Prelude to Civil War: The Nullification Controversy in South Carolina, 1816–1836* (New York, 1965), 197.

11. Charles Fenton Mercer, *An Address to the Colonization Society at their 36th Annual Meeting* (Geneva [Switzerland], 1854), 7, 16. Most of the Kendall letter is reprinted in the appendix. It is included neither in Branch's report nor in the documents accompanying Jackson's annual message.

12. Amos Kendall to Ralph R. Gurley, November 19, 1831, ACS Papers; Report of Secretary of the Navy John Branch, December 6, 1830, *Register of Debates in Congress* (Washington, D.C., 1831), 21st Cong., 2d sess., app. xix.

13. Mercer, *Address*, 7.

14. JQA Diary, February 2, 1831, in Charles Francis Adams, ed., *Memoirs of John Quincy Adams Comprising Parts of His Diary from 1795 to 1848*, 12 vols. (Philadelphia, 1874–77), 8:309.

15. Mercer, *To the August Assembly*, 13–14; *Register of Debates*, 21st Cong., 2d sess., 850.

16. *Richmond Enquirer*, August 16, 19, 1831.

17. *Constitutional Whig* (Richmond), August 29, 1831; *Richmond Enquirer*, August 30, 1831. Stephen B. Oates, *The Fires of Jubilee: Nat Turner's Fierce Rebellion* (New York, 1975), 114, places the number of innocent blacks slain at around 120, "probably more."

18. Charles I. Foster, "The Colonization of Free Negroes in Liberia, 1816–1835," *Journal of Negro History* 38 (January 1835): 55–56; *Richmond Enquirer*, December 15, October 25, 1831.

19. *Register of Debates*, 22d Cong., 1st sess., 1475–76; *Richmond Enquirer*, January 7, 1832.

20. James Madison to Ralph R. Gurley, December 29, 1831, in Carey, *Letters to Mercer*, 31; CFM to Charles James Faulkner, February 12, 1832, Faulkner Family Papers, VHS; John Marshall to Ralph R. Gurley, December 14, 1831, in Carey, *Letters to Mercer*, 31–32.

21. CFM to Ralph R. Gurley, January 6, 1832, ACS Papers; CFM to Charles James Faulkner, February 12, March 3, 1832, Faulkner Family Papers; Ralph R. Gurley to CFM, January 7, 1832, CFM Papers, NYHS.

22. *Richmond Enquirer*, January 26, 1832; CFM to Charles James Faulkner, January 13, 1833, Faulkner Family Papers.

23. Census Records, 1830, reel 190, p. 72, National Archives; Loudoun County Personal Property Tax, 1831, VSL; CFM to Charles James Faulkner, February 12, 1832, Faulkner Family Papers; Charles Fenton Mercer, *An Exposition of the Weakness and Inefficiency of the Government of the United States of North America* (N.p. 1845), 167. Alison G. Freehling, *Drift toward Dissolution: The Virginia Slavery Debate of 1831–1832* (Baton Rouge, 1982), 167, insists that the debates amounted to "a vigorous 'fresh start' to the age-old dream of emancipation-colonization." Later, however (192–93), she admits that the political power of the Tidewater "ultimately precluded action in 1832." My view, like Mercer's, is that the debates amounted to anything but a "fresh start."

24. CFM to Ralph R. Gurley, January 19, 1832; ACS Papers.

25. CFM to Charles James Faulkner, February 12, 1832, Faulkner Family Papers; *Register of Debates*, 22d Cong., 1st sess., 2332–33; *Richmond Enquirer*, April 10, 1832.

26. *Register of Debates*, 22d Cong., 1st sess., 2334–40.

27. Ibid., 2345–49.

28. Ibid., app., 5.

29. Robert F. Dalzell, Jr., *Daniel Webster and the Trial of American Nationalism, 1843–1852* (New York, 1972), 109; Peter Temin, *The Jacksonian Economy* (New York, 1969), 29; Mercer, *Exposition*, 362, 84.

30. JQA Diary, December 21, 1831, in Adams, ed., *Memoirs*, 8:439.

31. Glyndon G. Van Deusen, *The Life of Henry Clay* (Boston, 1937), 252.

32. *Register of Debates*, 22d Cong., 1st sess., 3830–31; *Richmond Enquirer*, July 3, 1832.

33. William Nisbet Chambers, *Old Bullion Benton, Senator from the New West: Thomas Hart Benton, 1782–1858* (1956; rpt. New York, 1970), 115; CFM to Charles James Faulkner, February 13, 1832, Faulkner Family Papers.

34. *Register of Debates*, 22d Cong., 1st sess., appr., 112–17.

35. Ibid., 3852–53; *Richmond Enquirer* July 6, 1832.

36. Samuel Flagg Bemis, *John Quincy Adams*, 2 vols. (New York, 1950–56), 2:260; Robert V. Remini, *Andrew Jackson*, 3 vols. (New York, 1977–84), 3:14.

37. Mercer, *Exposition*, 137.

38. John C. Calhoun to Virgil Maxcy, September 11, 1830, in Edwin W. Hemphill

et al., eds., *The Papers of John C. Calhoun*, 16 vols. to date (Columbia, S.C., 1959–84), 11:229.

39. Joel Poinsett to Andrew Jackson, February 9, 1833, in John Spencer Bassett, ed., *Correspondence of Andrew Jackson*, 6 vols. (Washington, D.C., 1926–33), 5:16; *Constitutional Whig* (Richmond), April 13, 1832.

40. *Register of Debates*, 22d Cong., 2d sess., app., 4, 180–87.

41. John Tyler to John Floyd, January 16, 1833, John Tyler Papers, LC; *Richmond Enquirer*, February 19, 1833; Maurice Baxter, *One and Inseparable: Daniel Webster and the Union* (Cambridge, Mass., 1984), 210–11; CFM to Charles James Faulkner, December 17, 1832, Faulkner Family Papers.

42. *Register of Debates*, 22d Cong., 2d sess., app., 145–54; *Richmond Enquirer*, January 19, 1833.

43. *Richmond Enquirer*, January 3, 29, 1833, Mercer, *Exposition*, 142.

44. *Richmond Enquirer*, February 16, 1833.

45. JQA Diary, February 21, 1833, in Adams, ed., *Memoirs*, 8:526; *Register of Debates*, 22d Cong., 2d sess., 688.

46. *Register of Debates*, 22d Cong., 2d sess., 1810–11; *Richmond Enquirer*, March 2, 1833.

47. CFM to Nathan Appleton, September 21, 1845, Nathan Appleton Papers, Massachusetts Historical Society; CFM to Edgar Snowden, March 4, 1833, in *Niles' Weekly Register* 44 (1833): 20–21.

48. *Richmond Enquirer*, March 5, 1833; *Register of Debates*, 22d Cong., 2d sess., 1903.

49. *Richmond Enquirer*, March 5, 1833; *Register of Debates*, 22d Cong., 2d sess., 1911, 1920–21; JQA Diary, March 1, 1833, in Adams, ed., *Memoirs*, 8:531.

50. *Richmond Enquirer*, March 7, 12, 1833; *African Repository* 8:381. Merrill D. Peterson, *The Great Triumvirate: Webster, Clay, and Calhoun* (New York, 1987), 232, notes that Clay, who should have known, did not consider his land bill part of the compromise package.

51. *African Repository* 8:353; *Sixteenth Annual Report* (Washington, D.C., 1834), iii–xxii.

52. JQA Diary, October 13, 1833, in Adams, ed., *Memoirs*, 9:23; *Seventeenth Annual Report* (Washington, 1834), iii–iv; Richard Henry Lee to CFM, January 19, 1836, CFM Papers, NYHS.

53. *National Intelligencer*, April 11, 1833; *Richmond Enquirer*, April 16, 19, 1833.

54. Glover Moore, *The Missouri Controversy, 1819–1921* (Lexington, Ky., 1953), 348; *Richmond Enquirer*, April 30, 26, 1833.

16

The Whig

It seemed strange to Mercer at the time, and perhaps it always did, that so much of the nation opposed his canal. Despite the disingenuousness with which he promoted the project, stubbornly insisting that the enormously expensive undertaking would benefit all of society, he never truly comprehended the depth of the Jacksonian antagonism to his great endeavor. Yet it was certain that the canal, like his colonization society and the tariff, was seriously endangered by the Democratic ascendancy.

With the clear understanding that the promotion of such immense enterprises had come to an end with the close of the Adams administration, Treasury Secretary Richard Rush, even before leaving office, offered to travel to Europe to seek financial backing for the canal. The "District Corporations" of Washington that subscribed to the canal stock immediately realized their inability to finance the purchases without loans from the great European investment houses. Mercer also hoped that Rush could persuade the Europeans to subscribe to stock for themselves.[1]

But news of the great project met with a less than enthusiastic response in Europe. In late June 1829, the banking firm of Baring Brothers informed Rush that it was not "sufficiently confident" about the undertaking to make a loan. News from across the channel was equally bad. A prominent Amsterdam banker wrote Rush that he would become involved only if the loans were "formally guaranteed by the Government [for] both Capital and interest." Rush was unable to make such a promise.[2]

Nevertheless, Rush decided that his chances were greater in Holland. On July 10 he arrived in Amsterdam only to discover that "the enormous failures [of] South America[n] projects" had dried up the flow of capital in Europe. Two months later he sadly reported to Mercer "that my prospects prove bad," and he was nearly ready to give up. For "three months" he had done little but shout at "the capitalists of this part of the world, almost until my lungs were sore."[3]

In late September Rush prepared to return to London. His business, he wearily informed his wife, might keep him in England "throughout the whole autumn." But he met with no success, and a month later he informed Mercer that he had once more "opened a correspondence with Holland." Strangely, Rush thought, his efforts in London were "defeated by Americans." Upon hearing of the project, the English banks went to the "American houses," where the success of the canal was "blown upon." One British banker even informed Rush "that he would not touch it, because there were slaves in the district." "Who put him up to this," Rush added, "I know not."[4]

In the proposals and counterproposals that followed it became clear that the English doubted the success of such a huge project without the backing of the American government. And as the fall wore on, Rush reported continuing failures. In mid-November, however, the gloom suddenly lifted. Rush, still in London, informed Mercer that although his negotiations with Holland remained unfinished, his "prospects of success [were] evidently brighter."[5]

Finally, Rush was able to report success. The Amsterdam house of Crommeline took the loans, although, to Rush's dismay, at nearly 6 percent, a far higher rate of interest than he had expected. "Undoubtedly, the great cause of our canal would have been at an end," he sighed, "but for this Dutch money." It was clear to him "that under President Jackson's administration, it would have been in vain to look to the general government for any new grant or subscription." The district, Rush bluntly told Mercer, would simply have to accept the high interest rate, for "no other capitalists in either hemisphere, would risk their money in it."[6]

There was every reason in addition to the high interest for Mercer to be concerned about the future of the canal. At the time of its initial application to Congress for aid, the company had estimated its capital to be nearly $4 million, of which one-half million was expected from a subscription by Maryland. But the money bill failed in that state, Mercer complained, by a "single casting voice." Friends of the canal would try again, but the funds were needed immediately. Just more than a month past the groundbreaking ceremony, Mercer realized that "75,000 dollars, must be demanded of the other Stockholders of the Company."[7]

To encourage the recalcitrant state to purchase stock, Mercer relied on his standard formula: he prepared a voluminous memorial, with the aid of Nicholas Biddle, president of the second Bank of the United States. Biddle well understood the role of internal improvements in the American System. He also well understood that his bank could profit from the national "canal madness," and he sent Mercer several pamphlets on Pennsylvania canals "which will furnish an interesting fact for your memorial."[8]

Mercer's bulky presentation obviously was effective, for in 1831, the same year it was presented to the Maryland legislature, the state appropriated half a million dollars for the purchase of stock. Next, he told a young supporter, Virginia should invest $750,000. In light of the Old Dominion's "relative population and wealth, and extent of interest, of the two states, in the common enterprise," Mercer thought, even that amount could "scarcely be considered enough."[9]

Virginia, of course, was controlled by Jacksonians hostile to the National Republican program. More to the point, the legislature continued to be dominated by the Tidewater, which showed little interest in investing in a project that would aid the northern and western regions of the commonwealth. Virginia, Mercer fumed, gave not "one farthing." How his native state could "refrain from aiding the common enterprise with honor or credit to herself," he could not fathom.[10]

That the canal was not the "common enterprise" he presented it as was precisely the point he declined to dwell on. Instead, Mercer relied on a relatively new legislative technique: he hired a former member of the House of Delegates, Bernard Grove, as a lobbyist. Mercer also labored to garner support for the canal by using Charles James Faulkner, a young "champeon" of the project, as his floor leader in the Virginia House. It was absolutely vital, he told Faulkner, that Virginia help in completing the eastern portion of the canal, for he had promised Congress that he "would ask no more for that section." If any Virginians objected to "uniting our State funds with those of the United States," Mercer advised, "let your opponents recollect our purchases of the U.S. Bank Stock." The comparison, although flawlessly logical, was one he would repudiate in less than a year.[11]

But the vision of the agricultural South did not encompass Mercer's magnificent waterway to the Ohio, and year after year the Virginia legislature rejected his requests. To his "extreme mortification" five delegates from the Shenandoah region, an area he expected to support the project, voted against purchasing stock. The canal was simply too far outside of the worldview of all but a very few Virginians. With no other choice, Mercer applied to the willing Biddle and his "Bank of the U.S. through the [Washington] branch for a loan."[12]

As bad as these problems appeared, they were not the only perplexities facing him. Indeed, the indefatigable Mercer, who attended to even the smallest tasks connected with the project, found nothing but problems. Through long hours of study in the congressional library he became familiar with every aspect of his enterprise. He researched the connection between the operations of "manufactures, merchants, and Engineers" in Great Britain. He fell into the "regular habit of inspecting the order books" of the engineers. He even personally tested the imported "Tuscororra cement" and found it of "miserable quality."[13]

Worse still, Mercer found the rapid advancement of his undertaking bogged down in a morass of litigation. Most of the suits were filed by property owners who objected to being thrown off their land to make way for the canal. Georgetown College filed suit over its land "required for the Canal," as did the Farmers and Mechanics' Bank of Georgetown over water rights first granted to the bank by the old Potomac Company. Most serious of all was an injunction granted by the chancellor of Maryland to stop work on the dam at Little Falls. Mercer imperiously "instructed" his laborers to carry on, "notwithstanding the existence of the writ of Injunction."[14]

Indeed, the company president did his best to see that construction continued on the canal while the innumerable suits slowly made their way through court. To expedite matters, Mercer, who did not shirk his legislative duties in this period—although he seems to have forsaken the cause of colonization—tried several of the Maryland cases himself. For the two cases that made their way up through the legal system to the Supreme Court, however, Mercer prudently retained William Wirt of Virginia, Monroe's attorney general.[15]

Another trivial if persistent problem was finding enough laborers for the canal. Mercer finally applied to the American consul in England to aid him in importing "surplus" Irish workers. The pay, Mercer noted expansively, was ten dollars a month, with meat three times a day and "a reasonable allowance of liquor." But when the workers arrived, they met all of Mercer's worst expectations. Twenty-two of them promptly fought their way into jail, and the annoyed company president was forced to bail them out. As a solution, the man both decried as a "Northern fanatic" and praised as an "American Wilberforce" turned to slave labor on the arduous "works of the Shenandoah."[16]

These problems were merely a nuisance; a more serious obstacle was the Baltimore and Ohio Railroad. Considering Mercer's industrial vision, it is ironic—but not surprising—that a serious enemy of the canal should be a rival form of transportation. Both projects would serve the same market, and both, more seriously, required the same path to the west. On Mercer's return to Washington from the Richmond convention, he "found already formed in the House" a "very strong" inclination to halt work on both projects "until an experiment should be made of the relative advantages of the Canal and Rail Road."[17]

To stave off such a disaster, Mercer adopted a personal form of persuasion. One wavering congressman, John Davis of Massachusetts, reported that Mercer appeared unexpectedly at his door early one morning and invited him to ride to Georgetown. When they reached that section of the city, Mercer spurred his horse up the canal. After they had ridden a "considerable distance," Davis nervously suggested that they return to their seats. Mercer refused, "for he felt anxious to show" more of the work. Upon reaching Great Falls the two men stopped for dinner "and then pushed our way to the city which we reached about sundown having completed 30 miles." The "wind was very raw and strong in our faces," and the young congressman's "poor bones complained some." He was amazed at the energy of his plump, fifty-two-year-old companion. Interestingly, in addition to his salary as company president, Mercer had the expenses for such excursions paid by the city of Washington as if he were a lobbyist.[18]

The Baltimore and Ohio Canal Company, however, was up to this challenge and more. The rewards to be reaped by tapping into the Ohio were too great to be given up without a fight. The company also hired a lobbyist in Virginia to ensure that the state bought no canal stock, and though it was doubtful that much argument was required in that agrarian realm, Mercer was furious at the company's "injurious insinuations and charges." There was something slightly pathetic in Mercer's grievances against the railroad. Having labored for nearly a decade in behalf of the canal, he could not admit that he had toiled for a project that was already obsolete. That he had thought only of a canal in 1823 demonstrates that Mercer, like many National Republicans, was very much an eighteenth-century man; the magnificent canal system of Britain was still clear in his mind. But by 1832 his senses told him he had erred. With a rage borne of impotence he lashed out at what he now knew to be the future. The "American public," he cried, "have been duped by the enthusiastic friends of these *new inventions*."[19]

The new inventions and their small army of lawyers, however, were too much for Mercer. The "works of the [canal] Comp[an]y," he snapped at the president of the railroad, "are now retarded beyond the 'Point of Rocks' solely by your injunction." But the railroad was willing to compromise. Its directors only wished to share the right of way with the canal. They had no desire to deny the canal its existence; time and their superior technology, they knew, would take care of that. And so while a compromise was hammered out in the courts, Mercer was free to turn his attention back to Virginia. With all "obstructions having been removed," Mercer lectured Faulkner, "we need only funds for its completion."[20]

Mercer was wrong. Moreover, he probably knew it, for the friends of internal improvements were by then aware that the most dangerous enemy of the canal was neither the railroad nor the nuisance suits. It was Andrew Jackson, as his reaction to the Maysville Turnpike bill, introduced in Congress in 1830, made clear. The bill was not unlike that which aided the canal, for it authorized the government to subscribe to fifteen hundred shares of private stock for $150,000. The bill was probably written by Mercer, now the chairman of the Committee on Roads and Canals. Such acts, he boasted, "were, with few exceptions, written by the Chairman, though frequently reported by the [various state] members charged with the memorials which gave rise to them." The bill argued that the road, which was entirely within the state of Kentucky, was a part of the National Road system. It was not.[21]

On April 30 the bill came before the House. After some discussion, Davy Crockett, the colorful if somewhat fraudulent National Republican frontiersman from Tennessee, moved to cut off debate. The bill was then voted on. It passed by a comfortable margin of 102 to 86. Mercer and his old friend Doddridge were the only Virginians to stand behind the measure.[22]

One month later the bill came roaring back to Congress carrying a stern veto message. The bill, Jackson insisted, was unconstitu-

tional because it appropriated federal funds for an intrastate project. His predecessors had only endorsed bills that were truly
interstate in character. More than that, the republic was still
deeply in debt, which the old general was determined to pay off
before leaving office. It would therefore be necessary to levy taxes
for such a system. "In many particulars," Jackson added, "these
taxes have borne severely upon the laboring and less prosperous
classes of the community, being imposed on the necessaries of
life."[23]

The veto message contained little of interest for those who were
not accustomed to contemplating the situation of the laboring
people. Mercer certainly did not hold with it much. He believed
"the gross absurdities into which the opponents of the constitutionality of the power to make any such improvements, were
proper subjects not of argument but of ridicule." He continued to
argue that the road was part of the larger system and decried the
theory "that no work could be national which was constructed
within the limits of a single State,—that a road might be national,
but its several parts were no so." It was an argument of little avail.
Mercer's position was bloodied a second time the following day
when the House, after a "quite angry debate," attempted to override Jackson's veto. The effort did achieve a vote of 96 to 90, with
Mercer and Doddridge again in the majority, but it was far short of
the necessary two-thirds. Two days later Congress adjourned, and a
dejected Mercer returned to his office at the canal company.[24]

The gulf of opinion between the committee chairman and the
president on such matters was, in an ironic way, narrowed a bit
shortly thereafter. The canal company finally completed its blast-
ing in Georgetown, to the great relief of the residents, who had
been terrified by "the fragments of rock that were almost daily"
raining down around them. A wide stone bridge was built across
the canal. On the east end of the bridge, no doubt to the mortification of both men, was erected a large marble tablet bearing Mercer's name and that of Andrew Jackson. Within days, an
appropriately named packet, the *Charles Fenton Mercer*, moved
slowly through the Georgetown locks.[25]

Mercer's reaction to the president's war on internal improvements was nothing compared to what he thought of the old general's attack on a second aspect of the American System. For it was
the second Bank of the United States more than any other issue
that divided and defined the two parties. Strong central banking
was crucial to merchants and incipient industrialists, as it was to

the businessmen and lawyers who were connencted with those interests. The bank was also staunchly supported by the great staple-producing planters of the South, who had close ties to the urban business community. The Washington branch of the bank, in addition to making loans to Mercer's canal company, held some of the loans on the shares purchased by the district corporations.[26]

Mercer was unwilling to admit that Biddle's bank, following a brief flirtation with Jackson, had forged a logical if unnaturally close relationship with the National Republican party. Although legally wedded to the federal government, the bank was theoretically nonpartisan. But Biddle thought it was wise to please those in Congress who might be in a position to do him favors, and this meant the opposition. One who benefited greatly from this coziness was Daniel Webster, who for several years was one of the directors of the bank. Webster also profited in other ways. Informing Biddle that he was asked to argue a case against the bank, Webster noted that he declined, although he churlishly observed that his "retainer has not been renewed, or *refreshed,* as usual."[27]

Another who benefited from the bank's largesse was Henry Clay. In 1832 the opposition leader was granted a five-thousand-dollar interest-free loan. The congressman from Loudoun, who was again slipping into poverty, also profited from this relationship. Mercer told Biddle that he felt "much indebted" for "the liberal arrangement which at your kind suggestion [the bank] made of my four debts to the Washington Branch." Even in a time of elastic ethics, a mood that allowed Mercer both to act as company president and to vote on bills relating to it, Democrats had cause to be worried about Biddle's powers of corruption.[28]

Jackson's public hostility to the bank made its recharter the central issue in this period. The old twenty-year charter was due to expire in 1836, but many conservatives thought it best to press the issue before the 1832 presidential contest. Mercer's old enemy Louis McLane, now secretary of the treasury, however, cautioned against any precipitous actions. True to his Federalist beginnings, McLane favored recharter, but he informed Thomas Cadwalader, Biddle's aide, that any movement "before the election" would be viewed "as an act of hostility." The bank would receive few votes from the South and only a handful from Virginia. Only "Mercer, Newton & Doddridge," all former Federalists, were "on our side."[29]

But Biddle received conflicting advice from Clay. Harry of the West, the likely National Republican nominee, was desperately searching for an issue that could defeat the Old Hero. Clay concluded that pressing the issue of recharter would put the president in a difficult spot. If Jackson signed a bill to recharter the banks, it would appear to the electorate that he acquiesced in the most important aspect of the American System and that the bank would be rechartered. If he vetoed the bill, Clay would have an issue to use against Jackson. The Maysville fight taught Clay that internal improvements were no longer a winning issue. Clay thus informed Biddle that "if *now* called upon" Jackson "would not negative the bill." But the outcome should the president be reelected "might and probably would be different."³⁰

Perhaps the most logical advice Biddle received came from Mercer. Several years before, he had warned Biddle not to attempt recharter "in the hey day of Genl. J[ackso]ns administration." Now he "confidently recommended" prompt action. The president's "election is as certain as his life," he predicted, and he "hates your Bank." A victory over Clay would "increase the effect of his influence over this Congress." But Calhoun, still vice-president, "is friendly to your bank," while "Van Buren your enemy is in England." Moreover, Jackson's administration was for the most part "on your side." Mercer was sure the "persons who fill these political stations may be changed" after the election. He was forced to agree with Clay. If pressed now while the advantage lay with the bank, Jackson would have to sign. It was flawlessly logical advice. It was also wrong.³¹

On January 9, 1832, memorials calling for the recharter of the second Bank of the United States were presented in both houses of Congress. Democrats immediately attacked the petitions, and Mercer rose in reply to insist that the issue was "intruded upon them" by "the Chief Magistrate." Little debate was required; "the matter had been thrice discussed by men of ability—in time of peril, and in time of peace, after which it could hardly be said that the House now requires additional illumination on the Subject." On the whole, the opposition's handling of the bank issue smacked of dishonesty and self-satisfaction. But the National Republicans were united behind the measure, and, startled at having it thrust upon them before the election, many Democrats were hesitant to oppose it. Aware of the leverage this situation gave him, Clay forced the issue to a vote on June 10. The measure passed, 28 to 20, with the two Virginia senators, John Tyler and Littleton Waller Tazewell, in the minority.³²

Three weeks later the bill came before the House. It passed, 106 to 84, with the vote reflecting the power of business and industrial capitalism in New England and the middle states. The agrarian South was strongly opposed to recharter; only seven Virginians voted in favor. Biddle then made his way down to the floor, where Mercer and others crowded around to shake his hand. That evening the bank president thanked his supporters with an expensive party at his lodgings. Biddle was jubilant. "Now for the President," he toasted.[33]

Indeed, the president. By pressing for recharter before the election the old duelist's pride and position as party leader were challenged, and Andrew Jackson was not a man one could safely challenge. Compromise was no longer possible. On July 10 the president returned the bill with a veto message largely drafted by Amos Kendall, the sharp-eyed auditor who had stemmed the flow of money to the American Colonization Society. The bank, the message began, was unconstitutional. More than that, it was wrong. "It is to be regretted that the rich, and powerful, too, often bend the acts of Government to their selfish purposes." Distinctions in society, based on talent, education, and wealth, Jackson conceded, would always exist. "But when the laws undertake to add to these natural and just advantages artificial distinctions . . . to make the rich richer," he stormed, "the humble members of society, the farmer, the mechanic, and laborers . . . have a right to complain." As long as he was in office, he would fight "any prostitution of our Government to the advancement of the few at the expense of the many."[34]

The veto outraged most National Republicans, but it truly terrified Mercer. It now became clear that the Democrats were intent on destroying the bank, a move that held grim implications for his canal. It was even suggested on the floor of the House that the president might remove the government deposits from the bank. Mercer abruptly reversed his course of the previous year and argued that whatever the reasons might be "for selling bank stock," they were "wholly inapplicable to the stock it had in roads and canals." The power of promoting works of internal improvement "by subscription for shares of stock," he argued, not without some difficulty, "was a circumstance which rendered it entirely distinct from the purchase of bank stock."[35]

The corporate concern of the National Republicans, however, was concentrated on the president's denouncement of class-based legislation. Because they doggedly argued that the harmonious American System would benefit all groups equally, a cant dating back to the days of late Federalism, they abhorred the dangerous rhetoric of conflict and were quick to vilify its use. Whoever was evil enough to attack the bank "by arraying one class against another," Webster thundered, "deserves to be marked especially as the poor man's curse." Even Mercer, despite his immediate concerns about his canal, found time to assail Jackson for exciting working-class "prejudice against the better and more intelligent classes."[36]

And so with the lines neatly drawn the two parties prepared for the impending presidential contest. Clay had his issue, although not necessarily on the terms he desired. In December 1831, the National Republican convention, chaired by James Barbour, met in Baltimore and nominated Clay and John Sergeant, a wealthy Philadelphia lawyer for the bank. Adams, despite his support for the American System, took no part in the election. But the "old federal party," he admitted, was "now devoted to Mr. Clay."[37]

The Democrats also met in Baltimore. Jackson was renominated with ease, and Van Buren, who met with considerable southern hostility, was tapped to replace Calhoun. Nevertheless, the Democratic ticket was extremely popular in Virginia. As in 1828, there was even a sizable Jackson "county committee" in Loudoun. But the bank forces were not only determined to win, they believed victory to be easily within their grasp. To ensure success, Biddle threw the weight of the bank into the melee. He donated close to a hundred thousand dollars to the effort and ordered the publication and circulation of thirty thousand copies of the bank veto message as a campaign document for Clay. That document worked wonders among the great majority of businessmen, who tended to be National Republicans, and in the Virginia manufacturing areas along the Great Kanawha. It was a strategy that Mercer believed would rally to the National Republican cause "the intelligence, substance and respectability of the country."[38]

Indeed, so little did Biddle, Mercer, and the party understand the mood of the republic that just before the election a Virginia National Republican paper confidently predicted that "Clay will be chosen by the Colleges," where he was within "one vote of a majority of a whole." The party was stunned as the enormity of Jackson's victory began to become clear. When all was decided, the electoral vote stood at 219 for Jackson and 49 for Clay. Even two of the three counties in Mercer's district went for the old general; only Loudoun went overwhelmingly for Clay and by a larger margin than it had for Adams.[39]

The immensity of the Democratic victory was not lost on the forces of conservatism. As soon as the outcome was announced, the stock of the second bank fell four points. Mercer had new reason to doubt the ability of his party to sell its program to the public. The American people had voted for Andrew Jackson, a man who "combined a most curiously and most fatally a despotism and a demagogue spirit."[40]

More bad news was to follow, of a personal nature. Just as the returns were seeping into the capital, an anxious letter arrived from Garnett telling Mercer that his sister was "dangerously ill." Early the next morning Mercer left his residence at Gadsby's Hotel, where he had moved to escape the radical odor of the Union Tavern, and galloped toward Essex.[41]

Garnett's alarm was unfounded, and when Mercer reached Essex he was relieved to discover that Eleanor had rallied. But not long after Mercer returned to Washington, news reached him that John Randolph, who, as Adams caustically observed, "for forty years was always dying," had finally made good his word. During his last years Randolph was mad, and his heavy use of opium and drink made matters worse. In accordance with his final request, he was buried facing west so that he could keep an eye on Henry Clay. Randolph had been estranged from Mercer since the constitutional convention, but the news still came as a jolt. The two men had been friends for almost a quarter-century, and because Randolph was only five years Mercer's senior, his death doubtless reminded the gloomy Virginian of his own mortality.[42]

Under these circumstances, it is a tribute to Mercer that he withstood the next blow. He had been president of the Chesapeake and Ohio Canal Company for five years, and 108 miles of the canal had been completed. His company had also reached an accord with the railroad in which both firms would share the right of way near Harpers Ferry. But the company was seriously in debt. Virginia had yet to subscribe to a single share of stock, and with a hostile administration in office it was unlikely that the canal could count on any further aid from the federal governemnt. In a move born of desperation, a faction within the company recommended that its presidency be passed to Jackson's close friend John Eaton, who had recently been defeated in a Senate bid. The Tennessee Democrat, they hoped—incorrectly, as it turned out—could alter the president's position on the project.[43]

The election for company president was held in June 1833. John Eaton prevailed, 5,054 votes to 3,430 for Mercer. Jackson, surely with great pleasure, used his influence to throw the more than 2,000 votes allotted to the government to Eaton, who also received the votes of the corporation of Washington. The proxies of Maryland, who were leaning toward Mercer, were split, as were those of the corporation of Georgetown, and the votes of both groups were thrown out. Had they gone to Mercer, as expected, he would have been reelected by 182 votes. The individual stockholders supported him by two to one. "It seems as if Mr. Mercer," snapped one sympathetic editor, "was the only sacrifice upon which a majority could be brought to act together."⁴⁴

As a final indignity, the stockholders unanimously voted the outgoing president a bonus of five thousand dollars in addition to his regular salary of two thousand dollars a year as a show of thanks. Mercer was humiliated, although the critical state of his finances would not allow his pride to have the last word. It was had instead by editor Hezekiah Niles, long his defender: "It partakes strongly of the absurd, or the ridiculous."⁴⁵

It was Mercer's fate to be human, indeed far too human, and to be involved in the cruel life of politics. In October he was given a "public dinner" at Morgantown, Virginia. If he had not been very festive at the dinner celebrating his election five years before, he was even less so now. The evening was subdued, and the dinner was followed by several cheerless toasts. Glasses were raised to the American System, the Union, and finally to Mercer, the "advocate of western Virginia principles." To that toast he rose and, deep in a blue funk, delivered a few rambling remarks on "the subject of internal improvement and public education."⁴⁶

Whether Mercer would even continue in politics was now open to speculation. Just before his removal from the canal company he told a friend that he had "long resolved the question, [of] how my indifference to life can be cured." The answer was "the simple remedy of occupation." His was a "mournful view," he admitted, "but it has long been mine, uncheered by wife or children." He considered resigning his seat and "editing a newspaper." Now even the remedy of occupation was denied him.⁴⁷

That so quintessential a National Republican project had been turned over to a Jacksonian was a matter of great importance to the party. Equally important, the president had begun to turn the National Road over to the states. But there was little time for concern. The rumors that Jackson would launch a new assault on the bank had grown too loud to ignore. On March 2, party members sponsored a resolution which held that "the Government deposits may, in the opinion of the House, be safely continued in the Bank of the United States." The resolution passed by a vote of 109 to 46; many Democrats who voted against rechartering the bank as it was then organized supported the resolution because they were not yet ready to take such a radical step. Mercer found himself in the unusual position of voting with the majority of the Virginia delegation, which split 7 to 4 in favor.[48]

Amos Kendall continued to badger the president to remove the deposits by the fall of 1833. Convincing Jackson of this course was not difficult, for the House resolution assured him of the corruptive powers of the bank. But the cabinet was not unanimously behind removal, and two treasury secretaries, including Mercer's old tormentor Louis McLane, were sent flying before Jackson found in Attorney General Roger Taney the man to do his bidding. On September 20 the removal of the deposits was announced in the *Washington Globe,* the official administration voice. "The explosion has taken place," Webster sighed.[49]

It was not surprising that the upper classes viewed the president's latest sortie with horror. Tyrone Power, an Irish actor then touring the states, heard wealthy residents of Pittsburgh blaming the lack of street lights on the removal of the deposits. It was an act somewhat too radical for many of Jackson's southern supporters, so the peculiarity of Mercer voting with a majority of his Virginia brethren was to continue, at least on matters concerning the bank. The General Assembly passed a resolution decrying removal of the deposits. Mercer happily promised Governor John Floyd that he would, "with becoming zeal, cooperate with a large majority of my colleagues in endeavoring a restoration of the public money."[50]

But the administration was far ahead of the opposition. On April 4, 1834, House Speaker James K. Polk forced through a series of resolutions against recharter and the restoration of the deposits. Mercer voted against each one. The opposition was despondent; Adams was "mortifie[d] beyond expression." Just as the election of 1832 was fought out on the question of recharter, the elections of 1834 were waged on the issue of removal. The National Republicans went forth in a new coalition, the Whig party, a word that first appeared on the ballot in the New York City elections. The name was also an attempt to appeal to unhappy states' rights men, for the term had often been used by nullifiers in South Carolina during the crisis of the previous year. Essentially the National Republicans were assuming a different name; even in Virginia the business wing of the party was dominant. Indeed, executive usurpation, a concern both wings of the party could agree on, gave the Whigs a cohesive issue in the July 1832 veto of the second bank.[51]

Whatever complaints Power found among the Pittsburgh elite, the plain people of the nation supported Andrew Jackson. The

Whigs made the election a referendum on the deposits, and they lost decisively. The Democrats, one boasted to Polk, gave "the W[h]igglery such a whipping that they will stay Whipped." Indeed, the rout of conservatism was complete. Of the four major pillars of the American System—internal improvements, central banking, high land prices, and a lofty tariff wall—virtually nothing remained. The ancillary supports—colonization and national aid to public education—were equally moribund. Even Mercer's magnificent canal had been taken from him. It too was in the ebb of life, although not because of the hapless Eaton, who was gone from the post by the 1834 elections. Mercer's political career was also in the ebb of life and would expire within a few years.[52]

Notes

ABBREVIATIONS

ACS	American Colonization Society
CFM	Charles Fenton Mercer
COCC	Chesapeake and Ohio Canal Company
DAB	*Dictionary of American Biography,* ed. Allen Johnson and Dumas Malone, 21 vols., 1928-1936.
JQA	John Quincy Adams
JSH	*Journal of Southern History*
LC	Library of Congress
NJHS	New Jersey Historical Society
NYHS	New-York Historical Society
PRO, FO	Great Britain, Public Record Office, Foreign Office
UVA	University of Virginia
VHS	Virginia Historical Society
VMHB	*Virginia Magazine of History and Biography*
VSL	Virginia State Library
WMQ	*William and Mary Quarterly*

1. Joseph Gales to Samuel Ingham, April 1829, Chesapeake and Ohio Canal Company Records, LC; CFM to Richard Rush, February 14, 1829, Richard Rush Papers, LC.

2. Baring Brothers Company to Richard Rush, June 22, 1829; W. Willink, Jr., to Richard Rush, June 20, 1829, both in Chesapeake and Ohio Canal Company Records, LC.

3. Richard Rush to CFM, July 15, September 8, 1829, Richard Rush Papers, LC.

4. Rush to Catherine Rush, September 10, 1829; Rush to CFM, October 7, 1829, both ibid.

5. Rush to CFM, October 29, November 13, 1829, ibid.

6. Rush to CFM, February 22, 1831, ibid.; Daniel Crommelin to Rush, October 17, 1829, in Richard Rush, *Letter and Accompanying Documents from the Hon. Richard Rush Respecting the Loan of a Million and a Half of Dollars* (Washington, D.C., 1830), 95-96; Rush to CFM, February 25, 1831, Rush Papers.

7. CFM to Joseph Gales, August 25, 1828, COCC, Papers, National Archives.

8. Edward Pessen, *Jacksonian America: Society, Personality, and Politics*, rev. ed. (Urbana, 1978), 129; Nicholas Biddle to CFM, November 10, 1828, CFM Papers, NYHS.

9. CFM to Charles James Faulkner, December 24, 1832, Faulkner Family Papers, VHS.

10. CFM to Charles James Faulkner, December 20, 1831, ibid.

11. CFM to Charles James Faulkner, January 13, 1833, December 19, 1831, ibid.

12. CFM to Clement Smith, February 11, 1833, COCC.

13. CFM to Benjamin Wright, June 17, 1830, ibid.; CFM to Charles James Faulkner, January 9, 1832, Faulkner Family Papers; CFM to Alfred Cruger, December 3, 1832, COCC.

14. John Ingle to Thomas Mulledy, November 4, 1830; CFM to Richard Coxe, June 27, 1831; John Ingle to Isaac McCord, July 2, 1829, all in COCC.

15. CFM to Richard Coxe, September 3, 1832, ibid.; William Wirt to CFM, December 22, 1832, William Wirt Papers, Maryland Historical Society.

16. CFM to James Maury (in Liverpool), November 18, 1828; John Ingle to M. Wines, October 3, 1829; CFM to Archibald Lee, January 17, 1829, all in COCC.

17. CFM to Andrew Stewart, May 14, 1830, ibid.

18. Joseph Gales to CFM, August 2, 1829, CFM Papers, Harvard University Library; John Davis to Eliza Davis, July 1830, John Davis Papers, American Antiquarian Society.

19. CFM to Charles James Faulkner, February 3, 12, 1832, Faulkner Family Papers.

20. CFM to President and Directors of the Baltimore and Ohio Railroad Company, November 6, 1830, COCC; Charles Fenton Mercer, *Report from the President of the Chesapeake and Ohio Canal Company, to the Legislature of Maryland* (Annapolis, 1831), 11; CFM to Charles James Faulkner, March 3, 1832, Faulkner Family Papers.

21. Robert V. Remini, *Andrew Jackson*, 3 vols. (New York, 1977–84), 2:247, n. 11, says it was not; CFM, Autobiographical Sketch, Mercer-Hunter Papers, VSL.

22. *Register of Debates in Congress* (Washington, D.C., 1830), 21st Cong., 1st sess., 842; *National Intelligencer*, April 30, 1830.

23. *Register of Debates*, 21st Cong., 1st sess., app., 133–42.

24. CFM, Autobiographical Sketch, Mercer-Hunter Papers; *Register of Debates*, 21st Cong., 1st sess., 1147–48; *National Intelligencer*, May 29, 1830.

25. *Richmond Enquirer*, September 16, 1831; William M. Franklin, "The Tidewater End of the Chesapeake and Ohio Canal," *Maryland Historical Magazine* 81 (Winter 1986): 299.

26. Daniel Walker Howe, *The Political Culture of the American Whigs* (Chicago, 1979), 16–17; Charles G. Sellers, Jr., "Who Were the Southern Whigs?" *AHR* 59 (January 1954): 340; *National Intelligencer*, April 21, 1830.

27. *Constitutional Whig* (Richmond), January 13, 1829; Daniel Webster to Nicholas Biddle, December 21, 1833, in Charles M. Wiltse et al., eds., *The Papers of Daniel Webster*, 7 vols. to date (Hanover, N.H., 1974–86), 3:288.

28. Nicholas Biddle to Henry Clay, August 1, 1832, in James F. Hopkins et al., eds., *The Papers of Henry Clay*, 8 vols. to date (Lexington, Ky., 1959–85), 8:557; CFM to Nicholas Biddle, September 17, 1835, CFM Papers, Harvard University Library.

29. Thomas Cadwalader to Nicholas Biddle, December 21, 1831, in Reginald C. McGrane, ed., *The Correspondence of Nicholas Biddle Dealing with National Affairs, 1807–1844* (Boston, 1919), 147–50.

30. Henry Clay to Nicholas Biddle, December 15, 1831, in Seager, ed., *Papers of Clay*, 8:432–33.

31. CFM to Nicholas Biddle, December 12, 1831, in McGrane, ed., *Correspondence of Biddle*, 140–42.

32. *Richmond Enquirer*, January 14, 15, 17, 1832; *Register of Debates*, 22d Cong., 1st sess., 1508.

33. *Register of Debates*, 22d Cong., 1st sess., 3851–52; William Nisbit Chambers, *Old Bullion Benton, Senator from the New West: Thomas Hart Benton, 1782–1858* (1956; rpt. New York, 1970), 183–84.

34. Robert V. Remini, *Andrew Jackson and the Bank War: A Study in the Growth of Presidential Power* (New York, 1967), 43; Lynn L. Marshall, "The Authorship of Jackson's Bank Veto Message," *Mississippi Valley Historical Review* 50 (December 1963): 474; *Register of Debates*, 22d Cong., 1st sess., app., 73–79.

35. *Register of Debates*, 22d Cong., 2d sess., 863–65.

36. Robert F. Dalzell, Jr., *Daniel Webster and the Trial of American Nationalism, 1843–1852* (New York, 1972), 34; Arthur M. Schlesinger, Jr., *The Age of Jackson* (Boston, 1945), 107; Charles Fenton Mercer, *An Exposition of the Weakness and Inefficiency of the Government of the United States of North America* (n.p., 1845), 187.

37. Samuel Flagg Bemis, *John Quincy Adams*, 2 vols. (New York, 1950–56), 2:292–93; *Niles' Weekly Register*, December 17, 1831, pp. 281–82; JQA Diary, March 3, 1832, in Charles Francis Adams, ed., *Memoirs of John Quincy Adams Comprising Part of His Diary from 1795 to 1848*, 12 vols. (Philadelphia, 1874–77), 8:486.

38. *Richmond Enquirer*, May 25, April 3, January 17, 1832; Schlesinger, *Age of Jackson*, 113; Remini, *Jackson and the Bank War*, 2:376; Clement Eaton, *The Growth of Southern Civilization, 1790–1860* (New York, 1961), 246; Virginius Dabney, *Virginia: The New Dominion* (New York, 1971), 231; Mercer, *Exposition*, 76.

39. *Richmond Constitutional Whig*, June 28, 1832; *Richmond Enquirer*, February 16, 1833, November 9, 13, 1832; *Register of Debates*, 22d Cong., 2d sess., 1723.

40. *Niles' Weekly Register*, December 8, 1832, p. 240; Mercer, *Exposition*, 260.

41. CFM to Thomas Purcell, November 3, 1832, COCC.

42. *DAB*, 15:365–66; JQA Diary, June 27, 1833, in Adams, ed., *Memoirs*, 9:5.

43. CFM, Autobiographical Sketch, Mercer-Hunter Papers; *DAB*, 3:610.

44. CFM, Autobiographical Sketch, Mercer-Hunter Papers; *Niles' Weekly Register*, June 22, 1833.

45. *Niles' Weekly Register*, June 22, 1853.

46. Ibid., October 26, 1833.

47. CFM to William M. Blackford, March 13, 1832, James Mercer Garnett Papers, Duke University Library.

48. Merrill D. Peterson, *The Great Triumvirate: Webster, Clay, and Calhoun* (New York, 1987), 196; *Register of Debates*, 22d Cong., 2d sess., 1922.

49. *National Intelligencer*, September 26, 1833; Daniel Webster to Samuel Jaudon, September 26, 1833, in Charles M. Wiltse et al., eds., *The Papers of Daniel Webster* 7 vols. to date (Hanover, N.H., 1974–86), 3:276.

50. Glyndon G. Van Deusen, *The Life of Henry Clay*, (Boston, 1937), 281; CFM to John Floyd, March 6, 1834, in H. W. Flourney, ed., *Calendar of Virginia State Papers and Other Manuscripts*, 11 vols. (1875–92; rpt. New York, 1968), 10:621.

51. *Congressional Globe*, 23d Cong., 1st sess., 291; JQA Diary, April 4, 1834, in Adams, ed., *Memoirs*, 9:120–23; Glyndon G. Van Deusen, *The Jacksonian Era, 1828–1848* (New York, 1959), 96; Lynn L. Marshall, "The Strange Stillbirth of the Whig Party," *AHR* 72 (January 1967): 446; Sellers, "Who Were the Southern Whigs?" 344, 338.

52. Sherman Page to James K. Polk, November 2, 1834, in Herbert Weaver et al., eds., *Correspondence of James K. Polk*, 6 vols. to date (Nashville, 1969–83), 2:545.

17

Into the Mines

The last years of Charles Fenton Mercer's political life symbolize the plight of conservatism during the high-water mark of Jacksonian radicalism. Broken on the wheel of Old Hickory's tremendous popularity, Whiggery underwent a period of transition. To its dismay, the party found that the old issues and the old candidates could not win victories. American conservatism had a program and the rhetoric it needed to convince the voters. But it lacked energy and a new and glamorous standard-bearer. Ironically, to triumph against the Democracy, the conservative party discovered that it had to leave behind the men who had salvaged conservatism from the ruins of 1800.

Before they could realize their potential, the Whigs had to endure the election of 1836, maneuvering for which had preceded the debacle of 1834. The situation was confused by the unnatural alliance between Clay and Calhoun, which was frowned upon by many in the more nationalistic wing of the party. Mercer's district particularly disliked Clay; in Leesburg it was believed that Clay "deceived them by betraying their interest to subserve Calhoun." This strongly protariff district, Webster was told, now "would prefer you."[1]

It was not surprising that Mercer was singled out by those who wished to carry Webster into the executive mansion. Copies of a letter were sent to one man in each state, including the congressman from Loudoun, who were to serve as the nucleus of a Webster and Union ticket. It "is apparent the Presidential Canvass has been opened," Henry Dearborn informed Mercer in the summer of 1833. And only Webster could "rally the most powerful party under the battle cry of 'The Constitution & the Union.'" The principles of the movement, aside from the tariff, would be those "of the President's Proclamation."[2]

Nothing came of the movement in Virginia. It was not that Mercer was not the logical choice to head such a movement in the Old Dominion. Indeed, as a ceremonial thanks for his stand on nullification he received several votes in the balloting for House Speaker. Nor was it because, regardless of the mood of his district, Mercer liked Clay and distrusted Webster. It was not even because any incipient Union movement fell apart during the struggle over the deposits. It was because, following his removal as president of the canal, Mercer had very little enthusiasm left for politics. There was much truth in one critic's charge that with no "object to excite his ambition," the portly Virginian had sunk into "a mere eater and drinker of the good things at Washington."[3]

As the presidential contest of 1836 approached, Mercer sank further and further from sight; he appeared to care little about who would face Martin Van Buren. Henry Clay, as always, coveted the nomination, but when the Ohio Whigs supported John McLean he abandoned hope and published a letter saying he would not "under any circumstances, be a candidate for the presidency." In the end, reflecting the uncomfortable fact that there was no unified Whig party, there was neither a Whig strategy nor a single Whig candidate. In the contest, Webster represented New England, Hugh Lawson White the South, and William Henry Harrison the West. Some Whigs hoped that the election would be thrown into the House, where they might have a better chance. Others, like Nicholas Biddle, prayed that the opposition electoral vote might add up to a majority so that it could be united on one man, probably Harrison. Should that happen, Biddle counseled, Harrison should "say not one single word about his principles." Let "the use of pen and ink be wholly forbidden as if he were a mad poet in Bedlam." But the banker's hopes were to no avail, for the Magician carried the three prizes of New York, Virginia, and Pennsylvania and with them the presidency.[4]

But even as Van Buren was taking office he had good reason to wish that Biddle's prayers had been answered. An economic crisis in Britain caused in part by the restrictions of the Bank of England led to the failure of several important business houses. American cotton prices plummeted, debts secured against the crops became uncollectible, and the merchants holding the debts failed. In a domino effect, the panic spread. Banks discovered their assets gone or illiquid, and with no other recourse the major New York banks suspended specie payment on May 10, 1837, just two months after Van Buren's inaugural.[5]

The hardest hit by the disaster was the urban working class. By the time the major banks suspended payment, the price of bread was double what it had been two years before. Terrified laborers responded to the crisis with bread riots and destroyed—but did not loot—the store of wholesale flour suppliers. These popular uprisings horrified conservatives. " 'Loco foco' means flour rioter," one Whig explained to Biddle.[6]

On May 16, the president issued the call for a special session of Congress, only the fourth in the history of the republic. All during the summer, as the depression deepened, Van Buren contacted the best financial minds among the Democrats, asking for their advice on the crisis. With many of these letters went the proposal he had received from John Brockenbrough, president of the Bank of Virginia, who suggested nothing less than the complete separation of bank and state.[7]

Such a course, however, was far too radical for many Democrats, and as congressmen began to straggle into Washington for the special session, the popular topic of debate was whether the president could force his will on the conservative wing of his party. The moment of truth arrived when the president's message was delivered to the House. Van Buren began by reviewing the causes of the depression: the "spirit of adventurous speculation," the drain of gold abroad, and the aid "profusely given to projected improvements." He cautioned his readers that these causes argued against the creation of another bank. Instead, Van Buren bravely insisted that the course Jackson had set out should be followed. He called for the complete separation of the government from all banks and suggested that federal money be dispensed and collected through a subtreasury system. As an emergency measure, Van Buren urged that the fourth installment of the surplus be retained to cover the government's operating costs.[8]

The financial community and the Whig party opposed these measures but did little but blame the Democrats for the panic; aside from urging the creation of another bank, they brought forth precious few proposals. Those they did urge cut through the progressive-sounding Whig rhetoric and laid bare the soul of American conservatism. "If there could be afforded any relief to the mercantile classes," Clay informed the Senate, "some alleviation of the general distress would follow." Mercer's suggestions were equally humane. Caught in speculating on "three large estates in improved land," he was forced to throw himself "on the indulgence of [Biddle's] Board." Yet he thought Clay correct. "Reflection convinces all," he wrote, "that the poor rates create paupers."[9]

The aspect of the president's plan that Mercer found most destructive was the decision to withhold the fourth installment of the surplus. He thus set about on the research for a long speech intended for publication. On September 26 he was ready. "I am, in truth," Mercer apologized, "of late years unused to debate." With that qualification, he delivered a speech lasting almost five hours. His concern, clearly, was for the tattered remnants of the American System. He admitted that he had wished to use federal funds obtained from land sales for three "noble purposes" and especially for a "widespread system of popular education elevating our social condition." If the surplus were withheld, even the states would not be able to pursue these objectives. There would be no need for these expediencies, he argued, were it not for years of Democratic bungling, and he followed this assertion with a detailed economic analysis that took several hours. All that was needed to see America through the crisis, he concluded, was a "manifestation of a temper," on the part of Van Buren, "friendly to the banks and the mercantile class of the community."[10]

Mercer went on for what seemed an eternity. His long absence from the floor and his unhappy tendency to bludgeon his audience with statistics were painfully obvious. He was followed by Abraham Rencher of North Carolina, who also opposed the bill. "I will not follow the example so repeatedly set me," Rencher pointedly remarked, "of wandering into discussion of other matters." Another speaker was even more barbed. "The gentleman from Virginia has gone into an investigation of the report," William Taylor observed, "but, I must confess, I was unable to understand the errors which he endeavored to point out," a remark that drew laughter from the floor.[11]

The sterility of both Mercer's agruments and the Whig wall of defiance was demonstrated late in the evening of September 29, when the bill on the fourth installment was put to a vote. It passed, 118 to 106, with Mercer and Adams in the minority. The Virginia delegation split 10 to 7 in favor.[12]

Such a small margin of victory was hardly reassuring to the administration, for Van Buren was all too aware that his central proposal, the subtreasury bill, was extremely unpopular among many groups in the Jacksonian camp. New York Democrats with ties to Wall Street banks found the measure abhorrent, and many southern party members thought it smacked of urban radicalism. Even Ritchie found himself in the odd position of supporting the president while drawing back from the heart of his program. The bill passed the Senate, but in the House it met a hostile coalition of Whigs and conservative Democrats. On October 14 the measure was tabled by a vote of 119 to 107. For the administration, it seemed as if conservative counsels would prevail, for when the subtreasury bill came up again at the regular session it met with much the same response.[13]

But the real drama that winter, at least from Mercer's perspective, was played out not in the House but in his home district. And when his position was challenged, it came not from the Democrats but from his own party. In late August a long letter appeared in the important *Alexandria Gazette*. "Is it not time," the anonymous author queried, "that the people of this District were turning their attention to the approaching Congressional Election?" It was clear, the writer thought, that "Col. Mercer intends holding on with a deadly grasp." The time had come for him to retire, although it appeared as if "he would rather die a natural than a political death." It was announced that contrary to practice—for a sitting member was never challenged by his own party—Robert Henderson, a Whig, was in the race. Such a contest would split the vote and hand the district to a Democrat. To stave off this disaster, "a District Convention should be held" to decide on a nominee. Mercer, of course, would be "the favored candidate," the author cunningly observed.[14]

Over the next several weeks Mercer discovered that the drive for a district convention was not the work of a single man. Other letters called for a meeting, one alleging that it was an "often voiced complaint" that Mercer had been "in Congress long enough." Another even suggested that the "Administration Party" would support Mercer. "His visionary schemes have abated," the writer declared, "and with the exception of being a Whig, he is doubtless an acceptable representative" to the Democrats.[15]

By mid-September Mercer realized that he was in the fight of his life. Two of the leading Whig papers in his district, the Leesburg *Genius of Liberty* and the *Warrenton Times*, were "dead against" his reelection and favored Robert Henderson and William McCarty, respectively. Even the powerful *Alexandria Gazette*, long an ardent Mercer defender, declared itself neutral. The subsequent flock of letters, however, proved that he still had numerous and vociferous friends. One long piece correctly guessed that "the friends of Mr. Mercer in said Convention, [would] be out numbered in the appointment of delegates." Despite all claims to the contrary, the convention was little but a device for disgruntled Whigs to unseat him. The "people—the bone and muscle of his constituents," the writer charged, "are not tired of him and will show you so."[16]

The key to the struggle was hidden between the lines of these letters. The attack on Mercer was generational. Looking forward with gleeful anticipation to 1840, the younger, more aggressive, and less deferential Whigs wished to replace the man who had become a mere eater and drinker in Washington. For many of these men, Mercer's long service in the legislature and his numerous bills under Monroe and Adams were history. Mercer was as obsolete to them as the old Federalists had once been to him. Yet the older Whigs remembered and found the younger men's claim to "have been raised with a kind of hereditary regard and respect" for Mercer presumptuous. The idea of them "offering C. F. Mercer advice relative to his political discretion," snarled one, "would excite a laugh, were it not below mirth."[17]

But the sarcasm of old men did not dissuade the young Whigs. The party was moving quickly to discard Henry Clay, the Old Prince, in 1840, and the Virginia branch was just as anxious to find a younger, more attractive champion for the "great Whig district." On October 11 Thomas Colston, the driving force behind the movement, in an open letter demanded to know whether Mercer would "consent to submit" his claims to represent the district "to the decision of a Whig Convention?" "Will you yield to such a decision?" Colston queried.[18]

Less than a week later Colston discovered that there was more fight left in the old gentleman than the young bucks of the party had presumed. In a letter published in Whig journals around the district, Mercer imperiously refused to abide by the decision of any group "calling themselves the Whig party of this district, but who cannot be regarded as speaking the voice of the majority of that party." When he truly thought that his constituents wished him to step down he would, but not a moment before. If a second Whig entered the race and split the vote, it would not be his fault, but he would not give way. Mercer also gave notice that he would speak "on the subject" at the November courts.[19]

In his heart of hearts Mercer knew why he was being opposed. His conscience assailed him and told him that the five years of inactivity following his removal from presidency of the canal company had won him the enmity of the younger Whigs. But he would not admit it. Instead he fell back upon a comforting lie: behind the opposition to his reelection lurked an old enemy, John Scott, who had slandered him in a public letter in 1829. It was easy for Mercer to convince himself of Scott's culpability for Scott, now a superior court judge, had been driven into the Whig camp by the bank war, and his son Robert was actively involved in the move to oust

Mercer. Moreover, Scott believed that in 1836 Mercer had pur-
posely delayed introducing a bill to aid the railroad of which he was
president.[20]

True to his word, Mercer arrived at the Fauquier court with a
long speech in hand. He told the crowd that some time back he had
met a stranger who informed him that the "source of the opposition" to him was John Scott. Mercer insisted that he had regarded
Scott as his "personal enemy ever since the Convention of 1829,"
when he was shown an essay that Scott had anonymously published claiming that he "advocated that convention with a view to
perpetuate my office of President of the Chesapeake and Ohio
Canal Company." The attacks, he shouted, did not stop. For years
Scott had been "in the habit of assailing my character." The move
for a convention was personal. And he had no greater wish, Mercer
concluded, than to continue in his constituents' service.[21]

Robert Scott was in the audience. When Mercer finished, the
young man mounted the steps before the courthouse and answered
Mercer's charges as best he could. But it was already late, and night
fell, dispersing much of the crowd, before Scott could proceed very
far. At this juncture the elder Scott, bearing documents pertaining
to his railroad, arrived on the scene. With a candle in one hand and
his papers in the other, Judge Scott prompted his distracted son as
the young man tried to complete the speech. As he rode away from
the chaos, Mercer was surely pleased at the damage the Scotts had
done to their case—and to the convention movement.[22]

Just before Mercer's denouncement of Scott, a group of young
Whigs met in Leesburg and recommended a district convention.
(That a public meeting in Leesburg was Mercer's traditional
method of starting any political drive was surely an irony neither
Colston nor Mercer savored.) On November 12 they met again and
picked December 13 as the day they would open a poll "to elect
delegates to represent the County of Loudoun" at the convention.
Mercer's triumph at the Fauquier court notwithstanding, determined groups in the other countries forged ahead in later weeks.
The Fairfax Whigs met in late November and approved the Loudoun resolves. They recommended that Loudoun receive twenty
delegates, Fauquier sixteen, and Fairfax eight. Elections were to be
held on December 13. In early December the Fauquier Whigs met
and agreed to join the other counties in a convention.[23]

The next step in the movement was another barrage of letters in
the press attacking Mercer. The "official" Loudoun party sadly
commented: "It is a fact, well known to some, if not all of you, that

many of the supporters of Col. Mercer have felt, and frequently expressed, the wish that he would decline being a candidate." "Senix" concurred. "Would it not have been more in the spirit of this modest Republican principle for Col. Mercer to have waived all preemption rights" to his seat?[24]

By this time Mercer was back in Washington, and neither he nor his friends made an argument against these latest attacks. Instead his reply took a curious form: a renewed vigor that resembled nothing so much as the Mercer of past times. He determined to assault the Democrats by tearing down "the overgrown power arising from the vast and annually increasing patronage of the President." It was, he admitted, an abrupt reversal of his long-held belief that "the Executive [was] too weak to counterpoise the Legislative department." But it was firmly in line with the newly discovered Whig cry that the presidency was too powerful.[25]

The alacrity with which Mercer seized upon this subject betrayed a zeal fired by more than the usual Whig dogma. In January 1839, Mercer presented a resolution requesting Van Buren to provide the House with "a list of all removals from office which have occurred since the organization of the present Government." In addition to the names of all those removed, Mercer requested the title of their office, a list of all public servants who were not renominated, and that "such list denote the date of each removal."[26]

Mercer's resolution clearly caught the Democrats off guard. The charge that Jackson had abused his powers of patronage had been bandied about for years, but the opposition had never taken it up. Ritchie was alarmed at the speed with which the allegation worked its way into the forefront of the "Whig Press." It also became the topic of the day in the Senate, where Webster and Benton engaged in virtually endless sparring matches over the issue. Perhaps more crucial, the *Alexandria Gazette,* previously neutral in the battle over Mercer's seat, pronounced his resolution one of great importance. Such information "will exhibit in an authentic form the workings of the 'spoils' system introduced on the 4th March, 1829."[27]

With the administration forces in disarray, Mercer pressed the attack. On March 2 he discharged a volley of resolutions. The first called on Van Buren to produce a list of all officers "who derive their appointment from the nomination of the President" and who have been removed from their positions "since the 3rd of March, 1789." A second resolution requested a list of officers "whose term of service being limited to four years, were not renominated to the Senate." Finally, he introduced a resolution cutting the salary of the postmaster general, a position traditionally awarded solely as political favoritism. It included a proviso stating that subordinate postmasters could be removed only for "incapacity, dishonesty or neglect of duty." All removals in this department were to be reported to Congress along with "the date of the removal and the cause thereof."[28]

The resolutions were agreed to by essentially the same coalition that annually defeated the subtreasury bill. But because the session was almost over, Mercer deemed it too late to try to force a bill through both chambers. Instead, the select committee on the subject, which he chaired, decided to delay "further action on the subject till the next Congress."[29]

When the answers to Mercer's resolutions began to drift in, the results were anything but encouraging. Secretary of State John Forsyth informed Mercer that no records were kept at his department on "dismissals and removals." The reply from the Treasury Department was equally inexact. "No separate record has ever been kept of removals from office," Levi Woodbury cheerfully reported to Mercer. Postmaster General Amos Kendall's response was even more disheartening. The man whose salary Mercer wished to slash politely replied that no books could be found for removals in his department before 1815. He did, however, possess complete records for the four administrations since then, all of which were presented to Mercer. To the dismay of the Whigs, Kendall demonstrated that although Van Buren had removed as many men in two years as Adams did in four, the number of post offices had doubled since 1828. The number of removals did not support the Whig cry of spoils. But if the Whigs as a party were displeased by the outcome, Mercer was certainly less so, for the issue had helped to blunt the attack on his recent career.[30]

Mercer's work that session was far from finished. If his district wanted "visionary schemes," he would provide them. Based on a memorial presented to Congress by Mathew Carey, the spiritual father of the American System and Mercer's old friend from the heyday of colonization, the chairman on roads and canals produced a voluminous and spectacular report that proposed a ship canal in Panama connecting the Atlantic with the Pacific oceans.[31]

The report began with the ostentatious claim that the project was "practicable." If the United States was willing to build the canal, it would "control the richest commerce of the world, [and] prescribe to all other states the terms upon which they may be admitted to share its enjoyment." The political situation in Central America, Mercer hinted, was fluid, and the government would be wise to procure the necessary territory before the European powers could take advantage of the situation.[32]

It was necessary, Mercer observed, that the oceanic link be a canal and not a railroad; simply carrying goods between the two ships would not be sufficient. He proposed a series of locks to raise ships to the flat highlands, which could be flooded to produce a large lake. The lake would be connected to the Pacific by a canal at the Bay of Panama and to the Atlantic by a canal at Limon Bay (which is exactly the course and design of the present Panama Canal). The canal would be open "to all nations, on the payment of reasonable tolls." In conclusion, Mercer urged that his design should not be "abandoned as impracticable" or prohibitive in cost, athough he admitted that he was unable to determine accurately "the cost of its construction." The report was followed by a series of detailed maps that demonstrated his proposed route, the elevation of Panama, and the trade route from New York to Panama to Canton, China.[33]

On Saturday, March 2, the last full day of the session and the same day as his final patronage resolution, Mercer delivered his report to the House. With it was a resolution calling on the president to open negotiations with the nations "whose territorial jurisdiction comprehends the Isthmus of Panama" for the "construction of a ship channel or canal." Surprisingly, the House, rather taken aback by the enormity of his vision, agreed to the resolution by a voice vote.[34]

That the proposal should win Mercer new converts among the younger Whigs was hardly unexpected, for the project was the American System on an international scale. It was precisely the kind of "visionary scheme" that fired the imagination of those younger Whigs whose economic perspective encompassed the Pacific and beyond. It did little, of course, to silence Mercer's personal critics. John Scott denounced it as simply another one of the "crude notions and wild schemes" of the "worn-out chairman." But Mercer was not trying to appeal to the judge and his minions.[35]

To be sure that his older, more traditional constituents were equally appeased, Mercer rode to the aid of a canal and river improvement project designed to connect the landlocked areas of Prince William, Loudoun, and Fauquier counties with the Chesapeake and Ohio Canal. Mercer's assistance was not totally altruistic, for a short canal would connect the Little River with his mill in Aldie. His July 13 letter to Virginia's Board of Public Works implied that he owned stock in the company. But local mill owners, powerful men in the region, favored the plan, and Mercer could hardly be unaware that they were in a position to do him great political favor.[36]

The result of Mercer's impressive burst of energy, combined with his stubborn refusal to leave the race even in the event of a three-way contest and his victory over Scott at the Fauquier court, was that even before the end of the session the convention movement was virtually moribund. His supporters, perhaps still in the majority in his district, banded together and refused to attend any meeting. One announced that "not a single friend of Col. Mercer" would agree to a convention. It would be "fatal" to the party, this writer warned, for the younger men to nominate a minority candidate.[37]

Faced with defeat, Mercer's Whig critics began to abandon their movement. Unless he received the nomination, one correctly observed, Mercer would "reject the whole proceedings, as emanating from his personal enemies, and continue as a Candidate in opposition to the nominee of a Convention." Such a course would turn Virginia's safest district over to the Democrats at a time when the Whigs were emerging victorious almost everywhere else. Let Mercer be returned to Congress, and "if God shall have him to live so long," one writer added in a nasty aside, a broader movement in 1841 could force him to obey "the will of the majority of the whole Whig party."[38]

In the following weeks the convention movement continued to collapse. One by one Mercer's challengers dropped out of the contest. William McCarty withdrew in December, saying it could afford him "no gratification to be the [nominated] opponent of Mr. Mercer." With only Robert Henderson left in the race, and he only halfheartedly, any last formal resistance to Mercer evaporated. In late December votes in Fairfax went to the polls. The turnout, not surprisingly, "was very small." Only fifty men bothered to show, and forty-three of them "expressed a preference for Col. Mercer." The challenge was over. The other counties in the district did not even hold elections.[39]

If the young Whigs fumed over their defeat, most of them did their gracious best to conceal it. In letter after letter they worked to unite the badly divided party behind Mercer. "I have lately been to Washington, and find that Mr. M. leaves there," observed one, "with a reputation for industry and talents increased instead of diminished." "Heretofore opposed to Mr. Mercer's reelection," echoed another, we "not only cease our opposition, but unite in his cordial support."[40]

Just as the hopes of the young Whigs were being dashed, the hostility of Mercer's personal enemies was increasing. In mid-December John Scott issued his formal reply to Mercer in a private letter that categorically denied Mercer's charges. Accompanying his letter was a copy of his 1829 "Caution" essay, which oddly enough supported the allegation that Scott had claimed Mercer's enthusiasm for constitutional reform was born of personal consid-erations. But Scott insisted it contained no "injurious attack," and he demanded a "prompt and full reparation." Mercer did not re-spond immediately, and so in early January Scott's friend Samuel Chilton twice wrote to him, inquiring whether Scott's letter had been received. A curt reply of January 18 informed Chilton that it had.[41]

Mercer, tied down by his research on Panama and happily watch-ing the resistance to his election evaporating, was in no mood to grant Scott a formal reply, let alone a retraction. Instead, he pub-lished a lengthy defense of his actions—it required a full page in four editions of the *Alexandria Gazette*—in which he insisted that he had done all he could to aid Scott's railroad. The bill had been buried in a morass of legislation following the diplomatic "diffi-culties with France" under Jackson. As late as January 1839 Mercer was peppering Amos Kendall with requests for a mail contract for the line, apparently in an effort to appease Scott and the railway. As for the charges growing out of the "Caution" essay, Mercer insisted that it was he who had been wronged. He would make no apol-ogy.[42]

Mercer's public statement further outraged his latest antagonist. Scott's behavior in November had made him look foolish, and now Mercer was still refusing to apologize and all but calling him a liar as well. Had he been dealing with anyone but Mercer, he stormed, he "should have drunk deeply of the cup of humiliation." He knew that it would be futile to challenge Mercer because of "his known determination not to demand nor give satisfaction in that way." There was no alternative but "to inflict upon him personal chas-tisement."[43]

A collision was only a matter of time. It came several weeks later, when Mercer appeared at the door of a tavern in Fauquier. As he glanced about for a table, he was surprised to see Scott heading toward him at a quick step and looking murder if ever a man did.

Almost before he could think, Scott backhanded him smartly across the face. Mercer lost his balance and went down. Scott then pulled a cutlass from his coat to be used if Mercer retaliated. Mercer scrambled to his feet, pulling from his pocket a penknife, the only weapon within reach. This opera bouffe ended only when several startled observers found their feet and wrenched the two corpulent and puffing old men apart.[44]

This encounter left him shaken, although a final vindication of sorts was achieved later in the month when for the twelfth time Mercer was elected to the House of Representatives. With no other Whig in the contest, the Democrats did not even bother to field a candidate.[45]

That vindication was all Mercer desired. In a short time odd gossip began to be whispered about northern Virginia. One of the first to hear these curious reports was James K. Polk. Cave Johnson informed the Speaker that he had it on good authority—Lewis Williams, an old friend of Mercer's—that the newly reelected congressman planned to retire. "Rumor says th[e] Genl has been appointed Cashier of some Bank and will resign," a surprised Johnson told Polk.[46]

In mid-November Mercer made what was by then common knowledge official. He publicly announced that as soon as Congress was organized (and his vote for Speaker cast against Polk), he would resign his seat. John Gamble, his old Federalist friend from the House of Delegates and now a bank president in Florida, had offered him the job of cashier. The word in Alexandria, *Niles' Register* reported, was that Mercer did not feel "himself at liberty to decline an offer which is personally so advantageous." The journal also gave ironic notice that William McCarty was the unanimous choice of the Whigs "to succeed Mr. Mercer."[47]

On November 16, Mercer published a farewell address to his constituents in the *Alexandria Gazette*. Part of it constituted the traditional thanks for support, but more of it read as a final justification of his career. He carefully mentioned all of his major bills, his fund for internal improvement, his support for public education, his drive "to amend our State Constitution," his colonization "plan" of 1816, his slave trade act of 1819, and his canal, the creation of which required "the labor of six years, and seventeen acts of legislation." He also revealed for the first time that he had been offered a position in Monroe's cabinet. But his financial problems made it necessary for him to resign his seat: "I entered your service rich, I shall leave it poor." His honesty forced him to mention that he had acquired many enemies, but "what public man is without?" He would leave it to his constituents' "justice to acquit me."[48]

Mercer was not being completely honest. His resignation was the product of a number of complex motives. There was surely much truth in his statement that his debts "made his retirement an act of justice to his creditors." But the full truth contained more than that. He had always lived on the precipice of financial ruin. In fact, his finances were then quite sound. By mid-1838 he had again dug himself out from under the debt into which he had fallen during the first panic. His activity in local internal improvements following the crash of 1839 also demonstrates that he was solvent. As late as September he told a friend not only that his credit was solid but that he possessed a thousand dollars to invest in the short canal to his mill. He even had enough ready capital to purchase a family of eight slaves.[49]

More critical was that he was weary of the abuse repeatedly heaped upon him by the dominant southern planter class. Just after his election the previous April, the *Washington Globe*, the leading Democratic organ in the nation's capital, ran a series of articles on why Clay should never be president. Foremost among them was that he was a "friend" of "abolitionist" Mercer. It was this "most devout Federalist of the Adams stamp in Virginia," the paper alleged, who had first moved "the agitation of this subject" by presenting a British memorial for colonization in 1832. It was he who "begat swarms of petitions from fanatics in the North, and made their enthusiasm on the subject a most potent ally in the cause of Federalism."[50]

Southern planters had never understood Mercer's program, and if there was any indication that they never would this was it. Perhaps the charge that Henry Clay was unfit for office because Mercer was his friend was the final blow. Adams suspected this was the real reason behind Mercer's resignation. "The savage and barbarous genius of slavery has not only baffled them all, but has kindled a flame of popular odium against him," he wrote, "from which he has shrunk into the cashier of a bank."[51]

Surely, too, Mercer's failure to achieve the tremendous promise of his youth played a part in his resignation. He was not merely in the wrong state of the Union, although certainly he would have gone farther had he remained in the North. More significantly, he was betrayed by his manner and the admiration he held for the more staid leaders of his father's generation. John Latrobe believed that if Mercer were endowed with "more Americanism of character," he would have "taken a much higher stand as a Statesman than he did." He had grown into an astute politician, but unlike Clay he was "too refined and elegant a gentleman for the rough and tumble" of the egalitarian 1830s. Although he was brilliant and "looked up to for information," his career never came close to meeting his early expectations.[52]

Most of all, it was the challenge by the young Whigs that drove him from both politics and his native state. The indignity of having to fight for his seat was more than he could bear; he wished only to be returned at the polls so he could withdraw gracefully. His later statement that he resigned after being reelected by "an increased majority of his constituents" was more than a little disingenuous. His seat had been retained only with great difficulty, a battle he would have to endure again in 1841 if he remained.[53]

Mercer's depression was eased considerably by the refusal of his old friends to let him slip quietly away. On December 27, a large gathering threw him a farewell dinner in Leesburg. Despite the icy wind and deep drifts, few of the Whig elders missed the chance to honor "their faithful and long-tried public servant." Following the removal of the cloth, toasts were hefted to Washington, Monroe, and Clay. Almost endless glasses were raised to William Henry Harrison, who had been nominated for president in Pennsylvania earlier in the month. Among other toasts, Harrison was honored as "the People's candidate," "the enlightened statesman," and, most improbable of all, "the sound practical farmer." Finally, hours after it began, the dinner was over, and guest and hosts alike fell out the door, sliding and crashing into one another (they had poured down thirty-two toasts).[54]

In early January, Mercer's Washington cronies did him equal honor by hosting a dinner at Brown's Hotel. He had arrived back in the capital only days before, and he was to be there but a few days. With so little time, many of his friends heard of the dinner only after it was held, although even on short notice the turnout of fifty people was gratifying. James Barbour acted as host. Henry A. Wise and Hugh Lawson White attended, as did Samuel Southard, who spoke of hearing Mercer speak at Princeton on the need for a permanent navy almost a half century before. Following the speeches, Mercer rose to reply but was so overwhelmed he could barely speak. Instead he raised his glass: "The Constitution."[55]

And so at the age of sixty Mercer ended his public career. As he boarded the steamer for Tallahassee he reflected with pride that only one man had served more consecutive terms in Congress than he. He later described his political career as a "very long and not altogether undistinguished public life of thirty years." The words may have been immodest, but they were correct. Leaving aside the darkness of his visions and goals, few of Mercer's detractors would deny that he had compiled an enviable legislative record. Indeed, the large number of bills that he passed into law was particularly impressive considering that most of his labors were discharged under the banner of a minority party. More than that, he performed a signal service for American conservatism, for he, as much as any other man and more than most, was instrumental in making the conservative party palatable to the American electorate. Mercer would be absent from the political scene by the time the Whigs finally captured the White House, but it was the handiwork of those like him that made the stunning victory of 1840 possible.[56]

Although he did not know it—and certainly the young Whig who irreverently predicted his imminent demise would never have guessed it—Mercer could look ahead to a long and full retirement, if that word could be used to describe his busy next years. The remainder of his years would not be spent in the political scene, but neither was his "noble spirit," as Adams sadly predicted, "doomed to drudge in the mines." Anyone who really knew Charles Fenton Mercer understood that his days were far from over; he was merely beginning a new stage in his life.[57]

Notes

ABBREVIATIONS

ACS	American Colonization Society
CFM	Charles Fenton Mercer
COCC	Chesapeake and Ohio Canal Company
DAB	*Dictionary of American Biography*, ed. Allen Johnson and Dumas Malone, 21 vols., 1928–1936.
JQA	John Quincy Adams
JSH	*Journal of Southern History*
LC	Library of Congress
NJHS	New Jersey Historical Society
NYHS	New-York Historical Society
PRO, FO	Great Britain, Public Record Office, Foreign Office
UVA	University of Virginia
VHS	Virginia Historical Society
VMHB	*Virginia Magazine of History and Biography*
VSL	Virginia State Library
WMQ	*William and Mary Quarterly*

1. Eli S. Davis to Daniel Webster, March 27, 1833, in Charles M. Wiltse et al., *The Papers of Daniel Webster*, 7 vols. to date (Hanover, N.H., 1974–86), 3:233.

2. Henry Dearborn to Daniel Webster, August 12, 1833 (copy to CFM) ibid., 270–72.

3. *Congressional Globe*, 24th Cong., 1st sess., 3; John Scott, ed., *Judge Scott's Reply to Mr. Mercer* (N.p., 1839), 45.

4. *Niles' Weekly Register*, December 26, 1835, p. 283; Richard P. McCormick, "Was There a 'Whig Strategy' in 1836?" *Journal of the Early Republic* 4 (Spring 1984): 68–71; *Register of Debates in Congress* (Washington, D.C., 1831), 24th Cong., 2d sess., 1656–57; Nicholas Biddle to Herman Cope, August 11, 1835 in Reginald C. McGrane, ed., *The Correspondence of Nicholas Biddle, Dealing with National Affairs, 1807–1844* (Boston, 1919), 255–56.

5. Peter Temin, *The Jacksonian Economy* (New York, 1969), 140; William Nisbet Chambers, *Old Bullion Benton, Senator from the New West: Thomas Hart Benton, 1782–1858;* (1956; rpt. New York, 1970), 222.

6. Arthur M. Schlesinger, Jr.; *The Age of Jackson* (Boston, 1945); 218–19; Herbert G. Gutman, *Work, Culture, and Society in Industrializing America: Essays in American Working-Class and Social History* (New York, 1977), 60–61; Charles Davis to Nicholas Biddle, September 27, 1837, in McGrane, ed., *Correspondence of Biddle*, 293.

7. John Niven, *Martin Van Buren: The Romantic Age of American Politics* (New York, 1983), 416; James C. Curtis, *The Fox at Bay: Martin Van Buren and the Presidency, 1837–1841* (Lexington, Ky., 1970), 76–77; *Alexandria Gazette*, April 11, 1839.

8. *Register of Debates in Congress* (Washington, D.C., 1834), 25th Cong., 1st sess., app., 1–9.

9. Ibid., 23d Cong., 1st sess., 224 (James F. Hopkins et al., eds., *The Papers of Henry Clay*, 8 vols. to date [Lexington, Ky., 1959–85]; 8:690, lists this comment in his index as " 'trickle-down' theory of prosperity"); CFM to Nicholas Biddle, September 17, 1835, CFM Papers, Harvard University Library; Charles Fenton Mercer, *An Exposition of the Weakness and Inefficiency of the Government of the United States of North America* (N.p., 1845), 189–90.

10. CFM, Autobiographical Sketch, Mercer-Hunter Papers, VSL; *Register of Debates*, 25th Cong., 1st sess., 938–71.

11. *Register of Debates*, 25th Cong., 1st sess., 971–75.

12. Ibid., 1150.

13. *Richmond Enquirer*, March 2, 1839; *Register of Debates*, 25th Cong., 1st sess., 1684–85; *Congressional Globe*, 25th Cong., 2d sess., 477–78; Howard Braverman, "The Economic and Political Background of the Conservative Revolt in Virginia," *VMHB* 60 (April 1952): 276–77; JQA Diary, June 25, 1838, in Charles Francis Adams, ed., *Memoirs of John Quincy Adams Comprising Parts of His Diary from 1795 to 1848*, 12 vols. (Philadelphia, 1874–77), 10:26.

14. *Alexandria Gazette*, August 28, 1838.

15. Ibid., September 4, October 3, 1838.

16. Ibid., September 12, 18, 1838.

17. Ibid., November 18, 1838.

18. Thomas Colston to CFM, October 11, 1838, ibid., November 13, 1838.

19. CFM to Thomas Colston, October 19, 1838, ibid.

20. *The National Cyclopedia of American Biography*, 61 vols. (New York, 1906), 19:235; Scott, ed., *Judge Scott's Reply*, 17.

21. Scott, ed., *Judge Scott's Reply*, 9; CFM to John Scott, December 1838, CFM Papers, NJHS.

22. Scott, ed., *Judge Scott's Reply*, 2; *Alexandria Gazette*, March 20, 1839.

23. *Alexandria Gazette*, November 20, 23, December 4, 1838.

24. Ibid., November 29, 20, 1838.

25. CFM, Autobiographical Sketch, Mercer-Hunter Papers; Charles Fenton Mercer, ed., *The Farewell Address of the Hon. C. F. Mercer to His Constituents* (N.p., 1839), 8.

26. *Congressional Globe*, 25th Cong., 3d sess., 152.

27. *Richmond Enquirer*, April 26, 1839; *Alexandria Gazette*, March 8, 1839.

28. *Congressional Globe*, 25th Cong., 3d sess., 241. The draft resolutions can be found in CFM Papers, NYHS.

29. Charles Fenton Mercer, *Appointment of Certain Officers*, House Committee Report 352, Serial 325 (Washington, D.C., 1839), 1.

30. John Forsyth to CFM, January 23, 1839, 2; Levi Woodbury to CFM, February 25, 1839, both in ibid., 2–3; Amos Kendall to CFM, February 22, 1839, in *Richmond Enquirer*, April 26, 1839.

31. Memorial to Congress, Mathew Carey, January 1838, in Charles Fenton Mercer, *Canal—Atlantic to Pacific*, House Committee Report 352, Serial 322 (Washington, D.C., 1839), 8–9; CFM, Autobiographical Sketch, Mercer-Hunter Papers.

32. Mercer, *Canal—Atlantic to Pacific*, 2.

33. Ibid., 3–7.

34. *Congressional Globe*, 25th Cong., 3d sess., 241; *Alexandria Gazette*, March 7, 1839.

35. Scott, ed.; *Judge Scott's Reply*, 12.

36. Ned Douglass, *The Aldie Mill* (N.p., n.d.), 1–4; W. E. Trout, "The Goose Creek and Little River Navigation," *Virginia Cavalcade* 16 (Winter 1967): 31–32.

37. *Alexandria Gazette*, December 4, 1838.

38. Ibid., December 10, 1838.

39. William M. McCarty to Edgar Snowden, December 5, 1838, in ibid., December 13, 1838; ibid., December 25, 1838.

40. Ibid., March 12, April 1, 1839.

41. John Scott to CFM, December 18, 1838, in Scott, ed., *Judge Scott's Reply*, 28–31.

42. Amos Kendall to CFM, January 14, 1839, CFM Papers, Harvard University Library; *Alexandria Gazette*, March 20, 21, 22, 25, 1839.

43. Scott, ed., *Judge Scott's Reply*, 4, 33.

44. Ibid., 4; CFM to John Scott, December 1838, CFM Papers, NJHS. Mercer added a postscript about the fight later.

45. *Richmond Enquirer*, April 30, 1839.

46. Cave Johnson to James K. Polk, November 19, 1839, in Herbert Weaver et al., eds., *Correspondence of James K. Polk*, 6 vols. to date (Nashville, 1969–83); 5:306.

47. *Richmond Enquirer*, December 3, 1839; *National Intelligencer*, January 7, 1840; *Niles' Weekly Register*, November 23, 1839, p. 194.

48. Mercer, ed., *Farewell Address*, 5–8.

49. CFM to William Benton, September 28, 1839, William Benton Papers, VHS; CFM to Joseph Eaches, July 29, 1838, CFM Papers, UVA; Loudoun County Personal Property Tax, 1834–38, VSL; CFM, Autobiographical Sketch, Mercer-Hunter Papers.

50. *Washington Globe*, April 27, 1839; also printed in *Richmond Enquirer*, May 3, 1839.

51. JQA Diary, November 22, 1840, in Adams, ed., *Memoirs*, 10:360–61.

52. John H. B. Latrobe Diary, early 1840s, in John E. Semmes, *John H. B. Latrobe and His Times, 1803–1891* (Baltimore, 1917), 368–69; Daniel P. Jordan, *Political Leadership in Jefferson's Virginia* (Charlottesville, 1983), 215, observes that many former Federalists "had partisan ceilings placed on their ability to rise in national politics . . . Charles Fenton Mercer, for example, merited higher leadership posts."

53. CFM, Autobiographical Sketch, Mercer-Hunter Papers.

54. Mercer, ed., *Farewell Address*, 10–12.

55. *National Intelligencer*, January 8, 1840; *Niles' Weekly Register*, February 1, 1840, p. 357; Mercer, ed., *Farewell Address*, 15.

56. *Niles' Weekly Register*, January 4, 1840, p. 304; CFM to Lord Radstock, July 12, 1856, CFM Papers, NYHS.

57. JQA Diary, November 22, 1840, in Adams, ed., *Memoirs*, 10:361.

PART FOUR

The Way-Worn Traveler
1840–1858

18

Texas

When Charles Fenton Mercer was offered and accepted the position of cashier of the Union Bank of Tallahassee, it appeared that the Virginian had abandoned forever a life of activity and acrimony for a peaceful and profitable retirement in the warm winds and gentle society of west Florida. Yet anyone who really knew the former congressman should have guessed that it would not be so.

At first, Mercer honestly tried to settle quietly into the job of cashier, a position of no small imporance to his financial institution. Normally, he was required to extend credit by issuing bank notes and loans to borrowers and real estate operators. But the Union Bank had invested too heavily in cotton before the crash and had yet to resume specie payment. And the decidedly Whig bank was under sharp attack from the Democratic state assembly. Gamble planned to put his old friend's enormous financial acumen to good use by sending him north to do business with the banks and cotton merchants of New York, Philadelphia, and Boston. Indeed, although Mercer brought with him to Florida his family of human property—his farm remained unsold—and fully expected to settle into Tallahassee society, his first year with the bank was devoted to two journeys from Florida to Boston.[1]

New England was not the only stop on Mercer's itinerary, and in February 1841 he crossed the Atlantic. The ostensible reason for the trip required very little of his time, and with several spare months on his hands his old interests soon reasserted themselves. Foremost among them was colonization. Liberia was then a subject of dispute, for although that tiny nation had declared its independence, its boundaries were not settled. The government of Lord Melbourne took the position that several purchases of territory by Liberia were irregular, not because the native Africans had got the worst of a bad bargain but because some of the land was once claimed by the crown. In early July 1841, the British Foreign Secretary, Lord Palmerston, arrived at his office to find Mercer waiting impatiently at his door. Following a long conference, Mercer believed, erroneously it turned out, that he had convinced Palmerston "that the Colony of Liberia claims no more than it is justly entitled to."[2]

By an odd twist of fate, Mercer's months in London brought him into contact with a project that would occupy his time and energy for most of the next decade: the colonization of the republic of Texas. During his stay in Britain, Mercer fell in with Daniel S. Carroll, a New Englander residing in London. Earlier that year, Carroll had joined with some of his friends in London and with W. S. Peters, an inept musician who lived in Louisville, Kentucky, in petitioning Texas for a grant of land that they would colonize. During its years as a Mexican department, Texas had encouraged immigration as a hedge against angry natives. Now that Texas had declared its independence, its government wished to continue the policy as a hedge against angry Mexicans.[3]

To the great surprise of all involved, Texas passed a law on February 4, 1841, granting Peters and his nineteen associates a tract south of the Red River. Through Carroll, Mercer discovered that one of the Englishmen named in the bill had died before passage of the laws and several others had suddenly lost interest in the venture when it threatened to become a reality. Carroll now urged Mercer to join in the enterprise. Caught up in the excitement of the moment, and doubtless envisioning the evaporation of his debts, he quickly agreed. On September 22 he purchased the share of the deceased grantee and the interests of five others and so "became a party to the contemplated enterprise." Exactly one month later he sailed for home.[4]

A man who would become a stockholder in such a scheme was not ready for a tranquil retirement. Although he was a minor partner, he saw in the Lone Star a grand vision of financial solvency. But much more than that, it seemed a project that could occupy his undiminished energies and restless intelligence in a way that the Union Bank never could. In the shadow of the palms, Mercer had grown restless. The opportunity to become more deeply involved came in the summer of 1842, when his business again carried him across the ocean of England.[5]

Upon returning to London, Mercer again became entangled in the affairs of Liberia. In late 1841 the Melbourne ministry fell, and under Robert Peel the government again denounced the purchases made by Liberia. Foreign Secretary Aberdeen was working through a committee in the Commons to dispossess Liberia of the territory bought with funds raised by the New York society. Mercer considered calling on Aberdeen or Peel, but his Atlantic journey had brought his health to a state "so bad as to confine" him to his chamber. Instead, he wrote to colonizationist Chauncey Whittlesey in America and urged him to call on Lord Ashburton, the British minister in Washington. The British case based on "the pretense that a Brtish flag having once floated at the mast head of some vessel on that coast, it could not be purchased of the natives," Mercer huffed.[6]

But during this time Mercer was more occupied with the colonization of Texas than with the colonization of Africa. In London Mercer discovered that the Texas situation was in flux. The Louisville men had been taken by surprise when Texas agreed to their grandiose proposal, and the tiny band of musicians was wholly unprepared for action. They soon realized that their grant was far too small, and in November 1841 Peters signed a second contract with Texas, pushing the boundary southward. This introduced new problems; they then discerned that their three-year contract was too short and that if an extension was not permitted they would lose their rights. So a third contract was signed in July 1842. The Louisville men, however, had an impressive name for their association: the Texas Agricultural, Commercial and Manufacturing Company.[7]

Around the same time that the Texas Congress was granting the Peters group a second contract, it passed a general colonization law. Based on the 1841 Peters Colony Act, the law of February 5, 1842, authorized the president to enter into an agreement with any company that wished to introduce settlers into the republic. The measure, however, only served to confuse the situation. The London partners, in ignorance of the second and third contracts, desired to take advantage of the colonization law to extend the area of the Peters grant. Because Ashbel Smith, the Texas minister to Britain, was unable to give the London group "any information," Carroll and Mercer "deemed it best to dispatch" stockholder Sherman Converse to Texas as a "special Agent."[8]

Blissfully ignorant of events in America, Mercer wrote in late September to President Sam Houston, whom he had known two decades before in Congress. He introduced Converse and informed Houston that he himself was now a part of the company. They wished to take advantage of the 1842 law and receive an extension of both time and territory. Mercer, however, clearly thought that Carroll, and not Peters, was the senior partner and majority stockholder in the enterprise.[9]

In late October 1842, Mercer left England for the third time in his life. Traveling with him aboard the steamer *Great Western* were Carroll and Converse. Just before they reached the dock, Converse startled Mercer by requesting that he not call him by his proper name until after they had sailed safely. Such behavior was more than a little suspicious, but the shocked Mercer, who guessed that his companion was deeply in debt, agreed. He knew that feeling well enough, and in any case he was relieved to be rid of London. President John Tyler's clumsy attempts to attain Texas, he believed, had a "mischievous" effect "on the American Character in Europe." Nothing, he sighed, "can be more mortifying to an American than a visit to Europe."[10]

When they reached America, Carroll remained in New York and Mercer returned to his bank in Florida, but Converse headed straight for Louisville. There the smooth-talking bankrupt convinced the Peters group to turn over control of the enterprise to him and his London partners. From there he hastened to Washington, Texas, where Congress was in session. Through some magic he persuaded Houston to sign yet another contract greatly enlarging the Peters grant to sixteen thousand square miles and allowing the company to introduce ten thousand immigrants. The bargain was finalized on January 20, 1843. It named Converse, Carroll, Mercer, and two Englishmen. No mention was made of the Louisville men.[11]

Converse's coup was a fantastic financial gift for Mercer, for instead of being one of twenty shareholders he was now one of five partners. But just at this moment of triumph, tragedy struck. On April 23 James Mercer Garnett died at the age of seventy-three. Eleanor Garnett had passed away seven years before, and since her death, Mercer had "little left on earth to cheer me in my solitary rambles." Now the man who was at once his cousin, brother-in-law, and guardian was gone. Mercer was the last of his generation.[12]

As it happened, there were others reasons for Mercer to be unhappy. Converse, then in New York, wrote him with the bad news that he was having difficulty raising money in the North to pay for surveys of the grant, a requirement of the contract. Thomas Hodgkins, an English colonizationist, was having equal difficulty attracting "British capital" to the enterprise. Mercer realized that they would need another extension. In August he informed Houston of their problems and blamed them on "the low state of American credit in Europe, applied to our whole continent, and the continued war between Mexico and Texas." But the recent armistice, he observed, was yet "unknown in London." When it was, he promised, the company would immediately prosper.[13]

In a desperate attempt to raise capital, the company agreed to take a sixth partner, Edward Tuke of London. To ratify this arrangement it was necessary for Mercer to sail for New York in early October, a trip he could barely afford. It also forced him to turn over his lucrative "professional engagements for two of our autumnal courts to a brother lawyer." But he admitted that "unless some funds were procured our incomplete survey in Texas" would lead to a forfeiture of their contract. On October 17, still another deal was made. All twenty of the original shares listed in the law of 1841 were in the possession of the six men.[14]

The situation in the North, however, was far more precarious than Mercer expected. To his consternation he found that Converse had made virtually no effort to attract settlers, and Mercer realized that they would never be able to plant the requisite 250 by the end of the first year, a deadline only three months away. He also began to receive disquieting reports from Converse's "associates of his former life." He began to suspect that any venture that involved the shady promoter would be crippled in England. Mercer thus determined to travel to Texas and ask Houston for "certain modifications of our contract."[15]

It was characteristic of Mercer to believe that only he could save the situation, but in this instance he was probably right. He was certain that he could salvage the contract by "availing myself of my acquaintance with Houston and also with the leaders of the party opposed to his administration." He also had the energy and opportunity to travel to Texas, which the other partners, especially the three in London, did not have. But he lacked the funds for such a journey. He thus wrote to the New York group and requested money for travel and lobbying and the right to sell one share for five thousand dollars to pay for the remainder of the surveys. Without waiting for a reply, he booked passage for New Orleans aboard the *Select* on December 4.[16]

A week later Mercer arrived in the Louisiana port, where to his annoyance and "extreme regret" he found no letters awaiting him. Again he wrote to Converse, this time in a far blunter tone. "My various letters," he snapped, "have long since apprised you of my determination to save our Texian Contracts from forfeiture if possible as I believe I have it in my power to do." Mercer also, at this late date, wrote to E. B. Ely, the secretary of the Louisville group, and apprised him of his actions.[17]

Mercer's letters did not find a friendly audience in Kentucky. The Louisville men had long since realized that Converse had swindled them into signing over control of the enterprise. They had just published a repudiation of both the dubious agreement and Converse when Mercer's missives arrived. Ely accordingly fired off a letter to Texas Secretary of State Anson Jones warning him to make no further agreements without his approval. "General Mercer is obviously in the dark in regard to the present attitude of the concern," Ely insisted.[18]

The confusion was now complete. After lingering for three weeks in vain hope of receiving some message from Converse, Mercer boarded the Neptune for Galveston, arriving on December 23. From there he steamed four hundred miles up the Brazos River to the tiny frontier capital of Washington. There he discovered that the president had fallen from his horse and fractured several ribs and was "laid up." Mercer's proposals would have to wait. But after checking into Lockharts Hotel, he put the time to good use by "making acquaintances and cultivating those of social standing."[19]

Several days later, Mercer was finally granted an audience with the President. The "Executive Mansion" was a rude, two-room cabin with a rickety porch and no glass in the windows. But the president was something else again. Even reclining, Houston was worth traveling a long way to see. At well over six feet and with steel-gray eyes, Houston appeared big to most men; to the diminutive Mercer he seemed enormous. It was also his habit—for Houston well understood self-promotion—to greet his guests in Indian garb or in a huge hat resplendent with long purple plumes. Mercer was distressed to find that Ely's circular denying the London group "any title whatever" to Peters Colony had already reached Houston and his secretary of state. This missive the president "totally disregarded," but he warned Mercer that any contract extensions would have to be granted by Congress.[20]

Houston's advice showed that the huge territory granted to Converse the previous year had turned Congress against Peters Colony and all other such ventures. The age of the speculators was coming to a close, hastened by the enormity of Houston's contract with Converse. It made no sense to grant thousands of miles of the best lands to six men. The Texas Congress graciously granted Mercer two hours to make his case, and though many believed that he "made out a just claim for further time," they were now so opposed to the idea that his proposal received virtually no support.[21]

Whatever considerations prompted the refusal of Congress to grant more time, the outcome was clear to Mercer. Without an extension the contract would stand forfeit. His "fortune" would be destroyed anew at an age when his "capacity for both mental and physical exertion [was] fast declining." With no more consideration than that he had brought into the venture, Mercer made a decision. He would negotiate a new contract with Houston for himself alone. The Peters grant had fallen victim to acrimony and confusion; with no clear leader, the enterprise was run from four spots on the globe. A new colony with himself as chief agent, he thought, would face no such problems.[22]

This was not to be the case, and Mercer should have known better. The unfavorable vote on an extension made the congressional hostility to further colonization clear. Had he not already expended so much time, energy, money, and ego on the effort, his good sense might have enabled him to walk away. More than that, even while he was in Washington Congress passed a bill stopping all empresario contracts. But Mercer thought he was safe. Houston told him that he intended to veto the measure, and Mercer warned the president that "any new contract you may approve, should be consummated before the return" of the bill with a veto message, lest Congress override the "negative." He even read the Texas constitution and identified to Houston the grounds for a veto.[23]

On January 29, 1844, Mercer and Houston signed yet another contract for colonization. The grant gave him sixty-five hundred square miles south of the Red River, a significant slice of the republic. In exchange, Mercer agreed to settle one hundred families a year for five years. Each family, upon carrying out its part of the agreement, would receive one section, or 640 acres. The company was to be awarded a premium of ten sections for each one hundred families placed. Significantly, Mercer wrote into the contract that Texas would grant one section to be sold to erect buildings for "elementary or primary schools." He also promised to survey the land and divide the sections into marked areas of 640 acres. The capital was to be called Fenton, although several other towns, including the sleepy hamlet of Dallas, already existed within the grant. Should he fail to settle one hundred families by May 1, 1845, "all right and title" would cease.[24]

This contract was patently not in keeping with the policy Congress had made so abundantly clear just days before. Within hours, an angry body repassed the measure over Houston's veto. Mercer's contract was legal, but it was far from safe. He could not say that he had not been warned.[25]

The new chief agent, however, did not intend to allow his grant, which he modestly if correctly entitled the Mercer Colony, to fail for a lack of energy. Staying in the same hotel was one P. J. Pilans, whom Mercer hired as "agent for running and marking the boundary line." Mercer also gave his surveyor the funds he needed to begin and informed him that he could draw on Lindenberger and Company of New Orleans for what more he might need.[26]

Mercer may have believed that his job would be made easier by the annexation of Texas to the United States, for settlers would be more likely to live in an area under the protection of the federal government. Yet annexation, he warned his old friend Henry Wise, was a matter "of peculiar delicacy." Because Texas had "no army or navy" she was at the mercy of the great powers as well as Mexico, and it "would be madness on her part to ask admission into our Union, unless she were certain of success." But if the offer were made, Mercer counseled Houston, he should not ignore it: "Delay can only invite the interposition of England or France which instead of staying the United States would involve us and you in a war with one or both of them."[27]

During all this activity, Sherman Converse was far from idle. Upon his return to New Orleans, Mercer found several letters from the promoter awaiting him. The first urged him not to go to Texas and not to sell any shares to pay for the unfinished surveys. He also imperiously observed that Mercer might be paid "in some way if not in money" should he insist upon going. A second letter, dated a week later, finally gave permission for him to sell one share at four thousand dollars, an action Mercer had already taken conditionally to raise funds for his journey.[28]

Converse then hurried to Louisville, where, amazingly enough, he convinced Peters to restore to him control of their colony. It was Mercer, he argued, who had swindled them out of their shares. "In fine these gentlemen," Mercer exploded, "patched up a reconciliation at my cost." He also fired back at Converse, observing that it was not his morals that should be in question; it was not he who had slipped out of England under an assumed name. He was enormously pleased, he informed one of the London partners, to "decline any further action on my own account in relation to this most misconducted enterprise."[29]

While still in New Orleans, Mercer sold the shares he held in the now failing Peters Colony. He then sailed for Tallahassee, where he planned to sell fifty shares of his own enterprise to raise the capital necessary for surveys, advertisements, and travel. By the time Mercer reached Florida, his company, called the Texas Association, was fully organized on paper. All he needed was "persons of social standing and pecuniary means to become his associates."[30]

Not surprisingly, given the way his contract had been won, the Mercer Colony had problems from the very first. Even before his return to Florida, Mercer realized that he had made "an error in the boundaries" he assigned to the adjacent Peters grant. Almost two thousand square miles of his grant lay within the boundaries of Peters Colony. "The impossibility of decypering the hand writing of Mr Converse, "he admitted to Anson Jones, "led to this mistake, which changes much."[31]

For a time, however, Mercer kept any nagging doubts he had about his new venture well hidden, even from himself. He had a broadside printed that bragged of the quality of his land and stated exactly what would be required from the settlers. He then sailed for Galveston, where he bought a horse and rode north. When he reached Paris he learned that "his contract had been so grossly misrepresented, as to be odious to the people." Yet he persisted. Then in his late sixties, Mercer spent the next three months examining his huge grant "on horseback, lodging at night on the open prairie, and by day, encountering the hottest sun of July and August."[32]

By September Mercer was in Kentucky, where he had recently invested in land. To his great anger, he found that Jacob Eliot, a member of the Louisville group, had filed a bill of injunction staying the payment of several thousand dollars due him. Eliot claimed that Mercer owed him money from the Peters Colony and as evidence he had a letter from Converse stating that Mercer "had treated him scandalously." In reply, a livid Mercer wrote to Thomas Ogden, the New York lawyer for the Peters Colony. "One thing, I wish Mr Converse to understand," he thundered, "and I shall enforce the lesson, upon Mr Eliot," and the "Louisville Co., [is] that I will not silently permit any remarks of theirs, to the prejudice of my grant, to pass unnoticed."[33]

Eventually Mercer put this latest perplexity behind him and rode again for the Lone Star Republic. On his own during the hot early summer of 1845, he doggedly followed the boundaries of his huge grant. Twice he had to swim his horse across high water, holding onto its mane for dear life as he had "never learnt that art." At night he slept "on the open prairie without any covering but the Heavens," and five times he became hopelessly lost and only with great luck stumbled upon isolated farms. "I have been literally covered with seedtains and cheegars and twice laid up with bilious attacks," he wrote to a nephew, "but an indomitable Scotch high spirit has sustained me so far." 34

With the boundaries of his grant more or less clear in his mind, Mercer rode east to advertise his colony. On June 13 he forded the Red River and galloped for Little Rock. After several weeks in Arkansas, he took a boat down the Mississippi to New Orleans. There he printed a map of his colony and one thousand copies of his contract with Houston. In early July he again mounted his horse, "heavily burthened with myself and baggage," and rode north. After traveling almost seven hundred miles Mercer reached St. Louis. From there he rode east through Illinois and Indiana, where he placed advertisements in newspapers. He advertised heavily in German-language papers and through them sent public notices to the German states. He then dropped down into Kentucky and rode to Cincinnati. After several weeks there, he again mounted up and journeyed to western Virginia.35

Mercer reached New York by the end of September. It was not a happy man who arrived on the coast. Although he had taken the cheapest form of transportation possible, the swing through the West and the various printing bills totaled nearly six hundred dollars. Worse, he found very little interest for his venture in either the cities or the outlying settlements. In all, he grumbled, he had sent five precious months on "two expensive and most unprofitable, and thankless journeys."36

But Mercer also had other projects on his mind. In the winter months before his western trip, Mercer wrote his only book, a gloomy autobiography of sorts entitled *An Exposition of the Weakness and Inefficiency of the Government of the United States of North America*. He probably intended to publish it when he reached New York, although certainly not under his own name. A career of misunderstood legislation had won him more enemies than friends, and such a blunt memoir would win him still more. By the mid-1840s the southern social order was so hostile to any criticism that it would have been nearly suicidal and, with his Texas enterprise, financially unwise to put his name on the title page. When he reached Cincinnati, he placed his manuscript in the hands of Nathaniel Ware, a Whig and former banker who was much interested in Texas.[37]

A small number of the lengthy screed were published anonymously by Ware in the early fall; evidently neither Mercer nor Ware intended to make any money from the book. Instead, it was intended to provoke thought and action among other members of the upper class. It presented an open window to the Whig soul. Most of the book was autobiographical in construction, for Mercer was certain that if one understood the course his life, one would have to agree with his conclusions. He truly believed that his program had not been rejected by Americans as much as it had been destroyed by demagogues; indeed, whole chapters were devoted to long and repetitive attacks on Thomas Jefferson and Andrew Jackson. But the heart of the book was his gift to the nation: a short proposal for "a simple government."[38]

The simple government was, in essence, the American System mandated by law and protected from the public. *An Exposition* advocated colonization and public education on a national scale; "all should be forced to educate their children under penalties." All the "internal improvements possible" would receive federal funds, and "manufacturing industry" would be protected by high tariff barriers. Not surprisingly, given Mercer's habitual poverty, "public servants, when grown old, [were] to be pensioned." Like Mercer's public life, which was a delicate balance between a distrust of the common people and the promotion of ostensibly democratic forms and rhetoric, his book tried at once to maintain the trappings of a progressive republic while taking the government firmly out of the hands of the people. He advocated no restrictions on the franchise, but the president, serving one ten-year term, was beyond the influence of the voter. True to his Federalist ideals, Mercer's simple government would allow for no states. The legislature would be of one chamber, and representatives would serve for four years. Finally, the executive's power of patronage—as well as the postmaster general's—would be greatly reduced.[39]

The tone of *An Exposition* was one of unrelenting gloom, yet ironically, just as it was going to press, Charles Fenton Mercer's financial situation was sounder than it had been in years. By the last day of December 1845, all one hundred shares of stock in the Texas Association were sold. Mercer held sixty; the other forty had sold at five hundred dollars each to pay for surveys, handbills, and the expensive lithographs of his map. He was finally able to begin paying off his long-due bills. Money went north to Gales and Seaton, to the old Bank of the United States, and to the Farmers' Bank of Alexandria. He no longer owed money in Loudoun—Aldie had finally been sold—and with his legal fees and bank salary of three thousand dollars annually, Mercer was slowly reducing his "bank debt in Washington and Georgetown."[40]

Left to himself, Mercer would probably have emerged from his Texas venture with a tidy profit. But just when he supposed that he was finally working his way out from under a lifetime of debt, his colony came under attack from all quarters. In late 1844, Houston left the presidency, and with him went Mercer's best shield against the hostility of the Texas Congress. Anson Jones, the new president, although Houston's first secretary, had no desire to carry on his predecessor's policies. Unable to attack the legality of Mercer's contract, Jones decided to kill it with a side blow. With his encouragement, on February 3, 1845, both houses of Congress passed a joint resolution requiring the Texas Association "to have the lines of their colony land actually surveyed and marked" by April 1. Failure to meet this impossible deadline "shall work a forfeiture of their contract."[41]

Mercer also discovered that as a political man, his former career was never far from the minds of many Texans. Nor was his connection with Houston all to the good, for during the last years of his presidency, Houston had appeared unusually friendly to those in the British government who wished to abolish slavery in Texas. For these reasons, and because of his fame as a colonizationist, Mercer was vilified by Houston's political enemies as an "abolitionist" and an "opponent of the interests of the settlers." The first charge was a result of the usual misunderstanding; the second was essentially true.[42]

Indeed, most of Mercer's problems reflected an enduring failure to grasp the dreams and needs of the agrarian nation, which in turn had some difficulty understanding why the most fertile land in Texas should be under the thumb of a Florida land speculator. When Mercer's surveyor arrived at one squatter settlememt, he was met by an angry crowd of farmers—and the Texas Ranger sent there to protect them from Indians—who suggested that he pack his gear and move on. To Mercer's great annoyance, the surveyor was swayed by the "moral influence" of the settlers. They had come to Texas "at their own cost," and had neither heard of Mercer nor received his aid, and "did not propose to have their lands surveyed and give up a part to him."[43]

A second surveyor was hired, but he too was harassed. This time the "old Texans," or squatters, did not simply rely on moral suasion. Six of them on horseback appeared suddenly before the startled surveyor, and while several of them told the employee to leave the area, one pulled his gun from its holster and very carefully examined it. The surveyor took the hint. He even discovered that his letters to Mercer were being "intercepted" and that Mercer's were being "suppressed."[44]

The final blow to Mercer's dreams were put into motion on October 11, 1846, when Attorney General J. W. Harris, acting on behalf on Governor Albert Horton—annexation to the United States was now complete—filed suit against the Texas Association in the District Court of Navarro County. The suit, which was filed within the boundaries of Mercer's grant, attacked its legality on several grounds. First, Harris alleged, the contract was unconstitutional, an odd claim since such grants were common during the republic period and it was negotiated with President Houston. More to the point, Harris asserted that Mercer had not settled enough emigrants "on or before the expiration date of the said contract." The suit also alleged that Mercer had not met the requirement of the joint resolution that called upon him to "survey, designate, and mark the boundary of the territory." That his surveyors had been kept from doing so by an officer of the state did not concern the attorney general.[45]

Mercer was baffled, although by this late date he should have been used to the forces of democracy using the machinery of the state to thwart his plans and programs. Nonetheless, Mercer studiously avoided the trial and left Florida for good. His new home was to be his land in Carroll County, Kentucky. But Mercer had not even as much as a cabin on his land, and so for almost a year he resided with the family of George Hancock, who owned a farm adjoining his tract.[46]

By now Mercer realized that he had lost his colony. Yet he was not willing to give up without a fight. Though he did not attend the trial, he wanted to prove his case to the governor. To obtain evidence he made several more trips to Texas, for a total of six, during which he worked himself into a state of exhaustion. As he lay sick at the Verandah Hotel in New Orleans, Mercer begged Theodore Garnett, his favorite nephew, to visit his colony and determine the number of families there. In mid-April Garnett was back at his uncle's side. He found a total of 661 families in the colony, far more than necessary under the contract, although it appeared that most

had simply drifted into Texas when annexation appeared imminent.[47]

Soon Mercer's employees knew that the colony was moribund.
One of his agents reported that the merchants of Baton Rouge were
unwilling to advance money due his drafts, and provisions could be
obtained only for cash and at a very high price. In late September
1848, just three months after Mercer's seventieth birthday, the
District Court of Navarro made formal what most of east Texas
knew. The jury declared Mercer's contract null and void. He was
"cited by publication, but did not appear." The judgment "by default was rendered." In what appeared to others as a saving technicality, the court had not only failed to locate Mercer, it had never
served the proper notice to give the court jurisdiction.[48]

Mercer knew better. It seemed to him that his entire life was a
series of failures, and this latest rout only magnified that impression. "I could not more usefully or honorably terminate a long life,"
he moaned to Houston's secretary, "than by planting and nourish-
ing a colony, of which, I should become the moral head and in the
midst of which I meant to live and die. I have been much disappointed." It was almost as though he had fallen victim to his own
commercial frame of mind; born into a deferential society, Mercer
and his ideas had helped to usher a far different age into being, one
in which small companies were consumed by bigger ones. But in
truth, Mercer's nature was not one that would ease into a peaceful
retirement, and the years that remained to him were to be among
the most active and interesting of his life.[49]

Notes

ABBREVIATIONS

ACS	American Colonization Society
CFM	Charles Fenton Mercer
COCC	Chesapeake and Ohio Canal Company
DAB	*Dictionary of American Biography*, ed. Allen Johnson and Dumas Malone, 21 vols., 1928–1936.
JQA	John Quincy Adams
JSH	*Journal of Southern History*
LC	Library of Congress
NJHS	New Jersey Historical Society
NYHS	New-York Historical Society
PRO, FO	Great Britain, Public Record Office, Foreign Office
UVA	University of Virginia

VHS   Virginia Historical Society
VMHB   *Virginia Magazine of History and Biography*
VSL   Virginia State Library
WMQ   *William and Mary Quarterly*

1. CFM to Nathan Appleton, July 8, 1840, Nathan Appleton Papers, Massachusetts Historical Society; *Floridian,* (Tallahassee) March 7, 1840; Census Records, 1840, reel 36, p. 79, National Archives; CFM, Autobiographical Sketch, Mercer-Hunter Papers, VSL.

2. JQA Diary, November 22, 1840, in Charles Francis Adams, ed., *Memoirs of John Quincy Adams Comprising Parts of His Diary from 1745 to 1848,* 12 vols. (Philadelphia, 1874–77); 10:360–61; CFM to John Gorham Palfrey, February 6, 1841, CFM Papers, Harvard University Library; CFM to Chauncey Whittlesey, August 2, 1842, ACS Papers, LC.

3. *United States Reports,* Vol. 109, *Walsh* v. *Preston,* Records and Briefs (New York, 1902), app., 1–4. The records are from the case appealed to the Supreme Court by William Preston, who bought out George Hancock as chief agent of the Mercer Colony. In 1883 the court ruled that the "total failure of Mercer to perform left him [and thus Preston] no rights under the contract." See *Walsh* v. *Preston,* Records and Briefs.

4. CFM to Thomas Ogden, June 5, 1844, William H. Harison Papers, NYHS; Charles Fenton Mercer, *Contract of Colonization between Charles F. Mercer and Associates with the Republic of Texas* (Louisville, 1858), 4; CFM to Sam Houston, September 29, 1842, A. J. Houston Collection, Texas State Library.

5. CFM, Autobiographical Sketch, Mercer-Hunter Papers; Edward Everett to Daniel Webster, August 3, 1842, in Charles M. et al., Wiltse, eds., *The Papers of Daniel Webster,* 7 vols. to date (Hanover, N.H., 1974–86), 5:232–33; CFM to Eliza Garnett, September 20, 1842, Mercer-Hunter Papers.

6. CFM to Chauncey Whittlesey, August 2, 1842, ACS Papers.

7. Seymour V. Connor, *Adventure in Glory: The Saga of Texas, 1836–1849* (Austin, 1965), 210–11.

8. *Walsh* v. *Preston,* Records and Briefs, app., 2–4; Ashbel Smith to Anson Jones, October 3, 1842, in George P. Garrison, ed., "Diplomatic Correspondence of the Republic of Texas," *Annual Report of the American Historical Association for the Year 1908* (Washington, 1911), 2:1024–25.

9. CFM to Sam Houston, September 29, 1842, A. J. Houston Collection.

10. CFM to Thomas Ogden, November 6, 1843, Harison Papers; CFM to Chauncey Whittlesey, August 2, 1842, ACS Papers.

11. CFM to Eliza Garnett, April 5, 1843, Mercer Family Papers, VHS; Anson Jones to Ashbel Smith, January 20, 1843 in Garrison, ed., "Diplomatic Correspondence," 1083–84.

12. *DAB,* 7:157; CFM to Theodore S. Garnett, February 11, 1854, Mercer-Hunter Papers.

13. CFM to Thomas Ogden, November 19, 1843, Harison Papers; CFM to Sam Houston, August 14, 1843, A. J. Houston Collection.

14. Articles of Agreement, October 17, 1843; CFM to Thomas Mawe, May 17, 1844, both in Harison Papers.

15. CFM to Thomas Ogden, October 23, November 6, 1843, ibid.

16. CFM to Thomas Ogden, November 22, December 4, 1843, ibid.

17. CFM to Sherman Converse, December 18, 1843, ibid.

18. E. B. Ely to Anson Jones, December 21, 1843, Colonization Records, Secretary of State Record Group, Texas State Library.

19. *Houston Telegraph and Texas Register,* January 3, 1844; CFM to Thomas Ogden, January 7, 1844, Harison Papers.

20. *DAB,* 9:263–67; CFM to Thomas Mawe, May 17, 1844, Harison Papers.

21. CFM to Thomas Mawe, May 17, 1844, Harison Papers.

22. CFM to Thomas Ogden, March 29, 1844, Harison Papers. Connor, *Adventure in Glory,* 216, is unfairly harsh on Mercer, whom he accuses of "slyly [cutting] out both the Louisville men and Converse." Because he did not use the papers at the NYHS, Connor was unaware of Converse'e shady background and the organizational chaos within the association. Moreover, Mercer cheated nobody. The Peters Colony continued to exist; Mercer simply contracted for his own.

23. *Houston Telegraph and Texas Register,* January 24, 1844; CFM to Sam Houston, January 8, 1844, A. J. Houston Collection.

24. Mercer, *Contract of Colonization,* 4–11.

25. T. R. Fehrenbach, *Lone Star: A History of Texas and the Texans* (New York, 1968), 284; *Walsh v. Preston,* 307.

26. Deposition of P. J. Pillans, *Walsh v. Preston,* Records and Briefs, 159.

27. CFM to Henry A. Wise, January 27, 1844, Washington D. Miller Papers, Texas State Library; CFM to Sam Houston, February 9, 1844, A. J. Houston Collection.

28. Sherman Converse to CFM, December 23, 29 1843, Harison Papers.

29. CFM to Thomas Mawe, May 17, 1844; CFM to Sherman Converse, April 23, 1844, both in ibid.

30. Bill of sale (in CFM's hand), June 5, 1844, ibid.; CFM to Anson Jones, July 11, 1844, Colonization Papers; Deposition of Richard T. Birchett, *Walsh v. Preston,* Records and Briefs, 196.

31. CFM to Anson Jones, February 24, 1844, Colonization Records.

32. *Texian Colonization* (one-page broadside), Harison Papers; CFM to Ebenezer Allen, March 31, 1845, Colonization Records.

33. CFM to Thomas Ogden, September 16, 1844, n.d., Harison Papers.

34. CFM to Theodore S. Garnett, July 4, 1845, James M. Garnett Papers, Duke University Library.

35. CFM to Ebenezer Allen, September 25, 1845, *Walsh v. Preston,* Records and Briefs, 82–87; CFM to Theodore S. Garnett, July 4, 1845, Garnett Papers.

36. CFM to Nathan Appleton, September 21, 1845, Appleton Papers; CFM to Thomas Ogden, n.d., Harison Papers.

37. Clement Eaton, *The Growth of Southern Civilization, 1790–1860* (New York, 1961), 313; William Diamond, "Nathaniel A. Ware, National Economist," *JSH* 5 (November 1939): 507; *DAB,* 19:451.

38. Charles Fenton Mercer, *An Exposition of the Weakness and Inefficiency of the Government of the United States of North America* (N.p., 1845); 336.

39. Ibid., 336–79.

40. Charles Fenton Mercer, *Gen. C. F. Mercer's Letter* (N.p., n.d.), 1–2; CFM to Gales and Seaton, April 2, 1845, CFM Letters, UVA; CFM to Theodore S. Garnett, July 4, 1845, Garnett Papers.

41. *DAB,* 10:161–62; *Walsh v. Preston,* 307.

42. Deposition of Peeler and Maxey, *Walsh v. Preston,* Records and Briefs, app., 32.

43. CFM to Washington D. Miller, April 1852, Washington D. Miller Papers, Texas State Archives; Mercer, *Gen. C. F. Mercer's Letter,* 6; Deposition of B. J. Chambers, *Walsh v. Preston,* Records and Briefs, 265.

44. W. Nicks Anderson to CFM, January 4, 1847, Colonization Records.

45. *Walsh v. Preston,* 308.

46. Deed, January 8, 1846, Breckinridge Family Papers, VHS: Deposition of J. Stoddard Johnson, *Walsh v. Preston,* Records and Briefs, 225.

47. CFM, Autobiographical Sketch, Mercer-Hunter Papers; Deposition of Theo-

dore S. Garnett, *Walsh* v. *Preston*, Records and Briefs, 184; Theodore S. Garnett to CFM, April 12, 1847, Colonization Records.

48. J. Clayton Taylor to CFM, June 20, 1848, Colonization Records; *Walsh* v. *Preston*, 308.

49. CFM to Washington D. Miller, April 1852, Washington D. Miller Papers, Texas State Library.

19

Reflections on the Past

Only a man completely lacking in energy and imagination, that is, most men, would have thought that renewed poverty at the age of seventy presaged a dismal future. But Charles Fenton Mercer was merely "disappointed" by the failure of his Texas venture; he was not defeated. He had not yet, in any period of his life, he admitted during that singularly cheerless year, tried "a life of solitude and comparative inaction, a life which has often proved fatal to minds accustomed to mental excitement." There was no reason to think he would do so now.[1]

Following hard on the heels of the Navarro court decision was the election of 1848. The Whigs, again running behind a popular general, took the White House but failed to capture either house of Congress. A month later, Mercer and his Kentucky neighbor Henry Clay traveled together downriver to New Orleans. As always, Clay had desired the nomination, and he bitterly informed Mercer that the "results demonstrate that I could have been elected with ease." Mercer gently urged the old warrior to return to the Senate and cited the example of Adams, who had died earlier that year after collapsing in the House chamber. The Old Prince admitted that Adams's death occurred "in a most remarkable manner," although he believed that Adams's later career "had a tendency to diminish instead of augmenting his reputation." Only if he were able to "contribute to the proper adjustment of the momentous question which has grown out of the acquisition of New Mexico and California," Clay told his friend, would he be willing to return to the Senate.[2]

Whatever Clay's plans were, the victory of Zachary Taylor presented Mercer with an interesting opportunity in 1849. Not only

312

was his old party victorious, but John Crittenden, the new governor of Kentucky, and John Clayton, both old Clay backers, were close to Taylor. Indeed, the latter was tapped as secretary of state. Just before the inauguration Mercer journeyed to Washington, although not before requesting Clay, Crittenden, and Kentucky Senator Joseph Underwood to write Taylor in his behalf. On March 8, Mercer was granted an interview with Clayton. It was, he announced, his "desire to spend a few years in Europe," perhaps as minister to one of the foreign states. But he was embarrassed to have to ask for a job, and he hastily added that he felt it "a delicate *task* for any man, however modest, to undertake, *that* of speaking of himself."[3]

Clayton, who was swamped with similar requests, was noncommittal. To bolster his case, Mercer sat down the next day and produced an extraordinary document, an autobiographical sketch of nearly eight thousand words. He mailed this narrative, which covered "some of the events" of his public life, to Clayton. Not surprisingly, the sketch focused on his military career and his three trips to Europe; absent were any hints of controversy or acrimony. Mercer hoped that his "egotism will be excused" and asked that both the narrative and cover letter be "committed to the flames." The sketch, ironically, ended with an account of his fight against patronage in the postal department and the diplomatic corps.[4]

But the old Whigs were out of luck in 1849. Taylor had pronounced himself a Whig, though not an "ultra" Whig. And Mercer, above all, was an "ultra." Nor did his Kentucky connections aid his drive for a diplomatic post. Crittenden's declaration for Taylor had all but destroyed his relationship with Clay, who could do no more than find a minor position for his son. He also ignored a small request from Webster. Perhaps most important was that the wandering Mercer, a perennial supporter of perennial candidate Clay, had done nothing to help place Taylor in the executive mansion and would bring no useful regional constituency to the administration. And so he sadly returned to his agricultural "experiments" at Fentonville, his modest Kentucky home.[5]

There Mercer remained in wounded seclusion for the next three years, almost hidden from the world. In an uncharacteristically diffident fashion, he fired off occasional pleas for financial aid to Texas. In early 1850, the state finally granted relief and clear title to the settlers of the Mercer Colony, but gave no money to any of the associates. For some unknown reason, the Peters Colony partners were given a premium of 1 million acres in west Texas. Two years later, Mercer was still begging for "a very modest remuneration for expenses incurred in adding, largely, to the population of Texas."[6]

Early in 1852 with no hope of relief from Texas and again seriously in debt, a restless Mercer decided to leave Kentucky. He believed he had little time left to live because none of his family had "ever reached my present age." He also wished to leave the South; the social order of the slave regime had matured to the point that Mercer was no longer comfortable there. Accordingly, he contacted Nathan Appleton in Boston and requested information on "what terms I could procure board" in either Boston, New York, or Philadelphia. "In one of these three cities," he wrote, "I expect to spend the few years that a man of 74 years of age, may rationally expect to live."[7]

Shortly thereafter, Mercer sold his home to George Hancock, his neighbor with whom he had lived for more than a year, for two thousand dollars. At the same time he transferred his remaining shares in the Texas Association to Hancock for an undisclosed sum. Any money realized from the dubious shares would be split between the new chief agent and Theodore Garnett. Mercer informed his nephew that Hancock "hurried me into a contract I never would have made voluntarily and to my serious injury," an uncharitable assessment considering the kindness Hancock had shown to him when he first moved to Kentucky.[8]

Several months later, in the late fall of 1852, Mercer arrived in Washington. While he waited for the remittance of Hancock's money from the Merchant's Bank of New York, he took a room at the boardinghouse of Eliza Peyton. There he was pleased to discover that one of his fellow boarders was Richard T. Birchett, whom he had first met in Florida in 1841. But Mercer was no longer thinking of moving to Boston. He told Birchett that he planned to use the money from the sale of his house to travel to Europe. Evidently the idea that had worked its way into his mind in 1849 was still there.[9]

Washington in 1852 was not the city Mercer remembered. Clay and Webster were gone, both having died during the previous months. Key and Monroe had long since passed away. He did, however see his old friend Edward Everett early in the next year when both men addressed the thirty-sixth annual meeting of the all but defunct American Colonization Society. Mercer used the opportunity to denounce the claim that the idea originated with Finley. For Mercer this was an exceedingly lonely time. One could "find pleasure almost every where," he groused, "except indeed in Washington or Alexandria, where I remained three months or more, in solitude."[10]

During his brief stay in the capital, Mercer had an inspiration. He could go to Europe as the official, if unpaid, representative of the American Colonization Society, even though he had no involvement with the organization for the past two decades. Nevertheless, with several letters of introduction from Ralph Gurley, Mercer left Washington in the spring of 1853. Following a final, brief journey back to Kentucky, he reached Philadelphia. On the morning of July 30, after nearly a week of packing and paying old debts, he boarded the steamer for Liverpool.[11]

On August 17, 1853, at just past one o'clock in the afternoon, Mercer arrived in England for the fourth time in his life. He performed no service for the society; instead, he wandered restively about, stopping first in Wales, then crossing the Irish Sea to Dublin, then sailing for London. After just a month in England, Mercer traveled to Paris, where he took a room at the Hotel de Ricole. From there he visited Versailles and other haunts of his visit half a century before. But again, he tarried less than a month, and on October 10 he was in the Sardinian city of Genoa. Nine days later, after passing through the towns of Leghorn and Pisa, he reached Florence by train. To his dismay, he discovered that he had spent nearly two thousand dollars since arriving in Liverpool.[12]

But Mercer was happier in Florence than he had been in Washington. He found himself "in the midst of an intellectual society of persons who, if they do not love me, at least treat me with kindness." Indeed, he fell in with many of the first names in Europe. He became especially friendly with Arthur Wellesley, the second Duke of Wellington. Mercer not only enjoyed but benefited from the hospitality of this group, for they fed him and gave him places to stay, and he in turn delighted them with his elegance and stories and knowledge and with his eagerness at the late age of seventy-six to learn to speak Italian.[13]

After lingering in Florence for several months, Mercer reluctantly pushed on for the papal states and Rome. He wished to speak to Pope Pius IX about colonization and the international slave trade. But upon reaching Rome he fell victim to a serious case of pneumonia, and the Italian doctors, in imitation of the favor their American counterparts had performed on William Crawford, gave him "a dose of Medicine that nearly killed [him] as well as the disease." By mid-February, Mercer was well enough to cross the

Tiber and climb "the highest hill near Rome" and enjoy "a most enchanting view of Rome itself at my feet."[14]

Pius IX, despite an early reputation as a reformer, had become an ardent conservative upon his accession, and he viewed with horror the movements sweeping the Continent, one of which presumably, was antislavery. After waiting "more than two months in a fruitless effort" to be granted an audience with the pope, Mercer contacted the American minister in Rome. Colonization, he argued, was "not connected with any political movement." Unwisely, perhaps, Mercer imperiously sent the pontiff word that a statement against the trade was "the duty of the chief of the Roman Catholic Church." No record, unfortunately, tells whether the impatient Virginian ever received an audience.[15]

Mercer left Rome shortly thereafter and traveled in a roundabout fashion through Venice, Verona, Milan, and finally back to Sardinia. There the foreign minister promised him "that his Govt. would cooperate with ours in making the Slave trade piracy." With awakened resolution, Mercer hastened to Geneva, Switzerland, where he had printed two hundred copies of his speech before the colonization meeting of the previous year. To his amazement, he discovered in Geneva a stack of his 1839 report on a Panamanian canal. These too he copied.[16]

Mercer's mission was complicated because American prestige was at a low ebb in Europe. The administration of Franklin Pierce was considering removing the American squadron from the African coast, which most of the European powers took as a sign that the United States was not seriously interested in putting an end to the slave trade. This action, along with the "filibustering movement toward Cuba" and the "misunderstood, and intentionally misrepresented repeal of the [Missouri] Compromise," Mercer complained to John Clayton, served as "evidence, in the judgement of Europe, that you meant to revive the accursed traffic."[17]

To escape such mortification, Mercer left Geneva in August and fled to the picturesque Swiss town of Interlaken. But after a time he was again restless. The lonely man suddenly decided to strike out for Russia; a young couple he met in Italy, the de Gernetts, had requested that he visit them there. It was an audacious decision because Russia was then at war with England and France, but Mercer was nothing if not audacious. He resolutely pushed north through Berlin to the Baltic Sea, where he sailed for the port city of Konigsberg. From there he was forced by the British blockade to travel overland by coach to St. Petersburg. "Six horses, and often twelve," were required to drag the carriage "thro the ruts and mud." Mercer, who had never cared much for rough travel, enjoyed the trip. In St. Petersburg he met Thomas Seymour, the American minister, who kindly offered the old man a chamber in his spacious suite of apartments.[18]

Following a failed attempt to meet Czar Nicholas I—he could not afford the requisite officer's uniform—Mercer decided to journey on to Reval, a trip of several hundred miles. There he stayed with Madame von Krehmer, the mother of a young woman he had met in Florence. The family spoke tolerable English, and he was content to roam the huge home that contained "eleven other apartments, besides a conservatory, Library and bathing-room, under the same roof." In his contact with the Russian aristocracy, Mercer's inherent conservatism rose to the fore; he was almost prepared to accept their invitation to spend the rest of his life with them. "We mistake in judging of the Russian despotism," the Virginian reported happily to a relative.[19]

But Mercer, still dedicated to the slave trade and, to a lesser degree, colonization, felt compelled to move on. In early November he returned to Berlin, and from there, after "travelling 3500 miles, ½ by Steam and the other [half] over bad roads in common carriages," Mercer made his way to Paris. There, to his great luck, he immediately fell in with Count Walewski. Upon hearing of his mission, the French diplomat invited Mercer to attend his famous "weekly soires."[20]

"I proceed to England, next," Mercer informed a niece in early December. For some time he had been in correspondence with middle-class reformers Richard Cobden and Joseph Hume, the latter in the last year of his life. Mercer hoped to travel to Britain and gain their "aid in the promotion of one, or both the objects, which have tempted me at 76 years of age, to cross the Atlantic a seventh time." The second of these "objects" was his dream of a Panamanian canal.[21]

That Mercer was again thinking of the canal suggests the seriousness of his European venture. He was driven on the subject of colonization, but just as clearly, his travels were a way of allowing the restless and unhappy man to be beyond where he was the day before. Upon reaching London he called on his old friend colonizationist Thomas Hodgkin. Together they went to see William Chamberlain, an important British antislavery activist who had long since broken with the colonizationists. Undaunted by Chamberlain's hostility, Mercer decided to contact Lord Palmerston, then in the Home Office, and requested an interview. Palmerston made no reply. Mercer, however, was greatly surprised to find that James Buchanan, a man he little cared for and who was at the time the American minister in London, was willing to introduce him to members of Parliament. But still he made no progress. England was too preoccupied with news from the Crimea to develop any interest in the slave trade. By January 1, 1855, he was back in Paris. To get along better in French society, Mercer, a born linguist, hired one Madame Graúinger as a live-in French teacher and maid. The two of them promptly set to work on polishing his long dormant French skills, and although he thought that his teacher drank a bit too much wine, which she charged to his bill, he enjoyed her "perfect good humor and gentleness."22

As he had half a lifetime before, Mercer delighted in his stay in Paris. June came and went and with it his seventy-seventh birthday. "Old age is not without its enjoyments," an unusually contented Mercer mused, "and among them is reflection on the past." He was "in good health and with unimpaired facilities of mind and body," although he could no longer read "without spectacles." He had also begun to notice a persistent sore on his lip.23

When after a month the sore was still there he paid a call on a Doctor Bigelow. But the fraud did Mercer no good, and on Bastille Day the Virginian, with some sense of the ironic, freed him. "He has done me no service and cost me 140 francs," Mercer fumed. The disgruntled patient also had to pay for several consultations by a surgeon whom Bigelow had brought in on the case. He too was "wholly ignorant" of Mercer's "malady, simply a sore lip."24

By August, Mercer's lip was no better. He had, however, decided that he had learned the French language sufficiently to "acquire the art of speaking it correctly." If he was to make any headway in Paris on the slave trade issue he would have to "enter society, that especially in which French is generally spoken." Yet Mercer had not given up on his other project. He wrote to his old friend Edward Cabell, a Florida shareholder in the Texas Association then in London, asking him to head up the hypothetical Panama canal project. Perhaps, Mercer observed, if it were presented as a counter-balance to the danger apprehended to India by the opening of the Suez Canal, the British government might support the project.25

For the next four months, Mercer lived quietly in Paris, occasionally pestering French officials about one of his two pet projects. In late December came his greatest opportunity to take significant action on the slave trade. The new Russian czar, facing revolt at home and the prospect of an Austrian invasion, chose to surrender. It was decided that the peace conference would take place not in Vienna, the traditional center of negotiation, but in Paris. At the same time, Mercer believed that he had finally "gained one powerful" friend to his cause, George Villiers, the Earl of Clarendon. For months, Mercer had peppered Clarendon, then in the Foreign Office under Aberdeen, with letters on the slave trade, and finally Clarendon's secretary replied. The foreign secretary, he was told, would "zealously promote" his views.[26]

The conference met on February 25, 1856. But to Mercer's dismay, much had changed in two months. The tenuous alliance between Britain and France was already coming apart, and with the victors laboring to hammer out a comprehensive maritime agreement, Aberdeen suddenly changed his mind. He was not willing to complicate the delicate negotiations by including the sticky question of searching foreign slavers. Upon reaching Paris, Clarendon quietly sent word to Mercer not to call on him. Mercer was undaunted. When he saw the foreign minister at a reception, he introduced himself, but he uttered only "a few words" before Clarendon abruptly pushed by him into another room.[27]

Mercer was furious—even crushed—at such shabby treatment. He had sent Clarendon a copy of a long memorial he had prepared, but now he doubted it would ever be introduced. Painstakingly he translated the document into French and gave one copy to Count Walewski, the French delegate with whom Mercer had been friendly for over a year. Through Walewski, Mercer was able personally to deliver a second copy to Napoleon III just before the end of the conference. The French emperor, however, in a position reminiscent of Adams, adopted his country's traditional position of conceding nothing that might grant greater authority to the British navy.[28]

Napoleon's opposition did not surprise Mercer, who was astute enough to understand the fine points of European power politics. But Mercer's American Whig correspondents were distraught by the refusal of the great maritime nations to mention the slave trade in their settlement. "What a sad pity it is that you did not succeed," John Crittenden confessed to Mercer. "The more I think of your failure the more I regret it."[29]

Within months of the end of the conference Mercer journeyed for a final time to London. There he soothed the wounds inflicted upon him by Clarendon in the gentle balm of the aged British upper class. In these months he became particularly friendly with

George Waldegrave, the second Baron Radstock. Then eight years Mercer's junior, Radstock, a vice-admiral, squired his new friend about London and introduced him to others of the better sort. In exchange, Mercer weighted Radstock down with complaints about the foreign secretary and copies of his book and various pamphlets.[30]

Mercer found this society pleasurable—Radstock even introduced him to the archbishop of Canterbury—and he found that he could be philosophical about his failure at the Paris conference. Such "discouragements" would have "disheartened me," he confided to Radstock, "had they not been encountered, in a cause to which I had desired with some success near thirty years of my public life." Such remarkable quietude was perhaps born of the knowledge that his life was nearly over. "The Flowers are but thinly strewed along an old man's path," he thought, "who, while he retains the remembrance of his youth, finds himself the solitary survivor of all his companions, and the way worn traveller of a foreign land."[31]

This acceptance of his mortality brought about the decision to return home. Finally, at the age of seventy-eight, he felt the strain of his years. A sudden neuralgia caused him some pain, and his sore lip stubbornly "resisted two years' attempt to cure it." The sore was especially troublesome when exposed to the cold night air. "One consolation attends it," Mercer told a relative, "it is not a cancer and is nearly stationary."[32]

On July 16, 1856, Mercer boarded the City of Baltimore and put England behind him for the fourth and last time. He left his memorial on the slave trade at a "cheap press" to be printed and distributed. As always, he was happy to be rid of Britain; in no other country in Europe had he "experienced so little kindness, or consideration." Thirteen days later he arrived in Philadelphia. He was nearly broke and made a show of borrowing a sovereign to pay "the servants of the boat" and his board for the night at Jones' Hotel. There was money enough, however, for the purchase of a panama hat well lined with green silk. A week later he took the train south through Washington, reaching Richmond in early August.[33]

The peace that Mercer found in Radstock's society escaped him at home, and for three months he wandered restlessly up and down the Atlantic coast. He was at one moment in Staunton, then in Washington, then in Philadelphia, and then in New York, where he saw yet another doctor about his lip. In vain he searched for a surgeon who could help him, although the sore was less painful than it had been in London. In early January 1857, he sailed south for Tallahassee on the steamer *Augustine.* Two months following he was again in New York, where he bought medicine and received a small amount of money from his bank. But several days later he was again on his way to Florida; a month later, he traveled to Savannah. During the voyage, he turned seventy-nine.[34]

Hazily aware of the passing of time, Mercer, in the firm and legible handwriting that had changed very little since his youth, drew up his will. All his possessions were given to his "well beloved-nephew" Theodore S. Garnett, the youngest son of his sister Mary Eleanor and James Mercer Garnett. "The only regret I have in making this will," he lamented, "is that I shall leave so little to one to whom I in truth owe so much."[35]

The affairs of this world, however, were not completely out of Mercer's mind. One final time, he wrote to Crittenden and implored him to find a southern member of the House to introduce his old resolution calling upon the president to negotiate with the maritime powers in the slave trade. He was also sharply critical of any further attempts to enlarge the republic. The Gadsden purchase, he roared to a relative, "will add as our other purchases have done to the relative power of the Slaveholding states and ultimately involve the dissolution of our Union and the ruin of the South." He caught himself in midlecture and laughed. "I am you see an old Fogy."[36]

Indeed, the old fire continued to flare up from time to time, although Mercer was once more concerned about the sore on his lip, back again and more painful than before. On June 20 he left Georgia for New York, a passsage that he spent reading "Dickens' last novel," probably *Little Dorrit.* He hoped he would not require surgery, although he suspected that an operation was "among the possible if not probable evils that await my return." His fears were evidently greater than his hopes, for upon reaching New York he could not bring himself to see a doctor. Instead, he hastened to Washington, and from there he took a carriage to Alexandria and the Episcopal high school run by his grandniece and her husband, John McGuire. The next day, bolstered by their words, he booked passage back to New York. There he found a doctor who knew the truth. The sore was cancerous and had to be removed immediately. Almost fleeing from the doctor, Mercer rushed to Alexandria. On Thursday, September 17, a Washington doctor cut away "a part of my lip." For the next several weeks he remained at the school, reading a history of the Mexican War and being nursed by his grandnephew, James Mercer Garnett.[37]

Garnett was not long needed, for either Mercer's Scottish spirit or his own stubbornness not only pulled him through the operation but found him out of bed and on the road for western Virginia within two weeks. He even thought about returning to Europe. The political turbulence of the late 1850s had all but cured him of his interest in politics; he was "weary" of "treachery and demagoguism" and "ready to enjoy the quiet of despotism" in Tuscany. If only, he hoped, his "malady, which has so long subjected me to the doctors, regular and irregular, surgeons and quacks, will permit me, I shall be in Florence next June."[38]

In the meantime, Mercer traveled to Cumberland, Maryland, the farthest point west his canal ever reached, and finally reached Clarksburg, Virginia. There he sold a parcel of land long mortgaged and received a final draft due him from the Merchants' Bank of New York. "Today I may say," he wrote proudly in his journal, "that for the first time since my return from England in 1803 I am out of debt." Money was paid out as far south as Tallahassee. Upon returning to Washington, he splurged and bought a handsome chess set. He even gave away five dollars to "beggars."[39]

By the start of 1858 Mercer's health was worse. He again traveled north to New York to see a doctor, although he had no surgery. As he headed back to Alexandria through Philadelphia, his old interests flared up again, for he bought a "Dred Scott pamphlet" for fifty cents. In Washington he stopped to see Richard Birchett, his old friend from Tallahassee. With a final look at the city that was for so long his home, Mercer turned away and boarded the carriage for Alexandria. "He knew his condition was hopeless," Birchett wrote, "and that his death was certain within a very short time."[40]

"To day the cancer broke," Mercer diligently recorded in his journal under the date of February 21. "The discharge of blood and water wet thro the Handkerchief that passed under the chin and around the throat and was tied on top of the head." The discharge was followed by a lessening of the pain "for only awhile," and so he resorted to large doses of morphine. The old flame flared up one final time as he fought back the pain and drugs long enough to read most of a book about the Federalists. On April 8 he paid his nurse Betsy her wages. It was his final journal entry.[41]

On May 4, 1858, just one month before his eightieth birthday, the flame finally flickered and went out. At Mercer's bedside was his favorite nephew, Theodore Garnett. Funeral services were held two days later at the school chapel. He was buried in the Episcopal cemetery in Leesburg. His gravestone, supplied by Garnett, mourned the passing of this "Patriot, Statesman, Philanthropist and Christian. After spending his life in the service of mankind, he died at peace with the world and in the favor of God."[42]

As was fitting, the *Alexandria Gazette* and the *National Intelligencer*, both long and ardent defenders of Mercer, provided the most glowing eulogies. They spoke of his long service to both state and nation, his energy, zeal, and (in Alexandria) his canal. "A friend of peace, a true patriot, a lover of his country, he achieved an honorable fame, and a place among the benefactors of his race." He returned "to the district he once represented," the papers observed, "to spend his last hours." The "citizens of this place will always respect his memory, for he was their friend in all instances." Even the *Richmond Enquirer*, Mercer's most persistent critic, observed his death "with sincere sorrow" and reprinted the *Gazette's* eulogy in full.[43]

It was not difficult for Mercer's old enemies to find kind words upon his passing. Brilliant, incorruptible, zealous, hardworking, elegant, gentlemanly, mannered, and of almost prophetic vision— these were words used by his friends to describe him, and few of his antagonists would give them the lie. They might have added courage and toughness, for his final battle was surely his bravest. His less lovely character traits of arrogance and egotism both friends and enemies charitably ignored.

These flaws were among the very few that his detractors ever correctly identified. Indeed, it said much about Mercer that few of his enemies truly understood him. To them he was either a dangerous progressive willing to give away the power and prerogatives of his class or a hated abolitionist ready to destroy his native South. On the second score they were right enough; he was no abolitionist, but the industrial world he battled to create was no less a threat to the paternalistic, precapitalist world of the plantation. Perhaps only Calhoun was brilliant enough to grasp the subleties and complexities of such a vision, and his refusal to acquiesce quietly nearly shook the republic to its foundations in 1833.

In the end, Calhoun failed. The agrarian realm could not win against the forces of industrialism. Yet ironically, Mercer thought his life and career a failure. His book demonstrated this feeling, as did his last years in Europe. Garnett was wrong; Mercer did not die at peace with the world. Perhaps it was his unendingly gloomy personality that led to such a view. But in fact Mercer was successful. The infant industries that he and the Whigs labored to create were very much in evidence in the North by the time of his death. Occasional attacks by planters and the plain people of the North notwithstanding, the soul of the American System could be found in the sweeping change that had taken place in America during Mercer's long lifetime.

Nor was Mercer a failure in his drive to drag conservatism out of the reactionary pose it adopted in 1798. His energy, his rhetoric, and most of his legislation and programs, progressive as they were in appearance, helped to reshape American conservatism, bring it into the mainstream of political thought, and make it acceptable to the expanding electorate.

Only in his inability to grasp the needs and hopes of those Americans unlike himself was Mercer a failure. He was fundamentally unable to grasp the forces that fought against him, and there is no evidence that he cared to. It was only his rhetoric that made him sound as if he did; his private letters, his speeches before his peers, his anonymously written book, and most of all, his legislative agenda, made clear his real intent. In his heart of hearts Mercer remained an old Federalist. He continued to believe that those who owned the country ought to rule it. It was his task, and his success, to see that under the glittering guise of late Federalism, National Republicanism, and Whiggery, they essentially did.

Notes

ABBREVIATIONS

ACS	American Colonization Society
CFM	Charles Fenton Mercer
COCC	Chesapeake and Ohio Canal Company
DAB	*Dictionary of American Biography*, ed. Allen Johnson and Dumas Malone, 21 vols., 1928–1936.
JQA	John Quincy Adams
JSH	*Journal of Southern History*
LC	Library of Congress
NJHS	New Jersey Historical Society
NYHS	New York Historical Society
PRO, FO	Great Britain, Public Record Office, Foreign Office
UVA	University of Virginia
VMHB	*Virginia Magazine of History and Biography*
VSL	Virginia State Library
WMQ	*William and Mary Quarterly*

1. CFM, Autobiographical Sketch, Mercer-Hunter Papers, VSL.
2. Henry Clay to CFM, December 10, 1848, CFM Papers, NJHS. The hope of the

younger Whigs, those who had pushed Mercer out of office, was that Clay would not return to the Senate, fearing he would "kick up a row" with Taylor. See Glyndon G. Van Deusen, *The Life of Henry Clay* (Boston, 1937), 394.

3. Henry Clay to CFM, October 19, 1835, Henry Clay Papers, Kentucky Historical Society (comment written on letter by CFM at a later date); CFM to John Clayton, March 9, 1849, John Clayton Papers, LC.

4. CFM to John Clayton, March 9, 1849, Clayton Papers; CFM, Autobiographical Sketch, Mercer-Hunter Papers. Clayton, thankfully, did not burn the narrative.

5. K. Jack Bauer, *Zachary Taylor: Soldier, Planter, Statesman of the Old Southwest* (Baton Rouge, 1985), 250; Maurice Baxter, *One and Inseparable: Daniel Webster and the Union* (Cambridge, Mass., 1984); 402; CFM, Autobiographical Sketch, Mercer-Hunter Papers; Henry Clay to CFM, December 10, 1848, CFM Papers, NJHS.

6. *United States Reports,* Vol. 109, *Walsh* v. *Preston,* Records and Briefs (New York, 1902), app., 14–15; CFM to Washington D. Miller, April 1852, Washington D. Miller Papers, Texas State Library.

7. Eugene D. Genovese, *The World the Slaveholders Made: Two Essays in Interpretation* (New York, 1969), 146; CFM to Nathan Appleton, February 20, 1852, Nathan Appleton Papers, Massachusetts Historical Society.

8. Deposition of Theodore S. Garnett, *Walsh* v. *Preston,* Records and Briefs, 185; CFM to Theodore S. Garnett, August 7, 1854, Mercer-Hunter Papers (first letter of that date).

9. Deposition of Richard T. Birchett, *Walsh* v. *Preston,* Records and Briefs, 197.

10. Charles Fenton Mercer, *An Address to the Colonization Society at Their 36th Annual Meeting* (Geneva [Switzerland]; 1854); 1; CFM to Maria H. Garnett, December 8, 1854, Mercer-Hunter Papers.

11. Unidentified newspaper clipping, n.d., CFM Papers, NJHS; CFM Journal, May 28–July 30, 1853, Mercer-Hunter Papers.

12. CFM Journal, August 17, 1853–January 2, 1854, December 1854, Mercer-Hunter Papers.

13. CFM to Maria H. Garnett, June 6, 1856; CFM to Theodore S. Garnett, December 25, both in ibid.; unidentified newspaper clipping, February 4, 1854, CFM Papers, NJHS.

14. CFM to Theodore S. Garnett, February 11, 1854, Mercer-Hunter Papers.

15. CFM to Cass, April 14, 1854, CFM Papers, NJHS.

16. CFM to Maria H. Garnett, December 8, 1854; CFM to Theodore S. Garnett, August 7, 1854 (second letter of that date), both in Mercer-Hunter Papers.

17. CFM to John Clayton, July 4, 1854, Clayton Papers.

18. CFM to Theodore S. Garnett, August 7, 1854, (second letter of that date); CFM to Maria H. Garnett, December 8, 1854, both in Mercer-Hunter Papers.

19. CFM to Maria H. Garnett, December 8, 1854; Mercer-Hunter Papers.

20. CFM Journal, November 8–20, 1854, ibid.; CFM to Mrs. William M. Blackford, 1855, James M. Garnett Papers, Duke University Library.

21. CFM to Maria H. Garnett, December 8, 1854, Mercer-Hunter Papers.

22. CFM to Lord Radstock, July 12, 1856, CFM Papers, NJHS; CFM Journal, December 12, 1854–March 22, 1855, Mercer-Hunter Papers.

23. CFM Journal, June 16, 1855, ibid.

24. CFM Journal, July 7–16, 1855, ibid.

25. CFM Journal, August 1–September 11, 1855, ibid.; CFM to Edward C. Cabell, August 16, 1855, in Nancy E. Eagleton, "The Mercer Colony in Texas, 1844–83," *Southwestern Historical Quarterly 39 (1935): 290.*

26. *CFM to Mrs. William M. Blackford, 1855, Garnett Papers.*

27. *Muriel E. Chamberlain, Lord Aberdeen: A Political Biography* (London, 1983), 513, CFM to Lord Radstock, July 12, 1856, CFM Papers, NJHS.

28. Charles Fenton Mercer, *To the August Assembly, Convened in the City of*

Paris, to Confer on Restoring the Peace of Europe, the Memorial of the American Society for Colonizing in Africa the free people of colour of the United States (London, 1856), written in CFM's hand on last page (copy in Princeton University Library); Charles Fenton Mercer, *Memoire relatif a L'abolition de la traite africaine adresse aux puissances maritimes de l'Europe et de l'Amerique au nom de la Société Americaine de Colonization* (Paris, 1855).

29. John J. Crittenden to CFM, January 5, 1857, John J. Crittenden Papers, LC.

30. Lord Radstock to CFM, n.d. 1856, June 11, 1856, CFM Papers, NJHS.

31. CFM to Lord Radstock, June 30, 1856, ibid.

32. CFM to Maria H. Garnett, June 6, 1856, Mercer-Hunter Papers.

33. CFM Journal, July 12–August 5, 1856, ibid.; Mercer, *To the August Assembly,* written in CFM's hand on last page; CFM to Lord Radstock, July 12, 1856, CFM Papers, NJHS.

34. CFM Journal, September 11, 1856–June 20, 1857, Mercer-Hunter Papers; John J. Crittenden to CFM, January 5, 1857, Crittenden Papers.

35. Will of CFM, March 25, 1857, *Walsh* v. *Preston,* Records and Briefs, 187.

36. CFM to John J. Crittenden, February 10, 1857, Crittenden Papers; CFM to unknown, March 10, 1857, CFM Papers, Yale University Library.

37. CFM Journal, June 20–October 1, 1857, Mercer-Hunter Papers; CFM to unknown, March 10, 1857, CFM Papers, Yale University Library.

38. CFM to B. J. Barbour, August 25, 1857, John Tyler Papers, LC; CFM to Maria H. Garnett, November 29, 1857, Mercer-Hunter Papers.

39. CFM Journal, Occtober 3–December 2, 1857, Mercer-Hunter Papers.

40. CFM Journal, January 2–23, 1858, ibid.; Deposition of Richard T. Birchett, *Walsh* v. *Preston,* Records and Briefs, 193.

41. CFM Journal, February 21–April 8, 1858, Mercer-Hunter Papers.

42. Deposition of Theodore S. Garnett, *Walsh* v. *Preston,* Records and Briefs, 183; *Alexandria Gazette,* May 5, 1858; James Mercer Garnett, ed., *Biographical Sketch of Hon. Charles Fenton Mercer, 1778–1858* (Richmond; 1911), 95. The deposition lists Mercer's death as May 2. The *Gazette* lists it as May 4, and since the May 5 edition announced the funeral for May 6, which would be four days after Mercer's death if one accepts the date Garnett gave two decades after the fact, the newspaper is surely correct. The tombstone, which, according to the *Biographical Sketch,* lists May 4 as the date of death, cannot be located. The Episcopal graveyard in Leesburg is overgrown, unkempt, and filled with broken, sunken, and smooth markers.

43. *National Intelligencer,* May 6, 1858; *Alexandria Gazette,* May 6, 1858; *Richmond Enquirer,* May 7, 1858.

The Authorship
of *An Exposition*

Although *An Exposition of the Weakness and Inefficiency of the Government of the United States of North America* was published anonymously, Charles Fenton Mercer's authorship seems never to have been in doubt. Although there is no evidence when his authorship became widely known, by the time that Charles Francis Adams, Jr., wrote a short sketch of Mercer for the *Dictionary of American Biography*, it was evidently accepted without question.

In 1939, however, William Diamond published an article in the *Journal of Southern History* arguing that Nathaniel A. Ware was the author. His evidence was Ware's ownership of the copyright to the book. He also held that the description of the author in the preface did not fit Mercer, just as the gloomy conclusions it reached did not fit the portrait of Mercer as a progressive painted in Wayland F. Dunaway's 1917 M.A. thesis at the University of Chicago, "Charles Fenton Mercer."

Although the description has to be stretched to fit Ware, and though Diamond admitted that the views on slavery and colonization in the book were not in keeping with Ware's—no small problem, that, for Ware was a planter—he proclaimed Ware the author. No corroborating evidence existed for Mercer, he charged, although he was admittedly unable to find any, save the copyright, that pointed to Ware.

It was a logical thesis, but only on the surface. When Dunaway's thesis was written, few of Mercer's personal papers were available. Moreover, Ware, who knew almost nothing about Mercer, was unaware of his long-held desire to keep his name "out of view." That the preface does not fit Mercer is not surprising. What is significant is that the long autobiography that follows—a Virginia Episcopalian with a classical education who had visited Europe and Texas, was a colonizationist, supported public education, had a firsthand knowledge of canals, and fought in the War of 1812— should match not the preface, which was written to disguise authorship, but the life of Mercer. Diamond suspects that Ware published the work anonymously because Southern society was hostile to the ideas presented in it. Why this theory should not be applied to Mercer, especially at a time when the Virginian was trying to sell shares in his Texas enterprise, Diamond fails to make clear.

More damaging to Diamond's thesis, however, is that there is evidence in Mercer's favor. He was in Cincinnati, Ware's home, in the summer of 1845. The copyright was dated September 11. It is not unlikely that a former congressman trying to find wealthy partners for his Texas venture would meet this Kentucky Whig.

There are also problems with the copyright. Ware held it only as "proprietor." Other works in the court records (now in the Rare Book Room of the Library of Congress) in which Ware's name appears were held as "author" or "author and proprietor." The information was obviously filled in by a clerk, for the writing on every page is the same. If Ware was the author as well as the proprietor, the clerk would have listed him as such. Finally, the title page in *An Exposition* states that the work was "Printed for the Author." Clearly, Ware, in his sole role of proprietor, published the book for someone else.

Diamond was evidently unaware that *An Exposition* was republished in England during the Civil War as northern propaganda. Three letters of Mercer's, those to and from Lord Radstock dated June 11, June 19, and June 20, 1856, mention several pamphlets, memorials, and a memoir that Mercer either loaned or gave to his friend. Radstock was surely not the only recipient of Mercer's works during his three-year stay in Europe; colonizationist Thomas Hodgkins doubtless also was similarly burdened.

Finally, the title page of the copy of *An Exposition* in the Harvard library says it was presented by the author.[1] Mercer was in Boston during his final rambles. Ware never visited the city.

Even without knowledge of these contradictions, Diamond's thesis, based solely on a copyright held as proprietor, is on shaky ground. Not surprisingly, in the nearly half a century since the article appeared it has found no supporters. Clement Eaton, in *The Freedom-of-Thought Struggle in the Old South*, attributes the book to Mercer although he is aware of Diamond's thesis. William P. Taylor, in *Cavalier and Yankee: The Old South and American National Character*, assigns the book to Mercer. He does not consider the matter to be debatable.[2] Bertram Wyatt-Brown, who is currently writing about Ware, notes that Mercer was "undoubtedly the author" of *An Exposition*.[3]

Notes

ABBREVIATIONS

ACS	American Colonization Society
CFM	Charles Fenton Mercer
COCC	Chesapeake and Ohio Canal Company
DAB	*Dictionary of American Biography*, ed. Allen Johnson and Dumas Malone, 21 vols., 1928–1936.
JQA	John Quincy Adams
JSH	*Journal of Southern History*

LC   Library of Congress
NJHS   New Jersey Historical Society
NYHS   New York Historical Society
PRO, FO   Great Britain, Public Record Office, Foreign Office
UVA   University of Virginia
VMHB   *Virginia Magazine of History and Biography*
VSL   Virginia State Library
WMQ   *William and Mary Quarterly*

1. Z. Maynard to Douglas R. Egerton, December 3, 1985.

2. Clement Eaton, *The Freedom-of-Thought Struggle in the Old South* (New York, 1964), 281–82, 299; William P. Taylor, *Cavalier and Yankee: The Old South and American National Character* (New York, 1961), 59–60.

3. Bertram Wyatt-Brown to Douglas R. Egerton, September 2, 1988.

Bibliographical Essay

This essay discusses the sources most pertinent to a study of the life and career of Charles Fenton Mercer. It does not include all the references cited in the footnotes, nor does it comment on the enormous body of secondary literature on the Early National and Jacksonian periods. That task has been admirably accomplished by Charles G. Sellers, Jr., "Andrew Jackson versus the Historians," *Mississippi Valley Historical Review* (1958), and Ronald P. Formisano, "Toward a Reorientation of Jacksonian Politics: A Review of the Literature, 1959–1975," *Journal of American History* (1976). My "An Update on Jacksonian Historiography: The Biographies," *Tennessee Historical Quarterly* (1987) reviews the most recent literature.

Unfortunately, the personal papers of Mercer are spread far and wide. When he died at the Alexandria home of his grandniece in 1858, he had in his possession several trunks of letters, correspondence that belonged both to himself and to his father and uncle (including the papers of the Ohio Company). When Union troops occupied Alexandria three years later, they bivouacked in the grandniece's home. The soldiers, being cold, broke open one of the trunks and threw its contents on a fire. An officer realized the worth of the papers and put a stop to the destruction, but then the autograph hunters among the soldiers divided up the remainder of the letters. Papers were carried north to New Jersey, New York, and Pennsylvania. As a result, most eastern repositories have at least some Mercer letters, and it is only within recent years that the great bulk of his correspondence has become available; indeed, as late as 1984 a significant number of his letters surfaced in a new collection.

Nonetheless, the core collection of Mercer family papers is in the Virginia Historical Society, Richmond. In addition to this collection, letters and documents pertinent to Mercer can be found in twelve other VHS collections. Edmund Burnett's *Letters of Members of the Continental Congress* (8 vols., Washington, D.C., 1921–26), Lois Mulkearn's *George Mercer Papers Relating to the Ohio Company of Virginia* (Pittsburgh, 1954), and John C. Fitzpatrick, ed., *The Writings of George Washington* (39 vols., Washington, D.C., 1931–44) provide a wealth of information about Marlborough, the Mercer plantation, Charles Fenton's parents, and the confusing tangle of Mercer family finances.

Several secondary works proved invaluable in explaining the world into which Mercer was born. My view of the South as an antibourgeois, noncapitalist social system was especially informed by two penetrating works of Eugene D. Genovese: *The Political Economy of Slavery: Studies in the Economy and Society of the Slave South* (New York, 1966) and *The World the Slaveholders Made: Two Essays in Interpretation* (New York, 1969). Charles Sydnor's *Gentlemen Freeholders: Political Practices in Jefferson's Virginia* (Chapel Hill, 1952) was also useful on the political culture in which Mercer was raised. Rhys Isaac's *Transformation of Virginia, 1740–1790* (Chapel Hill, 1982) is fascinating reading, although I disagree with the author's interpretation of Mercer as a student. Malcolm C. Watkins's *Cultural History of Marlborough, Virginia* (Washington, D.C., 1968) details the considerable archaelogical work the Smithsonian Institution has undertaken at the plantation since 1957.

Material relating to Mercer's Princeton years can be found in the New-York Historical Society and in Arthur Lowndes, ed., *The Correspondence of John Henry Hobart* (6 vols., New York, 1912), both of which detail his conversion to Federalism. His tragicomical involvement in the Quasi War can be traced in Fitzpatrick's *Writings* of Washington and in Harold Syrett et al., eds., *The Papers of Alexander Hamilton* (26 vols., New York, 1961–79). For Mercer's opinions on John Adams and the politics of the late 1790s, see his 1849 autobiographical sketch at the Virginia State Library, Richmond, and his anonymous 1845 autobiography, *An Exposition of the Weakness and Inefficiency of the Government of the United States of North America.*

The question of ties between the first and second American party systems is among the most controversial of all historical issues. Mercer's activities on the state level, however, provide an appreciation of the links between late Federalism and the early

Whig party. For a hostile view of his actions, see Thomas Ritchie's unrelentingly antagonistic *Richmond Enquirer,* the papers of Joseph C. Cabell, and the John Randolph–James Mercer Garnett letters, all at the Library of Congress. For a more favorable view, see Norman Risjord's "The Virginia Federalists," *Journal of Southern History* (1967), which claims that not all party members were conservatives. James H. Broussard's *The Southern Federalists, 1800–1816* (Baton Rouge, 1978) is a meticulous study that follows much the same path. David Hackett Fischer's depiction of the party as it attempted to make itself more palatable to the American electorate, *The Revolution of American Conservatism* (New York, 1965), is both original and persuasive.

The only narrative dealing with Mercer's bills for internal improvements, Philip M. Rice's "The Virginia Board of Public Works, 1816–1842" (M.A. thesis, University of North Carolina, 1947), is flawed by the lack of information on its creator. Most of the data on Mercer are drawn from his autobiographical sketch, which Rice inexplicably attributes to Mercer's nephew. One should instead consult two shorter works: Carter Goodrich's "The Virginia System of Mixed Enterprise," *Political Science Quarterly* (1949) and Wiley E. Hodge's "Pro-Governmentalism in Virginia, 1789–1936," *Journal of Politics* (1971). On the related issue of state banking, see Mercer's informative *Report on Banks* (Richmond, 1816) and George T. Starnes's *Sixty Years of Branch Banking in Virginia* (New York, 1931).

General works on the American Colonization Society are of little use in a study of the origins of the movement, and they tend to ignore the partisan nature of the effort. For Mercer's early role on both the state and national levels, see his detailed reminiscence, *An Address to the American Colonization Society at Their 36th Annual Meeting* (Geneva [Switzerland], 1854), in the Cornell University Library, and his letters to John Hartwell Cocke in the Alderman Library, University of Virginia. Mercer's daybook, at the New Jersey Historical Society, Newark, details his travels during the crucial early days of the organization. Although Philip Slaughter's *Virginian History of African Colonization* (Richmond, 1855) was written by a member of the society and a friend of Mercer's, it should be used with caution.

For Mercer, public education was the flip side of black colonization. Ironically, his bill of 1817 is better remembered than he is. His blunt *Discourse on Popular Education* (Princeton, 1826), delivered before a body of like-minded men, and his *Exposition,* are excellent windows into the post-1800 Federalist mind. On the connection between primary education and industrialization, see his *Oration Delivered to the Episcopal Church* (Alexandria, 1806) at the American Philosophical Society, Philadelphia. One should consult also Lawrence A. Cremin's *American Education: The National Experience, 1783–1816* (New York, 1980).

There is a wealth of material pertinent to the twenty-two years Mercer spent on the national stage. For his rocky first term in Congress, see the Louis McLane Papers at the University of Delaware and John Spencer Bassett's *Correspondence of Andrew Jackson* (7 vols., Washington, D.C., 1926–35). Mercer's *Controversy between Armistead Thompson Mason and Charles Fenton Mercer* (Washington, D.C., 1818) was the preface to an unusually savage duel, an unhappy story all too common to the antebellum South.

To understand fully the heyday of the American colonization movement, the society's voluminous correspondence at the Library of Congress is indispensable; even when in Washington, Mercer was more inclined to write to the society's secretary than to walk to his office. For printed material, one should see Mercer's *Colonization of Free People of Colour* (Washington, D.C., 1827) and his *To the August Assembly* (London, 1856). The standard work on the movement is P. J. Staudenraus's *African Colonization Movement, 1816–1865* (New York, 1961), a detailed but finally unconvincing attempt to portray the society as the conservative wing of the abolitionist movement. Staudenraus devotes far too much attention to the evangelical side of the society and far too little to colonization as an integral part of the American system. Far better on the colonizationists and their efforts to outlaw the slave trade is Betty Fladeland's scholarly *Men and Brothers: Anglo-American Antislavery Cooperation* (Urbana, 1972). Secondary sources, however, should not lead one to overlook Mercer's enormous collection of documents, *Slave Trade* (Washington, D.C., 1830). The society's organ, the *African Repository and Colonial Journal*, and the society's *Annual Reports*—many of which were edited by the indefatigable congressman from Loudoun—also provide a wealth of information.

Walter S. Sanderlin's *The Great National Project: A History of the Chesapeake and Ohio Canal* (New York, 1946) is the most complete study of Mercer's great dream, although the author's effort to portray the enormous undertaking as bipartisan leaves the reader confused about the great hostility it aroused. Mercer tried his disingenuous best to argue a similar line in his narrative account, *Chesapeake and Ohio Canal* (Washington, D.C., 1834). More revealing are the company papers in the National Archives, the politically frank letters of Richard Rush in the Library of Congress, and the correspondence of Mercer's legislative liaison in Virginia, Charles James Faulkner (Virginia Historical Society). Finally, a trio of superb biographies helps untangle the political machinations of the Monroe and Adams years: John A. Munroe's *Louis McLane: Federalist and Jacksonian* (New Brunswick, N.J., 1973); Samuel Flagg Bemis's *John Quincy Adams* (2 vols., New York, 1950–56); and Harry Ammon's *James Monroe: The Quest for National Identity* (New York, 1971). Bemis, however, occasionally attributes too much to his admittedly brilliant subject; his claim that Adams was the real father of the American System is based not on a comprehensive program but on a single bill for internal improvements. His chapter on the slave trade convention is not as good as Fladeland's treatment. And for an antidote against Ammon's overly sympathetic view of the fifth president, see Dangerfield's delightful *Era of Good Feelings* (New York, 1952).

There is still no first-rate account of the Virginia constitutional convention of 1829. Dickson D. Bruce, Jr., *The Rhetoric of Conservatism: The Virginia Convention of 1829–30* (San Marino, 1982) is weak on state politics. Bruce tends to label the antireform tirades of the Tidewater as Federalist, thus failing to note that former Federalists were in the forefront of the reform movement. On Mercer's role, see the Campbell Family Papers at Duke University and the Hugh Blair Grigsby collection at the Virginia Historical Society. The preconvention paper war that was vitriolic even by Old Dominion standards can be found in the pages of the *Richmond Enquirer*.

Any analysis of the plight of conservatism under the administration of Jackson and Van Buren must take the published letters of Henry Clay (edited by James F. Hopkins et al.) and Daniel Webster (edited by Charles M. Wiltse et al.) into account (both still unfinished). Charles Francis Adams, ed., *Memoirs of John Quincy Adams Comprising Parts of His Diary from 1795 to 1848* (12 vols., Philadelphia, 1874–77) is accurate in detail, although his political analysis is almost always faulty. For Mercer, these years were unrelentingly grim, as both his canal and the colonization society came under the full fire of the Democratic attack. For the fate of the former, see the canal company papers in the National Archives and the Library of Congress and *Niles' Weekly Register*. On the turmoil that destroyed the colonization movement, see Leonard L.

Richards's *"Gentlemen of Property and Standing": Anti-Abolition Mobs in Jacksonian America* (New York, 1970), although he fails to note that after 1833, even as the society increased its attacks on Garrison, it moved closer to the position of the abolitionists, having removed Mercer and those like him from positions of power.

For the acrimonious interparty struggle that drove Mercer from office see John Scott, ed., *Judge Scott's Reply to Mr. Mercer* (1839) and Mercer's *Farewell Address . . . to His Constituents* (1839). The *Alexandria Gazette*, an important Whig paper, provides a wealth of material on Mercer's last political battle. Three biographies of men who helped make his last years in Congress a trial are Robert V. Remini's monumental *Andrew Jackson* (3 vols., New York, 1977–84); John Niven's *Martin Van Buren: The Romantic Age of American Politics* (New York, 1983); and William Nisbet Chambers's *Old Bullion Benton, Senator from the New West: Thomas Hart Benton, 1782–1858* (1956; rpt. new York, 1970), which is especially good on the financial debate under the Magician. For life on the other side of the aisle see Daniel Walker Howe's *Political Culture of the American Whigs* (Chicago, 1979). Maurice G. Baxter's *One and Inseparable: Daniel Webster and the Union* (Cambridge, Mass., 1984) is the best biography of the Godlike, a figure even Mercer, whose own ethics could be elastic, found unattractive. Glyndon G. Van Deusen's *Life of Henry Clay* (Boston, 1937) is adequate; there is a need for a new biography of Harry of the West.

Unlike those of most politicians, Mercer's retirement years were as fascinating as the period of his public career. The primary sources for his Texas venture are vast. The Texas State Library has three holdings that pertain to the Mercer Colony, and the New-York Historical Society has an enormous number of papers. Not surprisingly, the legal battle that worked its way up to the Supreme Court generated a mountain of paperwork. Documents and letters both to and from Mercer can be found in two volumes under *Walsh v. Preston, United States Reports* (New York, 1902). Seymour V. Connor's *Adventure in Glory: The Saga of Texas, 1836–1849* (Austin, 1965) is a lively and colorful narrative of the republic period. Because he did not use the large collection of papers in New York, however, Connor is unduly harsh on Mercer's decision to contract for his own colony. I have avoided using the only detailed account of the colony, Nancy E. Eagleton's "The Mercer Colony in Texas, 1844–1883," *Southwestern Historical Quarterly* (1935–36), because it is replete with erroneous dates, incorrect citations, and misspelled and incorrect names.

Although he never kept a diary in the conventional sense, Mercer's last daybook, in the Virginia State Library, provides an excellent account of the wanderings of his final years, as well as graphic and often horrifying descriptions of his numerous cancer operations. On his final attempts to obtain an accord on the slave trade, see his *Memoir relatif A l'abolition de la traite africaine* (1855; in the Boston Public Library) and *To the August Assembly,* which includes his handwritten comments (copy in Princeton University Library).

INDEX